A World Transformed

When Hopes Collapse
&
Faiths Collide

A World Transformed

When Hopes Collapse
&
Faiths Collide

Pat Logan

CHURCHES TOGETHER
IN BRITAIN AND IRELAND

Churches Together in Britain and Ireland
Bastille Court
2 Paris Garden
London SE1 8ND

www.ctbi.org.uk

ISBN 978 0 85169 334 7
Published 2007

Further copies are available from:
CTBI Publications, 4 John Wesley Road, Werrington,
Peterborough PE4 6ZP

Telephone: 01733 325002
Fax: 01733 384180

Typeset in 11/15pt Adobe Garamond
Design and production by Makar Publishing Production, Edinburgh

Cover
Joseph Mallord William Turner, English, 1775–1851
Slave Ship (Slavers Throwing Overboard the Dead and Dying,
Typhon Coming On), 1840 (detail)
Oil on canvas
90.8 x 122.6 cm (35¾ x 48¼ in.)
Museum of Fine Arts, Boston
Henry Lillie Pierce Fund 99.22
Photograph © 2007 Museum of Fine Arts, Boston

Printed and bound in Great Britain by Cromwell Press

To Raymond Plant

who set us on our way

Contents

Acknowledgements

The Towards Social Transformation exercise was an ecumenical initiative launched in July 1990 under the banner of the Anglican Association for Social Responsibility. It could never have continued without the Association's vote of confidence, backed up by a subsidy, which made it possible, for many years, to print and distribute reports on each year's seminar to all the Association's members.

Among those whose energy and assistance were crucial in those early days, special mention must be made of John Austin, then Social Responsibility Adviser for the Diocese of London and later Bishop of Aston, Patrick Woodhouse, then Social Responsibility Adviser in the diocese of Winchester and later Precentor of Wells Cathedral, and Robin Morrison, then Social Responsibility Officer for the Diocese of Derby, and later Church and Society Officer for the Church in Wales. John convened the planning meetings, Patrick persuaded Professor Raymond (now Lord) Plant to lead the first seminar, and Robin arranged for the first and all subsequent 48-hour seminars to be held at Cumberland Lodge in Windsor Great Park.

We are grateful to the Principal and staff of Cumberland Lodge in Windsor Great Park for their hospitality and for their concern that our time there should be refreshing as well as productive.

Thanks are due, too, to the Christendom Trust, whose two grants enabled us to obtain the services of some top-flight seminar leaders.

The seminars were ecumenical from the beginning but the ecumenical character of the initiative was greatly enhanced in later years thanks to the assistance of Simon Barrow, then secretary of the Churches Commission on Mission and John Kennedy, then church and society co-ordinating secretary for Churches Together in Britain and Ireland, both of whom were also deeply involved in the seminars as well.

Above all, what made the experience so enriching was the contributions of all who participated. It says a great deal for the seminar leaders – some of whom found meeting with a group such as ours a new experience – that they were sensitive and flexible enough to let the conversation flow once they realized they had struck a chord. The participants themselves, in spite of their very different theological and political perspectives, invariably showed tolerance, good humour and a palpable desire to listen to, learn from and support one another. They made the experience as enjoyable as it has been enriching.

Pat Logan
December 2006

A Note on the Cover

The Slave Ship (Slavers throwing overboard the Dead and Dying – Typhon coming on)

Over a period of four days in November–December 1781, the captain of the slave ship *Zong* threw overboard 133 slaves who had become seriously ill. Most were still alive. Had they arrived dead, the responsibility would have been that of the owners, causing them a significant financial loss. But if it could be said that they had been thrown overboard in order to save the ship and the rest of the 'cargo' – for example, to quell a mutiny, to prevent the ship from sinking, or to ensure rations for the rest of those on board – then the ship's captain could claim insurance. This is precisely what the owners attempted to do.

The insurers refused to accept this account. When the owners took the case to court in March 1783, the court felt unable to find in favour of the insurers. Their shocking judgment, however, did serve to bring the whole gruesome incident to light. An outraged court witness wrote in the *Morning Chronicle and London Advertiser*: 'That there should be bad men to do bad things in all large communities must be expected; but a community makes the crime general and provokes divine wrath when it suffers any member to commit flagrant acts of villainy with impunity.' The letter was seen by the famous former slave Olaudah Equiano who at once contacted Granville Sharp, who, in turn, sought to enlist the support of the Bishops of Chester and Peterborough. Sharp attended the hearing on 21–22 May, which apparently decided to hold a retrial, but its outcome is not reported. Sharp also pressed the Lord Commissioner of the Admiralty, unsuccessfully, that the captain and crew be tried for mass murder.

The brutal event was recounted in 1808 by Thomas Clarkson in his *History of the Abolition of the African Slave Trade by the British Parliament*. The book's reprint in 1839 brought it to Turner's attention, who was moved to depict its horror. The following year Turner's painting was exhibited at the Royal Academy.

In his title Turner changed the 'shower of rain' into a 'Typhon', and he also added these lines from the *Fallacies of Hope* to the picture title in the exhibition catalogue:

> *Aloft all hands, strike the top masts and belay;*
> *Yon angry setting sun and fierce-edged clouds*
> *Declare the Typhon's coming.*
> *Before it sweeps your decks, throw overboard*
> *The dead and dying – ne'er heed their chains*
> *Hope, Hope, fallacious Hope!*
> *Where is thy market now?*

John Ruskin, in the first volume of *Modern Painters* (1843), declared: 'But, beyond dispute, the noblest sea that Turner has painted, and, if so, the noblest certainly ever painted by man, is that of the Slave Ship...if I were reduced to rest Turner's immortality upon any single work, I would choose this.' In 1844, Ruskin's father gave him the painting as a New Year's present, but after some years Ruskin found the subject 'too painful to live with' and decided to part with it.

A full account of this episode is given by Folarin Shyllon in *Black Slaves in Britain* (Oxford University Press, for the Institute of Race Relations, 1974).

Preface

The prophetic message of justice is a call for the total transformation
of unjust structures and patterns of behaviour.

Peace with Justice, First European Ecumenical Assembly, Basel, May 1989

Transforming social realties with the power of the Gospel…has always
been a challenge and it remains so today at the beginning of the third
millennium of the Christian era.

Compendium of the Social Doctrine of the Church [1]

The Towards Social Transformation Initiative

I was invited to write this book because of my part in an initiative first discussed
at a meeting of the Anglican Association for Social Responsibility in November
1988. We called it 'Towards Social Transformation'. The Berlin wall had not
yet come down, Nelson Mandela had not yet been freed, and Mrs. Thatcher
had not yet been ousted by her own party. But it was clear that change was in
the air. The bonds between Eastern and Western Europe were becoming ever
firmer, bringing with them the hope not just of a new Europe but of a Europe
with a renewed vision of 'Civil Society'. And the churches were at the very heart
of it all, particularly in the former East Germany, Poland and Hungary. Whilst
movements for the development of civil society were coming together under the
banner of the Helsinki Citizens Assembly,[2] the churches were preparing for their
own historic European Ecumenical Assembly in Basel. From there the call would
go out for 'the total transformation of unjust structures and patterns of behaviour'. And in response would be born *Kairos Europa,* the grass roots Christian
network which would be working with churches, social movements and trade
unions across Europe and beyond for a more just and tolerant society.[3]

It was in that climate that our own, more modest, Towards Social Transformation initiative, took shape. The immediate inspiration was the publication
in 1988 of a pair of influential books on civil society by John Keane. In *Civil
Society and the State: New European Perspectives* Keane had brought together a

thrilling collection of critical essays from Eastern and Western Europe, while in *Democracy and Civil Society* he had spelt out his own vision.[4] What gave the books life as well as authority was Keane's deep, personal involvement, for much of the decade, with civil society movements in Central Europe, particularly in Czechoslovakia. I had just come across these on the eve of our Association's annual meeting. Fortunately there was an opening at the meeting to share some of my excitement with colleagues. Several responded enthusiastically and immediately set up a working group to see how the Association might best engage with new thinking such as this.

So it was that it in the autumn of 1989, under the heading 'Towards Social Transformation', a few of us in the London area, from various denominations, began to gather for a series of informal sessions at the home of the Reverend Leslie Griffiths, one of which was led by John Keane. In January 1990, I circulated to all members of the Association a position paper entitled *Towards Social Transformation*. Five months later, I was privileged to be in Prague, when the first post-Communist election campaign was in full swing. Surely the time for social transformation had come? But already there were warning signs. In conversation with a Civic Forum activist, I was dumbstruck as he proceeded to express his firm conviction that the person who had the right ideas was none other than Mrs. Thatcher. Sure enough, within a few years, there was the Czech Prime Minister committed to taking up where Mrs. Thatcher had left off.[5]

Meanwhile, our Association's working group had decided that the best way for them to explore the issues would be to hold a 48-hour seminar in Cumberland Lodge, Windsor Great Park, and that participation should not be restricted to Anglicans. It was held in July 1990 and led by Professor Raymond (now Lord) Plant. That set the pattern for the next fourteen years. Subsequent seminar leaders represented a very wide range of perspectives and expertise: economists such as Grahame Thompson and Charles Leadbeater, political philosophers such as David Beetham and Patrick Riordan, S. J., experts on environmentalism (Michael Jacobs), social policy (Anna Coote), sociology (Bob Jessop), science (Michio Kaku), and globalization (Ian Linden). They have included democratic socialists such as Paul Hirst, Hilary Wainwright and Ian Gough, liberals such as Revd. David Nicholls, conservatives such as John Gray, and social democrats such as Raymond Plant.[6] Although only two seminars were wholly given over to theological explorations – by theologians with perspectives as different as liberal theology (Ian Markham) and Radical Orthodoxy (John Milbank) – nearly every seminar had time set aside for theological reflection on the theme under discussion. It has been gratifying – but also worrying – to hear participants say, fifteen years on, that nowhere else did they find such an opportunity for thinking critically and creatively together.

The aim of the initiative was never to search for some elusive 'Big Idea', nor to rally support for any particular movement, nor to promote any private agendas. It was simply, as we described it from the beginning: 'to promote dialogue between Christians involved in the field of social responsibility/social work and people, particularly from the academic community, who are developing creative analyses of social, political and economic change.' It was the sort of process later recommended by Aart Nicolaus van der Berg – an approach that 'opens rather than closes off thinking, thereby generating critical reflection and awakening hope that 'a new future that is totally different might become visible'.[7]

The present book draws on the seminars, but it is in no way a report of the seminars – nor does it pretend to reflect the positions of those who took part in the seminars and who enriched them with their insights. Rather it is an attempt to continue the dialogue with a particular focus on some key points of contact between theology and social, economic and political policy. It will highlight developments and new thinking in each of these fields which cry out for theological engagement. The challenge is to help narrow the gap between Christians who are working for a different kind of world and those who may not share such faith so as to see how we can learn from each other and why we need each other if our common search for a radically different world is to be fruitful. I would like to think that it may encourage all who read it to travel together on our journey 'towards social transformation'.

Pat Logan
December 2006

A World Transformed

> ...I pondered all these things, and how men fight and lose the battle, and
> the thing that they fought for comes about in spite of their defeat, and
> when it comes turns out not to be what they meant, and other men have to
> fight for what they meant under another name...
>
> William Morris, *A Dream of John Ball*

Précis

What happened to the hopes that burnt so brightly in 1989 – for life
after the Cold War and after Apartheid, for a united Europe and for
the flourishing of civil society? To complain that those hopes have been
dashed would be untrue. But so, too, would it be to pretend that they
have been realized. The world has been transformed – dramatically,
unpredictably, uncertainly – from those days in which ventures like the
'Towards Social Transformation' initiative of the Anglican Association
for Social Responsibility were taking shape. Some of the hopes have
indeed been realized, but in forms that are strange and at times even
perverse: '...the thing that they fought for comes about in spite of their
defeat, and when it comes turns out not to be what they meant....'

This chapter looks at the way the transformations of the past two
decades have indeed brought about a kind of 'civil society' but one
which is a far cry from that envisioned at the end of the 1990s. It lays
the foundation for the subsequent chapters by exploring the dynamics
of hope and the reasons why disappointments need not be seen as
defeats and why endeavours for a different kind of social transformation
are needed even more than they were two decades ago.

What are the tasks that such a recovery of a new movement towards
social transformation must address? Three will be examined in the
remainder of this introductory chapter. The first task is to seek insights
that can help sustain a more mature hope, one that is gained precisely
from reflecting deeply on what has happened to the hopes that were

so strong in 1989. The second is the task of critical analysis, with the help of a framework of interpretation that is able to put the threats, for example of terrorism, in a proper perspective and from there to begin to identify the causes. The third is the task of transformative action, changing the world by suggesting some promising directions and movements towards social transformation.

Preamble: Looking Back on Hope

Many of the hopes at that time centred on the transformative energies that were thought to be latent in 'civil society'. In two influential books published in 1988, John Keane pointed towards a new democratic-socialist vision. He aimed to retrieve the notion of civil society from the ways it had been taken up both by the Left – under the inspiration of Antonio Gramsci for whom the replacement of the state by a self-regulating society was achievable only through the hegemony of the working class led by the Communist Party[1] – and by the new Right, with its neo-liberal notion of civil society as the realm of self-interest, private property, markets, hard work and individual responsibility. Central to Keane's project was the deepening and renewal of democracy not just as a means to some further end but as an end in itself. The project was about the democratization of civil society *and* of the state, and about establishing the right relationship between the two.[2] Equality, freedom and solidarity were reinterpreted as complex, culturally-defined realities. Choice, social enterprise, collective self-organization, a citizens' wage were all brought into the frame. The aim was not to repeat the mistake made by socialist centralizers, who tried to plan outcomes in advance. On the contrary, the very unpredictability of the result of such a genuinely socialist democracy was, for Keane, a cause for celebration.

But what actually followed? Since 1989, civil society has undeniably become fashionable: '...the 1990s may be seen as heralding the birth of "global civil society" as something more than a vague idea,' notes Ian Linden, leader of the 2004 Towards Social Transformation seminar.[3] Military dictatorships have succumbed in Chile, Argentina and Indonesia. Halting steps towards democracy in various colours and shapes have been taken, often with covert as well as overt American 'guidance', especially in countries that were formerly under the influence or even part of the Soviet Union. Germany has been reunited. Europe has been enlarged. Huge advances have been made in information and communications technology and in medicine and the life sciences. There has been phenomenal economic growth and millions have risen out of poverty, above all in China and in India.

But the breakdown of a world that lived in the shadow of two mighty super powers has been followed by barbaric ethnic wars in the Balkans and by the readiness of the one remaining super power to use its military might to effect regime change in countries of strategic importance.[4] The colours have faded from the new democracies – Rose (Georgia), Orange (the Ukraine), Tulip (Kyrgyzstan), and the new regimes are often vehicles for the return of oligarchs and apparatchiks, and for the coming to power of religious and sectarian movements which lack a democratic tradition and, in some cases, even a commitment to genuinely democratic practice. Apartheid has been dismantled but South Africa, has seen a flight of young white professionals, bent on seeking their fortunes in financial and technical services in Britain and elsewhere, while South Africa, along with most sub-Saharan African countries has been devastated by HIV/AIDS. As the 1990s progressed, the rich have got richer, often obscenely so – the Russian oligarch Roman Abramovich who took advantage of the cut-rate sales of state-owned assets in Russia had by 2003 become the richest person in Britain, outranking even the Duke of Westminster[5] – while in sub-Saharan Africa the poor literally got poorer.[6] Indeed, life expectancy in that part of the world actually fell between 1990 and 2000, after having risen by an average of nine years between 1960 and 1990. The WHO Region of the Americas bears only 10% of the global burden of disease but it has 37% of the world's health workers (24.8 per 1,000 population), while the African regions bear 24% of the burden but have only 3% of the world's health workers (2.3 per 1,000 population) commanding less than 1% of world health expenditure.[7]

The United Nations formulated its Millennium Goals in September 2000, with an impressive set of targets: to strengthen respect for the rule of law in international affairs, to reduce poverty, to halt the spread of HIV/AIDS, the scourge of malaria and other major diseases.[8] But on present trends, the numbers of people in extreme poverty will not be halved, they will actually increase – from 334 million in 2000 to 471 million in 2015.[9] Since 1981, more than 25 million have died from AIDS-related illnesses. Spending on HIV/AIDS increased 15-fold between 1996 and 2003, but it was still only half the amount needed by developing countries, and the number of people with HIV keeps rising dramatically: by 2005, 38.6 million people were living with HIV/AIDS.[10]

Europe has been enlarged but the project of deepening Europe in terms of economic, social and political integration has been put into reverse, and its sense of cultural identity, its socio-economic model and its mission in the world have all been thrown into confusion.[11] Meanwhile, the focus of attention has shifted towards Asia. At least half a billion people in that region are unemployed or underemployed.[12] Even in China, where statistically most progress has been made to overcome poverty (although the real incomes of the poorest 130 million Chinese appear to have fallen by 2.4% between 2001 and 2003), the social disruption has been staggering and the scale of inequalities contributed to some 74,000 mass protests in 2004.[13]

Between 2000 and 2005 carbon emissions grew 10 times faster than in the preceding four years. Although the Kyoto protocol finally came into force in February 2005, the year 2005 saw greenhouse gases reaching record levels, and the treaty has not been ratified by the US, whilst some who have ratified the agreement have yet to embark seriously on action plans[14] – and others of those who have signed up appear to be having second thoughts. Here, too, it is Africa that is most vulnerable to the effects of climate change.[15]

People have migrated in massive numbers, some of them 'environmental refugees'. The Global Commission on International Migration set up by Kofi Annan in 2003 issued its first report on 6 October 2005, noting that the number of people who live outside their own country has risen to some 200 million, twice as many as 25 years ago, and that for many of these people migration has actually become a survival strategy. It called for the UN to establish a new inter-agency Global Migration Facility 'to ensure a more coherent institutional response to the opportunities and challenges presented by international migration'.[16] Yet however welcome migrant workers may be economically, host countries, especially in Europe, are concerned both that migrants may pose a threat to national security and that the numbers are approaching levels which are testing their ability to integrate the newcomers and are threatening their own cultural identities.

Civil Society: From Locke to Hobbes?

And the hope for a new type of civil society? What has happened to that? The radical visions of the 1980s have all but disappeared. Civil society is indeed a key arena for cultural, economic and political action. But now the battle for its shape and soul is between the neo-liberal forces of global capitalism and a new, often intolerant conservatism. NGOs may have increased, but their role is often viewed as junior partners of corporate interests. Voluntary and community groups may have been given a greater role but in the process of their transformation into the

'Third Sector' they are often viewed as agents of government policy. As for the five main sectors in 'civil society' – education, the media, the law, the arts, and religion – it is alarming to note how all have been sites of an increasingly confident and well-organized conservative movement, especially in the United States.[17]

Meanwhile, the world has become a place of profound insecurity. Although the Cold War has ended, more countries are being tempted to develop nuclear weapons, and those that already have them are now designing them for actual use as well as for deterrence. Even more alarming in practical terms – because they are easier to manufacture, transport and use – is the range of deadly biological and chemical weapons. Russia alone still has stockpiled some 40,000 tons of chemical weapons – Sarin, Soman, mustard, Lewisite and phosgene.[18] In the face of this new scenario, NATO itself is being doubly transformed, extending its reach far beyond Europe and shifting its focus to defences against internal threats. Added to this is the threat of pandemics of SARS or Avian flu – enhanced by the volume of global travel and transport. And, in terms of the actual threat to the lives and livelihood of present and future generations we are faced with the threat of climate change reaching the point where it could set off an irreversible chain reaction, involving the destruction of major aspects of our eco-system.

The number of people affected by natural disasters rose by one billion between 1984–1994, most in developing countries which lack insurance. So, as from October 2005, the UN has been setting aside an annual Day for Disaster Reduction, and the Institute for Environment and Human Security at the UN University of Bonn has announced the setting up of a new chair on 'Social Vulnerability'.[19] But one of the most alarming and ill-thought out responses has been a 'war on terror'. In the words of a recent report by a Working Group of the Church of England's House of Bishops: '"War on terrorism" like the talk in the 1980s about a "war on drugs" is a piece of dangerous rhetoric.'[20] It has led to the curtailing of civil liberties and, more disgracefully, the secret transferring of suspected 'terrorists' to other countries which can, with impunity, apply torture as part of their methods of interrogation, in a process shamefully described by the US government as 'extraordinary rendition'.[21] Furthermore behaviour of this sort, and indeed the invasion of Iraq itself has proved counter-productive in that it has actually tended to increase terrorist activity.[22] Yet US policy remains stark: 'America is at war....The United States is in the early years of a long struggle, similar to what our country faced in the early years of the Cold War.' A National Intelligence Council report is even more specific: 'We expect that by 2020 al-Qaeda will be superseded by similarly inspired but more diffuse Islamic extremist groups...[and] the United States increasingly will have to battle world public opinion....' A tragic by-product of the 'war on terror' is the way it has served to divert attention from Africa and elsewhere in the developing world, where the scale of deaths resulting from poverty, malnutrition and disease has reached unconscionable proportions, as well as undermining the urgency of the need for action to prevent the growing damage being done to the earth's environment. As the UK Government's own Chief Scientific Adviser, Sir David King, has warned: 'Climate change is the most severe problem we are facing today, more serious even than the threat of terrorism.'[23] Lord Rees, President of the Royal Society has also warned: '...this century may be a defining moment. The 21st century is the first in our planet's history where one species has Earth's future in its hands, and could·jeopardise life's immense potential.' One must hope that there is substance to the reports that the US may at last be beginning to recognize the inadequacy of a strategy based on a 'war on terror' and that it may be moving, together with the European Union, to a policy of engagement with Muslim communities.[24]

Meanwhile, the awful paradox is summed up by Irene Khan, Secretary General of Amnesty International, who whilst acknowledging that '[t]here is no stronger international community than global civil society', felt at the same time compelled to warn that human rights were under the most sustained attack, since the establishment of the United Nations.[25] In 1989 it looked as though the civil society we were entering was that of Locke with its promise of rights and freedom. By 2005, our 'civil society' is in danger of being re-shaped in the image of Hobbes where security, order and the use of force become the overriding criterion.

Where does that leave the project of social transformation? Is it the case, as Qoheleth reminds us, that 'for everything there is a season', and that the season for social transformation has passed and that we now live in a time of concern simply for ensuring survival? Has what appeared to be the kairos moment of 1989 when, for example, out of the Ecumenical Assembly at Basel, there emerged Kairos Europa become simply a fading memory? Or is this not the time to address with greater urgency the real causes of insecurity, climate change, terrorism, and the violation of human rights? Like it or not, we live in an age where the forces of one kind of social transformation or another are racing blindly ahead – global capital-ism, technological developments, the exhaustion of the earth's resources, and the mass displacement of people. And does this not make it all the more imperative to seek another kind of social transformation?

1. The Testing of Hope

Aloft all hands, strike the top masts and belay;
Yon angry setting sun and fierce-edged clouds
Declare the Typhon's coming.
Before it sweeps your decks, throw overboard
The dead and dying – ne'er heed their chains
Hope, Hope, fallacious Hope!
Where is thy market now?'
Joseph Mallord William Turner [26]

To seek a mature hope is to resist simple invitations to 'look on the bright side', to 'try harder', or to cast one's lot with some new messiah, be it a new folk hero or a new social movement. A mature hope may still receive support from a perhaps innate longing of the human spirit or from the creative power of the imagination, but it can only be grounded in truth. It must reflect precisely on the story of its own hopes, asking why certain cherished hopes have failed and how they might teach us the wisdom needed for a mature hope. A realistic hope – grounded on the reality of God's love and promise – is not a diminished hope, borne in a spirit of weary resignation. On the contrary, it is precisely the sort of hope that refuses to remain stuck at the stage of disappointment and disillusionment, but is able, in a true spirit of realism, to keep its sights set on and its energies devoted towards a radically different world, with a richer common life. It must be discovered, not invented, and that entails a spirit of discipleship – a willingness to let go at the right time of our ideas and vision so that we can learn anew. And it calls for a spirit of repentance – a readiness to recognize that the path to social transformation on which we have started may not be the right one.

We can call for help in this process on the example of people – not all of them Christian – who have struggled to develop a mature hope. This involves looking, with the English painter Turner, at 'the fallacies of hope', accepting with the playwright Samuel Beckett the inherent frustrations of human creativity, appreciating with the American theologian Reinhold Niebuhr the importance of irony, learning with Paul Mendes-Flohr the need to lament, and recovering, with John Milbank, the role of atonement. It is these lessons in hope that will be looked at here.

The Fallacies of Hope – Turner

Accompanying several of Turner's most powerful paintings are verses which bear the curious title *Fallacies of Hope*.[27] The theme was not original to Turner. 'Fallacious hope' was a note often intoned by 18th century poets.[28] What is significant is what Turner did with the theme. Partly this reflects the connection Turner made between hope, memory and 'the sublime'. Turner was, after all, the painter of the sublime – the picturesque sublime, the architectural sublime, the topographical sublime, the historical sublime and the apocalyptic sublime.[29] Evoking the sublime is a way of stating that reality exceeds both the power of human action to control, and the capacity of the human mind to comprehend. Nature is alive with energies, powerful but obscure, which are likely to erupt unpredictably, unexpectedly, in flashes of grandeur, with awesome creative and destructive force – tumultuous seas, earthquakes, avalanches – putting finite human beings in their place. For Turner this implied, according to Eric Shanes, 'that all hopes of successfully defying the forces of external nature, of overcoming the contradictions of human nature, and of religious redemption, are fallacious.' But it was not only to scenes of nature that he affixed these verses. He also applied it to the exploits of heroic figures – from Hannibal to Napoleon: 'Clearly,' notes Shanes, 'it was an irony that was directed at Turner's fellow empire-building countrymen, warning of the perils that awaited them if they similarly neglected their duty to serve the needs of the state and of each other. The notion that each citizen should eschew self-interest, vanity and luxury in pursuit of the common welfare was frequently encountered in eighteenth-century Augustan poetry, whence Turner undoubtedly derived it....'

When musing on the fallacies of hope, Turner was not simply indulging in Romantic melancholy; he was criticising the folly of hopes which arose from a desire to dominate history and nature. He was aligning himself with the forces of liberation and creativity.[30] The fallacies of hope, in other words, need to be understood within the wider context of Turner's enduring fascination with the sublime – an appeal to the imagination and indeed the wondrous and terrifying aspects of reality that are beyond imagining.

Not without reason has the notion of the sublime become an emblem of postmodernism's challenge to the prison of modernity. It is expressed from a theological perspective by John Milbank, leader of the 1995 Towards Social Transformation seminar.[31] It points to the crucial role played by imagination in breaking the boundaries of the possible, in defying the limits of false 'realism' and in envisioning a wealth of alternatives. But it also suggests that social transformation is not something wholly in our control and that it therefore demands receptivity as activity, dependency as well as autonomy – in short, a willingness to be transformed.

At a period in history when so many transformative hopes have proved fallacious, there are certain currents of Christian theology that may be particularly relevant. One such current is represented by the theology of Augustine of Hippo. It is quite understandable why his theology has had such a revival in the past two decades. It is not that we are all Augustinians now or even that we all read Augustine in the same way.[32] There is much in Augustine which is unpalatable and which cannot simply be put down to the context in which he lived. But there is much in Augustine that speaks directly to the project of social transformation, especially in the wake of fallacious hope. That is why his theology will appear often in the following chapters.

Fidelity to Failure – Beckett

When describing the artist's frustration in being unable to capture in his painting the full reality he wishes to express, Samuel Beckett speaks of 'fidelity to failure': '…to be an artist is to fail, as no other dare fail, that failure is his world and the shrink from it desertion. The history of painting, here we go again, is the history of the attempts to escape from this sense of failure, by means of more authentic, more ample, less exclusive relations between representer and representee….all that is required now, in order to bring even this horrible matter to an acceptable conclusion, is to make of this submission, this admission, this fidelity to failure, a new occasion, a new form of relation, and of the art which, unable to act, he makes an expressive act, even if only of itself, of the impossibility, of its obligation….'[33] A similar note is struck by Terry Eagleton: 'Radicals are those who seek to preserve in some way a compact with failure, to remain faithful to it; but there is then always a temptation to fetishize it, forgetting that it is not in that, but in human plenitude and affirmation, that the end of political action lies.'[34]

There is a hint of this in the aesthetics of John Ruskin, from whom the theologian John Milbank takes inspiration when referring to the 'constant recognition of imperfection, of the fragmentary and therefore always-already 'ruined' character of the gothic structure, which, as John Ruskin argued, expresses the Christian imperative to straining for the ultimate at the risk of thereby more comprehensively exhibiting one's finite and fallen insufficiency….'[35]

Irony and the Hollowness of Triumph – Niebuhr

Cynicism interprets fallacious hope as the destruction of hope. Irony interprets it as the salvation of hope. Cynicism is a sign not of age; but of immaturity. The hopes of those who feel that history must turn out as they want – or indeed that their efforts will guarantee the result they want – are not hopes too big. They are hopes too small. They reflect the very spirit, namely the *libido dominandi* – the drive for power and control – which Christian social transformation aims to overcome by opening up the possibility of basing life on grace. History has its own way of dealing with those who presume to bend it to fit their limited hopes.

Christian theology did not need postmodernism to discover the importance of irony. Fifty years ago, in the aftermath of the Second World War, America seemed on the verge of global hegemony. For Reinhold Niebuhr it was a time not for celebration but for sober reflection on 'the irony of American history'. In words that could have been written yesterday, Niebuhr warns his fellow Americans: 'The fact that the European nations, more accustomed to the tragic vicissitudes of history, still have a measure of misgiving about our leadership in the world community is due to their fear that our "technocratic" tendency to equate the mastery of nature with the mastery of history could tempt us to lose patience with the tortuous course of history....We might be tempted to bring the whole of modern history to a tragic conclusion by one final and mighty effort to overcome its frustrations. The political term for such an effort is "preventive war"....'[36]

If that warning was true at the dawn of a bi-polar world, all the more so is it relevant to the new age of (apparently) unchallenged American hegemony. The triumph of American power has indeed proved particularly hollow. Looked at in terms of pure military might, the experience first of Afghanistan and then of Iraq have demonstrated the shortcomings of the theory of 'Rapid Dominance'.[37] However effective 'shock and awe' may be in winning wars, they are worse than useless in winning peace. The unleashing of such military might has had the opposite effect of what was intended. It has generated hatred, fuelled terrorism, generated insecurity and fostered a regime of fear.

Lamentation and the Redemption of Suffering – Mendes-Flohr

The failures of hopes for peace, justice and social transformation mean more than disappointment for those who had set their hearts on them. For those who are the victims of war, injustice and inhumanity, they are a tragedy. A mature hope insists that they not be forgotten. Not to 'move on' or to 'put a line under it' but to remember – the victims of war, the victims of ethnic cleansing, the victims of torture, the victims of the gulags and concentration camps.

Attempts to reconcile the Holocaust with the promises of God are a problem not just for Jews but for all who believe or who would believe. Can an event of this magnitude possibly be a source of hope? Paul Mendes-Flohr, Professor of Modern Jewish Thought at the University of Chicago Divinity School, draws on the Book of Lamentations, showing that the theological function of a lament is not to demand an explanation, but, in the very expression of outrage as well as pain, to be a way of continuing to bear hope. Mendes-Flohr draws on his initial mentor Hermann Cohen for a unique insight into what Cohen calls 'prophetic hope', which 'commands us to remember the forlorn, the disinherited, to remember all those who weep and to include them in our vision of the Promised Land.'[38]

Atonement: Putting Ourselves in the Picture – Milbank

One reason for the fallacies of some hopes for social transformation is a failure to appreciate how the agents of transformation are themselves part of the problem. Transformationists may enjoy imagining themselves as artists before a clean canvass or as scientists arranging an experiment. But it is not like that. However much the modern narrative of social transformation may claim to be based on a pure aesthetic vision or on solid scientific principles, the reality is that all action is undertaken by human beings who bring with them the cultural, economic and political relations that make them what they are. Nothing could be more destructive to the process of social transformation than to imagine that its fashioners can make a clean break with the evils of the past and that they somehow stand outside, and above, what has gone before. A project undertaken from such a distorted perspective is bound to be fallacious. We do not come fresh onto the scene, much less with clean hands. We are already in the picture, part of the mess. We occupy a particular space. Our particular colour, age, gender, class are, rightly, all exposed to view. We have affected the landscape; our positioning affects the positioning of others. And, therefore, we need to look at that painting for illumination about the story in which we have been actors and for whose development we already bear some responsibility. Whether as revolutionaries or as 'guilty by-standers', whether as 'resident aliens' in a world not of our choosing, or whether as people with a vested interest in keeping things as they are, together we bear a share of the responsibility for the blessings and wounds of the world. It applies, for example, to Western leaders who speak about transforming failed states, but who fail to take account of the way that their own policies and interests may actually have made them accomplices in the failures of others. And it applies to those who have uncriticallly supported liberation movements or who have ruthlessly imposed their 'utopias'.

This is why atonement matters. Atonement is a reminder of the material side of responsibility, a witness to the fact that the acts of some have consequences on others and that saying 'Sorry' is not enough. The consequences, too, need to be addressed. A heavy price may already have been paid, irrevocably, by the victims of injustice. How is that to be acknowledged? How and to whom ought retribution be made? Such questions cannot be answered simply by cold legal awarding of damages by court decisions or even by the agonizing attempts of 'Truth and Reconciliation' committees to arrive at a shared acknowledgement of the guilt borne by those responsible for merciless killings, torture and oppression. The consequences remain. This is why atonement is needed. Atonement as a public collective act is a recognition that there are limits to the usefulness of trying to draw a clear line between the just and the unjust. It also insists that we are not allowed simply to hide in the crowd but that each of us bears personal responsibility for particular acts that have caused harm regardless of our intentions. The practice of atonement, prominent in Judaism as well as Christianity, is a response to that material reality. It is not about some monstrous idea of a God who is exacting payment – although some theologies of atonement have suggested this – but of a God who reminds us of the need, and gives us the example of how to pay the price for one another's wrong-doing because we are implicated in the story.

Hope and atonement belong together. It is striking how theologians as far apart as Reinhold Niebuhr and John Milbank can find common ground on the importance of the historical and collective dimensions of atonement – even if their interpretations of the doctrine are not quite the same. Niebuhr, for example, sees the Christian doctrine of the Atonement as 'the beginning of wisdom in the sense that it contains symbolically all that the Christian faith maintains about what man ought to do and what he cannot do, about his obligations and final incapacity to fulfil them, about the importance of decisions and achievements in history and about their final insignificance....The classical Christian idea of Atonement...emphasizes that God is both the propitiator and the propitiated. There can be no simple abrogation of the wrath of God by the mercy of God.'[39] What the Atonement reveals is 'that God cannot overcome evil without displaying in history His purpose to take the effects of evil upon and into Himself.' For Milbank, approaching it from a very different perspective, '...only God incarnate could define and so endure sin, precisely so that we can be drawn back to the cross as the very consummation of the preaching of the kingdom.... It is highly significant that from Paul, through Origen to Augustine, the early Christians seem to have thought in terms of a "continuing" atonement. Paul talks of "filling up what is lacking in the sufferings of Christ", Origen of the logos suffering to the end of time, Augustine of the church, the whole body of Christ as the complete sacrifice to God....'[40]

The atonement, moreover, is a reality that has more than moral and ontological significance. It also has historical significance, which is to say that it fully becomes real in particular and concrete events, involving specific people, individually and collectively. Few have expressed this more powerfully than Dietrich Bonhoeffer, who was led to work for the defeat of his own nation, Nazi Germany, precisely out of a sense of the need for atonement: 'Only in defeat can we atone for the terrible crimes we have committed against Europe and the world.'[41] Andrew Shanks has insisted on this point in his elaboration of what he means by 'Civil Religion'. In its liturgy, he urges, the church needs to celebrate and to enter into the reality of the atonement by grounding that proclamation in the events of our own contemporary history.

Surpassing Hope

There is, therefore, always an element of failure that a mature hope needs to take on board. And although the reason may at times be that we have hoped for the wrong things or placed our hopes on the wrong support, there is another, more fundamental reason. And that is because there is, especially in the most true and wonderful of hopes, always something that surpasses our ability fully to achieve, to articulate or even to imagine. John Keane must have realized, even in the 1980s, that, some of his own hopes for civil society might not turn out as expected, for he, too, has recourse to Beckett:

Ever tried. Ever failed.
No matter.
Try again.
Fail again.
Fail better.[42]

It is not failure that is the enemy of hope. It is the fear of failure.

2. Critical Analysis

How to make sense of the disappointment of the hopes of 1989? Why has civil society failed to deliver its transformative promise? There are at least three main streams of interpretation suggesting three factors that have caused hope to retreat. One sees it as due to a clash of faiths, either between religions themselves or between their fundamentalist followers. A second places the blame squarely at the door of American hegemony as an arrogant and malign influence on the world. Both these explanations will be looked at below – but will be seen as secondary. It will be argued that the central issue is with a third force, that of capitalist modernity, which needs to be confronted in both its positive and negative aspects. The approach will not be crudely reductionist, as if patriarchy, racism, exploitation, racism, terrorism or pandemics all have their origins in capitalist modernity and that such problems would inevitably fade away once we manage to get beyond capitalist modernity. No, the argument will be that capitalist modernity, which will be described more fully in Chapter One, is imposing a blockage – a constriction of hope and a paralysis of action. It is not that social transformation will have been completed once these constraints are overcome; it is that the conditions will then be somewhat more favourable and the path a bit clearer for us to proceed together on the journey towards a more humanly, socially and ecologically healthy social transformation.

The First Factor – A Clash of Faiths

...it is not merely events that shape responses to terrorism, but differing
interpretations of those events....
Mission and Public Affairs Council[43]

Why, since 1989, has there been such a marked rise of Islamism, of fanatical Christian apocalypticism, of Hindu nationalism and of anti-Semitism? Religious hatred is a reality even in the civil societies of the West. In Britain, the government recently deemed it expedient to introduce a bill which would make Incitement to Religious Hatred a criminal offence. Elsewhere, backed by their own interpretation of religious faith, devout young men and women have been led to further their cause by killing and by giving their own lives as suicide bombers. But does this necessarily imply a clash of faiths and is that the main source of struggle in the world today? Not necessarily. The issue is more complex, and this in two senses.

First, although it is true that religion can sometimes be the spark that ignites bloody conflicts, and can even be the central issue, religion can also serve as a useful tool to be manipulated both by governments and by leaders of opposition movements. Where an established group feels that its power or identity is being threatened, where a minority is suffering the injustice of exploitation, discrimination and oppression, where a nation feels destined to play an historic role in human affairs, it can be a source of considerable power to seek to ground this in religious faith. The fact that religion plays a key role both in inflaming and in abating conflict is nothing new. The Crusades as well as the persecutions and wars in 16th and 17th century Europe bear ample witness to that. But then, as now – whether in Northern Ireland, or the Caucasus, in the former Yugoslavia or in Kashmir – it is important to recognize that faith is only one element, of variable importance, in the wider mix of economic interests, ethnic tensions, class conflict and the struggle for political supremacy.

Secondly, in exploring the role that faith plays in such conflicts, it is worth noting that it is not simply the content of faith that is at issue. Clearly this may be the case, as for example, with some Protestant extremists who view the papacy as anti-Christ. More important, although less easy to grasp, is the way in which different faith perspectives give different interpretations of the situations, relationships and events of our world.

The General Synod of the Church of England has been urged to appreciate this point as it grapples with the questions of how to respond to the threat of terrorism from Islamist factions: 'Trying to see the world through Muslim eyes and listening to the testimony of Muslim voices means encountering different narratives of injustice and violence from those we habitually adopt as our own, yet recognizing our common humanity.'[44]

In short, it is not sufficient to take the clash of faiths thesis at face value. There are other, deeper factors which need to be explored. One of these is about the way the clash of faiths can be made a self-fulfilling prophecy by the misuse of power. That is what will be explored next.

The Second Factor – American Hegemony

President Clinton was committed to American hegemony, but his administration did not adhere to an American chauvinism.
Church of England House of Bishops' Working Group[45]

With the ending of the bi-polar world, America remains as the sole super-power. Its economic and military might are unprecedented. But how must that power be used and with whom must it be shared? The Iraq war has exposed the way even that awesome power can be over-extended. More than that, it has also illustrated the limits of sheer brute force. American hegemony, like the hegemony of previous empires is sustainable only with the aid of 'softer' but more fundamental supports – economic dependency, cultural excellence, political legitimacy. It is the erosion of these that is working against the continuation of American hegemony. In particular, there are two such forces. The first is the geo-political re-alignment that is resulting from global capitalism. The second is American policy itself.

As for global capitalism, the growing size and nature of the Chinese economy is having a major impact on the pattern of economic interests and dependencies. The development of its manufacturing has already made it 'the world's preferred manufacturing centre'.[46] In 2003 it entered into a strategic alliance with the European Union, and in November 2006 business and political leaders from over forty African countries attended a two-day summit in Beijing which led to new Chinese commitments to trade, investment and loans. But insofar as it is winning such markets by adopting a minimalist stance to human rights and environmental well-being. China has been accused of undermining the still fragile campaign to get international investors to incorporate these issues into their programmes for developing countries. The strength of its currency has created a huge dependency on the part of other South East Asian countries and on the part of the US itself. Its trade networks have been bringing about a subtle geopolitical shift, both in terms of its new trade relations with South America, which is loosening that region's long-standing dependence on the US and in terms of the drive to secure supplies of oil and gas in the South Caucasus and South East Asia, which is bringing China into direct competition with the US.

As for the way American policy itself is undermining its own hegemony, its leaders would do well to read the chapter 'International Order and the Ambiguity of American Power' in the recent report by a working group of the Church of England's House of Bishops.[47] Here is what they have to say about the Bush Administration's National Security Strategy, produced one year after 9/11: 'This policy of American exceptionalism reserves for itself the right to determine who are its friends and enemies. This downplays the role of multi-lateralism and any reciprocal obligation and collective decision-making....The Strategy confirms America's hegemonic status and propagates "a distinctively American internationalism that reflects the union of our values and our national interest"....Rather than using its predominance to cement or develop the post-1945 concert of powers in support of regulated capitalist growth, world stability and the relief of poverty, contemporary American nationalism appears at times to be directed at seeking out new enemies and markets. This crisis of modernity releases American power from any sense of responsibility. It is an extremely unstable basis upon which to base any hegemony, not least because it increases enmity at the expense of amity.'

A complementary but fuller analysis, put into the framework of other historical empires, is made by Giovanni Arrighi. He, too, stresses that hegemony depends not on power, be it military, political or economic, but on the readiness of subordinate nations to accept the legitimacy of one nation playing a leading role, because this is beneficial either in helping to promote their own prosperity or at least in protecting them from some other threatening power. This, he argues, is what America once provided, through its crucial role in helping to defeat Fascism, its Marshall Plan and its defence against Communism. With the ending of the bi-polar world, its reckless foreign policy, its selfish refusal to be party to international agreements on pollution control, its unashamed contempt for international law,[48] its barbarity in its treatment of prisoners of war, have combined to give the impression – to put it most charitably – that America is less than a benign influence for the future of the planet. It has, furthermore, actually poured fuel on the flames of international terrorism. Economic and environmental policy have undermined that hegemony. Its neo-imperialism is perceived more as threat than as blessing.[49]

It is sometimes thought that America has gone on the offensive as a result of 9/11. But this is to fail to consider where 9/11 came from as well as where the National Security Strategy originated. The Strategy, as shown by Stanley Hoffman, goes back at least to 1992 in the draft Defense Planning Guidance prepared by Dick Cheney and associates.[50] Similarly, if one takes seriously the fact that 15 of the 19 people involved in the 9/11 atrocity were Saudis – including Osama bin Laden – one can begin to trace the development of this rabid hatred of America which was seen as having long supported a corrupt

Saudi regime but, above all was seen as having violated the sacred land of the Prophet by stationing of US troops in the Iraq War of 1990–91.

The Bishops offer words of comfort: 'The nationalism currently displayed by the US is the exception rather than the norm.' This may well be true of what Stanley Hoffman calls 'the new exceptionalism' but it is certainly not true of the deeper strands of American exceptionalism, which derive from the following five factors: a sense of moral superiority; a divinely commissioned historic mission; a long-standing maxim to avoid 'entangling alliances'; a version of human rights in the US Constitution which gives no recognition to economic and social rights; and the lack of a significant socialist movement.

The problem is not American hegemony nor is the solution anti-Americanism. America will clearly have a major and often leading role to play. That role will be the more constructive to the extent that America can overcome its sense of exceptionalism. So deep-rooted is that sense, however, and so much a part of American identity that it will not easily be overcome by logical argument, much less by physical or cultural attack but only by a willingness to re-interpret its own history.

The Third Factor – Capitalist Modernity

While in 1989 some were placing their hopes for social transformation on a faith in new forms of socialism, others were hoping for a very different social transformation based on a faith in a reinvigorated capitalism. One of the most influential manifestations of that faith was the 'Washington Consensus', so called because it was adopted by the Washington-based IMF and, to a lesser extent, by the World Bank. It was actually on the eve of – not after – the collapse of Communism that, in November 1989, a British economist, John Williamson, was preparing that policy for the still new government of George Bush Senior.But by 2006 the IMF itself was heading for a deficit because not enough nations needed to borrow from it.[51] Capitalism had been given free rein. Capital was plentiful, credit cheap, money was mobile, shares soaring, and profits staggering.

What has capitalism delivered during that period? The period may be divided into two phases – a decade of irresponsibility, reaching crisis point in 1998, followed by a period of reform.The rise of 'gangster capitalism' in the former Communist countries and a series of scandals in the West involving some of the world's biggest and most respected firms, a periodic eruption of financial crises including that of Long-Term Capital Management in 1994, the Mexican currency crisis of 1995, the South Asian crisis of 1997 – whose effects were felt in areas as far apart as Russia and Brazil by 1998, the bursting of the dotcom bubble in 2000 and the Argentine defaults of 2001 and 2002. It is a matter of fierce debate as to just how much of the blame should be pinned on the policies of the Washington Consensus. Certainly Joseph Stiglitz, former Chief Economist at the World Bank has no doubt about the disastrous role played by the IMF in seeking to impose the Consensus on countries whose social, economic and political infrastructures could not cope with it. But faiths are hard to shake. Williamson insists that much of the Consensus remains valid even though admitting that the results have been disappointing in terms of growth, employment and poverty reduction. For these failures, however, he puts part of the blame on external factors such as the financial crises of the following decade, and on the failure of some governments to implement the reforms fully or follow them through. But the financial scandals continued. As *Forbes Magazine* commented: '2003 will be remembered as the year in which a raft of new financial fiascos surfaced rather than the year that Wall Street finally cleaned up its act.'[52]

But there is no denying the run of scandals, in a line-up so lengthy that they provide the letters for a damning new capitalist alphabet: **A** for Arthur Anderson and other auditors;[53] **B** for Barings;[54] **C** for Citigroup;[55] **D** for Dirty Money;[56] **E** for Enron;[57] **F** for Financial Advisers who systematically mis-sold mortgages, pensions and insurance policies; **G** for Garnier, Grasso and other golden handshakes, golden hellos and golden good-byes regardless of performance;[58] **H** for Hollinger International;[59] **L** for Long Term Management;[60] **O** for Oligarchs, who made fortunes buying cheaply state-owned assets in the former Soviet Union; **P** for Parmalat;[61] **R** for Refco;[62] **S** for SONY;[63] **T** for Tyco;[64] **U** for unions which were blocked by the concerted efforts by transnational corporations to prevent trade union organization in developing countries;[65] and **W** for WorldCom.[66] The list is far from complete.[67] The aggressive pursuit of corporate criminal activity on Wall Street by New York State's Attorney General Eliot Spitzer brought him a barrage of criticism from those who deplored his intimidating tactics, but also earned him the title 'Person of the Year' from the *Financial Times*.[68]

What is most worrying is that the scandals did not involve small players but some of the giants and most highly regarded firms in both the financial and industrial world. Nor were they isolated incidents but were, in large part, systemic. The charge that '[i]n terms of financial flows, the decade of the 1990s was the most corrupt in the past half century and probably the most corrupt in history' comes not from some anti-globalization movement but from Raymond W. Baker, who spent over forty years in business, most of it in the developing world, and is no anti-capitalist.[69]

As will be seen in Chapter Four, the shock of so many scandals has led to a series of reforms meant to address the problems of corruption, destabilization and environmental destruction. But the real scandal is the way unchallenged capitalism has continued to deliver obscene wealth to the few, has boosted the prosperity of the relatively comfortable but has failed to use its economic power to meet the UN's very realistic Millennium Goals and to develop a sense of economic responsibility to halt the destruction of the environment.

The argument here is that there is a close interconnection between the problems of climate change, of mass migration, of political instability of war and terrorism[70] and that in all of these capitalism is deeply implicated, not as the sole force at work but as the dominant force. And it is the dominant force not only in terms of its consequences but in terms of the values and motivation that are shaping our culture. It is capitalism as a civilization that needs to be addressed.

Modernity

If capitalism is the central issue, why then attempt to address modernity as well? The reason is partly that modernity and capitalism have historically been so closely intertwined, and also that modernity creates its own limits to social transformation and has indeed been partly responsible for the failure of some forms of socialism.

Martin Wolf of the *Financial Times* argues the case for modernity from a capitalist perspective: '...we must recognize that the underlying struggle is over how Islamic civilization achieves it reconciliation with modernity....Of the four great civilizations of Eurasia, European, Chinese, Indian and Islamic – it is the last that has found it most difficult to accept the transformation brought about by the first....Ultimately it is this failed modernization, and the incompetence, corruption and tyranny of Islamic governments – many, alas, long supported by the West – that fuels the jihad movement.'[71]

But capitalism's link with modernity is not necessarily essential or even as historically close as is sometimes thought. The role of the Protestant ethic in the development of capitalism, for example, has long been appreciated. And in the US today, there is an ever stronger and more aggressive link between capitalism and a positively anti-modern conservative strain of evangelicalism. This point is explored in the recent House of Bishops' Working Group report which identifies 'the strange paradox that many Americans are deeply hostile to the modern world, which America itself has made, and which the American thesis claims as its proudest achievement.'[72]

So there is some point in addressing the issue of modernity in its own right, as will be pursued in Chapters One and Three. The post-1989 world may actually have given rise to a kairos of a sort quite different from that imagined by Kairos Europa. In the view of the Roman Catholic theologian Nicholas Lash, 'The world we had got used to is crumbling before our very eyes. Because this world was, to a significant extent, constructed in terror, the disappearance of familiar, threatening landmarks has understandably and quite properly, given rise to rejoicing. It is a kairos – an "occasion for coming to our senses".'[73]

The regime of capitalist modernity has been challenged philosophically by Alasdair MacIntyre and theologically by John Milbank. The search for social transformation involves not a regression to some pre-capitalist, pre-modern world but for an alternative that goes beyond both. But how to move in that direction? We are at a point in history where it is simply not possible to see clearly what that alternative may be, but that must not prevent us from exploring and experimenting, however tentatively, with transformative action.

3. TOWARDS SOCIAL TRANSFORMATION

> What we need is to make larger ventures.
> J. H. (Joe) Oldham[74]

Transformation is more than reformation. It points towards a rethinking of purpose, a reassessing of values, a reshaping of relations, a redistribution of power. There are projects in the world today which go by the name of transformation but which on closer examination are actually about reinforcing power relationships. 'Transformational diplomacy', the watchword of current US foreign policy is one example. The Progressive Governance Network, like other projects of modernization, is another.[75] But it is a different sort of social transformation that our world requires – a genuine alternative. That is what will be explored in the chapters which follow.

Where to begin? What sort of action would this require? Not with a programme or a manifesto. We are at a stage where, as the World Social Forum's motto suggests, 'Another World Is Possible': but as its method suggests, the shape of that world is not entirely clear.[76]

We might best advance towards such a world by a sharing of insights and visions. If that is the way ahead, then the nature of transformative action will be more about creating openings and possibilities than about devising ideologies and imposing solutions. The kinds of action this might involve, and which underpin the explorations to be undertaken here include the following six tasks: a) rethinking transformationist theology; b) deconstructing the regime of capitalist modernity; c) redrawing the relationship between civil society and the state; d) recovering the associational tradition; e) reaffirming pluralism; and f) retaining a spirit of provisionality.

Rethinking Transformationist Theology

The first step is to rethink transformationist theology, freeing it from any remaining ties it may have with a modernist mind-set and a naïve belief in progress. This will be addressed in Chapter One, which will suggest – as many have done in the past two decades – that there are some valuable insights in Augustine of Hippo, with his narrative of the *City of God*, and with his focus on the role played by desire, specifically how the *libido dominandi* – the desire for control and power – may be overcome by discovery of grace. Here an attempt will be made to build on the plea made by the World Council of Churches: 'God, in your grace, transform the world.' The next chapter will lay the foundation for the theology of grace which will be used in subsequent chapters. These will explore the institutional implications of such an approach: what kind of institutions does a theology of grace point towards and what kind of institutions help create openings for living in grace?

Deconstructing Capitalist Modernity

How Augustine dealt with the regime of his day – the Roman Empire – offers clues as to how we might deal with the regime of our day – capitalist modernity. He did not simply seek to overthrow it but neither did he simply wait for it to collapse under the weight of its own perversity. He deconstructed it, by portraying it as but one chapter within a bigger historical narrative, in which it was neither the first nor the last empire. Thereby it could be seen as both representing the ambitions of the City of Man – driven by the *libido dominandi* – but also as serving a divine purpose in the history of the City of God. Augustine valued much of what he had gained under the empire – its cultivation of virtue, justice and beauty – whilst also ridiculing the way these had been distorted and corrupted by the regime of the *libido dominandi*. This may suggest that the best way to get beyond the regime of capitalist modernity is not by demonizing it or by refusing to acknowledge its achievements and benefits, but by deconstructing it and displaying its naked contingency – exposing its shallow historical roots, its corrupting influence, and its limited life span. This, too, will be the subject of the first chapter.

Redrawing the Relationship between Civil Society and the State

Civil society is about society. That is to say it is about the energies, visions, activities and relationships that emerge 'from below'. But to be civil, it must accept that these all take place within a wider 'City' (in Augustinian terms) not simply a closed sphere of self-interest and private pursuits. The process of agreeing and securing the wider set of rights and responsibilities is what makes necessary the role of something we now call 'the state'. It is a commonplace to say that, in the course of the 20th century, the state has overreached itself, interfering with, inhibiting and even colonizing major areas of social life. But the answer is not to make the opposite mistake of viewing the state as a threat rather than an aid to the development of civil society. One must take into account the very uncivil tendencies that exist in society – racism, patriarchy, exploitation, etc. Chapter Two will explore the different traditions and projects of civil society. It will stress both the importance of civil society as a sphere distinct from the state, with its own agenda and voice – as represented, for example, by campaign groups, such as CivWorld (the Global Citizens Campaign for Democracy),[77] Citizens for Tax Justice,[78] the Citizen Organising Foundation[79] and Citizen Works.[80] But it will also note the advantages – and the dangers – of the state's active role in empowering civil society as, for example, in the political experiments, such as the 'participatory budget' process in Porto Alegre, Brazil and the 'Bolivarian socialism' being promoted in Venezuela by Hugo Chavez with its twin policies of state-assisted co-operatives and workers' councils from above and *Comites de Tierra* from below.

Recovering the Associational Tradition

One of the ways in which civil society can be activated and enriched is by the spontaneous coming together of people to undertake common tasks. A somewhat romantic interpretation of the 19th century sees this as a kind of golden age of associationalism, as it is called, which led to the flourishing of society. The reality is far more problematic, then as now. Not all associations are civic. The danger in the 19th century – when nations were largely white, Christian (in name at least) and English-speaking – was that some associations could largely reproduce and reinforce relationships of class and gender power. The danger in the 20th century – when nations are more multi-ethnic, multi-religious and multi-cultural – is that associations could encourage the development of ghettoes. The norm is an associational life which is open and diverse. Associations, whether for environmental change, for social justice or simply for leisure have the capacity to bring together people of very diverse backgrounds and enable them to discover what they have and can do in common. Associations can be agents of transformation, witness their popularity amongst socialists not just liberals and conservatives in the 19th century. Here the possibilities of associational action will be explored, in its relation both to economic life (Chapter Four) and to political life (Chapter Five).

Reaffirming Pluralism

In a period of insecurity, mass migration and the fear of terrorism, there is a particular temptation to retreat, culturally and even geographically, into communities of the like-minded. It is particularly worrying when this happens in the church, because that is a denial of its vocation. The church, as a reflection of the *City of God*, is by definition meant not simply to be open to people of all cultures but to see in those cultures a manifestation of the richness and diversity of God's creation. The issue, of course, is how to hold together respect for truth and respect for difference? This will be the focus of attention in Chapter Three. Here is where Augustine is less than helpful. For where Augustine was inclined to see difference as heresy and, therefore, a betrayal of the truth, we are better able to appreciate difference as pluralism and, therefore, an enrichment of truth. Where Augustine tended to limit his critique of authority to the civil sphere, we are more prepared to address the problem of authoritarianism and the abuse of power within the church itself. Therefore, Chapter Three will seek to marry

Augustinian insights with the approach to the essential interaction of cultural and material reality pioneered by Raymond Williams, developed by Stuart Hall and used by many others, including Edward Said.[81] Williams' argument for 'a common culture' will be used to provide a fuller framework in which the current debate about 'multiculturalism' can be addressed.

Retaining a Spirit of Provisionality

One of the watchwords of modernity is 'reflexivity'. One of the insights in contemporary thinking about civil society is the importance of 'self-limitation'. These are essential features of any contemporary project of social transformation. This is the lesson to be learned from the grandiose and often nightmarish utopian projects of the past century – the need for provisionality, or what Augustine would call humility. It is not just that we are prone to making mistakes and to imposing our own will on others, nor is it just that the world is changing too fast for us to keep up with. It is not even that growth and learning come from reflecting upon the intended and unintended consequences of our actions, although it is all these things. The real reason for provisionality, however, is that transformation is a process not a goal. It is about awakening our desires, sensitivities and intellects, not satisfying them.

Conclusion
www: Symbol of Social Transformation

> He who receives an idea from me, receives instruction himself
> without lessening mine, as he who lights a taper from mine, receives
> light without darkening me.
> Thomas Jefferson[82]

In March 1989, as our own Towards Social Transformation initiative was taking shape, Tim Berners Lee, at the European Organization for Nuclear Research (CERN), was presenting his proposal for a form of non-hierarchical, cooperative and free sharing of information, which, two years later, would become known as 'the world-wide web'.[83]

The web, with all its ambivalences, is worth holding up as a symbol of how – in the real world – our lives and relationships can be transformed. It has been used to advance and to undermine the cause of capitalism. It has been used to develop terrorist networks such as 'the virtual hand of jihad' and networks working for peace and justic.[84] It has been used to disseminate misinformation as well as knowledge, to promote pornography as well as high culture. But it can also act as a symbol of what could lie at the heart of an alternative model of social transformation. For the true and perhaps more lasting contribution of the world wide web may be not so much technological as social, not just in what it does but in what it symbolises. It is not just that the web has made possible a global conversation, has opened up a wider world for those who were isolated, has helped break down established hierarchies, has made knowledge of health care accessible to those in developing countries who are remote from towns and hospitals, and has supported networks and movements for social transformation. In symbolic terms, its great value is that it has offered all this free of charge.

In so doing it has demonstated the immense advantage of sharing a precious resource – knowledge. It is a model that has been taken up by others, for example, the One Laptop per Child and Ndiyo initiatives, both non-profit organizations seeking to bring computer access to people in the most remote and poorest parts of the world at a cost of $100 or less per computer and using new open-source systems.[85]

The web could have been constructed for profit. Instead it bears witness to the fact that by sharing resources we all become richer not poorer, by sharing power we all become freer not more insecure, by sharing knowledge we all become more wise.

Another world really is possible.

Chapter One

Transforming Mission
Regime Change

Nobody thought that we would so thoroughly transform our opponents.
Margaret Thatcher on New Labour[1]

This time of global transformation calls for transformational diplomacy.
Condoleezza Rice, U.S. Secretary of State[2]

Tell me, I pray thee, how fares the human race: if new roofs be risen
in the ancient cities, whose empire is it that now sways the world?
Blessed Paul the Hermit[3]

Précis

Transformation by grace is an essential part of Christian mission. Precisely what shape that transforming mission ought to take varies with different social and historical contexts and with fresh insights into the gospel itself.

Here the argument is: a) that, in spite of a great deal of the talk about post-capitalism and post-modernity in the past half-century, we are in fact in an age where the forces of marketization and modernization have consolidated rather than undermined the regime of capitalist modernity; b) that the obstacles which capitalism and modernity place in the way of a grace-centred common way of life far outweigh the opportunities they present and c) that in this context transforming mission entails transforming the regime of capitalist modernity.

Before such an argument can proceed it is essential to be clear what 'capitalism' and 'modernity' actually are. That will be the task set in the first part of the present chapter. It will stress the importance of viewing capitalist modernity in historical perspective. This means recognizing both capitalism and modernity as contingent phenomena, which owe their existence to particular sets of conditions and events. They did not have to be nor is the continuation of their regime inevitable. Having some grasp of how they came to be and how they have been transformed in the course of time can offer valuable clues as to how they might be transformed in the future.

The second part of the chapter will be theological. It will note that the regime of capitalist modernity continues to be challenged by theologians such as John Milbank and Timothy Gorringe, and philosophers such as Alasdair MacIntyre. It will argue that the profound impact of factors such as globalization, technological advances, 9/11, and capitalist modernity itself all make transformationist theology increasingly relevant to our times. It will, however, examine some recent criticisms of the way transformationist theology has been set forth in the influential framework developed by H. Richard Niebuhr and foreshadowed by Etienne Gilson. It will argue that transformationist theology needs to be developed by incorporating a more explicit theology of grace. A key resource for such a development is Augustine of Hippo, whose significance for our times has been noted by many in recent decades. In addition to his theology of grace and desire, his portrayal of the history of the City of God provides a fitting framework within which the story of the rise and fall of the regime of capitalist modernity may be depicted

Preamble: Transforming Mission

There may also be such a thing as vitalizing anxiety
– an ache about transformation which keeps us alive…
Rowan Williams [4]

When David Bosch was constructing his masterly overview of Christian mission, 'Transforming Mission' was not the title he had in mind. He describes how he overcame his initial misgivings about the title, eventually coming to relish the very ambivalence of the phrase, which affirmed that it was the role of Christian mission to transform society, but also that our understanding of mission itself needed constantly to be transformed.[5] The same could be said about any project towards social transformation. It is not just the signs of the times that need to be re-interpreted; it is also the theology of social transformation itself.

The theme of transformation features in the New Testament. Precisely how it relates to Jesus' proclamation of the Kingdom of God has been a matter of heated controversy for a century and a half. It becomes more explicit as part of a post-resurrection, post-Pentecostal faith, appearing in the epistles of Paul,

Peter and John, as well as in the Book of Revelation. At the heart of that faith is a confidence in that the death of Jesus was not a defeat but a different kind of victory both over death and over the powers that 'in this age' rule over the world. The gifts of the Spirit, however, are a sign that, in some sense, this new age has in part already begun. Perhaps the most moving of all these images is that of Romans 8:21–22: 'Always there was hope, that the universe itself is to be freed from the shackles of mortality and enter upon the freedom and splendour of the offspring of God. For until now, we know, the whole created universe has been groaning in all its parts, as if in the first pangs of childbirth.'

The problem of course is that, like the Kingdom of God, the victory of Jesus and the power of the Spirit have given rise to all sorts of notions of what transforming mission is all about – from providing justification for a triumphalist church working hand in glove with Christian imperial powers, to viewing progressive, revolutionary and liberation movements as harbingers of 'the Kingdom', to constituting a summons to form pure communities that have nothing to do with this wicked world. In the context of capitalist modernity, some Christians might argue that it is precisely the transformative energy of capitalist modernity which makes it something which should, with reservations, be welcomed and in which we are called, with caution, to participate. Other Christians might see it simply as, in God's providence, supplying the context in which transforming mission is to be carried out. If a case can be made that the regime of capitalist modernity should itself be seen as an object of transforming mission, it cannot simply invoke the rhetoric of 'transformation' but must attempt to show why that regime stands in need of transformation as well giving some clues as to what that transformation might involve. The first step then is to take a close look at the regime of capitalist modernity.

1. The Regime of Capitalist Modernity – The Great Debate

The term capitalist modernity is used here to highlight the fact that modernity has been so stamped by capitalism that it cannot properly be understood apart from capitalism. And this in three ways. First, it was in the context of mercantile capitalism that modernity arose. The disruption and social dislocation caused by capitalism created a setting in which new ordering forces were needed. Modernity's tendency to order and control have, ever since, served as a means for the 'socializing' of capitalism's anarchic and destructive tendencies. Secondly and conversely, modernity's own ideology of creating ruptures – its dis-embedding (disrupting of social bonds) and de-traditionalizing (disparaging of traditional norms and values) – itself generates a process which makes it easier for human and material realities to be transformed into capital and treated as commodities, by stripping them of their intrinsic worth and attributing to them mainly instrumental value. Thirdly, modernity has provided a framework which bestows on these processes a logic of universality, necessity and, therefore, legitimacy – 'There Is No Alternative'. It is hardly surprising that policies of modernization have, to a large extent, been shaped by the needs of capitalism and have provided a cover for extending the scope of privatization, market operations and the subordination of labour to new methods of production. Modernity is not innocent.

Over half a century ago, Ralf Dahrendorf argued that our society was already 'post-capitalist' and for some three decades others have been describing our society as 'post-modernist'. To accept such labels at face value might be tempting but it would also be very misleading. Today it is capitalism that is winning and social democracy that is on the ropes. As for post-modernity its most valuable insights can be incorporated into other frameworks, including that of 'reflexive modernity' itself (see below) while much of it has proved ethereal and ephemeral. New analyses are needed, as Jack Goody has argued in his summary of the question, *Capitalism and Modernity: The Great Debate*, where he commends Andre Gunder Frank, who in his last years, totally revised his theory of capitalist dependency which exerted such great influence on development thinking in the last 20th century. The task then is to understand both at the process of development of capitalist modernity and at its interaction with today's global forces. The next two sections will look at the meaning and development first of capitalism and then of modernity.

1.1 Interpreting Capitalism

Too often the critique of capitalism is misconstrued – sometimes deliberately – as an attack on markets, private property contractual relations or on capital as such. Yet the real reason why both Right and Left have mounted fundamental critiques of capitalism is that both realize that capitalism is much more than an economic system. It is a social, cultural and political reality that undermines moral values, that reshapes social relations and that threatens vested interests, whether secular or religious. The following attempt to interpret capitalism will look at it first from a spatial perspective – as a regime and a civilization as well as an economic system – and then from a temporal perspective – as a contingent reality whose emergence, development and fate are due not to some natural law but to particular historical circumstances.

Capitalism: Economic System, Regime, Civilization

If capitalism were simply a market economy, there would be less cause for concern. But it is much more than that. It is a system which constructs markets in a particular way so that they function to enhance particular sets of interests. Fernand Braudel, in his fascinating three-volume study, *Civilization and Capitalism: 15th–18th Century*, refers to capitalism as 'anti-market'. The market 'was a world of transparence and regularity, in which everyone could be sure in advance, with all the benefits of common experience, how the processes of exchange would work.' But capitalism was a game that only rich merchants knew how to play, operating in a sphere where inside knowledge is the key to evaluating risk and calculating future profit: 'They would send it [grain] to a variety of destinations – to places where famine had sent the price up out of all proportion to the original purchasing price; or to places where it could be exchanged for a certain limited commodity.'[6] The emergence today of hedge funds and trading in derivatives, with their lack of transparency and feverish re-allocation of funds, is not an aberration. It is a perfect expression of the tendencies of capitalism, which have now been given scope to operate freely.

If capitalism were merely a matter of private property, it might present less of a moral problem. But it is much more than that. It is a system which defines what sorts of physical, artistic and intellectual assets can legitimately be claimed as private property and what sets of rights and responsibilities are attached to property. It enshrines a notion of property that has few, if any, inherent social obligations and which sees social responsibilities as an added extra and not what one is in business for. Social responsibility enters in mainly as the result either of regulation from above, or of class conflict and social protest from below, or of the need to offer a good public image for potential customers and investors.

If capitalism were purely a set of economic relations governed by contracts freely entered into, it would not pose a serious threat. But it is much more than that. The ideology construes the capital–labour relationship as a free transaction, relying on the fiction that individuals have a property in (i.e. 'own') their labour, which they can decide to sell as they choose in exchange for wages. The reality, however, is that prior to any such contract, the mass of population has been constructed as a class of 'labourers', who must sell their labour in order to survive. It is a system of structured power which, left to itself, tends to deepen the unequal relations of power, status and wealth.

If capitalism were simply a system where everyone was a capitalist, the judgement would be mixed. Having a bit of capital can promote independence, creativity and security – which is the point made decades ago by G. K. Chesterton and the distributists,[7] and more recently by Hernando de Soto.[8] In that sense, there were capitalists long before there was capitalism, as Marx himself noted when describing merchants' capital and usurers' capital as the 'twin brothers in the antediluvian forms of capital'. Capitalism is much more than that. It is a process of capital accumulation and wealth concentration as stressed by both Braudel and Marx. Profits are used to generate more profits. The accumulation of profits sets up a competitive relationship amongst capitalists, which in turn creates pressure for further accumulation. In order to speed up the process of accumulation, the tendency is to move from the slow lane of concentration (relying only on profits as a source of further investment) to the fast lane of centralization (relying on credit and on mergers as a source of further investment).

Capitalism as an Economic System

If, then, capitalism is not simply markets, private property, contract or even capital itself, what exactly is it that is being critiqued here? The classical analysis provided by Marxism argues that an economic system is defined by its *mode of production*, which in turn is based on the *forces of production* (the role of money, changes in technology, as for example the mechanical, the electrical, the chemical stages of industrialization and the post-industrial development of information technology) and the *relations of production* (the composition, organization, social status, legal rights and power of the economic classes). The fact that there were capitalists under feudalism did not make the system capitalist because production under feudalism was primarily for use, with production for the market occupying a secondary role. What defines capitalism as an economic system is that it is: a) centred on the production of commodities, that is goods and services, whose use-value (meeting a human physical or cultural need) is overshadowed by their exchange value; where b) such commodities are allocated through the mechanism of markets (giving the use value a social character in that it is not for the use of those who produced it); and where c) they are produced under a social arrangement where the means of production are privately owned by a minority, and the labour is performed by a larger section of the population who have no effective choice but to sell their labour power if they are to subsist and to live a decent life. The key feature in all this is that labour power itself becomes a commodity, i.e. it has a use and an exchange value.

Capitalism as a Regime

Capitalism becomes a regime in two senses. It is a regime, first, insofar as it offers its own set of rewards and disciplines. It is immensely productive – indeed it has frequently suffered from crises due to overproduction. The disciplines it imposes consist not just of the requirement to work (under conditions set by capital) but also of the requirement to consume. It is a regime, secondly, insofar as the continuing process of capital accumulation creates a structural inequality of wealth, which then translates into inequality of power.

What is striking about the regime is its impersonality. That is to say, first, that most of us have diverse roles – most of us are workers as well as consumers, tax-payers as well as users of public services and, if we have a pension or a savings account, we have a stake in capital. Secondly, it is an impersonal regime to the extent that relationships are formed and decisions made primarily on the basis of our interests. We are, for the most part, wholly ignorant even of the processes, much less of the people, who have a role in producing and distributing what we consume or who are affected by the decisions made by the holders of our pensions funds or our savings accounts. We let the laws of the markets – politically, economically and socially constructed – call the tune.

Seen in this light, the problem of the regime of capitalism is less with its failings – the financial scandals, the recessions, the bankruptcies – than with its successes – as personified by Big Tobacco,[9] Big Sugar[10] and Big Mac. Whereas in 19th century Europe, industrial capitalism, in the name of progress, wrought its most damaging effects on the urban life, turning cities into physical and moral cesspools, contemporary agri-capitalism, in the name of cheaper goods for the consumer, is unleashing its destructive forces on rural life. It is wiping out small farmers, defacing the countryside and creating dangers to public health with its methods of intensive farming – pesticides, fertilizers, genetically modified seeds, cheap meal for livestock. To see the issue, for example, as the city versus the countryside, when both are suffering, albeit in different ways, from the effects of the regime of capitalism is pure mischief. In the analysis developed consistently for two decades by Ulrich Duchrow, capitalism is now threatening our planetary life-system itself.[11]

Capitalism as a Civilization

Ultimately, the central problem with capitalism is that it has come to define our contemporary civilization, in contrast to other civilizations in which learning, religion or warfare are seen as the higher values. Its goals and requirements have become paramount. It has generated its peculiar type of values, virtues and character traits – ruthless ambition, cut-throat competition and success at any price. It is a system which thrives on the stimulation of desire both for more property (what R. H. Tawney described as an 'acquisitive society'), and for higher status goods (described by Thorstein Veblen as 'conspicuous consumption').

As a civilization, the capitalist mode of codification spreads into the social and political spheres – interpreting goods, activities and even people in terms of their productivity and profitability. The political processes and institutions themselves become transformed – citizens becomes consumers, policies are marketed, voters are shareholders, the state a business, politicians are managers, etc. In welfare and social services, patients become customers. Even the Church Commissioners are turned into capitalists. People are transformed into 'human capital' in the eyes of employers, and into 'social capital' in the eyes of social scientists. According to the most prominent booster of social capital, Robert Putnam: 'Most of us get our jobs because of who we know, not what we know – that is our social capital...Your extended family represents a form of social capital, as do your Sunday school class, the regulars who play poker on your commuter train, your college roommates, the civic organization to which you belong, the Internet chat group in which you participate, and the network of professional acquaintances in your address book.'[12] Richard Sennett has highlighted the way the vastly reduced time-framework generated by contemporary capitalism is leading to widespread insecurities and fears of uselessness as well as a growing 'social deficit' in terms of trust and loyalty, all of which is having profound effects on both domestic and political life.[13] It is a civilization of inverted values in which social relations, cultural values, political establishments, and the media have come to be driven, disciplined and shaped by the imperatives of capital. The result is the deformation of cultural, social and political life.

Capitalism: A Contingent Reality

Sixty years ago, shaken by the cataclysm of two world wars within three decades, Karl Polanyi delineated the history of the 'The Great Transformation' which had overtaken Western society – gradually from the 16th century, and more rapidly in the course of the 19th.[14] It was a transformation wrought by what

Polanyi described – in a phrase which has since become commonplace – as the 'disembedding' of markets from their social and cultural anchorage. What had developed – and what Polanyi saw as the root cause of the global economic chaos, ideological struggles and wars of the 20th century – was a 'market society'. Where traditionally markets had been subordinate to and disciplined by ethical values, religious norms and social institutions, they had gradually become autonomous – 'self-regulating' in Polanyi's words. In a market society everything and everyone is liable to be treated as a commodity. It was a utopian fallacy which could only end in catastrophe. For a time, Polanyi's warnings seemed to be heeded. Social democrats, social marketeers and socialists, in their various ways, all constructed systems which sought to ensure that the operations of the market were subordinated to wider social imperatives. Indeed, Polanyi's own historical research demonstrated that society could not be suppressed indefinitely. In the face of the movement towards a market society, society time and again sought to reassert itself. But because it had been seriously wounded, it tended – unfortunately – to rely on the intervention of the state.

Polanyi did not live long enough to see history repeating itself – the exposure, in the 1970s, of the weaknesses of the state-dominated systems and the resumption of the tragic story of 'The Great Transformation' from the 1980s onwards. Once again the well-intentioned state had become part of the problem. Those who wanted to de-regulate capital had their moment. Once again capital was set free, circulating at unimaginable speed and moving ever faster in order to gain a competitive edge. It seeks to extend its sphere of operation by gaining ownership and control of state enterprises and welfare systems. It stimulates both the movement of labour in search of employment and the appetite to consume in search of gratification of unknown and unfulfillable desires. Where Polanyi warned of the folly of market societies we now have the new utopia of a global 'society of market states'.[15] No longer need the state struggle to promote social justice or the common good; its main task is to ensure that market principles rule: '… the market-state ceases to base its legitimacy on improving the welfare of its people…the market-state is largely indifferent to the norms of justice, or for that matter to any particular set of moral values, so long as law does not act as an impediment to economic competition.'[16]

Nation states have tried to respond by pooling their efforts, even to the point of sharing their sovereignty. Regional groupings of states, such as the European Union, take on roles never envisioned by their founders and are met with increasing hostility.

Yet the continuing story of 'The Great Transformation', powerful though it is, is still a story which is constructed by actors, events and circumstances. It did not have to be. It does not have to be. To appreciate how capitalism came to dominate, it is helpful to have some idea of how it came to be in the first place. That is what will be explored next.

How did Capitalism Happen to Happen?

Transitions to capitalism have occurred in different parts of the world, in different ways, at different speeds and as a result of different combinations of internal and external factors. The systems which capitalism superseded were never states of innocence and were invariably less productive. They had their own class structure – sometimes more harsh and unequal than capitalism itself – with a minority enjoying access to power, status and leisure at the expense of an economically dependent majority whose labour was exploited through violence, usury, custom, law – and often religion. Transitions to capitalism generally entailed massive social dislocation and political crises. The general improvement in material living standards which followed was often at the price of a transitional period of immense impoverishment and moral degradation paid by the most vulnerable. One need not look back to the Industrial Revolution in Britain; one has only to look at what has been happening in post-communist Russia and China.

How did capitalism happen to happen in Britain? Not even the most distinguished Marxist historians are in complete agreement. In a famous mid-20th century debate, they managed to reach a general consensus that feudalism began to disintegrate in the 14th century and that modern capitalism was not established until the late 16th century at the earliest. But on other key questions the picture remained unclear: Why did the transition take so long? Were there distinct stages of capitalism in the two-century long transition period, and if so how should we define them? How much weight should be given to external factors – the recovery of Mediterranean trade in the late medieval period, the use of money, the Black Death – as compared with internal factors, such as the development of technology and the changes in relative power – and therefore structural conflict – between serfs and lords, between merchants and money-lenders? Is the transition period best seen as the slow death of feudalism, or as the long gestation of (pre-capitalist) commodity production?

According to Marx, for whom the internal dialectic was central, the expansion of lending led to a concentration of large money capital for the lenders, but also to the ruin of extravagant land-proprietors and to the impoverishment of small producers: 'The indebted feudal lord becomes even more oppressive, because he is himself more oppressed.' At the same time, the expansion of trade, particularly the clothing trade, both in the purchasing of raw material and in the selling of finished products, led to a concentration of large merchants and a decline in the independence of artisans. Marx himself appears to see a short-lived emergence of a capitalist mode of production as early as the 14th or 15th century. Eric Hobsbawm identified at least five or six stages in the period of transition. The point of this historical digression is not to try to resolve these issues. It is rather to note that at the end of the debate, two important conclusions emerged, conclusions which are usefully borne in mind when one asks about the future of capitalism and beyond. The first is that the transition cannot be ascribed to changes in technology, trade and production alone but that changes in legal institutions, social status and political consciousness also played a crucial role. The second is that the transition was neither smooth nor sudden, nor inevitable. [17]

1.2 Interpreting Modernity: Emancipation and Legislation

> And new Philosophy calls all in doubt....They seeke so many new;
> They see that this is crumbed out againe into Atomis
> 'Tis all in peeces, all coherence gone,
> All just supply and all Relation:
> Prince, Subject, Father, Sonne are things forgot,
> For every man alone thinkes he hath got
> To be a Phoenix, and that there can bee
> None of that kinde, of which he is, but hee.
>
> John Donne, *An Anatomy of the World*

> Postmodernity is perhaps best construed as an 'exodus' from the
> constraints of modernity, as a plea to release the other, as a demand
> to let particulars be themselves.
>
> *Cambridge Companion to Postmodern Theology*[18]

It is commonly claimed that we have entered a new period called postmodernity. Some date it earlier than others. Amitai Etzioni, founder of the communitarian movement discerned the onset of this period as early as 1945.[19] Some link it with whilst others distinguish it from postmodernism (see Chapter Three). Its distinguishing features have been highlighted in different ways by different people. John Milbank, for example, identifies four characteristics: '(1) the blurring of the nature/culture divide; (2) the merging of public and private; (3) the mode of the information economy; and (4) economic and political globalization.'[21] But rather than see postmodernity as an historical period upon which we have entered like it or not, it seems far more helpful to see it simply as a theoretical framework or stance that different people have chosen because they find it useful for different reasons in trying to interpret certain aspects of our times. It is misleading to think that somehow we have left modernity behind when, in fact, the process of modernization and the ideology of modernity remain fundamental forces whose hold has still not been broken.

Christians sometimes seem polarized between those who feel called to embrace modernity in order to keep tradition alive and those who feel called to resist modernity in order to keep tradition safe. In the middle are the larger numbers who seem to feel that there really is no choice and that we have to adapt or be left behind. Something of that attitude can slip into the thinking of even the most knowledgeable economic theologians. John Atherton, for example, having undertaken an insightful historical review of the way the majority of theologians have tended until recently to deal with economic issues, allows the myth of modernity to colour his conclusion: 'Running through them all [conservative, liberal and radical theologians who insist on trying to impose higher purposes on the market and entwine it in personal relations] is a Christian tradition, *essentially pre-modern* in origins and formation, that regards economics as a very subordinate secondary human task' (my emphasis).[21] The same assumption appears in Atherton's later work, where he appears to endorse the view that: 'Wider economic changes focused on "the rediscovery of the market" which became "*a trademark of modernity*" for globalization....' (my emphasis again).[22] Notice that a whole tradition is given the label 'pre-modern' and is thus dismissed, while a prevailing economic system is deemed 'modern' and is thus accepted. This is to periodize history and to rob it of its essential marks of contingency and openness. It imposes determinism and precludes a proper reinterpretation and reappropriation of the past. The very categories themselves – pre-modern, modern and postmodern – are value-laden and are often bearers of ideology. In such a perspective a radical critique of capitalism is something that belongs to an outdated way of thinking and cannot be developed.

An approach to modernity which captures the mix of critical thinking and humility which seem essential in getting the measure of the project of modernity is typified by the international conference of evangelical theologians held at Uppsala in 1991.[23] The achievements of modernity and post-modernity (what might better be called a 'third modernity') are weighed up – a respect for truth in science, the development of decentralized institutions, cultural openness and an extension of democratic processes. At the same time, however, the point is clearly made by Os Guinness that 'modernity's repression of transcendence explains not only the triumph of triviality…but the flawed enterprise of spurious forms of transcendence, such as Promethean Marxism.' What Christianity offers, argues Lars Johansson, is an alternative rationality, as reflected, for example, in the Trinitarian theology of Colin Gunton.

Modernity, like capitalism, is a complex, contingent, historical phenomenon. It is more than keeping up with the latest technological development. It is a conscious project. What makes modernity so appealing is that it presents itself as a project of emancipation. What makes it so dangerous is that it is also a project of legislation. Which aspect prevails is itself a matter of historical contingency. Here a brief look at the history of the project of modernity will seek to show how, having started life with the hope of emancipation being dominant, modernity entered a dark period in which its legislative tendencies almost extinguished its emancipatory potential but that, in recent decades, creative attempts have been made to achieve a more mature balance. It makes for a revealing story.

Modernity as Project: Whose Idea was It?

Stephen Toulmin, in speaking of 'the hidden agenda of modernity', provides a particularly insightful account of the birth of the project of modernity, linking it with the emergence of capitalism.[24] In this interpretation, it was the break-up of the old order – under the impact of new economic and religious forces – that drove the two founders of modernity, Francis Bacon and René Descartes to seek, in very different ways, to lay new foundations for a more a secure order, based on scientifically proven and universally valid principles. Bacon (1561–1626), the elder of the two, had seen, but did not lament, the emergence of a new acquisitive gentry, in the words of R. H. Tawney,[25] fattened by the seizure of monastic estates, the successive enclosure of common lands, and the influx of vast wealth from the New World but absolved of responsibility for the dispossessed. This final dissolution of feudal society provides the setting, suggests Toulmin, for John Donne's lament: 'Prince, Subject, Father, Sonne are things forgot'. For the younger René Descartes (1596–1650), Toulmin suggests, it was the assassination of the French king Henry IV in 1610 that dashed hopes for an era of toleration and pluralism and unleashed decades of religious wars across Europe. In his travels, Descartes discovered everywhere simply a mass of prejudices and ill-founded opinions. What was desperately needed was solid knowledge to which all could have access and on which all could agree.

Thanks to Toulmin we can better appreciate why modernity as we know it is so driven by a quest for order, certainty and control. It was constructed on the territory of early capitalism, social breakdown and religious intolerance. But in its obsession with methods, norms and order, it has sacrificed – indeed feared – the authority of the good.

Both Bacon and Descartes not only called into question the methods and foundations of what traditionally had passed for knowledge; they also took aim at the power-base, namely the keepers of tradition. Both were clear that they were laying new foundations, based on science, not just for a new system of knowledge but for a new world. For Bacon the turn was outwards and the method inductive, for Descartes the turn was inwards and the method deductive. Both were hugely influential: Bacon in a line which can be traced at least roughly through Hobbes, Newton and Locke; Descartes in a line which can be traced, again roughly, through Kant and Hegel. Of the two, Descartes' is by far the more radical and more dangerous, both in terms of its assumption of the autonomy of the human subject and in its claims for absolute certitude for the truths it has established.

Francis Bacon, 'the Father of Modern Science', had no doubt that he was at the dawn of a new epoch: 'Men have been kept back, as by a hand of enchantment, from progress in the sciences by reverence for antiquity, by the authority of men accounted great in philosophy, and then by general consent [which amounts to] nothing less than a wicked effort to control human power over nature and to produce a deliberate and artificial despair. This despair in turn confounds the promptings of hope, cuts the springs and sinews of industry, and makes men unwilling to put anything to the hazard of trial.'[26] He spells out his project in *The Great Instauration* (1620): 'There was but one course left, therefore – to try the whole thing anew upon a better plan, and to commence a total reconstruction of sciences, arts, and all human knowledge, raised upon the proper foundations...by these means I suppose that I have established forever a true and lawful marriage between the empirical and the rational faculty, the unkind and ill-starred divorce and separation of which has thrown into confusion all the affairs of the human family.' Then Bacon takes aim at '...those very authors who have usurped a kind of dictatorship in the sciences and taken upon them to lay down the law with such confidence, yet when from time to time they come to themselves again, they fall to complaints of the subtlety of nature, the hiding places of truth, the obscurity of things, the entanglement of causes, the weakness of the human mind; wherein nevertheless they show themselves never the more modest, seeing that they will rather lay the blame upon the common condition of men and nature than upon themselves....'

René Descartes was also making a fresh start, proposing to: 'demolish every-thing and start again from the right foundations'.[27] Descartes may have had many doubts, but the need for intellectual emancipation was not one of them. On hearing of the condemnation of Galileo in 1633, Descartes decided to suppress his treatise *Le Monde*, which begins with a subversive description of 'The Difference between Our Sensations and the Things That Produce Them'. In developing his new method, Descartes' aim was precisely to make certain truth accessible, pure and simple so that no one would have to rely on the confused and confusing speculations of an intellectual elite: 'I shall bring to light the true riches of our souls, opening up to each of us the means whereby we can find within ourselves, without any help from anyone else, all the knowledge we may need for the conduct of life...'[28] Each person has the light of reason and by turning inwards, they can discover truths which are 'self-evident'. The process Descartes spelt out in his step-by-step 'Rules for Guiding One's Intelligence in Searching for the Truth' (1628). The approach is perfectly captured by Rule 13: 'If we understand a question perfectly, it must be abstracted from every super-fluous concept, reduced to its most simple form and divided by enumeration into the smallest parts possible.'

What Happened to Emancipation? The Dark Side of Modernity

By 'the dark side of modernity' is meant not so much its indiscriminate destruc-tion of whatever sails under the flag of tradition but rather the repressed dynamics of modernity itself. From the very beginning, the project of modernity had two sides. Whilst seeking to emancipate reason from the forces of unreason, dogma-tism and prejudice, it also sought to establish control by laying unshakeable and universally valid foundations for a new more rational world whose author-ity would be self-evident. Between these two sides of the project of modernity, there was always going to be tension.

The darkness emerged towards the end of the 19th century. Its de-tradition-alizing power was leading to rootlessness; its de-territorializing to homelessness. It was depicted graphically by Max Weber as an 'iron cage'. It was satirized by Charlie Chaplin in *Modern Times*. But nowhere was it portrayed with greater intensity than in the shape of Critical Theory as developed in the face of totalitarianism by the Frankfurt School.[29] Under totalitarianism not only were political parties and trade unions suppressed but, culturally, an ideology took hold which enshrined instrumental rather than critical reason and which incorporated everything and everyone within the scope of a 'totally administered society'. In such a world, there was no home for 'the other', whether as group, movement, idea or alternative system: 'Nothing at all may remain outside, because the mere idea of outsideness is the very source of fear.'[30] According to Critical Theory, totalitarianism was not simply an historical accident but was part of the logic of capitalist modernity itself. Thus the defeat of Nazism did not signal the end of the mission of the Frankfurt School. The underlying tendencies towards totalization remained, social relations were still being distorted and freedom constrained by the continuing rule of 'instrumental reason'. The result was, in the phrase popularized in the 1960s by Herbert Marcuse, the creation of 'One Dimensional Man'. In such a confining scenario, the only hope seemed to consist in leaping outside 'the system' altogether.

Having started as emancipator, modernity gradually became legislator. Its discoveries enabled it to reconstruct a world in which ethics was governed by norms and procedures rather than by any intrinsic attraction towards or obligation deriving from the good, a world in which politics was shaped by balances of power rather then the pursuit of the common good, where a safe but separate sphere was created for 'religion' (what Milbank described as 'the policing of the sublime').[31] The mode of ordering becomes one of external controls rather than of relationship arising from participation. The result is, in the words of Alasdair MacIntyre, 'therapeutic managerialism'.[32] But it is a therapy that does not heal the heart's desire in the face of forces which refuse to be managed. It was a world which, in the famous words of Max Weber, was disenchanted and administered by 'specialists without souls'.

Rescuing the Project of Emancipation

…we are witnesses to a social transformation within modernity, in the course of which people will be set free from the social forms of industrial society – class, stratification, family, gender status of men and women – just as during the course of the Reformation people were 'released' from the secular rule of the church into society.

Norbert Elias[33]

…the sorts of transformations involved in modernity are more profound than most sorts of change characteristic of prior periods.

Anthony Giddens[34]

The dire predictions of Weber and Marcuse have not materialized. For all the talk about the iron cage of modernity or about the opening up of a new postmodern age, modernity's original project of emancipation has not entirely failed. One rescue operation goes by the name of 'reflexive modernity'. Here the model is taken from cybernetics – feedback on the impact of one's interventions precisely so that adjustments may be made where necessary. The mechanism was described in the late 1960s by Amitai Etzioni, founder of the communitarian movement a quarter of a century later. Etzioni saw this as the key to a truly active society, described as one which is 'responsive to its changing membership...[and] engaged in an intensive and perpetual self-transformation.'[35] It is in this sense that the notion of reflexive modernity has tended to be popularized by Anthony Giddens.[36] In the hands of Ulrich Beck, however, the notion of reflexive modernity is given a much more existential twist. For Beck it refers to the new technological situation in which we find ourselves – faced with an unprecedented ability to intervene in the processes which shape human and ecological life this 'modernization of uncertainty' creates a situation of reflexive self-endangerment.[37]

A quite different approach to rescuing modernity has been developed by the German political philosopher, Jurgen Habermas, leading light of the second generation of the school of Critical Theory. What was required was not so much reflexivity as the crucial dialectical dimension of modernity. His predecessors, Horkheimer and Adorno, observes Habermas, pursued such a purist version of theory, purged of all elements of myth, that in the end the whole project became simply impossible. Taking a less defeatist approach, Habermas proceeds to reorient the project of modernity away from the traditional subject-object rela-tionship (an economic model of productive rationality) and towards a subject-subject relationship (a more political model of 'communicative rationality'). The project involves purifying communication of all elements of coercion and unequal power so as to create an ideal speech situation. Habermas acknowledges that this is utopian, which is why he stresses the importance of a dialectical approach. This means that modernity will always have to observe the mediation of critique and theory, being and illusion, discovery and justification.[38] In this way, the original emancipatory spark of modernity can again be rekindled and the path re-opened for the pursuit of: 'social solidarity, preserved in legal struc-tures and in need of continual regeneration...[and] democratic self-organiz-ation of a legal community.'[39]

Yet another creative approach to rescuing modernity has been undertaken by the Canadian philosopher Charles Taylor, who explores the moral significance of a modernity which has come to be self-critical. He argues that it is not enough to issue the standard denunciations of modernity – that it is driven by the will to dominate, that it is trapped in instrumental reason (brilliant on the question of means but speechless on the question of ends), that it is therefore culturally hollow and impoverished, that it fosters a sense of spiritual and social home-lessness, etc. A more mature modernity can surmount these criticisms, argues Taylor. But to do so it must recognize the need to take seriously the question of the good. Taylor distinguishes three levels on which this question arises. At the most obvious level, we make decisions about 'life goods' – family life, civic life, long life, labour, status, possessions, etc. But the fact that we make judgments about the relative importance of such goods means that we are falling back on another level of what Taylor calls 'constitutive goods'. These are the moral resources which provide us with the criteria by which we decide which goods are 'good' and how good they are. Underlying this, Taylor argues, is a third level, the ontological, which raises questions about the nature of the good itself. This is the heart of modernity's problem, argues Taylor. The old ontological and narrative frameworks are gone – irretrievably, he believes. Yet unless we can make some contact with the ontological character of the good (which for him has a theistic dimension) we are in danger of living beyond our moral resources. The task is to discover whether there is some other way into the ontology of the good. But has not modernity resolutely set itself up in opposition to any such venture? Taylor's solution takes the form of intuitive 'personal resonance'.[40]

All three rescue attempts – reflexive modernity, communicative rationality, and personal resonance – are projects of modernity, sometimes called post-modernity. In spite of the new humility and caution, the original project remains: emancipation, individuation, secularization and, lurking in the back-ground, domination. Indeed some of the features of modernity are actually intensified. Giddens acknowledges modernity's continued two-fold process of disembedding the individual, both from traditional communities ('de-territorial-ization') and from traditional practices and routines ('de-institutionalization'). It is these 'discontinuities of modernity' that present modernity with the task of reconstructing personal and institutional reality. Giddens remains the optimist, even in conceding '[p]ersonal meaninglessness…becomes a fundamental psychic problem in the circumstances of late modernity'. Jurgen Habermas seems more aware of the demands this makes: 'The concept of modernity no longer comes with a promise of happiness.'

2. TRANSFORMATIONIST THEOLOGY

> They [the transformationists] understand that his [Christ's] work is
> concerned not with the specious, external aspects of human behaviour in
> the first place, but that he tries the hearts and judges the subconscious life;
> that he deals with what is deepest and most fundamental in man.
> H. Richard Niebuhr[41]

2.1 The Legacy: 'Christ the Transformer of Culture'

Although elaborated over half a century ago and subjected to much biblical
and theological criticism ever since, H. Richard Niebuhr's five-fold typology
describing the different positions that Christians have taken vis-à-vis society is
still used as a starting point for discussions of Christian social mission. His *Christ
and Culture* remains high on the required reading list of theological students in
the United States.[42] The idea for such a typology may not have been entirely
original. In an unpublished manuscript, written nine years before the publication of *Christ and Culture*, Niebuhr acknowledges that the Roman Catholic
Étienne Gilson 'points a promising direction' in identifying four main 'spiritual
families' – 'the Tertullian family', 'the Augustinian family', 'the Latin Averroist
family' and 'the Thomist family', whilst also alluding to a fifth, more devotional
and pietistic trend.[43] It seems astonishing that there is no acknowledgement of
this debt in *Christ and Culture*, whose five types are so remarkably similar: 'Christ
Against Culture' (a counter-cultural approach), 'Christ of Culture' (theological
liberalism), 'Christ Above Culture' (typified by Roman Catholicism), 'Christ
and Culture in Paradox' (developed most fully in Lutheranism) and – making
no secret of his own preference – 'Christ the Transformer of Culture,' which
he sees represented in John the Evangelist ('born again'), Augustine of Hippo
('regeneration') and the Christian socialist F. D. Maurice ('the most consistent
of the conversionists').[44]

What did the transformationist/conversionist type mean for Niebuhr? First,
it meant that human nature, society and culture are seen neither as purely good
nor as purely evil but as 'perverted good': 'The problem of culture is therefore the problem of its conversion, not of its replacement by a wholly new
creation.'[45] It sees creation as temporarily subjected to an alien power – the
prince of darkness. Thus, where some Christian theologies, not least Augustine's,
might stress the fact that we are 'resident aliens' here on earth, transformationists – though Niebuhr did not put it this way – might stress that it is the ruling
powers which are the aliens, the usurpers, the pretenders. Regime change will

not bring heaven on earth but Christians are called to take part in the struggle to free the earth from the grip of the powers that close off openings to grace.

Social transformation, by definition, is about changes in social policies, economic systems and political structures but unless it approaches these in a way which takes account of the ways in which they reflect, reinforce and relate to personal relations and values, it cannot be called Christian. Niebuhr is quite clear about this – social transformation is about the healing and reorientation of human desire.

The Tradition Continued

H. Richard Niebuhr died on the eve of the Second Vatican Council. He would never have expected to see how enthusiastically the theme of transformation features in the Pastoral Constitution *Gaudium et Spes* (Joy and Hope). The 'joy and hope' arose not out of some false sense of optimism but out of an attempt to read 'the signs of the times'. The theme is announced in a paragraph headed 'On hope and anguish', which explores the contradictions and struggles of contemporary developments: 'Today, the human race is involved in a new stage of history. Profound and rapid changes are spreading by degrees around the whole world…Hence we can already speak of a true cultural and social transformation, one which has repercussions on man's religious life as well…As happens in any crisis of growth, this transformation has brought serious difficulties in its wake. Thus while man extends his power in every direction, he does not always succeed in subjecting it to his own welfare. Striving to probe more profoundly into the deeper recesses of his own mind, he frequently appears more unsure of himself. Gradually and more precisely he lays bare the laws of society, only to be paralyzed by uncertainty about the direction to give it.'[46]

Social transformation is set by the Council squarely in the context of the interaction between the heavenly and earthly cities: '…the Church has a saving and an eschatological purpose which can be fully attained only in the future world. But she is already present in this world. She serves as a leaven and as a kind of soul for human society as it is to be renewed in Christ and transformed into God's family….That the earthly and the heavenly city penetrate each other is a fact accessible to faith alone; it remains a mystery of human history, which sin will keep in great disarray until the splendour of God's sons, is fully revealed. And it is a mission founded in love: He Himself revealed to us that "God is love" (1 John 4:8) and at the same time taught us that the new command of love was the basic law of human perfection and hence of the world's transformation.'

Such pronouncements continued to find echoes in other statements issued by Pope Paul VI[47] and by the world-wide Synod of Bishops.[48]

The Tradition Called into Question

A redemption that has merely the transformation of the world in view will not deal seriously with the fact that what God has done in Christ he has done for his creation and for his own sake as creator. It is not enough to understand the triumph of the Kingdom as improving or perfecting a world that was, as it stood, simply inadequate.

Oliver O'Donovan[49]

Richard Niebuhr's five-fold typology has always had its critics. To some, he failed to do justice to particular theologians or traditions. To others, his interpretations of Scripture are debatable, while still others never liked the idea of typology anyway. But recent decades have seen more fundamental challenges to the basic transformationist model itself.

Stanley Hauerwas, acknowledging that some of the criticisms of Niebuhr's transformationist type are too simplistic, makes the far weightier charge that Niebuhr himself has failed '…to deal with a crucial problem – namely how to discriminate between different kinds of cultures and different aspects of any culture for what might be transformed and what might be accepted.' Nor does Hauerwas stop there. It is time, he argued more than two decades ago, that we left behind our preoccupation with social transformation. It is distracting the church from the central political task of Christian ethics, which is 'to challenge the moral presuppositions of our polity and society….[particularly] Christian acquiescence in the liberal assumption that a just polity is possible without the people being just.'[50]

A decade later, to mark the centenary of Richard Niebuhr's birth, Glen Stassen, Dianne M. Yeager and John Howard Yoder undertook a critical reassessment.[51] A large part of their concern is about the incompleteness of Niebuhr's approach, specifically his alleged failure to give any substance to transformation – there is no 'before' and 'after' – and his refusal to provide any reality test as to what is and is not a genuinely Christian transformation. The task of authentic transformation, according to this critique, is not to devise abstract typologies but to provide tools for discernment: 'What needs to be transformed is actual ways of living, working, relating and not merely ways of thinking about them.' Both Yoder and Stassen proceed to suggest, from very different starting points, some very similar criteria for 'authentic transformation.' All three authors note that *Christ and Culture* '…is not only a typology but also an argument', specifically an argument in favour of the transformationist type. Yoder's is the most direct, if not always the fairest, critique. As a Mennonite, he is clearly disappointed that 'Niebuhr devotes only a single sentence to the Mennonites (in a way which indicates that Niebuhr actually must be thinking of the Old Order Amish)'.[52] He complains that, for Niebuhr '…only one of the other positions needs radically to be challenged. It is only the first position [Christ against Culture].' Yoder's main charge is that in Niebuhr's transformationist model: '…we still have the last word; Christ does not.'

Ten years on and it is Timothy Gorringe's turn. Niebuhr's use of the term 'culture' is inconsistent, charges Gorringe, adding that Niebuhr's interpretation of the various Christian postures is too sweeping, his typology so vague that it cannot be falsified and his theology insufficiently Trinitarian. Gorringe is in no doubt: '…this immensely influential typology has to be dropped, to be replaced not with an alternative typology, but with a more complex mapping of the interrelation of gospel and culture'.[53] Gorringe, in contrast to Hauerwas, does not argue that the church can take up its proper place simply by being a counter-culture: 'that would be a functionalist undertaking.' Rather it is Barth's dialectical approach which provides the necessary tool. By stressing the otherness of God's action as eschatological, Gorringe is able to develop a powerful critique of capitalist modernity. Yet an element of transformation remains in so far as 'culture is the name of that whole process in the course of which God does what it takes, in Paul Lehman's [sic] phrase, to keep human beings human.'

One response to such critiques might be literally to put the critics in their place by using Niebuhr's own framework. Of course, one could say, they would be critical of the transformationist tradition because they are representatives of certain of the other types already identified by Niebuhr. Thus Hauerwas and Yoder could be construed as keeping alive the 'Christ against Culture' approach. Gorringe could be seen as doing the same for the 'Christ and Culture in Paradox' tradition. O'Donovan – like Richard's even more famous brother Reinhold – could be a mixture of 'Christ and Culture in Paradox' and 'Christ the Transformer of Culture', with O'Donovan leaning towards the paradox pole and Reinhold leaning towards the transformationist where both Milbank and Rowan Williams might be surprised to find themselves.[54]

One could also say, with some justification, that Richard Niebuhr is fairer to representatives of other traditions than his recent critics appear to be towards him. He shows considerable appreciation for the Christ and Culture in Paradox tradition, which stresses such themes as divine command/obedience, wrath/

mercy, judgement/forgiveness.[55] He acknowledges the 'vitality and strength' of that motif with its vision of 'living between the times.' He gives full credit to Luther as a 'dynamic, dialectical thinker'. He takes seriously this tradition's view that the primary point is not to transform institutions of 'the world' but precisely to recognize what Bonhoeffer would call their secularity and, from that position, to take responsible action.

Rethinking Transformationist Theology

From the preceding critique of H. Richard Niebuhr's exposition of the various models of Christianity, three conclusions may be drawn. First, that it is important to ground any contemporary critique of capitalist modernity to Christian tradition. Secondly that each of Niebuhr's five types continues to be used to develop such a critique. Critiques have been developed from a sectarian perspective in counter-cultural mode, in the form of communistic experiments, from a Lutheran perspective by Ulrich Duchrow, from a Barthian perspective by Timothy Gorringe, and from an Anglo-Catholic perspective by Kenneth Leech. The third conclusion is that if the fifth type, viz. the transformationist perspective is held up as being particularly fruitful – as i *is* here – it must draw more explicitly on a theology of grace than it has sometimes done in the past.

When the World Council of Churches chose 'God, in your grace, transform the world' as the theme for their 9th Assembly in February 2006, it was not simply adding a pious gloss onto the motto of the World Social Forum, 'Another world is possible'. It was stressing that the key to any radically other and different world lies in a deeper appreciation of the reality of God's grace. Of all the recent theologians who have explored the social and cultural implications of the theme of grace, two whose work offers the most profound insights, and whose work will be drawn on here, are Rowan Williams and John Milbank.

Three aspects of grace are particularly fitting in providing a basis for a rethinking of transformationist theology. First, grace points to an abundance at the heart of reality. It thereby provides a basis for a praxis of mutual giving and of redistribution. Secondly, grace allows us to be, and thus it enables us to welcome rather than to fear a world which is genuinely other. Thirdly, grace is vivifying, it keeps alive our interconnectedness and allows our relationships to flourish in ever new ways.

To take the first aspect, the grace of God is exceedingly abundant. It is expressed not only in the process of redemption but in creation itself. This implies that at the heart of reality there already is an abundance, an excess.

What we have is somehow given to us and grows rather than lessens when it is shared. That is the key to overcoming the insecurity against which modernity seeks to provide defences by setting up boundaries which vainly try to keep the unknown at bay. It is also the answer to scarcity with which capitalism is preoccupied and which it vainly seeks to solve by a process of endless accumulation, with its preoccupation with and perpetuation of scarcity. Recognition of the reality of grace opens up deeper and richer dimensions of life and enables us to celebrate the excess of meanings which reveal that life is always about more than we or our traditions can say because it is grounded in and participates in a transcendent reality. Such a claim is, of course, based on faith not on evidence. But grace comes through faith, which builds on desire.

Secondly, because we can neither fathom the depth nor discern the full shape of that realm of grace, it always contains an element of the strange, the mysterious, and the different. It keeps our hearts and minds open. It calls for a different and more radical form of learning. It fosters a spirit of discipleship in which the learner is called to be changed rather than, as with modernity, to pursue knowledge as mastery or with capitalism to treat knowledge as a possession, a commodity, and a form of capital.

Thirdly, because grace enables the continual entry of the unknown to reshape our world and ourselves it continually reveals new connections and redefines relationships which are seen as fulfilling, unlike the dichotomies of modernity which assigns roles and status and then encourages rebellion in the name of individuality, and unlike the utilitarianism of capitalism which attributes to people a use-value and then discards them after their sell-by date. What grace creates is the kind of exchange by which God enters humanity and humanity participates in divinity, so beautifully described in a medieval hymn as an *admirable commercium*.

2.2 Contexts Past and Present: The Need for Transformationist Theologyy

> There is no appetite for big, transforming ideas; the politicians want
> micro-ideas that fit into existing political narratives.
> *Prospect*[56]

Are we or are we not in an age which requires critical transformationist theology? Clearly we are in an age where major social transformations are taking place – culturally, economically and politically. The ending of the bi-polar world, the advances in technology, the intermingling of cultures, all make our world a very different place than it was a generation ago. The impact of technological developments were explored in the 1999 'Towards Social Transformation' seminar, led by the quantum-physicist Michio Kaku.[57] There have also been major transformations of class structures as the working class splits into a more affluent versus a highly insecure fraction, with a 'fourth world' which is left out altogether. Shifts in the nature of employment patterns are allowing a healthier work/family balance but also taking a toll on health in terms of the increase in stress and insecurity. Social assistance systems have been transformed from sources of social security to springboards for individual responsibility. Health, education and social security systems are now operated by new owners, under new management, with new aims and with a wholly new style. The countryside and the city alike are undergoing radical change. How we cope with all these transformations becomes particularly problematic as profound questions arise about identity – of gender, ethnicity and sexual orientation and about the continuing reliability of rational religions, moral codes and literary canons.

For some the threats these transformations pose – to the environment, to security and to individual and collective identities – are so great that what it seems to call for is a theology of survival. For others, the growing interdependence it is engendering means that what is most needed is a theology of partnership.[58] But, surely, the transformations of our time present challenges which need to be tackled not avoided. In such a context there is more not less urgency about developing and rethinking a transformationist theology. This is recognized by Christians with as diverse traditions as the Evangelical Alliance which declares that '…the Alliance is committed to helping churches bring about spiritual and social transformation' and by the recent *Compendium of the Social Doctrine of the Church*, which insists 'The transformation of the world is a fundamental requirement of our time also'.[59]

What would transformationist theology have to do? Its first task is about trying to interpret the transformations of our time from a theological perspective. The interpretation offered in the first part of this chapter is that the forces of capitalist modernity constitute a regime. It is that regime which is giving impetus, direction and shape to the transformations of our time. Theology can help reveal and evaluate the character of that regime. In that task, Augustine's insights can be of particular help. The second theological task is about developing responses, specifically, about openings to regime change. Where the first theological task is to do with revelation and disclosure, the second has to do with vision and wisdom. Here, too, Augustine's theology can be of help.

Augustine: Theologian of Regime Change

In the city of the world, both the rulers themselves and the people they
dominate are dominated by the lust for domination, whereas in the City of
God all citizens serve one another in charity.

Augustine of Hippo[60]

Regime Change

Edward Said has revealed the ways in which the secret of empires is their cultural
power. Empires which rely on cruelty and exploitation cannot last. Empires which
are in it for the long term colonize cultures, constructing narratives – of power,
glory, prosperity, chosenness, destiny – into which lesser peoples are invited,
enticed or coerced to enter, sacrificing their own identities in the process. It is
precisely where identities are felt to be at stake, Said recounts, pointing to the
horrors of the Khmer Rouge, that the most brutal and unrestrained struggles of
regime change often emerge.[61] Ultimately, however, success depends not on the
ferocity of counter-violence but on the attractiveness of counter-narrative. It is
in this light that Augustine's narrative of the struggle between the two cities, or
two civilizations, can be read.

From 410 to 9/11: Regimes in Crisis?

Augustine's *City of God* was triggered by an event which shook the Roman
Empire to the core – the sack of Rome in 410 by Alaric, king of the Goths
– an event comparable to 9/11 in our own times. Yet, as Peter Brown stresses:
'It is particularly superficial to regard it [*The City of God*] as a book about the
sack of Rome.'[62] After all, by that time the Roman Empire, though in theory
still one, had for fifteen years been divided into an Eastern division (based at
Constantinople) and a Western division (based at Ravenna). Politically, the
structures remained after the sack of Rome as they were before. But culturally,
it was the civilization not just the polity of the Empire which was at its final
crossroads. As with 9/11, it was a time for soul-searching and for heated debate.
Why had God allowed this to happen? Both Augustine and his adversaries
agreed that it was a form of divine punishment. But for what? To the pagan
cultural elite it was punishment because the new Christian rulers, most notably
Theodosius in the previous decades, had been suppressing pagan temples, feasts
and practices. To Augustine, it was punishment because the Christian rulers had
actually been too tolerant of moral and religious laxity.[63] Both Augustine and his
adversaries, furthermore, saw in the sacking of Rome a new opportunity. For the
latter it suggested the possibilities of restoration, when such cultural ascendancy

as they still enjoyed could once again be translated into political power. For Augustine it was the moment when that very culture could be unmasked as foolish, corrupt and hollow. The issue was about a clash of civilizations. But the focus for Augustine was not on the civilization – or lack of it – of the Goths (read 'terrorists') any more than it was an occasion for being anti-Roman (read anti-American). Augustine did not rejoice over the sack of Rome nor did he disparage the virtues and intellectual heritage of Rome. What he did set out to do was, first, to expose the foundations of that regime like those before it as being the *libido dominandi* (the drive for power and control) and, then, to reveal the existence of an alternative based on the desire for peace.

Augustine had used the contrast between the heavenly and the earthly cities long before the sack of Rome.[64] Now it would provide the key to deconstructing the Roman Empire. At issue was not what kind of political system should prevail or even what Christian emperors should or should not do. It was about what we would today call ideology – the dominant beliefs (paganism) and desires (*libido dominandi*) which gave rise to such empires.[65] The importance of the former was made clear by the very title of Augustine's work: *De Civitate Dei Contra Paganos* (underlining added). The importance of the latter is declared in the Preface: '... so far as my general plan of the treatise demands and my ability permits, I must speak also of the earthly city – of that city which lusts to dominate the world, and which, though nations bend to its yoke, is itself dominated by its passion for domination.' Augustine knew the task was not so much to win minds with compelling logic as to awaken hearts with an appealing aesthetic. When he set to on this mighty project, Augustine was nearly sixty; by the time he completed his twenty-two volumes he would be in his early seventies.

What follows will be a look at regime change, first from the perspective of deconstructing regimes based on the *libido dominandi*, and then from the perspective of reconstructing a society based on the love of peace.

Regime Change – Deconstructing Empire

A thousand years hence...perhaps in less, America may be what Europe now is. The innocence of her character, that won the hearts of all nations in her favour, may sound like a romance and her inimitable virtue as if it had never been....When we contemplate the fall of empires and the extinction of the nations of the Ancient World, we see but little to excite our regret...but when the empire of America shall fall, the subject for contemplative sorrow will be infinitely greater than crumbling brass and marble can inspire....It will not then be said, here stood a temple of vast

antiquity; here rose a babel of invisible height…but here, Ah, painful
thought! the noblest work of human wisdom, the grandest scene of human
glory, the fair cause of Freedom rose and fell.

Tom Paine [66]

What Augustine was attempting was the deconstruction not just of the Roman
Empire. That empire was but the latest in a string of empires – Assyrian, Persian,
Hellenistic – all destined to fade because all relied on false gods.[65] Deconstruction
involved depriving the empire of its privileged sacred status and depicting it as
but one brief chapter in a much longer history. He did not try to find its Achilles
heel; he went directly for its strong point, attacking, with biting irony, wit and
mockery, the very foundations of its claims to glory and virtue: 'I must keep my
promise: to prove, as briefly and as clearly as I can…that there never existed any
such thing as a Roman Republic.'[68]

Revelation and Exposure: The Libido Dominandi

Augustine records the lament of the Roman historian Sallust (c. 86–34 BC) over
the influence of the *libido dominandi*. This is not the true Rome, Sallust argues;
it is an alien attitude, introduced in imitation of the regimes of Cyrus in Asia
and the Lacedemonians and Athenians in Greece. Augustine would not wear
it.[69] The *libido dominandi* was present at the creation of Rome, witness the
slaying of Remus by his brother Romulus, which in turn was a re-enactment of
the murder of Abel by his brother Cain.

Others, too, have denounced the *libido dominandi*. Martin Heidegger traced
its hold on Western civilization to the transition from Greek to Roman civilization.[70] Charles Taylor, focussing on its expression in the ethics of self-mastery,
traces its history in some versions of Christianity through Stoicism and back
to Plato.[71] Feminists have located its roots in male psychology and patriarchal
culture.[72] Environmentalists have traced it back to the Book of Genesis with its
picture of God commanding humanity to 'subdue the earth'.

We try to find scapegoats. Yet, as Reinhold Niebuhr argues in his classic *The
Nature and Destiny of Man*, the place to begin is with ourselves: 'The inclination of
modern man to find the source of evil in his life in some particular event in history
or some specific historical corruption is a natural consequence of his view of himself
in a simple one-dimensional history. But this modern error merely accentuates a
perennial tendency of the human heart…to escape responsibility….'[73]

What then is the root of the *libido dominandi*? Three authors offer three
different insights into Augustine's thought. Reinhold Niebuhr, mixing Augustine

with a dose of Kierkegaard and Heidegger, sees it in terms of *Sorge* (a mixture of existential anxiety and care) that arises precisely from the simultaneous awareness of our finiteness and our transcendence, our fear of meaninglessness and nothingness and our sense of being rooted in something greater. The temptation is either to escape this tension – the path of sensuality – or to deny our finitude and claim to encapsulate the universal in ourselves – the path of pride. The path of pride takes three forms: pride of power (domination and greed), pride of knowledge (ideology), and pride of virtue (self-righteousness). Behind pride itself, for Niebuhr, and at the root of sin, is the desire to be self-sufficient, the reluctance to believe, and the denial of the need for grace.[74]

Robert Markus provides a different insight: 'The community living in concord and singlemindedness, with all property shared, is Augustine's favoured model of the monastery. These are the qualities which make it a microcosm of the City of God. The most insidious form of pride, the root of all sin, was privacy's self-enclosure.'[75]

Peter Brown offers a third insight, focussing on Augustine's treatment of the sin of the angels. He puts it simply, referring to Augustine's repeated reference to 'this basic denial of dependence, and so of gratitude, in politics, in thought, in religion'.[76]

Libido Dominandi
At the Heart of the Regime of Capitalist Modernity

The manifold expressions of this *libido dominandi* are evident both in capitalism's 'possessive individualism', its privileging of self-interest, its drive for accumulation and for endless consumption, and in modernity's celebration of the autonomous but morally impoverished individual. It makes for a regime of ruthlessness, since for both capitalism and modernity people and goods are valued in terms of their utility – what is inefficient and unprofitable must go. The predictable result has been a pattern of social relations which is basically uncivil and conflictual. Yet the regime claims for itself universality and therefore the right both to co-opt and to integrate as many aspects of life into its logic as possible, whilst marginalizing whatever appears as genuinely other. In return for the material comforts it offers, the regime sends out the decree: There Is No Alternative.

The point of interpreting the regime of capitalist modernity as part of the narrative of the two cities is precisely to avoid the simplistic view that capitalist modernity is the root of all our problems or that it is the apotheosis of evil. Even in purely empirical terms, the regimes which preceded capitalist modernity as well as some of the alternatives which have been attempted in the previous century have exhibited in their own ways the destructive power of the *libido dominandi*. The point is that it is capitalist modernity which is the dominant regime now, taking our civilization down the wrong path, distorting the shape of society, perverting the values of our culture, appropriating control of our political institutions, and leading to the destruction of our environment. What makes the regime more dangerous than its predecessors are two things. The first is its tendency to absorb and colonize the life of civil society. The second is its expansion to the point where it is depleting the resources on which the life of the planet itself depends. If the regime does continue, it is likely to involve more intense conflict over ever scarcer resources at the cost of more inequality and less freedom. The issue is less likely to be about the survival of life on earth than of the quality of such life – materially, morally and politically. That is why a transformation – regime change – rather than reformation is needed.

Regime Change – Another City

'A generation ago H. Richard Niebuhr popularized the thesis that Augustine stood for a "transformation" of human culture by Christ. It is a thesis which will garner little support today.' So declares Oliver O'Donovan.[77] Today the trend is to focus more on Augustine's image of the citizens of the heavenly city as 'resident aliens'. This is indeed a useful insight. Augustine's thought is rich and there is a case for saying that Augustine might fit just as comfortably in Richard Niebuhr's 'Christ and Culture in Paradox' family. Clearly Augustine was not a transformationist in the Social Gospel sense of seeking directly to refashion the structures of the earthly city. There was no question of developing a Christian political, economic or social system. The difference between the two civilizations was the difference between two kinds of love. There was no room for the shallow idea that all that is needed to bring about peace and justice is a change of system. There remained two cities. But Augustine's vision was not simply about the tension between them; it was also about their interaction in history. Indeed O'Donovan himself goes on to make a significant qualification: 'There is, then, a significant transvaluation of the structures of society, but it would seem to fall considerably short of what is meant by speaking of their "transformation".' But surely 'transvaluation' is absolutely central to the project of social transformation. It is the reshaping of culture, the healing of desire and the redirecting of the mind which are at the heart of the project of social transformation.

The point, however, is not to pigeon-hole Augustine or even to suggest that his theology should serve as a model. There is much that gives cause for concern. His encouragement of the use of state power to suppress both Christian heresy as well as paganism cannot simply be excused as typical of the age. Astute emperors had long realized the advantages – and often the necessity – of allowing subject nations to retain their religious practices. Augustine could well be charged with having started a new tradition of religious intolerance. Peter Brown calls him 'the first theorist of the Inquisition'.[78] The point is that Augustine reminds us of the importance of practising theology in a way which is confident that there is an alternative, that it is what happens at the cultural level which is the key to the realization of that alternative, and that it is, in the end, about the activating and redirecting of love.

Augustine's vision is not just of a different kind of life withdrawn from an evil world, but a vision precisely of a different *civitas* – city, civilization, civil society – inspired by a different kind of love and leading towards a different kind of destination. What is more, Augustine's argument was not that this alternative city was something to be wished for in the distant future, but was present now and indeed from the beginning of actual history.

2.3 The Path: Transformation by Grace

Once upon a time social transformation seemed to be written into the logic of history. Whigs, Progressivists, socialists and communists all saw their goal as something that was already partly discernible and would inevitably come to be consummated in the forward march of their movements. More recently transformationist thinking has tended to shift from temporal to spatial imagery. Part of the reason is the development of such a richness and vitality of global interaction. Another factor, of course, is the growing awareness of the finiteness and fragility of our planet's life system. In this spatial perspective, time itself looks different. That is to say that modernity's approach which deals with ruptures and which seems to leave the past behind in order to create the future afresh will not do. Nor will capitalism's endless tendency towards accumulation. There must be an end to accumulation and a new beginning to sharing.

In this spatial framework, models of transformation are less likely to be shaped by physics with its laws of motion, the balancing of forces and controlling of energy. Better models might come from chemistry with its intermingling of elements which involve changes in identity, or even from alchemy, which held a long-time attraction even for as 'rational' a scientific genius as Isaac Newton. Social transformation calls not for a flight to the new but for a deeper engagement and confrontation with present reality in the expectation that strange and even explosive latent energies may be released and a new beauty emerge.

Transformation by Grace – A Work of Art

...it has been said with profound insight that 'beauty will save the world'.
Pope John Paul II[79]

David Bosch, the renowned mission theologian, warmed to Max Stackhouse's insight that: 'People do not only need truth (theory) and justice (praxis), they also need beauty, the rich resources of symbol, piety, worship, love, awe and mystery. Only too often, in the tug-of-war between the priority of truth and the priority of justice, this dimension gets lost.'[80] Bosch returns to Stackhouse when discussing inter-religious dialogue: 'Perhaps the theology of religions is pre-eminently an area which we should explore with the aid of *poiesis* rather than of *theoria*....For both dialogue and mission manifest themselves in a meeting of hearts rather than of minds. We are dealing with a mystery.'

It is an approach that is central to the work of John Milbank and the Radical Orthodoxy network. Milbank chides Reinhold Niebuhr, who draws heavily on Augustine, for not for being Augustinian enough. At the very heart of Augustine's vision is a kind of love which combines, rather than opposes *agape* (charity) and *eros* (desire). The issue, Milbank points out, is not about the presence or absence of love but about the healing and redirecting of misguided love. That is why attraction to and participation in the good are central and why aesthetics must come before morality. This, in turn, entails a much more prominent role for the imagination: 'It is seen [by Niebuhr] as essentially to do with a capacity for empathy with other persons and situations; it extends our range of awareness, but it is not, in itself, a power to evaluate or judge. For Niebuhr, imagination is outside the realm of ethical intuition.'[81]

Milbank's observation helps set the scene for the sort of transformation that is being encouraged here – a transformation by grace, which, as described above, brings into play the three dimensions of grace – excess/giving, openness/otherness, and vitality/interconnectedness. For it suggests that the path to social transformation is a path both of action and deed (*praxis*) and of creation and expression (*poiesis*).

As for the first, grace as gift, one of the first to use the language of gift, although not grace since he was not a theologian, was the American poet Lewis

Hyde. The notion of gift as grace is developed theologically by John Milbank and Rowan Williams.[82] Both Hyde and Williams praise the insights of the mid 20th-century Catholic philosopher Jacques Maritain into the nature of art. Williams calls particular attention to '...what is perhaps Maritain's most significant contribution to the whole debate: his analysis of art as exposing the "excess" of the material environment ("things are more than they are")'. The reality of abundance is there; it is art's task to bring it out.

In terms of second aspect, grace and otherness, Williams stresses that art 'makes the world strange' – not unintelligible but rather with insights, hints, and pointers to meanings which are not altogether clear, nor complete, but which we sense are there: '...bad art is art that does not invite us to question our perceptions and emotions.' Milbank contrasts the work of *techne*, which has a tendency to appear to be more dramatic and different than it really is, with the work of *ars* which appears only to alter the surface but which in fact often provokes more profound social change.

As for the third aspect, grace and connectedness, Hyde notes: 'Gifts are the agents of that organic cohesion we perceive as liveliness....The artist must submit himself to what I shall be calling a "gifted state", one in which he is able to discern the connections inherent in his materials and give the increase, bring the work to life....If the artist was really gifted, the work will induce a moment of grace, a communion, a period during which we too know the hidden coherence of our being and feel the fulness of our lives.'

Williams observes that for Maritain art acts '[b]y engaging us in an unforeseen pattern of coherence or integrity, art uncovers relations and resonances...' Milbank takes from Goethe the image of elective affinity. Art, in this perspective, enables us to sense possible connections and relationships which we can freely choose to develop in particular ways, but which we are drawn to by a kind of love.

Insights such as these into the deeper nature of art illustrate why the work of social transformation needs poets and artists – drawn by an experience of the good – as much as it needs prophets and activists – outraged by a sense of injustice. Not artists as propagandists, but artists who can help ensure that the passion for justice is grounded in the good. Far from causing the passion to be cooled, it will keep the sense of longing warm, the spirit of hope strong, and the powers of the imagination alive, so that social transformation does not become domesticated into some bland 'Third Way'. An aesthetics of grace in particular can help prevent social transformation from being undertaken as the brutal replacement of one alienating system of someone else's making with an equally alienating one of our own. 'Another World Is Possible', but in words which give a deeper sense to that slogan, Williams concludes: 'The artist's commitment to generative excess in the world stands as a challenge to a vulgarized Darwinism: this life could be otherwise; this life could mean more than its adaptation to these particular circumstances suggests.'[83]

Transformation by Grace – Practice

Transformation by poiesis/art and transformation by praxis/action are not alternatives nor do they run on parallel lines. The one infuses the other so that social transformation involves poetic praxis, a praxis that calls forth new meanings rather than imposes a plan, that allows for reinterpretation rather then simple reflexivity, that is creative rather than imitative. Milbank notes with pleasure the progression in Hauerwas' theology, from an earlier, more Barthian tendency to reproduce the radical patterns of action presented in the Gospel – e.g. pacifism – precisely towards a recognition of the role of the church in co-authoring the narrative, in generating creative, poetic, praxis which keeps the story alive.[84]

Transformative practice expresses itself, therefore, in many and unexpected ways. But it also needs some coherence. One way of assisting this is to identify some broad strands of action within a somewhat wider framework. Three such broader patterns of transformative practice may be described as: redistributing representing and redistributing. These will be looked at next.

Redistributing – Grace as Gift

> …there is no basis for the Marxist hope that an 'economy of
> abundance' will guarantee world peace; for men may fight as
> desperately for 'power and glory' as for bread.
> Reinhold Niebuhr [85]

For Anthony Giddens, the post-scarcity system appears to be the key unlocking the door to a system of planetary care, co-ordinated global order (not a 'world government' on 19th century models), the transcendence of war and the socialized organization of the economy.[86] But implied in that assertion are some very dubious assumptions not only about the supposed state of 'post-scarcity' but about the nature of scarcity itself. To divide human needs into material and spiritual is precisely to perpetuate the kind of division between humanity and nature, subject and object, controller and controlled that is characteristic of the secular reason on which capitalist modernity thrives. Realities such as economic scarcity and political insecurity do not exist on their own; they are interpreted and mediated culturally, socially, politically. Our very ideas of what it is we lack and what it is we ought to fear are mediated through cultural codes, historical memories, economic structures and political systems. All these, furthermore, are handled by human beings with fears and desires that are shaped by genetic orientation and personal experiences. This is not to deny that in all too many places today the sheer material dimensions of the realities of civil war, famine and disease are not so shocking and so scandalous as to condemn our failure to help provide food, medicine and even peacekeeping forces. The point is that even when these things are made available, cultural forces quickly assert themselves in determining, for example, what form peace-keeping will best take, how food will be distributed, and how the use of medicine will be complemented by other health-promoting measures.

The persistence of 'material' insecurity and scarcity does not account for the *libido dominandi* any more than an Age of Abundance would eliminate it. Enough will never be enough as long as possessions and political authority themselves are being treated as signs of superiority, status, security or power. That gives another clue to social transformation. The new regime will come about when we are able to see and use material goods as grace-filled signs and invitations to participate in a different type of life and a different type of love. Augustine, in one of his most moving passages, describes his own search: 'I asked the earth, and it said: "I am not he!" And all things in it confessed the same. I asked the sea and the deeps, and among living animals the things that creep, and they answered: "We are not your God. Seek you higher than us!" I asked the winds that blow; and all the air, with the dwellers therein, said: "Anaximines was wrong. I am not God!" I asked the heavens, the sun, the moon and the stars: "We are not the God whom you seek," said they. To all the things that stand around the doors of my flesh I said: "Tell me of my God. Although you are not he, tell me something of him!" With a mighty voice they cried out: "He made us!" My question was the gaze I turned on them; the answer was their beauty.'[87]

Re-presenting – Grace as Otherness

Milbank and others in the Radical Orthodoxy network have criticized liberation theology for being entirely preoccupied with the struggle for transformation and for assuming that the shape of the new social world would arise out of the struggle itself.[88] The same criticism is commonly made of Marx. To the extent that it is true, it is wholly justified. In fact, it is not the whole truth. Many liberation theologians have kept vision alive. Even in Marx there remained a utopian element.[89] And Critical Theory itself, even in its darkest period, refused to allow the utopian impulse to be extinguished, holding onto it as the very source of the power of critique, a point stressed by Jurgen Habermas, leading light of the second generation of Critical Theorists.[90]

Social transformation cannot rest with re-interpreting and re-imagining. It must translate these into creative action, ensuring that praxis has an essential element of the poetic. Poetic praxis must be contextual. This means for Milbank, as for Augustine, that in some contexts purely transformative witness may not be possible and that the possibilities of peace may have to be kept open by the use of force. For Christians, there is always the question of which context, which world, we choose to call home. Taking a stand alongside those whom the regime has marginalized and excluded is more likely to generate poetic praxis than sitting in a meeting.

A more modest approach to representing alternatives takes the form of experimentalism. That is the English way and it has often proved highly successful. Robert Owen, for example, insisted that his radical proposals for a new system of society be implemented gradually at a pace which people could accept and in a way which could be shown to work. Out of this, he believed, people would themselves have the confidence to determine and to take the next step forward. Similarly, John Stuart Mill also advocated 'experiments in living' as the best way to test out what true freedom really meant, and as the way to discover better ways of life.[91] It is in the same tradition that Hilary Wainwright, leader of the 1994 Towards Social Transformation seminar, warns that the project of social transformation today is not about providing all the answers. The point, she stresses, is that '...the creativity and innovation necessary for social transformation will come first from practice. Therefore the priority for work on new democratic institutions must be to investigate practical experiments to develop such institutions...'[92]

Restructuring – Grace as Connectedness

The decisions which create a human environment can give rise to specific structures of sin which impede the full realization of those who are in any way oppressed by them. To destroy such structures and replace them with more authentic forms of living in community is a task which demands courage and patience.

Pope John Paul II [93]

For Augustine, it is not so much that social structures are either good or bad but rather that they are provisional. Some take this to mean that Augustine can be hailed as the architect of a world in which space was reserved for a separate 'secular' sphere. This is the view of Robert Markus, who claims: 'Augustine's theology had carefully kept a space for an intermediate realm of the "secular" between the "sacred" and the "profane".'[94] Similarly, Peter Brown describes Augustine as 'the great "secularizer" of the pagan past'.[95] For John Milbank, on the other hand, such interpretations would be classic examples of that secular reason which is so contrary to the neo-Platonism he sees in Augustine, and which makes it possible to share ontologically and to express analogically the sacred dimension in all created reality.

For Milbank the empire is neither wholly sacred nor wholly secular. The boundaries between 'church and state' are, and should be, 'extremely hazy'.[96] Augustine did not hold out the hope that somehow, it was God's plan that Christians and the Empire would enter some new covenant. It was precisely the collusion of some Christians with the myth of security and greatness of Rome that Augustine set out to challenge.[97]

A sense of Augustinian provisionality will prove useful as we try – as we must – to imagine and to experiment with alternative ways of restructuring our society. Anthony Giddens argues at some length in favour of 'Utopian Realism', venturing to 'identify the contours of a post-modern order' in the shape of the humanization of technology, multi-layered democratic participation, demilitarization and the emergence of a post-scarcity economic system.[98] Meanwhile, a group of social and political theorists, which included Paul Hirst, joint leader of the 1991 Towards Social Transformation seminar, were setting up a 'Real Utopias' project which periodically published 'hard-nosed proposals for pragmatically improving our institutions'. The focus is on the core organizing principles of alternatives to existing institutions not on detailed institutional 'blueprints'. Objectives include the constructing of stations along the way towards that destination. Among the possibilities suggested are Basic Income Grants, Secondary Associations and Democratic Governance, Market Socialism and Asset Redistribution in Advanced Capitalism.[99] Of course, some of these suggestions may prove to be blind alleys, and may even be positively dangerous. But if we are serious about social transformation we dare not be afraid to dream.

CONCLUSION

The Church between Two Regimes
The Church and the Old Regime of Capitalist Modernity

How is the church to position itself between the two regimes – the earthly and the heavenly city? For Augustine, there is a creative blurring of boundaries. The church is more than just a sign of the heavenly city but neither is it co-terminous with the heavenly city. It would be dishonest to pretend either that it possesses a solution to the injustices of the old regime of capitalist modernity; it would be unrealistic to claim that it should. One might require, however, that it desire the new regime more whole-heartedly. The church is very much part of the 'old regime' – not, in the sense of being pre-modern and pre-capitalist but, on the contrary, in the sense of being too comfortable with capitalist modernity. To take capitalism, a great deal of credit – or blame – for its development has been laid at the door of 'the Protestant ethic' of hard work, deferred gratification and material success – although Max Weber's argument was challenged by R. H. Tawney, who thought it had much more to do with things like the appropriation of monastic lands and the enclosure of the commons. Today, the relationship is perhaps reversed – the church owes its financial viability to the stake it holds in capitalism, as Ulrich Duchrow and the liberation theologians have persistently pointed out.[100]

As for modernity, John Gray, leader of the 2002 Towards Social Transformation seminar, levels this accusation: 'Enlightenment thinkers like to see themselves as modern pagans, but they are latter-day Christians…Marxism and neo-liberalism are post-Christian cults. Beyond Christendom, no one has ever imagined that "world communism" or "global capitalism" could be "the end of history"….The Positivists inherited the Christian view of history, but – suppressing Christianity's saving insight that human nature is ineradicably flawed – they announced that by the use of technology humanity could make a new world.'[101] Ernest Gellner charges: 'In Christianity…Hierarchy, organized mediation, bureaucratised ritual and magic, prevailed in the very central and single Organization….The scriptur-alist, puritan, individualistic, symmetrical, ecstasy-spinning and mediation-repudi-ation enthusiasts were at the margin….It was this which in fact engendered, by some internal chemistry, the modern world.'[102]

It is instructive to see all this in terms of Milbank's critique of Christianity's long-standing collusion with secular reason: '…it was first of all the church, the *sacerdotium*, rather than the *regnum*, which assumed the traits of modern secularity – legal formalization, rational instrumentalization, sovereign rule, economic contractualism....' What led the church down this wrong path, according to Milbank, was its theological endorsement of the concept of *dominium* ('power, property, active right, absolute sovereignty').[103] So, in good Augustinian mode, the first aspect of the church's approach to the challenge of social transformation must be to confess its own need for grace.

Augustine is deeply aware of the power of sin in the structures of domination. But he is also aware that the process of liberation from that power involves a continual process of healing. Freedom features prominently in Augustine's city but not in the sense of a facile laissez-faire view of freedom. 'Civility' cannot be taken for granted. At the heart of what passes for culture there is often barbarism, as Terry Eagleton – and the Modernists – have realized. The church itself, for Augustine, is not a gathering of the perfect or even of those who feel they can become perfect by their own striving. Augustine's theological victory over Pelagius is construed by Peter Brown as 'a victory for the average good Catholic layman of the Later Empire, over an austere, reforming ideal'.[104] Not that Augustine was soft on sin or on the causes of sin; on the contrary, he refused to underestimate its hold. Nor did he fatalistically see us as powerless in the face of sin. The point was to create openings, in our hearts, in our assemblies and in our structures, for grace. Such a view provides the sort of strength that is required for 'fidelity to failure' in the face of 'the fallacy of hope'.

The regime of capitalist modernity is supported by myths which tend to deny historicity. They purport to suggest the regime is inscribed essentially on the story of human development, when in fact it is a contingent reality, whose origins were due to particular historical circumstances, whose characters are coloured by wider cultural forces and whose future is by no means guaranteed. The point of demythologizing the regime of capitalist modernity is not to demonize it, but to be able to treat it as literally not necessary – either empirically or morally.

More fundamentally still, it is what capitalist modernity represents and perpetuates – namely the regime of the *libido dominandi* – that is neither necessary nor destined to prevail. The path towards social transformation must lead to a consideration of social structures. Subsequent chapters will seek to develop it more fully still in an attempt to see in what ways the reality of grace has implications for the shape of our institutions. Chapter Three will suggest that social rights are best seen not as individual possessions but, with Richard Titmuss, as an expression of 'the gift relationship'. Chapter Four will suggest that the greater the role that is provided for giving in the processes of production, distribution and exchange, the nearer we will be to resolving the problem of scarcity. Chapter Five will argue that the less we cling jealously to illusions such as sovereignty and autonomy, the more will peace and freedom be allowed to flourish. But first: what happened to civil society? The context in which many radical hopes for social transformation were raised relied on the vitality and creativity that were assumed to be latent in civil society. In fact civil society itself has been transformed by capitalist modernity. Are there still possibilities for its transformation in other directions? That is the subject of the next chapter.

They are set apart by a holy yearning.

Augustine of Hippo [105]

Chapter 2

Transforming Relations
What Kind of Civil Society?

It [civil society] was a big fad in the wake of the fall of communism…
I bought into that but now I am more cynical. In Russia, it created shallowly
based elites good at writing grant applications to western organizations.
Francis Fukuyama[1]

Précis

There are many visions of Civil Society. When the Towards Social
Transformation initiative began to take shape in 1989, it was the more
democratic and self-organizing models of Civil Society that held out
the promise of radical social transformation. Since then, however, it
is a revived bourgeois version of Civil Society which has made the
running. Its blending of the values of money-making and civility, of
commerce consumption, of self-interest and individual liberties do
indeed underpin the civilization of capitalist modernity.[2] But when this
fact is used to support the claim that Civil Society is the product and
great achievement of capitalist modernity, then history has given way to
ideology. In fact the roots of Civil Society are to be found in particular
features of European history, some of which go back to medieval
times and others back to the Roman Empire itself. In other words, the
development of Civil Society in any of its forms is a contingent reality.
Its future shape – and its very existence or demise – will be as much the
result of unforeseen events, institutional momentum and human choice
as has been the case in the past.

This chapter will explore the different understandings and projects
of civil society and will argue that, in fact, all of these contain important
insights but that the development of associational forms offers the most
important path towards social transformation. It will first look at the
emergence of civil society – described by some as a miracle. It will then
lay out the current competing project for civil society and, thirdly, will
attempt to put the issue in a theological framework.

Preamble:
Transforming relations

At the time when the Towards Social Transformation initiative was taking shape, many on the Left were looking to the development of civil society as the key to social transformation. Fifteen years on, the state has been rolled back – but into the space that was supposed to be opened up for democratic renewal have rushed the forces of capitalist modernization. Where John Keane's vision of civil society involved the strengthening of trade union responsibilities as in Sweden and, increased workers' rights as in France, there is now more labour market flexibility. Where Keane pointed to campaigns for a 'citizen's wage' as in Germany, there are now cuts in benefits and closures of pension funds.[3] Where new social movements were seen as a hope for social transformation, the voluntary and community sector is now struggling to avoid being transformed into an agency of the state. For some this reinforcement of capitalist modernity represents the triumph of civil society; for others it represents a capture of civil society, stifling its potential to open up a genuine alternative.[4] Does this mean that those to the left of Keane were correct when they warned that the whole civil society project, from its origins to its recent revival, is nothing but an ideological front for capitalism? Does it mean that Gilles Deleuze was right to see civil society as simply representing a strategy of governance adopted when the traditional state apparatus was no longer able to contain the anarchic energies and desires unleashed by capitalism? Was Michel Foucault right when he argued that, far from being a simple sphere of civility and freedom, the interstices of social life are precisely where the diffuse and often hidden operations of power are most pervasive? Whose version of civil society is right? Why has it emerged in the form it has? Where are the possibilities of a transformative version? Does Augustine's vision of two cities offer any clues?

I. The Emergence of Civil Society

The Retreat of the State

The last quarter of the past century saw a steady abandonment by the state of many of the roles it has assumed over the previous one hundred years. For some this was simply a return to the natural state of affairs. But the relationship between state and society is more complex than that. There were good reasons why the state had played an increasingly interventionist role, not least the need to secure a reasonable resolution of the conflict between capital and labour within its boundaries and to expand and protect its markets in its colonial territories. But times change. With the increase in prosperity, there came the realization that cooperation between labour and capital could, within limits, be mutually beneficial. And with the development of regional blocs, such as the European Common Market, and the subsequent increase in globalized trade and investment, came the need to protect former colonial markets. But with the economic and political crisis of the 1970s, the argument for reducing the role of the state acquired a real urgency. The state simply could not deliver on all the promises it had begun to make as part of the welfare state regime. The less it was able to deliver, the greater the crisis of legitimacy. More fundamental still was the economic crisis. Stagflation (low growth mixed with high inflation) was leading to a squeeze in profits. The neo-liberal answer was to free capital – free it from high taxation so that people would have more incentives to work and to invest, free it from obligations on the home front, free it to circulate globally.

To make the argument more socially acceptable, there was the added argument that the retreat of the state would mean not just the liberation of capital but also the liberation of society. Indeed there was considerable agreement, by both Left and Right, that for the past century there had developed an unhealthy confusion of roles. Various forms of corporatism meant that 'society' had become embedded in the state apparatus in the form of particular interest groups, such as business, trade unions, the voluntary sector and even the established church. Conversely the state had been colonizing many functions and spheres of social life in a way which threatened their efficiency and their very integrity. This confusion of roles proved detrimental to enterprise and to creativity, to socialism and to democracy, to freedom and to responsibility – whilst fostering unimaginative, interventionist, inefficient, costly and ever expanding layers of bureaucracy.

But what then was the proper role of the state? What new relationship was needed between state and society? There were sharply differing views. For some the state was little more than a necessary evil. Its role should be mainly negative. Like a night watchman its basic role was to ensure order and security. Such a view could be based either on a pessimistic view of human nature, which saw individuals as mainly self-interested, and society as riven with conflict and competition, or on a sunnier view, which assumed that people would naturally find ways of living and working together if they were left free to work out their own relationships. For others, however, the state was still seen as having a more positive role vis-à-vis society: as an enabler both of enterprise and of collaboration.

Given the circumstances which prevailed in the late 20th century, it was hardly realistic to expect that the retreat of the state would automatically release new social energies. 'Society' was not in a healthy state and was hardly prepared to support the acceptance of new responsibilities and powers. In the capitalist world, the 1980s had been a period when self-interest, competition, inequality and even greed had been systematically promoted. The pronouncement by a Prime Minister that: 'There is no such thing as Society. There are individual men and women and there are families,' was a more accurate comment on the effects of capitalism than many would like to have admitted.[5] But the effects of communism on society were no less devastating. The destruction of autonomous social systems meant the absence of any institutional infrastructure capable of containing the divisive ethnic and religious divisions within or of keeping at bay the economic and cultural predators who were moving in to exploit the situation. Thus in both East and West, the conditions of the time were more likely to unleash social Darwinism than to encourage civil society – which is, in fact, what happened. Society became far less civil.

The Emergence of Civil Society

Is society naturally 'civil'? Does mutual respect, tolerance, respect for law, etc., come naturally, or does the sheer force of self-interest mean that it is relationships of power – economic, sexual, religious, tribal, and political – which tend to prevail? One need not be a disciple of Hobbes to recognize that conflict is indeed deeply embedded in our world – arising not just from the ambition of political and military leaders but also from the narrowness and self-righteousness of communities and from competition over scarce resources. Yet although greed, aggression and the *libido dominandi* play a real and powerful part in human affairs, this does not mean that they are central to human nature. They can be healed – by the right kind of relationships – and redirected – with the help of the right type of social institutions.[6]

How then does 'society' become 'civil'? For Ernest Gellner (1925–1995) not only is the emergence of civil society not natural, it is nothing less than a mystery and a miracle, resulting from a combination of historical factors.[7] It differs from the normal state of affairs, argues Gellner, which is marked on the one hand by a spirit of tribalism and identification with ethnic and/or religious 'community' and, on the other, by a strong political power, which was called into being to check the disorder which arose from economic conflict and competition. Both of these are forms of tyranny. Indeed for Gellner, far greater than the threat to Civil Society from the state is the threat posed by highly moral, status-oriented 'segmentary communities', i.e. which, even if they happen to be pluralistic, still treat individuals as integral parts of social sub-sets.

But what is this mysterious, miraculous thing called civil society? One look at the history of the term is enough to dispel the notion that there is any universally agreed definition.[8] The heart of the problem is that there are two very different philosophical traditions – the Anglo-Saxon (which, to oversimplify, stresses the merits of civil society) and the Continental European (which, again to over-simplify, tends to stress the limitations of civil society). Within each of these traditions, furthermore, there are liberal and radical versions of the civil society narrative. Representing the liberal-bourgeois version of the Anglo-Saxon narra-tive is John Locke, with the radical-democratic version being championed by Tom Paine. In the Continental tradition, it is Hegel who represents the liberal version (seeing the State as higher than civil society) and Marx who represents the radical version (seeing the division between State and civil society itself being overcome). Both main narratives are living traditions, which means that even within these traditions, new insights into civil society are continually being developed. Thus, in more recent times, the late Ernest Gellner might be seen as having carried forward the Lockean tradition, with John Keane carrying forward that of Paine, while the Hegelian tradition might be seen as having an impact on (though obviously not simply championed by) Jurgen Habermas, with the Marxist-Leninist tradition taking a more positive view of civil society under the influences of the posthumous works of the Italian Communist Antonio Gramsci (1891–1937). And, as if two historical narratives of civil society were not enough, the developing countries are today breaking new ground by mixing selected bits from the older understandings of civil society into their own very different cultural traditions. This all makes the debate about civil society much richer – Mary Kaldor delights in the fact that '…there is no agreed definition of the term. Indeed, its ambiguity is one of its attractions.'[9] It also keeps the debate about civil society open and creative. John Keane, therefore, argues against seeking 'purist' definitions of global civil society that would restrict it only to the groups that are campaigning for social transformation. For him civil society includes capitalist as well as anti-capitalist groups, agencies funded by govern-ments as well as grass roots campaign groups, global media groups as well as informal networks. Keane expresses concern about '...the neglect of religion, which (intended or not) creates the secularist impression that religion is "withering away". Most definitely it is not, which is one of the reasons why ethical standards are currently alive and well with civil society at the global level, why global civil society is normatively contested.'[10]

Two Levels of Civil Society: Clarification and Contention

But precisely because civil society can mean such different things to different people, it is necessary for participants in any particular conversation to be as clear as possible as to how they are using the term. Here the focus will be largely on the Anglo-Saxon narrative of civil society, although drawing on others where appropriate. And here we will cease putting the term civil society in quotation marks by instead using upper case and lower case to distinguish two very different usages, which are often confused. The lower case – civil society – will hereafter be used when referring to a sphere distinct from the state. It may seem obvious that that is what civil society is all about. This is the popular use. It is the usage adopted in official Catholic Church teaching.[11] It refers to a sphere distinct from the state but with particular civic functions which give it a more specific and narrower meaning than simply 'society'.

But before that lower-case use of the term emerged, the Scottish philosopher Adam Ferguson (1723–1816) had already articulated a broader usage of the term and for this the upper case will hereafter be used. 'Civil Society' as celebrated by Ferguson describes an overall culture, institutions and regime, of which the polity itself is only a part, and which is represented historically by the bourgeoisie.[12] It is worth elaborating on the distinction.

Taken in the narrower sense, civil society refers to those institutions which act not just in tension with the state but also in a complementary relationship, thus helping to ensure that it is the actual experiences, needs, values and relationships of everyday life that help define the purposes and limits of state action. There is some debate as to whether either the family or the economy are best included in the concept of civil society. Traditionally, the family has not been included. Some argue that it should have been because in many cultures, families play an extremely important political and economic role – although others see such action precisely as undermining the very principles of civil society. Traditionally the economy has been included. Some argue that it no longer should be because the capitalist economy has grown to be at least as powerful as the state once was.[13] Here, there is not space to engage with such debates, so the conventional view will be followed, which takes civil society to include the economy but to exclude the family.

Taken in the broader sense, Civil Society includes the state and designates a particular kind of overall polity, whose defining feature is freedom. Its characteristic civil values are freedom of speech, mutual tolerance, and respect for law. Its key institutions include 'the rule of law', an independent judiciary, a range of civil liberties, a free press, security of property, and a market system. It is free in the limited sense that the regime – however contrary to historical fact – rests on consent to a mythical 'social contract' rather than on coercion. It is free also in the limited sense that it assumes – however contrary to psychological fact – that its laws are reasonable because its citizens are reasonable. It is free, furthermore, in the limited sense that – however indulgent it may be towards concentrations of economic power – it places limits on the concentration of political and cultural power.

As with civil society, the notion of Civil Society is also a matter of some debate. For Ernest Gellner, '[w]hat distinguishes Civil Society (using the term to describe the entire society), or a society *containing* Civil Society (in the narrower sense), from others is that it is *not* clear who is boss.'[14] In other words, there is no dominant power, no concentration of economic, political and cultural authority. For Gellner, it is 'ideocracies', whether secular or religious, which, by attempting to implement a moral vision, are the antithesis of Civil Society. Civil Society, for Gellner, is an 'a-moral order', in that it does not demand obedience to a particular set of values or beliefs. It is 'above all a society whose order is not sacralized', although Gellner then adds 'or rather is only sacralized with ambiguity, irony and nuance.' Gellner accuses Ferguson of timidity in refusing to cut the economic order off completely from the moral order – in other words, of not fully accepting modernity. Civil Society is characterized by the separation of spheres – a fine example of modernity at work. Capitalism, too, gets the green light. Gellner ascribes primacy to the economy, seeing it as being 'not merely independent but actually dominant, treating the polity as its accountable servant'. He qualifies this, however, when he distinguishes the conditions which prevailed at the time of the emergence of civil society from the situation that exists now, where: '...the economy is so appallingly powerful. The side effects of economic operations, if unrestrained, would disrupt everything – the environment, the cultural heritage, human relations.' He also insists that the state is not a mere night watchman: 'A modern society without some form of effective welfare state is morally repellent.' Yet, for all the acuteness, wisdom and qualifications in Gellner's argument, there is more than a hint of ideology. Is it any wonder that the notion of Civil Society has been viewed with considerable suspicion by those who are concerned for social justice and who warn of the dangers of neglecting the moral and the material basis of freedom itself?

But What about Democracy?

What sparked off the Towards Social Transformation initiative was John Keane's work on civil society, in which democratization, participation, self-organization and collective responsibility were absolutely central. The issue of democracy will be explored in Chapter Five. Here, however, it is enough to sound a warning that if democracy is to be a part of Civil Society and of civil society it must be fought for, not taken for granted. It is not accidental that, in the original project of Civil Society, democracy simply had no place. Even Gellner, who devotes a whole chapter to 'Democracy or Civil Society', confesses to finding the term democracy less satisfactory than that of Civil Society. As for civil society, it is very alarming to note the current trend for government and the corporate sector alike to narrow the notion of civil society, using it simply as shorthand for NGOs and voluntary associations.

If civil society is to be a source of social transformation, therefore, it will mean an uphill struggle. The next section seeks to clarify what this involves by using a grid to locate the different projects which are being promoted under the banner of Civil Society.

2. Competing Projects for 'Civil Society'

> The future of Civil Society seems linked to our historical
> destiny...[but] the choice is ours.
> Ernest Gellner[15]

One way of comparing the competing projects for Civil Society is to try to chart them on a grid (see opposite). It assumes that all find some place for individuality as well as for community, and that all give some role to authority as well as to spontaneity. By locating the different projects in different quadrants of the grid, the aim is both to show the different weight they give to each of these factors as well as to suggest what their starting point is. For example, those furthest to the left give greatest scope to individuality. Those closest to the top give greatest role to authority. All have their own concepts of 'Freedom' and 'Order'. Because

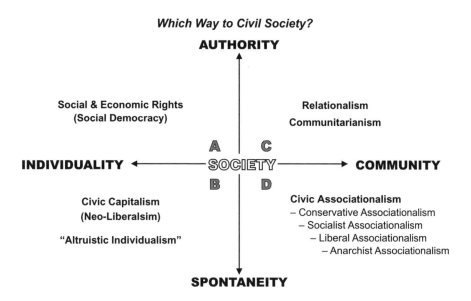

Which Way to Civil Society?

all of the projects included on the grid see themselves as offering a model of Civil Society, none are at the extreme corners of their respective quadrants (the extreme corner of Quadrant A might be Fascism, just as Anarchism might be at the far corner of Quadrant B, Tribalism at the far corner of Quadrant C and Communism at the far corner of Quadrant D).

Quadrant A (Social Democracy) represents what was, until recently, assumed to be the natural evolution of Civil Society. It wove a narrative of the steady evolution of rights from civil to political to social and economic. The role of rights is to provide the individual with protection from the abuses of power and with scope for the exercise of freedom. That narrative has been losing ground to neo-liberalism (Quadrant B – Civic Capitalism). Here Civil Society reverts to its earlier sense, favouring commerce as an antidote to war, property as a source of order and industry as a means to prosperity. Both Social Democracy and Civic Capitalism are rooted in individualistic assumptions. They represent alternative versions of capitalist modernity. The defining, but not the only difference, is in the role they give to the state in protecting and empowering the individual. The alternative projects on the right of the grid start from a more social under-standing of human nature. They are represented by Quadrants C (Relationalism and Communitarianism), and D (Associationalism). For Quadrant C, what is central to Civil Society is a sense of duty, responsibility and respect for others. For Quadrant D, the glory of Civil Society consists in the practical realization of the benefits of freedom of speech, assembly and association. In the real world, the serious options are about various mixtures of society, individual and state. This means that the alternatives are located at various points within any of the quadrants. Such choices are not pure, but they do matter. They determine where we will devote our resources in the present; and they may open up the possibilities for transformation in the future.

Since it is social democracy which is being transformed, and since the case for social rights will be examined in detail in Chapter Three, the following section will look at the movements for transforming Civil Society, as represented in Quadrants B, C, and D.

Quadrant B: Civic Capitalism and Altruistic Individualism

Quadrant B is wedded most closely to the logic of capitalist modernity, with capitalism taking the form of civic capitalism and modernity that of altruistic individualism. Both will be looked at next.

Civic Capitalism

Civic capitalism relies on a view of human nature and society which sees self-interest as the basic motive. It is fundamental to the philosophy of both Hobbes and Locke, but where Hobbes saw self-interest as tending naturally to civil war, Locke saw it as the basis of a civil society.

Why did Hobbes take this view? It is sometimes put down to Hobbes' materialism or atomistic view of human nature. On the contrary, argues, C. B. Macpherson: it was not what Hobbes *thought* but what he *saw* that shaped his views. What he saw was: 'Covetousness of great Riches, and ambition of great Honours, are honourable....Riches are honourable for they are power.... We do not...by nature seek society for its own sake, but that we may receive some honour or profit from it....All society therefore is for gain or for glory... [but] that glory is like honour; if all men have it no man hath it, for they consist in comparison and precellence.'[16] According to Macpherson: 'It was to the new strength of market mentality and of market-made wealth that Hobbes attributed the Civil War.'[17]

How then could Locke, writing only a few decades later, have managed to build a vision of 'civil society' in which markets and private property would be so beneficial? Locke's narrative is so influential and so clever that it is worth following his argument step-by-step. Enlisting a reasonable God in aid of reasonable human beings, Locke develops his picture of the state of nature as one of law not war: 'God gave the world to men in common but...it cannot be supposed

He meant it should always remain in common.'[18] In this state of nature, there is a law, says Locke, which of course places reasonable constraints on the process of appropriation. Firstly, the right to private property derives from a person's labour; secondly, it should not be allowed to spoil ('Every man should have as much as he could make use of...'); and thirdly, that there remains '...enough and as good left in common for others.'

Having set these conditions, Locke proceeds systematically, to circumvent each of them. Enclosure of land is justifiable because proprietors do not diminish the common stock but actually increase it by their labour. Money may be accumulated beyond all need, because it is not the sort of good which will spoil for lack of use, so that it is perfectly all right to make more and more money through trade. Locke, having served as Secretary to the Council of Trade and Foreign Plantations, speaks for the ascendant commercial bourgeoisie rather than for the landed bourgeoisie. Thus are laid the foundations for the ideology of capitalist Civil Society.

On those foundations, Locke built his version of civil society. Those whose only property is their labour, he continues, are accorded the right to sell their labour, which is as wonderfully in accord with the law of nature and with God's command as is inequality and the class system. Not surprisingly, the labourers are less than happy with this arrangement. Conflict inevitably arises, but not, as for Hobbes, a war of all against all but between two sections of the community: on one side, the 'Quarrelsome and Contentious' (represented by the proletariat – who adopting this attitude are, incidentally being disobedient to God as well), on the other, the 'Industrious and Rational' (represented, of course, by the bourgeoisie). Only at this stage is Civil Society formed – not to replace the law of nature but to ensure that it can be enforced. Civil Society in this scenario does not entail as it did for Hobbes, submission to a Leviathan. Rather it is agreement to class rule. The bourgeoisie alone are party to the pact and they alone retain the right to annul it. Democracy simply does not enter into it. The result is a Civil Society that contains, rather than creates, conflict and one whose rule of law and rationality are instruments of economic and political power, even if less overtly intertwined than in feudal society.[19] It is a masterpiece of ideology which seeks to build a cohesive society on the basis of what Macpherson calls possessive individualism, and which enjoys the endorsement of nature and the blessing of God.

The times were right for the acceptance of Locke's view. The commercial class was in the ascendancy. The last thing they needed was a Hobbesian-style strong monarch. The 'Glorious Revolution' of 1688 took care of that problem. As for 'the working class', they were still largely rural and unorganized. This left the bourgeoisie with prime responsibility for developing the new civic order. The regime must not appear as simply a new form of oppression. The first step was to create the fiction that it was based on consent. Thus the myth of a social contract, which most of the population had never heard of much less agreed to. Secondly, it would be better if the bourgeoisie were not seen to be rulers. Let 'the rule of law' take care of that so that they could get on with making money. This might involve a degree of corruption, but wasn't the corruption of the Court – where people did not even work for their wealth – far more immoral? Thirdly, to bolster their indirect way of exercising political power, it would be important to keep their ears to the ground so as to be able to respond quickly to new opportunities and new threats. Thus the development of a public sphere.

Jurgen Habermas has explored the dynamics nicely. The bourgeois regime of Civil Society: '...may be conceived above all as the sphere of private people come together as a public....The bourgeois were private persons; as such they did not "rule"....The principle of control that the bourgeois public opposed to the latter [i.e. to the political rulers of the day] – namely publicity – was intended to change domination as such....' [20] Instead of 'ruling' the bourgeoisie built up a set of institutions, including freedom of speech and a free press. Initially devised to defend their interests, these institutions eventually became part of an immensely beneficial liberal heritage.

Habermas explores the contradictions of this new public sphere. It developed in tandem with the rise of mercantile capitalism, since merchants needed publications which reported daily on commercial news and on state affairs. A by-product of this was the use of the media for criticism of the state and for the development of public opinion, which helped the new bourgeoisie articulate their interests and develop a political voice. This new public sphere, Habermas demonstrates, played a dual role for the bourgeoisie. On the one hand it served as their living space, enabling them to articulate their distinctive (economic) interests. On the other, it also opened up a space where their hypocrisy would be savagely criticized by the likes of Swift, Bolingbroke and Pope:

> *At length Corruption, like a gen'ral flood*
> *(So long by watchful Ministers withstood)*
> *Shall deluge all; and Av'rice creeping on,*
> *Spread like a low-born mist, and blot the Sun;*

> *Statesman and Patriot ply alike the stocks,*
> *Peeress and Butler share alike the Box,*
> *And Judges job, and Bishops bite the town,*
> *And mighty Dukes pack cards for half a crown.* [21]

Constructing a regime on the bases of self-interest and civility was always going to be a challenge. The bourgeoisie were not blind to the problem. No wonder that Adam Ferguson, in his paean to Civil Society, warns that although it was founded on commerce, it must not be confused with 'the commercial state', in which 'man is sometimes found a detached and a solitary being. He had found an object which sets him in competition with his fellow creatures and he deals with them as he does with his cattle and his soil for the sake of the profits they bring.' The cult of riches would end in tyranny and slavery. [22]

Yet the animus against the state continued even as democratic spirits stirred. For Tom Paine (1737–1809), it was still political power more than economic power which was the real danger to freedom. [23] For Paine, society was 'produced by our wants', the state 'by our wickedness'). [24] Self-interest remains fundamental for Paine: 'All the great laws of society are laws of nature. Those of trade and commerce…are laws of mutual and reciprocal interest.' [25] 'Government is nothing more than a national association.' But the link between self-interest and social dimensions of property is not left behind as it is for Locke: 'He [the citizen] therefore deposits this [natural] right in the common stock of society…. Society grants him nothing. Every man is a proprietor in society, and draws on the capital as a matter of right.' [26]

The radical implications of this insight are developed in *Agrarian Justice*. Paine claims that in the natural state not only is there no poverty, there is also an equality of natural property: '…the first principle of civilization ought to have been, and ought still to be, that the condition of every person born into the world, after a state of civilization commences, ought not to be worse off than if he had been born before that period.' [27] But unlike natural property, acquired property is not and should not have to be equal. Appropriation of land, cultivation and industry all give rise to a legitimate title to property. Nonetheless, a three-fold claim arises on the part of the community to a return on their investment sufficient to alleviate poverty; first, because civilization has created poverty; secondly, because those who have acquired property have done so thanks to the development of society; and, thirdly, because: '…if we examine the case minutely it will be found that the accumulation of personal property is, in many instances, the result of paying too little for the labour that produced it....' Thus Paine proposes – as a matter of strict right, not simply of charity – a National Fund, out of which every person, on reaching the age of twenty-one should receive a one-off grant of £15, with every person aged fifty and over receiving a grant of £10 per year.

All these contradictions were manageable but only until mercantile capitalism was followed by industrial capitalism when the exploitation and degradation inflicted on the working class became shockingly apparent. Now, instead of civil society, there was the real threat of civil war. So the state was turned to, by capitalists and proletariat alike – not, this time, as Leviathan, but as Conflict Manager. But instead of saving Civil Society, the state also tended to absorb civil society. Later, as capitalism moved onto a new stage, the state was pushed back but after a decade or so of pure neo-liberalism, crude individualism and pure greed, the call for a more 'civic capitalism' began to be sounded.

Civic Capitalism Today

It is a clear sign of the times when David Green, director of *Civitas*, the Institute for the Study of Civil Society, can confess: 'Worse still, the renewal of civil society was simply not on the agenda of the Thatcher governments of the 1980s. And when advantage was taken of voluntary organizations, they were seen largely as sub-contractors which could supply services for government more cheaply than commercial alternatives. The unintended upshot of this 'contract culture' was further weakening of civil society....'[28] What makes the observation so significant is the fact that Civitas, although established as an independent charity in 2000, was previously incarnate as the Health and Welfare Unit of the right-wing Institute of Economic Affairs.

Yet civic capitalism does not stray far from the tradition of Hayek. Green insists – somewhat less unequivocally than Hayek – that freedom is an end in itself and that it is frustrated by the attempt to establish social goals. For Green the state is there to enable people to pursue their own goals. Its limited role in welfare is to promote choice by the introduction of market principles where feasible into public services and to encourage individual responsibility by designing welfare as a safety net and a means for guiding people into the labour market. It also stresses the family and the fact that each individual: '...has an important task to play as a custodian of the common culture which has been passed down the generations.' Although Civic Capitalism professes to distance itself from the Thatcher era, there is, in fact, considerable continuity. Stuart Hall once described: 'Thatcherite populism' as 'a particularly rich mix. It combines the resonant themes of organic Toryism – nation, family, duty, authority, standards, traditionalism – with the aggressive themes of a revived neo-liberalism – self-interest, competitive individualism, anti-statism'.[29] What greater satisfaction could Mrs. Thatcher have than to see her project carried forward by New Labour?

As heir to Locke's understanding of Civil Society, Civic Capitalism suffers from some of the same drawbacks, never fully overcoming an individualism which views social relations as mainly a matter of choice and which has little to say about the social origins or obligations of property. It fails to address the question of the way capitalism becomes a regime and a civilization, undermining and distorting social relationships – a process powerfully described by Tawney, Marx and Polanyi.

Altruistic Individualism?

Alongside the influence of capitalism, there is also the challenge posed by the individualizing tendencies of contemporary modernity. Ulrich Beck describes these as 'institutional individualism.' By this he means that the institutions of contemporary society no longer provide a source of personal integration; increasingly we keep our 'selves' at some distance from any institution.[30] This individualism is intensified, notes Beck, in that we can no longer fall back on class solidarity, even in opposition to the system. Classes still exist but without a sense of solidarity because social identities are centred less around class.[31] Beck sees all this as an ambivalent development. It brings more freedom but heavier responsibility, more opportunity but less security, more mobility but less support, more varied social relationships but more conflict – which is often displaced onto the family.

Anthony Giddens offers a similar analysis. Exploring the effects of contemporary modernity at the personal level, he describes it as a move towards 'pure relationships', i.e. relationships without traditional norms or institutional support: 'In the individualized society the individual must therefore learn, on pain of permanent disadvantage, to conceive of himself or herself as the centre of action, as the planning office with respect to his/her own biography, abilities, orientations, relationships and so on. Under these conditions of a reflexive biography, "society" **must** be individually manipulated as a "variable".'[32]

Beck and Giddens are at pains to distinguish these tendencies of individuation from *individualism* – i.e. the enthronement of self-interest as celebrated by the me-generation: '...these new 'we' orientations are creating something like a co-operative or altruistic individualism. Thinking of oneself and living for others, once considered a contradiction in terms, is revealed as an internal connection'.[33] The combination, however, of the self-interest of capitalism and the individuation of modernity suggests that, because it lacks a strong view of the social, the sort of Civil Society which Civic Capitalism and Altruistic Individualism are capable of producing will be very tenuous.

Transforming Civil Society: Alternative Visions

The transformation of Civil Society is not just a matter of constructing a different set of institutions, which shift power in a more equal direction, or of invoking a different set of values which place more stress on the social. It is also theological, challenging the idea which underpins Locke's complacent view that the pursuit of self-interest is the surest path to collective well-being and the protection of private property the best source of security. There is little aware-ness of Augustine's warnings about the presence of the *libido dominandi*, the need for healing and the attraction of the good are all essential ingredients of a society that is to be truly civil. That is why it is important to look to the right hand side of the grid, to Quadrants C and D.

Quadrant C: Communitarianism and Relationalism

Quadrants C and D represent various attempts to develop a more social version of Civil Society, with Quadrant C relying somewhat more heavily on author-ity and Quadrant D giving greater scope to choice. The two movements within Quadrant C to be explored here are Communitarianism and Relationalism.

Communitarianism

The communitarian movement started in the United States, sparked by the soci-ologist Amitai Etzioni. It has been taken up enthusiastically by many Christians, notably Robert Bellah and others in the Communitarian Network.[34] Within a few years it had found support in the UK, where a Communitarian Forum was set up. In 2003, its chairperson, Henry Tam, was appointed Deputy Director of the government's newly formed Civil Renewal Unit.[35]

The original motive was to redress the prevailing balance that had given exces-sive weight to rights and liberties at the expense of responsibilities and duties. But the thinking has not stopped there. Communitarianism, Tam insists, is not so much a fourth ideology, as a search for common ground: 'Conservatives, liberals and socialists who approach politics in a communitarian manner will share a very important common agenda....'[36] Communitarianism for Tam rests on three basic principles: co-operative enquiry, mutual responsibility and citizen participation. The principle of co-operative enquiry leads to the overcoming of relativism and the arrival at common values – but values which are discovered together rather than simply handed down by tradition. The principle of mutual responsibility – buttressed by a Bill of Responsibilities – is applied to welfare ('citizen income' conditional on some form of 'citizen service'). The principle of participation is applied not just to neighbourhood concerns but to a 'participatory economy', with worker participation and communitarian management, and to politics – 'communitarian governance'. After such a build-up, it is somewhat disappointing to find that Tam relegates 'Communitarian Civil Society' to a sub-section of a chapter on 'The Third Sector', which could unintentionally reinforce the idea that the development of civil society is mainly about voluntary organization providing social services.

Communitarianism: Some Health Warnings

The bright side of communitarianism is its concern to be inclusive and to promote civil society. A sense of community can overcome the isolation that so characterizes the regime of capitalist modernity. It can enhance the spirit of trust, co-operation, reciprocity, generosity. But it has a dark side as well. Two of the main dangers are those of intolerance, which could lead to authoritarianism and exclusiveness, which could lead to tribalism.

Communitarianism's concern about discouraging anti-social behaviour is widely shared and its readiness to resort to mechanisms such as Anti-Social Behaviour Orders has found many converts. The case for such measures is strong. It is no use saying: 'Let's wait until we have eliminated the causes, before addressing some of the symptoms which make people's lives miserable.' Nonetheless, if the causes are not dealt with, the remedies may help to bring about the very opposite of what was intended. A police state is not a civil society.

The second danger is tribalism. With the tightening of bonds and the deepening of loyalties can come a heightening of barriers. There is tribalism on the grand scale, as seen not just in the current resentment of immigrants but in a more deeply-rooted hostility towards 'foreigners', as noted by Tom Paine, in a typically caustic comment: 'It is somewhat curious to observe, that although the people of England have been in the habit of talking about kings, it is always a Foreign House of kings; hating foreigners, yet governed by them.'[37] But there is also tribalism on a smaller scale. When Robert Bellah and his associates undertook their research into the state of American social values in the 1980s – admittedly focussing on the East- and West-coast white middle-class – what they found was not so much crude individualism but a worrying retreat into 'life-style' enclaves, both residential and professional. These enclaves were not true communities, they insisted, but were basically private expressions of narcissism, embracing only those with a similar life-style and relating only to certain segments of life, especially consumption: '…the tendency of contemporary American life is to pull all of us into lifestyle enclaves of one sort or another.'[38] This is very similar to what Francis Fukuyama calls the 'miniaturization of community' – the retreat into self-contained residential associations ('burbclaves'), the narrowing of politics into single issue groups at the expense of broad-based political parties, the narrowing of the circles which can operate on the basis of relations of trust, reciprocity and mutual responsibility.[39]

The danger of communitarianism, in short, is that it is more about conforming than about transforming. It is a danger of which the church itself must be wary if it is not to betray its mission.

Relationalism

Relationalism has much in common with communitarianism. It, too, addresses the broad scope of social life. It places particular emphasis on the family. It also has a vision for the economy – espousing a 'relational market economy', promoting congruence of interest between shareholders, managers and workforce, protecting rootedness for local communities and families, relational finance (regional banks, debt-free equity finance, reduction of government borrowing), relational corporate and industrial structures, opportunity to work together in small groups or, for those who work in large groups, to participate in decision-making, seeking parity in dealings between people who act as representatives of institutions whether public or private.[40] And it extends to the political arena – with proposals for a 'relational democracy', and to the fields of social policy – relational welfare – and culture – relational media.[41]

But where communitarianism falls short, according to Michael Schluter, founder of the Relationships Foundation,[42] is in its failure to get to the heart of the problem. What is needed is the thoroughly Biblical vision of relationships which provides the needed basis for relationships that are deep, stable and underpinned by long-term commitment. What this means is not simply that the intensity and permanence of relationships are good in themselves but the shape of the bonds – of faithfulness, of obligation, of respect – are expressions of obedience to God whose order is revealed in the Bible.

In a relational framework, quality matters. Schluter has developed a five-dimensional set of criteria for 'relational proximity'. The shape of relationships matters, too. Here the patterns of relationship as found in the Bible are given a normative status which not all Scripture scholars would see as warranted. The development of the Jubilee laws, which for Schluter 'is foundational' to the social structure of Old Testament Law, clearly does strike a popular chord.[43] Less popular would be the application by Michael Ovey of I Corinthians 11 and Ephesians 5 to justify the continuing relevance of the notion of male 'headship' in the family, expressing equal but asymmetrical relationships, or the use of I Timothy 2 to justify the restriction of certain ecclesiastical roles to men. More contentious still, Christopher Townsend concludes that acceptance of homosexual behaviour implies a repudiation of the created moral order, a shift to subjective morality and enshrining of human insights in place of divine revelation.[44]

Quadrant D: Civic Associationalism – Ancient and Modern

Who says liberty says association.
Lamennais

Recovering the Associational Tradition

In the associational tradition there are two streams – political and social. 18th century England saw a flourishing of social associations – literary, artistic and scientific societies. Modern political associational thinking can be traced back to the German Calvinist Johannes Althaus (Althusius) (1557–1638).[45] He begins his classic treatise with the following statement: 'Politics is the art of human con-sociation for the sake of defining, nurturing and conserving social life, for which reason it is called "symbiotic".'[46] But he then proceeds to develop a comprehensive, minutely defined schema into which every aspect of social life is divided, subdivided and allocated its proper place. Thus Althusius needs to be treated with caution. His Calvinism is shaped not only by the Bible – reflected in his emphasis on covenant – but also by modernity – reflected by his emphasis on method (perhaps under the influence of Peter Ramus). Some have adopted Althusius as a sort of patron saint of the Federalist movement.[47] Others see him as a precursor of the corporate state.[48]

As a significant force, however, associationalism emerged only in the first half of the 19th century, largely in reaction against the centralizing power of the

French state but, to a lesser extent, in response to the impersonal forces of industrial capitalism. Its proponents included Charles Fourier (1772–1837), Félicité de Lamennais (1782–1854) and Pierre-Joseph Proudhon (1809–1865) in France, Robert Owen (1771–1858) and George Jacob Holyoake (1817–1906) in Britain, Giuseppe Mazzini (1805–1872) in Italy and, most famously, Alexis de Tocqueville (1805–1859), author of the two-volume tome *De la Démocratie en Amérique*. And it became a central part of Catholic social practice, especially in Germany ('*Vereinskatholizismus*') and in Italy (the *Opera dei Congressi*). It was, in part, a defensive strategy, in response, on the one hand to the anti-Catholic policies of the state and, on the other, to the revolutionary movements of socialists.[49]

As the state took on more and more functions at the beginning of the 20th century, the associational idea once again became popular, thanks to the works of G. D. H. Cole, Harold Laski and the Anglican priest-historian John Neville Figgis (1866–1919). In Italy, the rise of totalitarianism may well have played a part in the papal promotion of the principle of subsidiarity.[50] Today, as the power of the state is once again being called into question, the associational tradition has been looked at afresh. It has a rich history and it offers possibilities, as will be seen below, for a variety of projects – liberal, conservative, anarchist, or socialist.

Associationalism's contributions to civil society are both negative and positive. Negatively, they serve to prevent the abuse of power, whether by the conspiracies of elites or by what Tocqueville called 'the tyranny of the majority'.[51] But there are other, more positive reasons why associationalism has such a unique contribution to make to the development of civil society. First, it allows individuals to mix with those of different cultures for common purposes, thus diluting tribalism and promoting pluralism. Secondly, it allows for a rich texture of social life, since associations will take a variety of shapes and styles, allowing for the development of alternatives. Thirdly, it fosters a sense of responsibility and confidence in the possibilities of collective self-organization as a way of dealing with a wider range of issues in the economic and political sphere. Fourthly, it provides a base for a genuine collective voice.

Associations: Civil and Political

Tocqueville distinguishes two types of associations: political and civil. Political associations were important for keeping the government at bay. 'The more government takes the place of associations, the more will individuals lose the idea of forming associations and need the government to come to their help. That is a vicious circle.…The morals and intelligence of a democratic people would be in as much danger as its commerce and industry if ever a government usurped the place of private associations'.[52] Political associations were also important as schools for democracy. Recognizing that people are not instinctively prepared to associate for larger political issues, Tocqueville stresses the important educative effect of smaller, local associations: 'Thus, far more may be done by entrusting citizens with the management of minor affairs than by handing over control of greater matters…to gain the affection and respect of your immediate neighbours, a long succession of little services rendered and of obscure good deeds, a constant habit of kindness and an established reputation for disinterestedness, are required.'

But more important for Tocqueville than political associations, because more basic, are civil associations '…of a thousand different types – religious, moral, serious, futile, very generous and very limited, immensely large and very minute. Americans combine to give fêtes, found seminaries, build churches, distribute books, and send missionaries to the Antipodes. Hospitals, prisons and schools take shape in that way.' Tocqueville goes further: 'Nothing, in my view, more deserves attention than the intellectual and moral associations in America. American political and industrial associations easily catch our eyes, but the others tend not to be noticed.'

The Status of Associations

Just how important associational life is for the development of civil society is seen most clearly in the debate about the legal status of associations. This surfaced as a crucial issue towards the end of the 19th century as the logic of the modern state led it to claim that associations should be encompassed within its legal and administrative system. Such a policy of incipient totalitarianism struck at the basic integrity of associational life.[53] The battle was joined, notably by Figgis who argued the case for the independent corporate personality of associations – whether these were trade unions or businesses, colleges or Inns of Court, secular or religious bodies. Figgis in turn, thanks to the guidance of the legal historian F. W. Maitland, was able to draw on the findings of the German historian Otto von Gierke, who called attention to the rich pattern of corporate life in the Middle Ages.

Attributing to associations the status of corporate personality – a status which is to be recognized not bestowed by the state – denies the state the right to intervene in ways which might alter their character. It is a position which, incidentally, poses a fundamental challenge to the whole notion of state sovereignty – an issue which will be explored in Chapter Five.

The associational vision is spelt out more fully still by G. D. H. Cole. Cole identifies four types of association as essential to society: religious, political, vocational and appetitive.[54] 'The highest development of society consists not only in the general diffusion of associations and institutions over every organiz-able tract of social life, but also in the harmonious co-operation of all the various bodies, each fulfilling its proper function within society, in harmony and agree-ment with the others.' But even associations need to be kept in perspective. Being primarily functional in nature, they represent only one aspect of human sociality: 'As long as human life remains,' warns Cole, 'most of the best things in it will remain outside the bounds and scope of organization....'

Civic Associationalisms – Conservative, Socialist, Liberal, Anarchist

No one group or project has a monopoly on the associational principle. The roots of the tradition were strongly socialist. But a liberal version is reflected in the thought of John Neville Figgis, William Temple[55] and David Nicholls.[56] And a more conservative version has been elaborated in the United States in the 1950s by Robert Nisbet and in the 1970s by Peter L. Berger with Richard John Neuhaus. Here it is the conservative and socialist versions which will be looked at in more detail.

Conservative Associationalism

Although the sociologist Robert Nisbet attempted, in 1953, to revive the associational idea from a neo-conservative perspective,[57] it was not until 1977 that a bigger impact was made, this time by the joint efforts of sociologist Peter L. Berger and theologian Richard John Neuhaus in a pamphlet for the free-market lobby group, the American Enterprise Institute.[58]

The problem they sought to address was the dichotomy created by modern-ity between public and private life. This left the individual having to struggle to balance the demands of both spheres while at the same time the political was being perceived as devoid of personal meaning, unreal or even malign. Berger and Neuhaus proposed 'mediating structures': '...those institutions standing between the individual in his private life and the large institutions of public life.' With the help of mediating structures, individuals could feel more 'at home' in society and democracy could become more meaningful. Not just any type of association, however, could measure up to the challenge. It would have to be structured, not just occasional, so as to connect with the realities and values of everyday life. As a structure it would have to be reliable and have a moral foundation so as to ensure the legitimacy of the political side of its mediation. Berger and Neuhaus acknowledged that there was a considerable range of potential mediating structures but the four which they held up as being the strongest candidates were: family, neighbourhood, voluntary association and church.

The family has been affected in a paradoxical way by modernity, according to Berger and Neuhaus. Although it has been stripped of many of its functions, its role has actually become more important, not just as a source of companionship but as an institution. Among the recommendations for strengthening the family as a mediating structure are more support for families with disabled children, keeping the state out of day care and the use of educational vouchers.

As for neighbourhoods, Berger and Neuhaus argue that: 'The goal of making and keeping life human, of sustaining a people-sized society depends upon our learning again that parochialism is not a nasty word.'

Voluntary associations are assigned a less strong role than is the case in Britain. In fact they get a salutary warning: professionals must remember to be ancillary to the people they serve. Amen.

Of the four principal mediating structures, however, the most important according to Berger and Neuhaus – working in an American context – are the churches (a term they say they use as shorthand for all religious institutions). The church, '...with its deep involvement in family life and its social position between the family and the larger society, is seen as a primary agent for bearing and transmitting the operative values of our society.'

Berger and Neuhaus address the very issues which have become so sensitive in the current promotion of faith-community involvement. They warn that '...the religious character of these [church-based] agencies is fast being eroded...such institutions are (often) being turned into quasi-government agencies.' They argue that the state should use religious institutions as much as possible, and that public funding should be allowed to religious groups even if they are meeting the social needs only of people of their own faith.

Commenting on these proposals twenty years later Berger and Neuhaus appear to have moved further to the Right. Reaffirming their basic proposal, they add some strong *caveats*. Now, they would press for an even smaller role for government in the area of welfare, noting the likely tendency of the state to colonize mediating structures – as, indeed, it has sometimes done with welfare services. They also warn against the misuse of the idea of 'mediating structures' as a form of community action by the Left.

Socialist Associationalism

The associational socialism of Paul Hirst highlights the principles of cooperation and mutual assistance over competition, the greatest measure of equality of condition attainable between individuals, economic autonomy rather than the subordination of the worker to management or to owner, and the highest amount of democratic self-government and freedom of expression attainable. These principles rather than any specific institutional arrangements, like central planning, or state welfare, are what is at the heart of the socialist enterprise.[59]

This requires, suggests Hirst, a wholly new framework for social welfare. Basic welfare needs would be met by a Basic or Guaranteed Minimum Income but not conditional on undertaking national or civic service. Specific welfare needs (health, education, social care, etc) would be met, as far as possible by a 'confederal welfare state made up of 'Self-Governing Voluntary Associations'. These would be semi-public bodies, which would have to register and would have to meet standard criteria, such as those required by the Charity Commission. State funding for such associations would be greatly increased and could be distributed through three parallel mechanisms: a) each tax payer could be given, say, five vouchers which they could then give to registered associations of their choice; b) a consociational board of registered associations could have power to allocate a share of the tax revenue; c) an independent, but state-appointed committee could also allocate a significant share of tax revenue, possibly to the larger registered associations.[60] 'Associational socialism', Hirst continues 'can tolerate, and indeed, should welcome the Catholic Church and the gay community, for example, providing health and welfare services for their members….they will run their own organizations very differently, will have different educational or welfare objectives and very different rules of personal conduct. A pluralist system that cannot accommodate the two, that cannot allow both to undertake major tasks of social organization, as the primary providers of services to their members, is clearly doomed.'[61]

Associationalism: Uses, Abuses and Limits

Associationalism does not provide some magic answer to the needs of civil society. It, too, has its darker side. Associations can be sectarian, xenophobic, sexist and racist. They can be formed to defend privilege, to obstruct progress, to constrain competition, to circumvent the law. But even when they are formed to preserve the identity of a particular religious or ethnic group, there may well be situations in which this is defensible and even necessary. The point is that associationalism needs to be judged contextually, taking account of the actual economic, political and cultural situation which prevails in any particular time and place.

In 19th century Britain welfare associations, in the form of friendly societies based on solidarity and voluntary organizations inspired by philanthropy, played an essential role.[62] In late 19th century continental Europe aggressively secular states were seeking to bring educational and cultural life under their control. In response, the Catholic Church in Italy, France, Spain and Germany developed a powerful alternative set of associations, urban and rural, economic and cultural, which were firmly under the control of the church. In the Netherlands there developed a 'pillarization' of welfare associations, set up along parallel lines by Catholic and Protestant churches. Today they may be in danger of being used to absolve the state of its responsibilities. In Northern Ireland, associations based on religious lines are a mixed blessing; in Palestine, associations are all that an oppressed people have. There is, therefore, a fine balance to be observed as to when civil society is promoted by development of associations which cater almost exclusively for one group and when it is important precisely that they do not cater for just one group.

Indeed, in some contexts preoccupation with associations may actually distract attention from deeper and more urgent social injustices. For example, American brutality towards its black and native populations provoked some of Tocqueville's most passionate outbursts. Shocked by the Americans' treatment of African slaves he exclaimed: 'Seeing what happens in the world, might one not say that the European is to men of other races what man is to the animals? He makes them serve his convenience, and when he cannot bend them to his will he destroys them. In one blow oppression has deprived the descendants of the Africans of almost all the privileges of humanity.'[63] The treatment of the Indian tribes was even worse: 'All the Indian tribes who once inhabited the territory of New England…now live only in men's memories….I have met the last of the Iroquois; they were begging….These savages have not just drawn back; they have been destroyed.' Had he remained in America for just a few more years, he might have mentioned the killing and wounding of Irish immigrants – thought to be threatening the jobs of local people – and the burning of their churches by groups in New York and Philadelphia calling themselves ironically – in view of what had been done to the Indian population – 'Native American associations'.[64] Paradoxically, with rapid promotion of racial integration in the United States since the 1950s, the rich range of Negro (as they were then called) cultural, educational, political associations in early twentieth century America has been undermined and in some cases destroyed, leaving those trapped in today's inner cities in a culturally impoverished condition.[65]

3. Civil Society in Theological Perspective

> God himself would admit a figure of society, as there is a plurality of persons in God, though there is but one God; and all his external actions testify a love of society and communion. In heaven there are three orders of angels, and armies of martyrs, and in that house many mansions; in earth, families, clubs, churches, colleges, all plural things; and lest either of these should not be company enough alone, there is an association of faith, a communion of saints which makes the militant and triumphant church one parish.
>
> John Donne[66]

The Basis: Christian Social Ontology

As with capitalist modernity, so with Civil Society: it grew up on Christian soil, neither apart from nor against the church. It was a process which Christian theology both affected and was affected by. What insights and judgments has Christian theology today to bring to bear on the future of Civil Society? The starting point surely is the view of the social nature of human life as being a participation in and a sign of the social nature of the divine life. There are two doctrines in particular which provide a basis for a Christian social ontology: that of the Trinity and that of the Incarnation. Both will be looked at briefly.

Trinitarian Theology: Being in Communion

The past two decades have seen a welcome recovery of Trinitarian theology. One early pointer was the beautiful passage from John Donne (above), which David Nicholls chose as the frontispiece for his book on pluralism.[67]

Nicholls argues – adopting an approach similar to that which Raymond Williams had taken several years previously with regard to the idea of culture – that there is a dialogical relationship between our ideas of God and our social, economic and political context. Nicholls sees this as offering a 'model for a political order where freedom of individuals and groups is combined with active participation by people in social life at many different levels'. Nicholls warns against a simplistic understanding of such an approach, denying the existence of any direct link either between 'monolithic' concepts of God as in Arianism and political tyranny, or between Trinitarianism and political pluralism. He is quite critical of the tendency – which he detects in Moltmann and Boff, amongst others – to propose a conflict-free model of politics on the grounds that the Trinity provides a model of complete consensus and perfect harmony. Politics involves a pleading for particular interests and a conversation about incommensurable goods. Might not this, too, Nicholls mischievously suggests, be reflected in the Trinity, in a 'conversation' about justice and mercy, where 'the Son, in interceding as our advocate, indeed appeals to, and assumes, an inherent mercy and disposition to forgive in the Father, which is manifested in the Spirit's healing and transforming action.'[68] In any case, the argument is one of analogy: our experiences of participation, collaboration, mutuality and interdependence enable us to experience something of the communication of persons within the Trinity.[69]

Colin Gunton's approach starts from the opposite end: '…it is only through an understanding of the kind of being that God is that we can come to learn what kind of beings we are and what kind of world we inhabit.'[70] Gunton makes clear that he is not engaged in 'mapping the inner life of God' nor 'seeking patterns of threeness' in the world, but rather 'asking what concepts we may develop in order to characterize the kind of being that God is.' He takes his answer from John Zizioulas: 'God has…no true being apart from communion.'[71]

Incarnational Theology: Mediation

In his recovering of the doctrine of the Trinity, Colin Gunton points an accusing finger at Augustine as the one most responsible for turning Western theology and spirituality away from the earlier and richer Trinitarian theology of the East and for leaving Western Christianity with an impoverished, overly individualistic strain.[72]

For John Milbank, on the other hand, the neo-Platonic element in Augustine is something worth rescuing. Indeed it is precisely 'the Christian critique and transformation of neo-Platonism' that Milbank proposes as the alternative to secular reason.[73] At the heart of neo-Platonism is the view that created goods are good because they participate, ontologically, in the ultimate good and that they are important because, epistemologically, they mediate our knowing of that good. At the heart of this series of mediations is Christ: 'Augustine's Christian ontology…implies both that the part belongs to the whole, and that each part transcends any imaginable whole, because the whole is only a finite series which continues indefinitely towards an infinite and unfathomable God....The "whole" is Christ the mediator, and he articulates his body and conveys this mediation as an endless series of new mediations which interpellates human "persons". Otto von Gierke correctly recognized such a social ontology as precariously present during the middle ages....'

The result is a wonderful 'sociality of harmonious difference'. The many forms of 'the social' are freed from the controlling logic of secular reason, but are allowed to flourish, interact, and multiply in 'a sequence of mediations between individuals, households and cities.'

But it is a being-in-communion that is riddled with wounds and stands in need of restoration. And so we must work with analogy and signs. If the church is to represent the peace of the City of God, Milbank argues, it must recall that it is founded 'not in a succession of power, but upon the memory of the murdered brother, Abel, slain by Cain.' That is to say that the church is a sign of peace, offering a refuge where the victims are remembered but where even 'the enemy' is offered forgiveness.

Conclusion: Renewing Civil Society

The revival of civil society stems not simply from disenchantment with the state. Nor does it involve separation from the state. We are living in a period in which our social, economic and political structures are all being reshaped. Socially, networks (freer and more personal forms of collaboration) are seen to be just as useful as bureaucratic, impersonal organizations. Economically, small, flexible businesses are coming to play an important role alongside the large transactional corporations. And politically, state sovereignty in a global world is increasingly being diluted and replaced by looser forms of governance. All these developments open up new possibilities for Civil Society and all call for a creative renegotiation of the relationship between state and civil society.

The various paths towards the renewal of civil society which have been outlined in this chapter stem from different ideologies – social democracy, civic capitalism, communitarianism, relationalism and associationalism – all pulling in different directions. Of the different projects, it is suggested here that associationalism appears to open up an especially promising path towards social transformation. It allows for greater creativity and participation; it may also offer more flexibility and more scope for recognizing and correcting any wayward tendencies and any abuses of power.

Each project has its own unhealthy tendencies and each has its own valid insights. Therefore the different projects – even those which rely on the very forces of individualism and legalism which have so distorted Civil Society and tended to suppress civil society – can provide useful correctives to one another.

But following the path towards social transformation and renewing Civil Society is not simply a matter of choosing the right project. More fundamentally it is about being drawn in the right direction by the attraction of a vision. The basic task involves a healing of desire, with a reorientation away from the *libido dominandi* towards an ontological good. It is only through that kind of reorientation that the coercive power of the state will be less needed, and solidarity, collaboration, pluralism and self-government will be more able to flourish. That is what makes the question of the common good so important. That is one of the central issues to be addressed in the next chapter.

Chapter Three

Transforming Meanings
Common Culture, Common Good

We need a common culture, not for the sake of an abstraction, but because
we shall not survive without it.

Raymond Williams [1]

It does seem to me that, despite all that can be said on the narrative and
particularist side of the argument, we are still a long way from the moment
when we should give up the idea of a common nature and common value.

Raymond Plant [2]

Modern social theory, like modern political theory, developed only when
society was given a naturalistic instead of a religious explanation....It is
in England...that the transformation of the structure of society is earliest,
swiftest and most complete. Its essence is the secularization of social and
economic philosophy.

R.H. Tawney [3]

Précis

What is the point of social transformation? That is what this chapter
will address. It will look beyond the question of social structures and
processes to ask questions about the ends of human activity – by which
is meant not so much distant goals but contact with the good here
and now. The question of the good underlies the issues treated in all
the other chapters, in that questions about justice, freedom and civil
society depend on notions of a good society, a good economy and good
governance.

Capitalist modernity has difficulty accepting the case which poses the
issues in that way. It sees little use for and even questions the validity of
talking about 'the good' much less 'the common good'. For that reason
it has created a culture which is hollow, confused and unsustainable.
Unless such notions are rehabilitated the futures we face are likely to

involve either a continuation of the culture wars, the imposition of a false peace by a dominant political, economic or cultural power, or the nervous truce of a modus vivendi which settles for the ultimate incommensurability of conflicting traditions.

We can do better. But to do so we must appreciate that central to the project of social transformation is the question of culture. The chapter will begin by distinguishing four very different, but all relevant, ways in which the term 'culture' is used. It will, however, draw particularly on the anthological concept of culture as did H. Richard Niebuhr in his treatment of the five types or relationships between Christianity and culture – culture as 'a whole way of life' – seeing this as offering a framework within which the notion of a 'common culture' can be developed. In so doing it will seek to adapt the argument of Raymond Williams to a world which has taken a decisive epistemological 'cultural turn' and which has also become radically pluralistic. The continuing usefulness of Williams' response rests on the fact that it stresses the interaction between the 'ideal' and the 'material' in a non-reductionist way, that it gives a central place to communication, and that it insists on the need for equality if that communication is to proceed in a genuinely democratic fashion.

Secondly, the chapter will explore how these insights can help in creating a common culture. The chapter will conclude with theological reflections on the way Williams' approach itself needs to be grounded in a more explicit understanding of the notion of 'the common good' and will suggest connections between transformation by grace and Williams' three key features of a common culture.

PREAMBLE: CULTURE, SOCIAL TRANSFORMATION AND WHAT REALLY MATTERS

At the very heart of any project towards social transformation is the question: transformation into what? Technological advances, changes in political and economic structures and a redistribution of goods and power are all essential factors but they are primarily about means rather than ends. It is when concern about ends is signalled, that the issue of 'culture' takes centre stage. 'Ends' are not merely goals or final destinations. Ends refer simply to what really matters – about what is to be cherished and enjoyed for its own sake. Ends in this sense have an ontological status that demands a proportionate response from us – a response that is not simply a matter of personal choice. But ends are also culturally defined. To say that the end of economic activity is 'wealth creation' assumes that we know the difference between the production, possession and consumption of true wealth as against what John Ruskin called 'illth'.[4] To say that the aim of social policy is 'welfare' assumes that we are clear as to what makes for human development and fulfilment. And to say that the purpose of political struggle is social justice, points to the need to have some sort of agreement on such complex notions as equality and to be able to determine what kinds of equality matter most and why.[5] Even our concern for the 'environment' is loaded with value judgments as to the quality of life.[6] And when we do manage to identify the criteria to our satisfaction, we then come up against the fact that other people have different criteria which they find equally satisfying – which is to say that our thinking is more embedded in our cultures than we sometimes realize. But given that the term culture itself is used in so many different senses, the first step must be to try to clarify what we mean when we talk about culture.

I. CULTURE AS 'A WHOLE WAY OF LIFE'

...culture is not only a body of intellectual and imaginative work; it is also and essentially a whole way of life...material, intellectual and spiritual.
Raymond Williams[7]

Four Senses of Culture

Culture is a term used in at least four different senses. To start with the root meaning of the term, culture is about cultivation. Originally referring to the culture of soil, it was then applied to the cultivation of human sensibility, judgment, virtue, etc., which in turn points to the role of education, character formation, refinement, etc. Secondly, culture is also used in an aesthetic sense, referring to that particular sphere of leisure activity associated with the arts, literature, theatre, film, painting, music, etc. Thirdly, from the perspective of hermeneutics and linguistics, culture may have to do with the process of codification and communication, acting as the lens or framework by means of which activities and goods are articulated, interpreted and evaluated. Fourthly, culture is used in the anthropological sense which for American anthropologists tends to refer to a separate sphere of beliefs, values, codes of behaviour, but for British anthropologists tends to include ways of producing and consuming goods and of securing order, in short a 'whole way of life'.

In recent decades it is the third meaning of culture – as applied to processes of interpretation and codification – that has assumed new importance ('the cultural turn'). It was perhaps a necessary corrective to the tendency to view social, economic and political realities in a reductionist over-materialistic fashion. But this important insight gradually came to create its own world in which material reality was effectively treated mainly as providing subjects for ever more recondite and narcissistic language games which were increasingly playable by smaller and smaller elites. The urgent cultural task now is to reconnect with material reality. It is not a question of reversing the cultural turn but rather of not going around in circles.[8] That is why in this chapter the focus will be largely on the anthropological meaning of the term, which views culture as a whole way of life.

There are advantages in taking such an approach to culture. First, culture as a whole way of life provides the framework in which culture in the other three senses arises. Whether as cultivation, aesthetics, or codification, culture does not simply exist in a vacuum. These concepts of culture cannot be understood – they are literally meaningless – without reference to the wider social processes and structures in which they are set. Secondly, when used in any of the other three senses of the term, culture is too often understood without reference to the nature of its continuing interaction with material, economic reality. Yet in a world where capitalism has so permeated our civilization and shaped our way of life, to consider culture without reference to this process would be to deprive ourselves of the means of understanding why and how our culture – in the other three senses – takes the form it does.

But although the focus will be on culture as a whole way of life, no discussion of culture can avoid using the other important senses as well. Furthermore, each of these understandings of culture is also relevant to the project of social trans-formation. Just how relevant they are may be made clearer by looking briefly at each of the four senses of culture.

Culture as Cultivation

The project of social transformation is not just structural transformation. It has a central personal dimension. It involves healing. It involves the cultivation of sensibilities, capabilities and virtues, But which ones? The answer has an essential contextual dimension. Different historical settings have given special prominence to different character ideals – the soldier, the saint, the scholar, the citizen, the merchant, the worker – and have often generated the need for counter character ideals – the pacifist, the prophet, the outsider, the rebel, the revolutionary. The history of competing workers' education movements in Britain, in which Christians played a key role,[9] provides a classic example of the tensions. The struggle for the soul of the working class then has similarities with the struggle for the loyalty of ethnic and religious minorities today – the battle lines being drawn once again between assimilationists, pluralists and revolutionaries.[10]

Culture as Aesthetics

Aesthetics has long served both to celebrate and to interrogate, to defend and to challenge, to prop up and to subvert whole ways of life. This can be done with a certain integrity if it is done with a view to casting a brighter light on aspects of human activity and social structure that might otherwise be obscured. But when it is done so as to impart a moral lesson or a political message then it has become prostituted and turned into sheer propaganda. The line is sometimes hard to draw but to see how important it is one has only to recall the celebrations of Fascism and Communism in the 1930s, the Cold War (Congress for Cultural Freedom) in the 1950s and 60s, the black, feminist, and popular revolutionary consciousness-raising movements of the seventies and eighties, and the government-sponsored efforts at social cohesion and multiculturalism in the 1990s. More recently, Keith Reinhard, President of Business for Diplomatic Action has faulted the American government for having abandoned the cultural diplomacy of the cold war. The government has lost so much credibility, he argues, that it is now time for civil society to develop a strategy to combat anti-Americanism.[11] The response to such attempts to use culture is not 'art for art's sake', or the need to rescue art from 'politics'. It is one of aesthetic truth.

Culture as Codification

The 'cultural turn', so popular in the 1980s and early 90s did not signal a turn away from politics and economics and towards something called 'culture' but more a turning of 'objective' realities into texts. That is to say that words, behaviour, events, social systems, etc. were to be understood and valued in terms of their richness of multiple, overlapping and changing meanings, which they both expressed and evoked. Reality was not something 'out there' to be grasped and possessed by a detached subject. It was rather something mediated, understood indirectly between reader and text. Explanation gave way to interpretation. Clearly such a turn had profound implications for social transformation, at one level giving new depth and richness to the meaning of social transformation itself, and at another level, sometimes illuminating and sometimes obscuring both the processes which influenced the making of the texts as well as the ideological factors which influenced the making of the lenses through which the texts were read, as for example, the tendency within capitalism to codify goods and people in terms of their profitability. At its worst, the cultural turn could – and sometimes did – turn the whole process of interpretation into a game of infinite regression, with a gradual disconnection from the reality it was meant to mediate and a turning of excess meaning into meaninglessness. There may be no turning back from the cultural turn but there are signs of rethink.

Culture as A Whole Way of Life

What is meant by culture as a whole way of life is not a claim that a society should have only one 'way of life' or that 'ways of life' should be closed and static. It simply refers to the integration of social practices in a way which takes account of the interaction of beliefs and values with economic, political and technological processes and thus addresses the problem of alienation.

Raymond Williams' classic study *Culture and Society* was an instructive exploration of the way changes in the prevailing ideas of culture offer important clues to the changes which were occurring in the social, economic and political order. His is an argument for interaction not for reductionism. It is the interaction of intellectual insight and imaginative spirit with material and everyday activities which gives rise to particular ideas of culture – ideas which may either mirror the dominant forces of the age or express resistance to them: 'The idea of *culture* would be simpler if it had been a response to industrialism alone, but it was also, quite evidently, a response to the new political and social developments…to the new problems of social class….These are the first stages of the formulation of the idea of culture, but its historical development is at least as important. For the recognition of a separate body of moral and intellectual activities, and the offering of a court of human appeal…are joined, and in themselves changed, by the growing assertion of a whole way of life, not only as a scale of integrity, but as a mode of interpreting all our common experience, and in this new interpretation, changing it.' [12]

The question which such an approach brings into the open is: when and why did the idea of culture change so that it came to refer to 'a whole way of life, material, intellectual and spiritual'? Williams suggests that when Samuel Taylor Coleridge, John Ruskin, William Morris, T. S. Eliot, and others began articulating their concern about culture as a whole way of life, they were doing so not in the name of anthropology but in the name of protest. It was a call to action about something that was happening to society as a whole – a summons to resistance against both the uglier aspects of capitalist modernity and against misguided attempts to recreate the past and to perpetuate elitist notions of a 'higher' culture.

What goes into a whole way of life? Not just picture-book images. Even as he pays genuine tribute to Eliot for breaking with the idea of culture as something to be diffused by elites to the masses, Williams also pokes gentle fun at Eliot's 'pleasant miscellany' which includes as part of culture everything from dog races to Derby Day, from Wensleydale cheese to Gothic churches, from the music of Elgar to beetroot in vinegar, but leaves out things like coal-mining, the Stock Exchange and London Transport.[13] Williams can be even tougher with his fellow socialists if they try to impose a middle-class perspective. He passionately denounces the view that 'The working-class movement, unable to develop an ideology for itself, will be "captured" either by "bourgeois ideology" or by socialist ideology, which latter is itself created by bourgeois intellectuals.'[14]

Wholeness, for Williams, is genuine interaction without either privileging or leaving out any one group or class and without attributing priority to any sphere of activity – economic, political or artistic – although particular historical circumstances may justify a particular group's having to play a leading role. Culture, therefore, involves participation in the whole range of human activities – work, civic life, leisure. To be able to work, to find dignity and fulfilment in work, to contribute to the welfare of others through work is just as much part of culture as is the art of painting or composing music. To take part in civic life is just as much part of culture as teaching or writing books. The lack of integration between labour and leisure, civic and domestic life, art and science has deep roots in the cultures of patriarchy, priesthood and social class.

Since Williams' time, of course, the challenge has become more complicated. For increasing numbers of the British population their first language is not English, their religion is not Christian nor is liberal democracy part of their tradition. Does this offer a social transformation marked by an enlargement of vision and a widening of solidarity? Or does it represent a threat to the institutions and customs that are seen as central to national identity? The disconcerting aspects of this new cultural context can produce a kind of displacement, by which 'others' can be blamed for the cultural crisis which the West has been experiencing for the past century. This conveniently obscures the need even to acknowledge, let alone explore the causes of our cultural crisis. Therefore, to try to get the issue in perspective, it is only after having looked at the crisis of capitalist modernity that this chapter will address the question of 'multiculturalism'.

Culture in the Bourgeois Era

The bourgeois mind, from the earliest to the present day, has been the
victim of illusions caused by the contrast between the private character of
its 'tokens' of property and the social character of the real wealth which
those tokens and counters signify.

Reinhold Niebuhr[15]

Capitalist modernity has sought to reinterpret and reconstruct culture, but in its
own image. One of the impressive achievements – and indeed the secret to the
success – of early capitalist modernity was precisely to have fashioned a culture
in the image of the bourgeoisie, and this in all four senses of the term culture.
Understood as a process of cultivation, it developed particularly the virtues associated with 'the Protestant ethic' – a sense of duty, a spirit of service, honesty,
hard work, deferred gratification, and the use of wealth for good causes – all of
which went to demonstrate the admirable efficacy of self-interest.[16] Understood
as aesthetics the culture of the bourgeoisie could boast a cultivation of manners,
and the development of a lively republic of letters.[17] Understood as codification
it set in motion the fiction of commodification which construed land, labour
and money itself as 'property' which could be privately owned and traded on
the market. Understood, finally, as a whole way of life, bourgeois culture could
be summed up in Adam Ferguson's picture of Civil Society, as described in the
previous chapter. It all served to support the claim that the pursuit of private
interest really could promote the public good.[18] It was an order eminently
reasonable, which kept enthusiasm and imagination under control and assigned
even God his proper role as one to be thanked for having arranged and then
not interfered in such a beneficent system[19] Milbank characterizes it nicely with
his phrase, the 'policing of the sublime'.[20] Thus, having been made reasonable
according to the terms of the bourgeoisie, religion far from becoming redundant was positively serviceable. And even if religion's reasonableness could be
doubted, its utility could not. David Hume, for whom even Deism lacked any
rational foundation allows his character Cleanthes to make the point: 'The
proper office of religion is to regulate the heart of men, humanize their conduct,
infuse the spirit of temperance, order and obedience.'[21]

But the very fact that the type of harmony in this whole order was represented in mechanistic form, as a balance of powers, gives the game away. For the
system built on self-interest is a system which systematically generates conflict.
Instead of repressing conflicts with the might of the state, it cleverly seeks to set
them off against each other in civil society. But it is in the end about conflict

and power, which are liable to erupt whenever the balance is upset – which is precisely what happened with the further development of capitalist modernity. Part of the task of social transformation, therefore, is to recognize the way our culture – in all its four senses – has been moulded within that framework. The other part is to point the way out.

After the Bourgeoisie: Culture in Crisis

As capitalism developed into its monopoly stage, the inadequacies of the bourgeois culture of self-interest became impossible to disguise. The limits of a system of harmony based on the balancing of conflicting interests were breached with the descent into urban degeneration and the eruption of class warfare. The cry of alienation and spiritual homelessness began to be raised by Romantics as early as the beginning of the 19th century.[22] As the century progressed, the cultural crisis deepened and the voices of the prophets of doom became more strident. Arthur Schopenhauer, Friedrich Nietzsche, Oswald Spengler all warned that the death knell was tolling for Western civilization. But death was slow in coming. In the 20th century T. S. Eliot was describing a cultural wasteland, Martin Heidegger was sounding the retreat into a spiritual night,[23] and Samuel Beckett and Albert Camus were showing how to come to terms with the absurd.

By the late 20th century it was the turn of postmodernism. However, many of the themes that are often associated with postmodernism – contingency, insubstantiality, incoherence, dislocation, transgression – had been articulated much earlier. Looking back to his youthful days in the 1770s, Goethe observed: 'At the time [genius] was thought to manifest itself only by overstepping existing laws, breaking established rules and declaring itself above all restraint....All exceptional people who created something great, something that seemed impossible, have to be decried as drunkards or madmen.'[24] Baudelaire, writing in the1860s describes the experience of life as 'that which is ephemeral, fleeting, contingent'. Oswald Spengler, looking at where civilization has got to at the beginning of the 20th century, laments: 'In place of a type-true people, born and grown on the soil, there is a new sort of nomad, cohering unstably in fluid masses, the parasitical city dweller, traditionless, matter-of-fact, religionless, clever, unfruitful.... This is a very great stride towards the inorganic, toward the end – what does it signify?....The world-city means cosmopolitanism in place of "home"....To the world-city belongs not a folk but a mass.'[25]

Class, Culture and Multiculturalism

To describe English life, thought, and imagination in the last three
hundred years simply as 'bourgeois'…is to surrender reality to a formula….
the consciousness of a whole society is always more diverse, and is not
limited to the economically dominant class".
Raymond Williams[26]

Lions in the Path

There was, in the words of Tawney, a 'lion in the path' that led to a common
culture. That lion was inequality. Today there are many lions in the path.
Inequality, though less stark than in Tawney's time increased in the 1980s
and 90s. The spirit of individualism and self-interest is more rampant. Moral
compasses are not working as well as they did then. And, perhaps most signifi-
cantly, there is far broader cultural diversity, as a result of immigration. It is
precisely these new realities that make the question of a common culture more,
not less, urgent. And it is this awareness of the interaction between beliefs and
values on the one hand and economic and political forces on the other, as well as
his insistence on the importance of communication in a democratic and egalitarian context that make Williams' holistic approach so relevant.

The Battle over 'Culture'

What triggered Williams' socialist quest for a common culture appears to have
been sparked off by Eliot's more conservative version. For Eliot: '…the society
which is coming into existence, and which is advancing in every country whether
"democratic" or "totalitarian", is a lower middle class society: I should expect
the culture of the twentieth century to belong to the lower middle class as that
of the Victorian age belonged to the upper middle class.…I mean by a "lower
middle class society" one in which the standard man legislated for and catered
for, the man whose passions must be manipulated, whose prejudices must be
humoured, whose tastes must be gratified, will be the lower middle class man.
He is the most numerous, the one most necessary to flatter.'[27]

Williams started with the working class as it actually existed – not the working
class as something either to be re-moulded or reconstructed: 'The manufacture
of an artificial "working class culture", in opposition to this common tradition,
is merely foolish.…What is properly meant by "working class culture"…is not
proletarian art, or council houses, or particular use of language; it is, rather,
the basic collective idea, and the institutions manners, habits of thought, and

105

intentions which proceed from this...the collective, democratic institution, whether in the trade unions, the cooperative movement, or a political party. Working class culture, in the stage through which it has been passing, is primarily social.'[28]

The common culture that R. H. Tawney, T. S. Eliot and Raymond Williams were seeking was one which could overcome the conflict between classes. The struggle then was between the elitists, whether secular or Christian, and those who were propounding the virtues of the working class. Fierce as it was, it at least took place within the framework of a common language, a common Christian tradition, a common assumption of male hegemony. Today, little remains of that framework. That very fact, however, makes the question of a common culture more not less pressing. But how can a mid-20th century British debate about a common culture really offer any help in addressing the challenges posed by a 21st century multicultural world?

The Need for a Framework

We live at a moment when the rhetoric about celebrating diversity and the ideal of a multicultural society is being sorely tested. A backlash against immigration and particularly against Muslims has flared up, fed both by domestic turmoil and by the shadow of global terrorist networks. The issue was once seen – and in some quarters still is – largely in materialistic terms: are there enough jobs? Is there enough housing? Can we afford more immigration? And, to reply in purely materialist terms, the answer is clearly: Yes. Many Western countries are facing both a demographic crisis, as ageing populations fail to reproduce themselves, and a shortage of workers both in skilled and unskilled areas of employment. But that can too easily obscure the deeper issue of a common culture. John Gray, leader of the 2002 Towards Social Transformation seminar, has warned about the way that a naïve liberalism can play into the hands of the political right and threaten liberalism itself.[29]

If the problem of common culture were only about immigration it would be serious enough but it is not. Many battles in the 'culture wars' are entirely homegrown. Bitter debates have broken out over a host of issues, from questions about how many different voices should be accommodated in a literary canon (assuming there should even be such a canon), to whether more faith-based schools are a good idea and whether same-sex 'marriages' pose so grave a threat to society as to require an amendment to the US Constitution itself.[30]

At stake in these cultural battles are profound issues of justice, power and identity. How are we to respond? Four broad options are available: cosmopolitanism, 'multiculturalism', national citizenship, and common culture. At the heart of this chapter will be a detailed argument on behalf of the last of these options. But, first, it may be worth highlighting some of the problems posed by the other three approaches.

Cosmopolitanism

The claim to be 'citizens of the world' goes back before Christianity to Stoic philosophy. It represents more than the spirit of internationalism, which has played an important part in so many associations and movements. Its appeal is rooted in an intellectual recognition that all people have the same basic human nature, that because all have the light of reason all can live by the universal moral principles, and that differences of faith, ethnicity, gender, etc. are largely accidental and of lesser importance – except in so far as they get in the way.

It is a view whose attractiveness has diminished, not just because of petty nationalism and ugly racism but because of the spread of pluralism with its appreciation of the fact that difference does matter and that, indeed, under the right conditions, it can enrich human society. Does this then point the way to multiculturalism?

Multiculturalism

> Multiculturalism's legacy is 'have a nice day' racism.
> Trevor Phillips, Director of the Commission for Racial Equality[31]

In his remark, Trevor Phillips was not so much attacking multiculturalism as such but rather pointing out how it can too easily be used to distract from underlying social injustices which need urgent attention. Specifically he was pointing out that cultural celebrations do not make up for the scandal that more than half of Whitehall's departments have no ethnic minority staff at senior level, or that British boardrooms hardly ever see a non-white face. There are some very real problems with multiculturalism. Multiculturalism can also create – or mask – problems for those who are suffering from exclusion and exploitation. The celebration of diversity can be a screen covering a continuing and even deepening problem of economic inequality, social discrimination and an implied sense that the faith, values and customs of host nations, or former imperial nations if not superior at least have a privileged place.

Multiculturalism can also obscure deep historical grievances that have not been fully resolved. Martin Marty's proposal that religious dialogue could provide the key to achieving a new American pluralism, has come in for strong criticism on the basis that this could lead to a 'premature reconciliation' which was unfaithful to realities of complicity in historical injustice.[32] One has only to ask: What does multiculturalism mean in Northern Ireland, in Palestine, in Kosovo, in Chechnya?

At the heart of all these ambivalent feelings about multiculturalism is the question of identity. For those who have been marginalized the question of identity means a demand for recognition. For those who have been part of the dominant group the question of identity means a challenge to the claim of superiority. It is not just a matter of living with difference. It is rather about the difference that difference makes to a society's existing consensus, patterns of values, norms and customs and to the distribution of status, wealth and power. What makes such questions particularly acute is the context in which this is occurring today: a context of political insecurity, in which terrorism has become a daily worry; a context of economic insecurity, in which jobs for life have gone and pension systems have collapsed; a context of institutional insecurity, in which the level of trust in the City, the health service, in politicians and even in the clergy has been severely dented; a context of emotional insecurity, in which personal and family relationships are less reliable; and a context of cultural insecurity, in which Western countries are less certain of their own values. Postmodernists may celebrate all this. Most of us worry. It is hardly the most favourable context in which to give either multiculturalism or a common culture a fair hearing.

National Citizenship

I believe that just about every central question about our national future
– from the constitution to our role in Europe, from citizenship to the
challenges of multiculturalism – even the question of how and why we
deliver public services in the manner we do – can only be fully answered
if we are clear about what we value about being British and what gives us
purpose and direction as a country.

Gordon Brown[33]

An increasingly popular response to the tensions provoked by multiculturalism is that of nationalism. Nationalism can take a brutal form as it has in some of the right-wing movements that have arisen in Europe. But it can also take a gentler form as reflected, for example in the current insistence on 'Britishness'. It seeks to combine the notions of citizenship (British) and national identity (which comprises four nations, with their own national institutions, including national churches, football teams and, in some cases language as well). The argument is that if people are to prosper, contribute to and enjoy the benefits of the country, and to be able to understand their children who grow up and are educated in a new country, then clearly they do need to speak the language and understand the values and customs of that country. The Director of the Commission for Racial Equality has himself argued: 'I disagree with those who say that integration and Britishness are irrelevant to the struggle against racism. There can be no true integration without true equality. But the reverse is also true. The equality of the ghetto is no equality at all....And yes, newcomers do have to change. The language barrier is a real obstacle to work, friendship and democratic participation.'

One can accept the case for all this whilst at the same time questioning why such processes have to be encouraged under the label of Britishness. The unease comes from the fact that a label of this sort involves not simply a question of behaviour but touches on the issue of identity itself. And that is a much more sensitive question which has to be answered contextually taking full account of the existing identities of the people involved. For example, the label 'American Catholic' is a label that has been accepted with pride by large numbers of people who see their American experience as having provided them not only with a route out of poverty but also as having given them new insights into their faith. On the other hand, to expect people, say from the Republic of Ireland who have settled in Britain, to describe themselves in terms of Britishness would often be seen as an act of betrayal. Perhaps the most sobering example in modern times has been the tragic history of the way Jews in Germany responded in sharply different ways to the recurring pressure to take on a German identity.[34] The resort to Britishness therefore may at best be justified on the pragmatic ground that it prevents British identity from being stolen by the racist forces of the Right, but whether it gets to the heart of the problem must be questioned.

A Fourth Way?

The alternative approach that is being advanced here sees the issue of cultural tensions – whether these arise from immigration or are generated by internal social change – in terms of the development of a common culture. This affirms rather than rejects multiculturalism, provided multiculturalism is distinguished from a conservative, communitarian 'plural monoculturalism', as Amartya Sen, Master of Trinity College, Cambridge, has insisted. Sen advocates a more liberal form of multiculturalism involving interaction with other cultures and characterized by what Doyal and Gough (see below) call critical autonomy. This refers to the capacity to question and then decide whether to affirm, modify or reject the culture in which one grew up.[35] But it is possible to take this one step further and to see multiculturalism understood in this sense as a stage on the journey towards a common culture not an obstacle to it. Multiculturalism, furthermore, can also point towards a common culture precisely because the inevitable experience of points of incommensurability between cultures can be viewed not just as an occasion for frustration, or even worse, for pretending to understand what one does not, but as a stimulus to see all cultures, including one's own, as pointing toward the good in ways which neither can fully express and which also serves as source of critique and development for each one's culture. Although it is articulated with the help of insights from Raymond Williams, its advantage from a theological point of view is that it fits nicely within the vision of the City of God as spelt out by Augustine. It is about a process which involves the forging of a new identity and new types of bonds, based not on domination but on love. It requires repentance and offers healing. It involves not the destruction but the redemption of existing identities in a new setting. In short, it replaces fear of change with the desire for transformation.

2. Creating A Common Culture

[A] common culture is…the creation of a condition in which the people as a whole participate in the articulation of meanings and values and in the consequent decisions between this meaning and that, this value and that.
Raymond Williams[36]

What did Williams mean by a common culture, and how was it to be realized? For Williams, a common culture was not about uniformity, whether derived from tradition or imposed by dictat. It certainly has nothing to do with ideological purism, as in the 1930s' tendency within socialist realism to eliminate all traces of 'bourgeois deviations' or in the contemporary tendency to ban all violations of 'political correctness'.[37] It was not a call for marginal, excluded or oppressed groups to be assimilated into the dominant culture. It was about equal participation in the development of a way of life. Here is how he describes it: 'a common culture is not the general extension of what [an elitist] minority mean and believe but the creation of a condition in which the people as a whole participate in the articulation of meanings and values and in the consequent decisions between this meaning and that, this value and that. This would involve, in any real world, the removal of all material obstacles to just this form of participation.'[38]

In this definition there are three features to be singled out. These will provide the framework for the argument developed in the rest of this chapter. They have to do with what is here paraphrased as: communication, empowerment and solidarity.

Communication

Long before Habermas, Williams stressed the importance of democratic communication: 'My own view is that if, in a socialist society, the basic cultural skills are made widely available, and the channels of communication widened and cleared, as much as possible has been done in the way of preparation, and what then emerges will be an actual response to the whole reality....' Williams notes that: 'It is very difficult to think clearly about communication, because the pattern of our thinking about community is, normally, dominative.' The alternative is not to tone it down a notch to the level of exhortation but, much more radically to see that 'a transmission [of ideas] is always an offering...not an attempt to dominate, but to communicate to achieve reception...and living response.'[39]

Empowerment

Democratic communication depends, in turn, on 'the removal of all material obstacles to just this form of participation.' In practice, this sort of communication will not be possible without equality, and equality will not be possible until the question of ownership and control of the means of production is addressed. Williams teases R. H. Tawney for not taking the issue of ownership of the means of production seriously enough: Tawney sees economic inequality as being 'the lion in the path' but 'hopes that the path can be followed to the end by converting both traveller and lion to a common humanity.'

Solidarity

Williams stresses the importance of an 'effective community of experience' by 'the people as a whole'. Are we then back to the argument for Britishness? Not if the people as a whole is interpreted within the framework of Civil Society, which, as Gellner has suggested, avoids both the concentration of power and authority, whether cultural, economic or political, and the 'segmentation' of society into separate, self-sufficient communities. Or, to put it more positively, not if the people as a whole allows for a rich overlapping pattern of associational life. It is possible, in other words, to understand the people as a whole in terms of solidarity in a civic community in which there are no first or second class citizens, in which there are agreed means of resolving conflicts and in which concern for the well-being of strangers as well as neighbours is engraved in the institutions and in attitudes.

These three aspects can help open up the path towards a common culture. In the rest of the chapter they will be explored in detail.

Participation in the Articulation of Meanings and Values

Communication and the Development of Critical Autonomy

[Communication] is always an offering...not an attempt to dominate, but to communicate, to achieve reception and response.
Raymond Williams[40]

The central activity in the development of a common culture is communication and that does not come automatically or easily. It is difficult at a personal level, in that it requires imagination to enter into the world that lies behind another's words and action. It requires courage to allow one's own world to be interrogated in the process. It is difficult at a structural level, in that communication is often distorted by relations of economic, political and cultural power and by interpretations that have been imposed by the media or by popular prejudice. The sections which follow will attempt to explore the nature of these difficulties and how they might be addressed.

Personal Qualities

Genuine communication, for Williams, implies a commitment to operating in the democratic not the dominative mode. This, in turn, requires the readiness to challenge dominative systems of thought and the maturity to be critical of one's own tradition.

Communication is not just about understanding the product of a culture (i.e. its concepts, values, ways of life) but rather a movement between cultures themselves (i.e. world-views which in turn are shaped by key historical experiences, memories traditions and loyalties which provide the key not only to what different beliefs 'mean' but how they relate, interact, function and change).

To enter into other worlds requires a two-fold leap of the imagination – the first to become aware of that other world, the second, to realize that there are limits to what a visitor can understand about that world. Does that mean that we live in incommensurable worlds? To a certain extent it does. David Nicholls cites with approval the philosopher Richard Rorty: '...to look for commensuration rather than simply continued conversation…is to attempt to escape from humanity.'[41] John Milbank also stresses that narratives are incommensurable, and that it is foolish to expect that with the right kind of a dialectic participants in conversation would ultimately recognize the grander narrative that somehow includes both lesser narratives.[42]

But communication is a two-way process. The less attempt there is at domination, the more each party can let their defences down and allow their own convictions and narratives – and possibly their identities – to be called into question, and to let other identities emerge. Most of us have multiple, overlapping identities – based on our gender, ethnicity, faith, education, role, etc. Which one comes to the fore often depends on the context and on what kind of communication is taking place with those around us. How we communicate actually generates different identities. A Muslim's identity can be turned into that of an Islamist or a jihaidist not simply by what the Koran says but by how the Koran is used to make sense of the way he or his people are being treated and portrayed. A black priest working in a white country will be under great pressure, internal as well as external, to define his identity first as a black person and only secondarily as a priest. A Jew fighting for survival may come to feel that she must define herself first of all as a Zionist.

Genuine communication is the exact opposite of indifference. It means taking seriously the fact that identities and traditions are not only different but that some may be truer, nobler and more attractive than others. It is often most difficult not between parties whose identities are firmly established but between parties who feel that their identities are vulnerable. Just how threatening this can be was seen in the response, by members of his own community, to the efforts of the Chief Rabbi to engage in this sort of conversation.[43] Another example is the controversy that was sparked off by a recent seminar sponsored by the Institute for Public Policy Research, which sought to engage humanists and believers in the debate about the purpose of religious education in schools. Is the purpose primarily civic – to equip students for life in a multicultural society, or is it more to do with the nature of religion itself – how to examine its truth claims as well as its necessity? It was significant that the plea: 'I hope that the National Framework could begin to address the relativism too often seen in RE [religious education]' came from a spokesperson from the British Humanist Association.[44] Might the government have been listening in? When its Faith Communities Unit issued its main policy statement, it specifically chose: '…to include humanists and secularists among its contacts'.[45]

The need for such communication is not just desirable, it is imperative. Certain things demand to be said – and heard – partly because, for all the talk of globalization, we are tending to withdraw into separate little worlds and partly because there is so much unfinished business. i.e. areas where we have touched one another's lives without even realizing it. In today's climate, it may even require more courage to call into question one's nation than to question one's religion. Yet at times it is necessary. A striking example is the warning issued by the pre-eminent American social theologian Reinhold Niebuhr in 1950: 'The idolatrous devotion to the "American way of life" grows at a tremendous pace…religiously sanctified self-idolatry is more grievous than its secular variety.…Inevitably the religious world is corrupted by this idolatrous creed of America. Many businessmen will no longer support the World Council of Churches or the Federal Council of Churches because the pronouncements of these bodies on economic affairs have preserved a proper critical reserve toward the American pretensions of a perfect economic system.…One is reminded of the day when [President] Herbert Hoover opposed unemployment insurance on the ground that it destroyed the good old American way of voluntary aid to the unfortunate.'[46]

The threats and challenges of genuine non-dominative communication are real. To recognize and to deal with them requires intellectual honesty and a measure of what Ian Gough, joint leader of the 1993 Towards Social Transformation seminar, has called 'critical autonomy'. The function of critical autonomy for Gough is precisely to clarify and examine one's own culture in comparison with others, so that one is more able to make a rational choice about the culture in which one will dwell. This is precisely the point made by Sen (see above) in his defence of liberal multiculturalism. Gough stresses the importance of learning about other cultures as an essential means for the development of critical autonomy. The aim is not a melting down of individual cultures – that is already being done, far more effectively, in capitalist modernity, by the mass media, by policies of integration and by social pressures towards conformity. The point is precisely the opposite. There are many different cultures and each has its strengths and weaknesses. The culture that one happens to inhabit and have inherited must be examined to see just how far and in what way it does lead towards a good life: 'Critical autonomy entails the capacity to compare cultural rules, to reflect upon the rules of one's own culture, to work with others to change them and, *in extremis*, to move to another culture if all else fails.'[47] For Gough, critical autonomy is so essential an aspect of human development that it is part of that 'optimum' which must be nurtured by social rights whose role in promoting a common culture will be explored below.

Social Structures and Communication

It is interesting to compare Williams' stress on non-dominative communication with the later theory of coercion-free communicative rationality developed by Jurgen Habermas. For Habermas, human emancipation, is not about individualism but is grounded in an 'unlimited community of communication.... unlimited in social space and historical time'.[48] Communication is about truth, about the negotiation of interests and, especially, about morality. The aim is for a morality based on principles which are, as far as possible, universalizable – not, however, on an agreed notion of the common good, but on a situation in which everyone's interests are given equal regard: '...we must rather ask,' insists Habermas, 'what is equally good for all?....Moral judgment must be capable of being approved by all those who might possibly be affected – and not, like ethical judgments, only from the perspective of my particular or our particular understanding of the world.'

What Habermas' ideal relies on is the nature of language itself: '...a *telos* of mutual understanding is built into linguistic communication.'[49] The community of communication is one in which all must be able to participate. What stands in the way, however, is the systematic distortion of communication, particularly by the power of the state, the role of money and the force of authoritarianism that Habermas targets as the major obstacles to be overcome if non-coercive communication is to be allowed to flourish.

What is meant by 'structures' is not just economic and political systems. There are also cultural structures, of which 'religion' is a key part. The task of critiquing structures in terms of their dimensions of power and domination needs to extend to cultural narratives as well if genuine communication is to be realized. There are at least three ways in which this critique can be developed.

One approach is to see our grand religious and 'secular' narratives as texts to be read. In reading them Richard Rorty suggests we need to be aware of saving 'splits': 'We can only hope to transcend our acculturation if our culture contains...splits which supply toeholds for new initiatives. Without such splits – without tensions which make people listen to unfamiliar ideas in the hope of finding means of overcoming those tensions – there is no such hope.'[50]

A second approach to opening texts up and freeing them of their dominative potential is to recognize that they reveal a surplus of meanings, an excess which reminds us that the text comes from and points beyond itself. One might observe that the parables of Jesus about the Kingdom of God are perfect examples of this. They are communicative in that they call for a response from the listener, in terms of action as well as interpretation.[51] When applied to sacred texts, such an approach shows the importance of tradition, i.e. collective attempts to tease out the rich and multiple meanings of the text, whilst also revealing the fact that tradition is something living and continuing and that the meanings of the text can never be exhausted, finalized or closed.

A third approach involves a more direct confrontation with those custodians and interpreters of texts and narratives who use them to consolidate their own power. A theologian who, more than any, has addressed the issue of the inherent and systematic tendency of secular and religious regimes to construct dominative systems of thought is Andrew Shanks. Challenging such structures entails undergoing an experience of 'shakenness'. Not the shakenness that comes from external sources, such as the events of 9/11. These are more likely to result in closure rather than openness. It is rather the kind of shakenness that comes from the recognition of the insecure and imperfect foundations of the narrative which has shaped one's life. Shanks' theology is hugely indebted to the philosophical insights of the Czech philosopher and co-founder of Charter 77, Jan Patocka (1907–1977), which Shanks came to appreciate as the result of his own East–West work for peace and human rights.[52] The new 'solidarity of the shaken' arises amongst those who have experienced such insecurity – existentially and historically. There are echoes in this of the way the experience of the First World War shook Karl Barth's and Reinhold Niebuhr's faith in liberalism; in the way Chamberlain's appeasement of Hitler shook T. S. Eliot's faith in the British establishment;[53] in the way the Communist system shook Eastern Europeans' faith in socialism. The impact of this sort of shakenness is liberating, enabling people to take responsibility for calling their own narrative-keepers to account, by their own 'living in the truth', which for Vaclav Havel meant combining the personal with the political.[54]

Participation in the Consequent Decisions

Empowerment – Reassessing Social Rights

> Class abatement is still the aim of social rights.
> T. H. Marshall.[55]

Social Rights as Capabilities for Participation

What have social rights to do with a common culture? Part of the answer has to do with the definition of culture used by Williams. It is about a whole way of life. The material conditions must not be taken for granted. The rest of the answer has to do with the function which social rights perform. Besides taming the lion of inequality, they also have a more positive role in helping to promote what Amartya Sen refers to as a person's general capabilities – those substantive freedoms 'to achieve alternative functioning combinations (or, less formally put, the freedom to achieve various lifestyles)'.[56] One of the key functions of social rights, in other words, is to empower a person to be able to participate more fully and effectively in cultural life.

Shortly before the 1993 Towards Social Transformation seminar, one of the joint leaders, Anna Coote, had just edited a collection of essays advocating a range of new social rights. It was the fruit of a project whose inspiration she credits to Raymond Plant, author of the first essay in the collection, and leader of the 1990 and 2001 Towards Social Transformation seminars.[57] The seminar's co-leader, Ian Gough, had just been awarded two major prizes for a work written in collaboration with Len Doyal on human need as the basis for social rights.[58] At that time the agenda was about expanding and modernizing social rights, whilst also bolstering their defence.

Since that time, however, the social rights agenda has stalled and conditions and obligations have increasingly been attached to them. But this combination of rights and duties could have been done in a very different way. Raymond Plant, writing shortly before his appearance at the first Towards Social Transformation seminar, argued that the attempt to combine rights and responsibilities is not necessarily incompatible with the pursuit of equality. Invoking the legacy of R. H. Tawney, he urged socialists to update their thinking on social rights. Taking forward the argument put forward in an essay published the previous year, Plant spelt out why the idea of democratic citizenship should be central to the ideological modernization of the Labour Party. Elaborating on the notion of citizenship, Plant insisted: 'Those who are able-bodied and claim [social] rights must be prepared to contribute to the production of these social resources. This is done by the majority through taxation, but for some it might be done through accepting an obligation to (socially useful) work.'

The argument that social rights can be seen in a socialist version of citizenship, which sees equality and solidarity going hand in hand, far from being novel, is part of an important tradition. It was elaborated by the two great framers of the modern theory of social rights, T. H. Marshall (1893–1961) and Richard Titmuss (1907–1973).[59]

Unlike the prevailing approach which overlays conservative social policies on top of neo-liberal economics – thus generating the very inequality, exclusion and lack of social cohesion that social policy is then expected to alleviate – Marshall and Titmuss envisioned social rights within a framework of equality and solidarity. It is worth taking a fresh look at what social rights were intended to do, why they have disappointed and how they still have a crucial role to play in preparing the path towards a common culture.

Social Rights and Social Cohesion

The natural tendency of capitalist accumulation of wealth and of unregulated markets is to boost the fortunes of the holders of property at the expense of those who have to sell their labour in order to survive. If unchecked the process ultimately undermines social cohesion as well. What inspired the socialist movement for social rights was a concern not simply to alleviate poverty but to promote equality and social cohesion. 'Even when benefits are paid in cash, this class fusion is outwardly expressed in the form of a new common experience.' It is this 'common experience', Marshall believed, that would foster a mutual acceptance of rights and duties: 'All who possess the status [of citizenship] are equal with respect to the rights and duties with which the status is endowed.' Marshall insists on the duty to work – a duty sustained by a 'sense of personal obligation...not [just] to have a job and hold it...but to put one's heart into one's job and work hard.' So too with education. The social right carries with it a social duty: 'The duty to improve and civilize oneself is therefore a social duty, and not merely a personal one, because the health of a society depends upon the civilization of its members.'

Richard Titmuss carried the argument forward: '...the fundamental and dominating historical processes which led to these major changes in social policy were the demand for one society; for non-discriminatory services...which would manifestly encourage social integration.' Whilst insisting on the principle of universalism as fundamental, Titmuss gradually came to appreciate the need to take into account the more subtle dimensions of social life. New social needs and new patterns of power were giving rise to the need for new social institutions. In an apparent reversal of an earlier position, Titmuss came to accept, for the sake of social integration, the case for positive discrimination: '...in favour of the poor, the handicapped, the deprived, the coloured, the homeless and the social casualties of our society.'[60]

Taking account of the rise of what J. K. Galbraith called 'the affluent society'; Titmuss saw the moral dimensions of social policy as assuming ever greater importance. 'The Gift Relationship' – symbolised most powerfully in the giving of blood – expressed what Titmuss saw to be at the heart of the Western tradition of social welfare. That spirit of giving could not be sustained, and certainly would not be extended internationally, if our societies lost their sense of moral purpose. Titmuss was greatly concerned that those who, even forty years ago, were trumpeting the 'end of ideology' were 'blind to the need for a sense of moral purpose in their own societies as the motive power in the art of giving to our international neighbours.'[61]

Optimising Social Rights

Ian Gough, joint leader of the 1993 Towards Social Transformation seminar, had worked, with his colleague Len Doyal, to develop a theory of human need which would help to renew the tradition of social rights: 'We have argued that a belief in the existence of human needs in conjunction with a consistent belief in a moral vision of the good lends strong support for a moral code that the needs of *all* people should be satisfied to the *optimum* extent.'[62] Gough's insistence that the needs of all people be met carries forward the concern of Marshall and Titmuss, for a basic equality. Like them he sees social rights as linked with social duties – not just in the narrow sense that rights are conditional on the acceptance of duties, but that rights can only arise in a context where people accept that they have duties towards one another, including, where appropriate, to relieve the suffering of others. Underpinning this is a sense of membership in a community: '...duties only entail rights against the backdrop of an already existing network of moral beliefs which clearly specify the conditions of entailment.'

Gough then goes on to argue that certain such rights ought to be satisfied to the optimum extent. By 'optimum' he does not mean maximum or indefinite. The notion of the optimum arises in the context of viewing social rights and duties as grounded in a sense of membership in a community, and as oriented to a realization of the good: 'Commitment to a conception of the good shared with others…a collective commitment to optimum need-satisfaction should follow from a collective commitment to a vision of the good.' It is precisely this grounding in the good which is what justifies the expansion of rights and duties. It is not an indiscriminate or indefinite expansion but one whose object is 'those things which will optimise their capacity for moral action.' It has an obligatory character: 'The measure of our moral commitment is our willingness to take seriously its categorical character – its applicability to everyone and not just to those with whom we already profess agreement. If our good is *the* good then we must believe that *all* individuals should do their best to act accordingly – irrespective of their own moral values.' Moral action is, in turn, defined in terms of 'critical autonomy'. Gough briefly shines a light on the issue of the good, but he refrains from endorsing the picture of a substantive common good.

Sadly, the vision of Marshall and Titmuss, Gough and Doyal is far from being realized. In fact, the whole basis of their argument has been seriously challenged, on both philosophical and empirical grounds. Social rights, far from having brought about the hoped-for social solidarity have, in many respects, come to be a source of resentment for those who feel that their hard work is paying for the support of 'scroungers' and 'foreigners'. Clearly there is major work to be done in addressing the basis of such sentiments both by providing accurate information and by responding to abuses where they do occur. But to sever the understanding of social rights from a solid grounding in human need, human good and social solidarity would be to abandon them to the whims of public opinion and political opportunism. There is a need to reassess realistically what can and cannot be achieved through which particular social rights. In theory, social rights are supposed both to underpin and to promote social solidarity. It is meant to be a virtuous circle. But this cannot be taken for granted. It depends upon there being what Williams referred to as a common experience. That is what will be explored next.

An Effective Community of Experience
Solidarity – Challenging Class Society

> It would be part of my scheme of physical education that every youth in
> the State – from the King's son downwards – should learn to do something
> finely and thoroughly with his hand, so as to let him know what touch
> meant; and what stout craftsmanship meant.
>
> *Time and Tide*, John Ruskin[63]

No Common Experience?

'Common experience' is a problematic concept. Some types of common experience can give rise to a crippling negative identity – a sense of victimhood, the
perpetual nursing of grievance, a rigidity of a siege mentality. There are also
plenty of other cases where a common experience is basically positive but has
been distorted by a sense of superiority, exclusiveness or even chosenness. These
unhelpful types of common experience have many causes but they are exacerbated
by the tendencies of capitalist modernity. The fact that we so often live in
different worlds and sometimes simply in our own private worlds has more than
a little connection with the growth of inequality, the promotion of self-interest
and the fragmentation of class solidarities. John J. Rodger points to some of the
effects of this experiential gap, which he refers to as 'post-emotionalism'. Poverty,
distress and exclusion are known to the public only indirectly and through a
knowledge which is abstract, intellectualized and constructed, with the help of
the media. We do not feel the injustice and distress; we view it – and then get
on with things. Post-emotionalism is '…a system designed to avoid emotional
disorder [and]…to make the social solidarity of complex societies possible.'[64]

How to make possible the sort of common experience that overcomes these
divisive tendencies and provides not the superficial sense of shared experience
that comes from following the same football team or watching the same TV
soap series, but which generates the recognition of a common humanity and a
common interest? For the middle class, Williams notes, the traditional way was
through service – civil service, voluntary service, national service.[65] Williams
construes this as the mentality of 'upper servants' who in serving those beneath
themselves are also serving those above themselves – the nation, the government
the monarch: '…in practice it serves, at every level, to maintain and confirm the
status quo….The real personal unselfishness…seemed to me to exist within a
larger selfishness which was only not seen because it was idealized as the necessary form of a civilization….', he observes.[66] This 'larger selfishness' is reflected
in the fact that the present state of capitalism is indeed a structure of personal

opportunity, in which a few do very well, many think they can do very well but only do fairly well, and others do not make it – but still think that with a bit of luck they might. Williams, as was seen above, contrasts this with the spirit of solidarity traditionally felt by the working class: 'the basic collective ideas, and…the collective, democratic institution, whether in the trade unions, the cooperative movement, or a political party. Working class culture, in the stage through which it has been passing, is primarily social.' Looking back we might note that the operative words are *the stage through which it has been passing*. For what we have today is not just the fragmentation of the working class, it is the fact that all classes – and we are still most definitely a class society – have been impregnated with the spirit of self-interest and individual self-advancement as the dominant motive.

Where then is it possible to look for the sort of 'effective community of experience' which Williams saw as the basis of solidarity? And a common experience of what? Certainly a common experience of adversity is often shown to bring out a sense of solidarity, as in the case of the Second World War. And shrewd political leaders have often resorted to the real or imaginary threat of a common enemy – whether from without or from within – as a tactic for rallying the people behind them. But must we rely mainly on such negative experiences, however powerful they may be? Are we not called to discover something more positive which we can share and celebrate together? Is it not possible to believe in a common good? That is the question that will be explored next. It is, however, a question of faith, which is why it is best addressed from a theological perspective.

3. Theological Reflection: Rethinking The Common Good

> …the common good of a community is not a distinct end which can be invoked to overrule a specific perspective; it is rather the very capacity of the community to negotiate gifts and needs within an overall hope of growing into a relation with God analogical to that displayed in Christ.
> Rowan Williams[67]

Capitalist modernity has difficulties accepting the notion of 'the good'. Charles Taylor's insightful analysis of this problem was discussed in Chapter One. In this chapter about a common culture, those difficulties will be compounded as the conversation turns to the notion of the *common* good. Is the concept really helpful? Can it possibly provide a basis for the sort of democratic communication and decision-making which are so central to Williams approach when it is so easily used as a subtle tool for cultural power and domination? A number of theologians have their doubts.

David Nicholls, joint leader of the 1991 Towards Social Transformation seminar is one. He notes that the pluralists were rightly suspicious of the notion of the common good as being a means whereby the state might seek to limit the autonomous life of associations. The only possible place for the concept is where it is taken in the structural, formal sense not in any substantive sense.[68] John Atherton is another sceptic, declaring: 'The common good, with its over-tones of undue political interference in economic life and private choices, may no longer be an appropriate concept for Christian social thought.'[69] Even more forceful is Enrique Dussel, speaking from the perspective of liberation theology. Dussel warns that in practice it is the forces of domination which use the language of the common good even as the systems they set up lead to the exploitation and death of the poor. What is needed is a radical conversion so that the poor, working together in 'associations of free persons' might be creators of 'communal goodness'.[70]

Yet however justified and even useful these warnings may be, it would be unwise to dismiss the potential help offered by the notion of the common good. Not only does the common good remain a staple of Roman Catholic teaching, it has more recently been taken up in America by 'Protestants for the Common Good'.[71] Far from being incompatible with pluralism, associationalism and multiculturalism, a proper understanding of the common good can actually provide precisely the kind of framework that is needed to make these forms of social life more coherent, more appealing and more secure. Before rejecting the relevance of the common good, therefore, it is worth pausing to take a closer look at what it might actually mean.

Two Approaches to the Common Good: Conceptual and Experiential

There are several different understandings of the common good now, just as there were in the Middle Ages. Matthew Kempshall shows how, even in the Middle Ages, there were very different traditions of the common good: Aristotelian, Ciceronian and Augustinian. Indeed even within Aquinas, Thomas Gilby found inconsistencies between the theme of 'community', where the individual is portrayed as a part of a whole, and the theme of society, where nothing of the personal is surrendered.[72] Rather than try to resolve debates such as this, it may be more useful here to distinguish two ways of understanding the common good: one conceptual, which seeks to define its key features, and the other experiential, which seeks to locate partial, analogous experiences of the common good which point to its deeper grounding. The first approach, which will be touched on briefly, is reflected in the Roman Catholic Catechism; the second will be explored more fully, drawing on the approach suggested by Patrick Riordan, S.J., leader of the 2003 Towards Social Transformation seminar.

A very useful and brief exposition of a contemporary Christian understanding of the common good is found in the revised Roman Catholic Catechism: 'By common good is to be understood the sum total of social conditions which allow people, either as groups or as individuals, to reach their fulfilment more fully and more easily....The common good is always oriented towards the progress of persons: The order of things must be subordinate to the order of persons, and not the other way around.'[73] The common good, it continues, 'consists of three essential elements: First, the common good presupposes respect for the person as such. In the name of the common good, public authorities are bound to respect the fundamental and inalienable rights of the human person....Second, the common good requires the social well-being and development of the group itself....it is the proper function of authority to arbitrate, in the name of the common good, between various particular interests; but it should make accessible to each what is needed to lead a truly human life: food, clothing, health, work, education and culture, suitable information, the right to establish a family, and so on....Finally, the common good requires peace, that is, the stability and security of a just order. It presupposes that authority should ensure by morally acceptable means the security of society and its members. It is the basis of the right to legitimate personal and collective defence....Each human community possesses a common good which permits it to be recognized as such; it is in the political community that its most complete realization is found. It is the role of the state to defend and promote the common good of civil society, its citizens, and intermediate bodies....' The strength of this very lengthy definition is also its weakness: different aspects can be seized upon selectively to attempt to justify quite contradictory policies.

A more experiential approach to the common good has been developed by Patrick Riordan.[74] This involves reflection on experiences which, by way of analogy, can convey a sense of what the common good might be like. Riordan is keen to distance a genuine experience of the common good from the experience of a football team's achieving victory, or a corporation's making profits. Such models of the common good can imply that the individual is merely a part of a whole or a means to an end (even if they enjoy winning or are entitled to a share in the profits). The kinds of experiences which Riordan holds up are those which open up the possibility of and make plausible the overcoming of opposition, exclusion, isolation and pure self-interest. The method is heuristic, exploring areas of social life, ranging from criminal justice to corporate governance, from poverty to the environment, from leisure to politics, and then suggesting that the notion of the common good is, in the first instance, a useful tool for interpreting what is actually going on in these activities. All of them, if looked at deeply, reveal that a description of action in terms of egoism versus altruism, self-interest versus sacrifice, is simply inadequate. What is taking place is an experience of active commonality, of sharing – which is good in itself, not merely a means to an end or a quest for personal benefit. That is at the heart of the idea of the common good.

Riordan moves on from mere observation, however, to suggest that this sort of thinking provides the essential frame of reference if we hope to tackle the urgent problems of our day. A notion of the common good gives us a language which can take us beyond the notion of politics as simple *bargaining,* where one group's rights and interests are played off against another's, to mature political *argument,* where communication and a common search for the good can be pursued. To the objection that the language of the common good marginalizes the role of rights, Riordan argues that, on the contrary, the common good provides a framework within which the shape, content and limits of rights and responsibilities can be worked out as well as a way of proceeding when rights conflict, as they often do. As Milbank has pointed out: '...the issue of the common good most pointedly surfaces...in the ever re-encountered "boundary disputes" and occasions for collective action in the everyday lives of citizens. These disputes have somehow got to be mediated and where the reality of "community" fades, the attempt is made to more and more do so by the extension of merely formal regulation....'[75]

Pluralism, Postmodernism and the Common Good

One would hardly expect terms like 'common' and 'good' to sit easily with postmodernism in whose view reality is mainly about fragmentation, transience, contingency, indeterminacy, particularity, isolation, nomadism, irony, scepticism, etc.[76] But there are some surprising points of contact.

A major part of the postmodern critique of Western culture is that ever since the time of Greek philosophy, *logos* (a form of reason which orders and structures reality) has been privileged at the expense of *eros* (a way of knowing that is rooted in desire). The malady was powerfully diagnosed by Nietzsche but his prescription was to abandon altogether the shackles of *logos* and to opt instead for an aesthetic affirmation of life in spite of – or because of – its lack of meaning. When Heidegger addressed the same problem, his solution was not to renounce all reason but to renounce both technological and metaphysical knowledge and to retreat into mysticism. Radical Orthodoxy, however, has combined postmodern and neo-Platonic insights in a way which restores *eros* to the centre. This it does by relating *eros* to a good which has an ontological basis and which is revealed in the Christian narrative.[77] It is precisely within this perspective that the Common Good assumes renewed importance.

Radical Orthodoxy also tackles a second of postmodernism's main critiques of Western thought – its tendency to seek to encompass all in a single one-dimensional system. Against this is raised the cry of Jean Francois Lyotard: 'Let us wage war on totality; let us be witnesses to the unrepresentable; let us activate the difference and save the honor of the name....'[78] Milbank would counter by arguing that the good of the City of God, as described by Augustine, is precisely a peaceful harmony of difference: 'The idea of the participation of all goods in a single, transcendent Good...does not imply...the denial of difference, nor the measurement of all goods as different quantities of a single substance....Our differences, affinities and inclinations are themselves grounded in the realm of forms, and justice, or the idea of the Good, is itself the harmonic blending of these differences: a blending which...I chose to describe as "analogical".'[79] In other words, what is so good about the ultimate, transcendent common good is the goodness of respecting and valuing difference which is precisely the manifestation of the fullness and overflowing nature of the good.

CONCLUSION

Common Culture, Civil Society, Social Transformation

The previous chapter argued that associational life is enriched by, not undermined by a Christian social ontology which stresses that life, human and divine, is a 'being-in communion'. It drew on Milbank's image of 'gothic space' to illustrate how it is possible for parts to participate in and to reflect the whole, in their own distinctive ways, without being reduced to mere pieces of a jigsaw or cogs in a machine – 'The gothic vision…[which] acknowledges sublime indeterminacy, and the inescapability of an aesthetic judgement – of both unity and distinction.…'[80] That image is even more relevant to the themes developed in the present chapter. It suggests that pluralism is better safeguarded and multiculturalism better nurtured within a vision which places these within the framework of the common good, rather than by settling for the *modus vivendi* approach commended by John Gray, leader of the 2002 Towards Social Transformation. Such a vision overcomes any notion of the common good as being about everyone joining in one big common enterprise or celebration. It makes the common good accessible. A precondition is the non-dominative mode of communication, described by Habermas. But, drawing on Riordan's insights, the common good can actually be experienced in everyday life, precisely through a multiplicity of rich associational activities, as people of different cultures come together for limited but voluntary purposes.

The Christian narrative is wonderfully supportive of this exercise. Its attraction consists not in any claim to be 'thicker' than other narratives, as if to say that its bonds are tighter, its norms clearer, its practices more elaborate, etc. The great attraction is that it is more generous and it can be more generous because it is richer, being based as Milbank has suggested, on a narrative which has an excess of meanings, a spirit of giving, a delight in beauty. In short, it is about grace. It is grace that can make possible the kind of non-dominative communication which Habermas recommends. It is grace which can provide the humility to embrace the critical autonomy which Gough and Doyal see as part of human development and which Sen sees as a key to genuine multiculturalism. It is grace with enables the development of the gift-relationship so prized by Titmuss. It is grace which can free us from captivity to narratives of national or ethnic superiority. And it is grace which can open the way through multiculturalism to a common culture. At least that is what it is meant to be. If this potential is to be realized, it will demand a radical reversal of the tendencies to closure which are threatening to dominate Christian life and worship today.

Why has the vision of a common culture not been fully realized? Cynics may say that it was because it had too high a view of human nature and its inclinations towards altruism and even common decency.[81] But it also has something to do with the cultural distortions, conflicts of interest and power relations of capitalist modernity. It is about the way people, shaped by particular narratives and traditions, are united and divided by the particular economic systems and political regimes of their particular country. Concern for common culture is concern for culture as a whole way of life – with conditions which allow all to participate on an equal basis. It provides the essential framework for discerning what types of economic and political transformations we are called to seek and how we might move towards a genuine common-wealth. That will be the subject of the next two chapters.

Chapter Four

Transforming Economies
Life After Capitalism

Every few hundred years in Western history there occurs a sharp
transformation....We are currently living in such a transformation.
It is creating the Post-capitalist society.
Peter Drucker[1]

John Paul II is the last great ideologue to criticize capitalism for what
it is....In the last ten years, it [the Left] has been too frightened to say
that capitalism is a moral evil. I think it will start saying it again.
Eric Hobsbawm[2]

If we can think the unthinkable about 'welfare' why are we not clever
enough and informed enough to think the unthinkable about capital?
David Jenkins[3]

Précis

Capitalism's sheer dynamism means that it has always had a profoundly
transformative impact – both creative and destructive, liberating and
oppressive – on the shape of society, culture and politics. That is the subject
of the other chapters in this book. Here the spotlight will be on the ways in
which capitalism itself has had to undergo its own transformations. These
are due not only to the impetus of its own logic. They also arise because it
is embedded in a web of social, cultural and political forces – forces which
it both needs as supports but which it also provokes into reaction so as to
protect themselves from the impact of capitalism.

Following the more entrepreneurial mode of 18th and 19th century
capitalism came a brief period of 'organized capitalism' – organized internally by reason of the development of managerial power of its own corporate bureaucracy, and organized externally by reason of its more formalized
relationships of co-operation rather than conflict with the organized labour
and the state. With the crisis of the post-World War II settlement in the

mid-1970s, the internal constraints were gradually released, and with the collapse of Communism the way was open for capital to call the tune, in terms of its relations with states and labour. This, plus the transformative impact of information and communications technology meant that by the 1990s a 'new capitalism' had emerged – described variously as 'hyper-capitalism', 'turbo-capitalism' or 'savage capitalism'.

The so-called new capitalism is marked by several transformations: a transformation of capital itself (the financialization of capitalism), the penetration of market principles deeper into all areas of human activity (the commodification of culture), and the reshaping of class relations (the fragmentation of society). The first section of this chapter will explore more fully these features and will argue that far from representing something new, they simply reveal what capitalism is like once the nation-state has been weakened and the working class divided. The second section will compare some recent theological approaches to capitalism. It will argue that a 'good economy' needs to be grounded in notions of a common culture and the common good, as developed in the previous chapter. The third section will look at the institutional aspects of the economy, examining a range of recent attempts at redressing the current imbalance between the three central co-ordinators of economic activity – market, state and society – so that alternative paths to the transformation of capitalism might be opened up. Particular reference will be made to the recovery of the social in exploring stakeholder capitalism, the social market, market socialism and associational socialism.

PREAMBLE: RENAMING THE SYSTEM

> ...certainly 'capitalism', like the word laissez-faire, is dead.
> John Atherton[4]

John K. Galbraith, looking back on nearly a century of economic turmoil and debate, devoted a short, sharp chapter, 'The Renaming of the System', to challenge the prevailing tendency to use terms such as 'free enterprise', and 'the market system' as a way of escape from using the disturbing term 'capitalism': 'Reference to the market system as a benign alternative to capitalism is a bland, meaningless disguise of this deeper corporate reality – of producer power....'[5] The tendency is increasingly found in church circles as well, for example in John Atherton's claim (above). Andrew Britton has recently stated: 'Indeed, the word 'capitalism' does not really have a part to play in mainstream economics.'[6] A report produced in 2005 by Churches Together in Britain and Ireland, exploring prosperity, poverty and the threat to the environment in the context of globalization, abounds in references to the market economy but fails to make even a single mention of capitalism, although the long-awaited successor to *Faith in the City* does make critical comments about 'secular capitalism'.[7] The issue is not simply one of words. Without an adequate acknowledgement of the economic system in which we are operating, it is impossible even to appreciate, much less to address, the pressures that determine what is necessary and the constraints which determine what is possible.

The dangers of confusing capitalism as a system with markets, private property, contractual relations and even the use of capital itself were spelt out in Chapter One. The point was also made there that capitalism needs to be viewed as a contingent reality, which happened to happen due to a combination of social, cultural, legal, political, technological and economic forces and events. Capitalism does not have to be. Neither does it have to implode under the weight of its own internal contradictions. Its future, like it past, depends on a combination of unforeseeable and often uncontrollable events in history and on the extent and ways in which we take seriously our responsibility for the economic order. The script is not completed.

I. THE NEW CAPITALISM

Transformations in Contemporary Capitalism

The true pacemakers of socialism were not the intellectuals or the agitators
who preached it but the Vanderbilts, Carnegies and Rockefellers.
Joseph Schumpeter [8]

Capitalism must change. That is not an expression of a moral imperative. It is a comment on the very nature of capitalism itself. If it is to expand, or even to survive, ways of financing, producing and marketing must change as capitalists seek to gain and retain the competitive edge on one another. Ways of behaving must change as capitalists respond to the wishes of consumers, the demands of shareholders and the requirements of the state. The rapidity and profundity of change in our world today presents new possibilities for economic transformations not previously available. Capitalism will change, but as Dahrendorf has asked: 'What must change for a capitalist system to cease being capitalist?'[9]

The revolution in information and communication technology is providing a new source of empowerment, both in terms of access to information and in terms of the ability for smaller enterprises to become key producers and suppliers of goods and services. It is generating new elites and new networks of solidarity. The shift of power to consumers is creating pressure for the creation of better quality products. The ownership of shares by local authorities, trade unions, voluntary and religious bodies and ethical investment funds, is making it possible to increase pressure on corporations to develop practices which embody more social and environmental justice.

These transformations make for a more complex world with new opportunities for profit, but also with new opportunities for human development, new possibilities for social solidarity and new understandings of the dynamics of capitalism itself. On balance, the sort of transformation that has been occurring in recent decades, in spite of profoundly destabilising forces and periodic crises, has resulted in an intensification and reinforcement rather than a weakening of capitalism There is little sign that, for all its failings, contemporary capitalism is in mortal crisis or that the people have had enough. On the contrary, people seem to want more. We seem to be wanting to pick up the narrative which Karl Polanyi described as 'The Great Transformation', namely the attempt to subject as many aspects of human activity as possible to the 'self-regulating' forces of the market, forgetting Polanyi's warning about how such a narrative tends to end. Society will reassert itself in both conservative and progressive ways and if it has been too weakened by market forces to be able to do so, then the state will intervene, in ways which may seek to give priority to order rather than to freedom. This time the trigger for that reaction may come from an area that was not an issue in Polanyi's day – the environment. The destruction caused by climate change is generating pressure for a new approach to economic theory and practice.[10] There are signs that profound changes in the forces, and relations of production are occurring alongside changes in public opinion and in economic power. The point is to try to read the signs of the times. But it is not easy.

Misreading the Signs of the Times: The Age of Fallibility

I was wrong to predict disaster.
George Soros [11]

Marxists are by no means alone in being mistaken in claiming to be able to discern the course that capitalism was going to take. They have plenty of company – professional economists and political theorists from various points on the political spectrum, including prophets like Peter Drucker, doyen of manage-ment theorists, who once envisioned 'capitalism without capitalists',[12] not to mention the mindless herd of investors who, against all logic, blew the dotcom balloon up to ludicrous proportions. Even shrewd investors like Warren Buffett, who once viewed derivatives as 'financial weapons of mass destruction', only to see them given a blessing by the then chairman of the US Federal Reserve Bank, Alan Greenspan. There are those who worry about global inflation, others who worry even more about global deflation, some who worry about the chaos that would come from unregulated trade, and others who worry about the threat to growth caused by protectionism. Standing in the opposite corner from those who discern the growing impotence of nation states in the face of global markets are those who shudder at the spectre of nation states putting up protectionist barriers. Only a few years ago, George Soros insisted that uncontrollable currency movements were about to create a global financial disaster. He has now come to the view that reform is possible, recognizing that the scale of the revolution in information technology may also be used to provide feedback, reflexivity and corrective action.[13] The lesson which Soros draws is that we would be wise to speak of 'The Age of Fallibility'.[14]

Clearly this is a time for humility as well as caution. It may also be a time for repentance. One of the most bizarre signs of current capitalist times is the marketing of an 'Incarceration Optimization Program', offering a 'discreet prison training course for convicted executives'.[15] Hernando de Soto speaks of 'the mystery of capital'. More mysterious still are the ways of capitalism. There are no sure ways to predict the course it will take, and certainly no off-the-shelf alternatives. Nonetheless the transformations that are taking place within contemporary capitalism do need to be studied closely if we are ever to move beyond it. That is what will be looked at next.

Transformations of Contemporary Capitalism

The new capitalism that is one of the driving forces of globalization to
some extent is a mystery.
Anthony Giddens[16]

More than Globalization

Globalization matters. It is not just a wider field onto which capitalism can expand. It is bringing about dramatic transformations, including a reversal of the relations of globalization that characterized the earlier age of empire. At the inter-state level, resource-rich countries as in Latin America are now exercising power against their former exploiters, Asian economic giants are starting to take over long-established and key firms in the industrialized world, and the transformation of the Chinese economy is having world-wide repercussions. At a deeper level, relations of investment, trade and production are also being dramatically transformed as manufacturing, assembling and administrative services are being outsourced by developed to developing countries, which is creating a new global class structure with new global elites at the top of the pyramid and an excluded 'Fourth world' at the bottom. And all this is happening at such a pace that legislation and regulation simply cannot keep pace. So, of course, globalization matters enormously. But it is not the main issue that will be examined here. And this for two reasons. One is that globalization is about much more than capitalism and is not shaped only by capitalism. The second is that the more fundamental economic issue is not about new forms of integration into an expanding system. It is about the nature of that system itself. Both these points are worth looking at more closely.

There is a tendency to confuse capitalism with globalization. This is profoundly unhelpful. Yes, capitalism has become global in its operations. But so have many other aspects of life – from travel to tourism, from education to entertainment, religion to recreation.[17] And, yes, capitalism has also become global in its impact. But the same may be said of many other human activities – not least our consumption of natural resources and our generation of waste. And, yes, the structure and organization of capitalism has taken on a global dimension. But, so too have many other institutions, from publishing to political protest.

As with capitalism past, so with global capitalism today: it brings both gains and losses – unequally distributed, as always. Globalization's 'potential for good is immense', declares the International Labour Organization's World Commission on the Social Dimensions of Globalization – before going on to warn of the 'deep-seated and persistent imbalances in the current workings of the global economy, which are ethically unacceptable and politically unsustainable.'[18] Regular assessments of the positive and negative impact of globalization have been made by the global management consulting firm A. T Kearney. It records improvements on the United Nations Human Development Index, and the extension of civil and political rights, alongside increased inequality, more widespread corruption and poorer health (partly due to an increase in pollution).[19] In the debate about global capitalism initiated by Will Hutton and Anthony Giddens, what emerged as just as important as the economic effects were the knock-on effects of globalization: a) cultural – resulting from both the development of satellite communications and the emergence of global communications empires; b) environmental – frequently offloading the effects of environmental damage, through climate change, the exporting of hazardous waste products, the encouraging of illegal deforestation, etc.; and c) political – the changes in power relations resulting in severe constraints on the policy options of nation-states.[20]

To try to understand contemporary capitalism simply in terms of globalization, therefore, is to miss the point. The global reach of capital is of immense significance, but it does not tell us what contemporary capitalism actually is and why, where and how it is expanding in particular ways with particular impacts. What follows, therefore, is an attempt to draw out the emerging features of contemporary capitalism and to understand the dynamic behind the changes.

Capitalisms New and Old

The investment banking system makes a mockery of the free-market economy because, as a result of the way it works, markets are not really free and the odds are loaded in favour of those who know.

Philip Augur [21]

The 'new capitalism': what sort of animal is it? It has been described, variously, as 'impatient capitalism',[22] 'millennial capitalism',[23] 'turbo-capitalism',[24] 'hyper-capitalism',[25] 'savage capitalism'[26] and 'Rotweiler capitalism'.[27] In essence it is about the financialization of capitalism, sometimes loosely described as being about 'making money rather than things'. But, of course, things are still being made, in greater quantity and, in many cases, of higher quality, than ever before. A more accurate description of the key feature of the new capitalism is the disjunction between making things and making money.

'Making money' refers not simply to the astronomical fees, commissions, and bonuses 'earned' by those in the City. It also refers to the fact that an increasing share of British GDP comes from financial services, shares, rents, etc rather than manufacturing.[28]

But the financialization of capitalism means something more funda-mental still. It describes an economy a) in which trading of shares, currencies and commodities becomes more important than owning them, b) where an increasing percentage of banking profits comes not from investment banking but from financial trading, c) with financiers less committed to long-term direct links with industry and d) a new breed of hedge fund managers and private equity investors who take a more flexible and often riskier approach to investment, e) using a complex range of new and sophisticated financial products, f) encouraged by an abundant supply of capital at low rates of interest which leads them into incurring staggering levels of indebtedness, g) in a highly competitive environment which has produced a transformation of the structure and mode of operating of banks, brokers and stock exchanges.

It is crystallized in the transformations which are taking place in the very centres of financial trading, the stock exchanges. Where better to see this all focussed than in the current crisis in the London Stock Exchange.

Transformation in Capital Markets
Case Study – Turmoil at the LSE

One of the main centres of financial trading has long been the London Stock Exchange. It offers traders a range of crucial services – listing companies, providing up-to-the minute information on price changes, giving access to a global supply of capital, offering sophisticated expert advice, and fostering a network of contacts and informal communication. It is a pretty big business. The London Stock Exchange describes itself as 'a global marketplace', listing more than 2,800 companies, worth over £3,500 billion. It claims to provide information to 90,000 installed terminals in over 100 countries worldwide. In 2004 it handled more than 66 million trades, an average of 261,000 trades every day.[29] And the volume of trading is increasing rapidly, up by more than 50% in the past two years – all of which is good news for its own shareholders who between January-September 2006 saw operating profits treble to over £80 million.[30]

But in the new world of financial capitalism its primacy is being challenged on three fronts – from above, from below and from within. The first threat is from above. The forces of globalization are generating pressure for mergers. The LSE has been targeted by take-over bids from rivals both on the Continent (the Deutsche Börse) and in America (NASDAQ). The reason why the LSE was able to see off the bid from the Deutsche Börse in 2005 was that British hedge funds began buying into the Börse and putting it on the defensive. A year later, the situation was reversed when NASDAQ, finding the LSE unwilling to countenance its approaches, began buying shares in the LSE itself, achieving by November 2006 a powerful 28.75% stake. In a further ironic twist to the story, the socialist Mayor of London, Ken Livingstone, then came to the defence of the LSE, recognizing its key role in London's economy both because it brings in income and ancillary jobs thanks to the presence of large international investment banks and because it had shown a commitment to helping smaller local venture capital firms.

Meanwhile, a second challenge was mounting from within. The profits that were such good news for LSE's shareholders seemed less good news for customers, who felt that they were being charged too much. Finally some of their largest customers had had enough. In September 2006 a group of 7 invest-ment banks – Citigroup, Goldman Sachs, Lehman Brothers, Merrill Lynch, Morgan Stanley and UBS – launched Project Turquoise, a plan to form their own alternative and cheaper multilateral trading facility (the Block Interest Discovery System). The fact that this would draw off some of the LSE's most important business immediately sent LSE shares down 10%. This, in turn, once again made it a target for takeover by other exchanges mentioned above. These pressures increased the likelihood that the LSE would eventually have to cast its lot with someone. And that realization tended to push up the price of LSE shares up. So the cycle continued. The fact that LSE's share prices were facing both upward and downward pressures in this uncertain period, made it the perfect target for hedge funds, which, as will be seen below, thrive on guessing how prices are to move and can make a profit by guessing correctly whether prices go up or down.

And then a third threat appeared from below. The new technology has made dealing on such exchanges appear less necessary, with the result that in the US some smaller, aggressive private firms are getting into the exchange business themselves. So far, at least, this threat has not proved anywhere near as signifi-cant as the other two.

The Financialization Race

One way of looking at the financialization of capitalism is to compare it to a race amongst lorries which are meant to be delivering goods. It is a high risk affair, with big gains and big losses, and lots of opportunities for cheating. It is full of dangers which could affect people not in the race as well as the environ-ment even more than it does the racers themselves. Yet because they are being funded largely with borrowed money the racers seem not to care. It is worth taking a good look at what is going on.

That is what the 'new capitalism' is like. Ten main features are highlighted below. Each of them demands a closer look:

1. Daring Drivers – Hedge Funds, Private Equity and Shareholder Activists;
2. Lorries as Race Cars – High Gearing and Leveraging;
3. Highly Combustible Fuel – Derivatives;
4. Lightning Speed – Hypercapitalism;
5. Faulty Brakes – Turbocapitalism;

6. Poor Vision – Lack of Transparency;

7. Cheating and Dirty Tricks;

8. Inadequate Policing;

9. Wrecks and Crashes – Destabilising the System?;

10. Who Makes and Services the Lorries? Workers as an Afterthought.

1. Daring Drivers – Hedge Funds, Private Equity and Shareholders Activists

Some of the most exciting action in the race is due to the impact of three aggressive drivers – hedge funds, private equity firms and shareholder activists. None of these are new. Hedge funds go back to 1949 with Alfred Winslow Jones' long short equity fund.

Private equity firms have been around even longer. The shift to shareholder power has been identified as having started in the early 1970s with the breakdown of the Bretton Woods agreement.[31] What is significant is that the increasingly prominent role which these drivers have come to play since the 1990s has resulted in a two-fold transformation. On the one hand, established corporations have begun to welcome and even adopt some of the practices of these flashy drivers. On the other hand, the drivers themselves have begun engaging with rather than merely exploiting the system. In short, they have become respectable. But what exactly are they? In the following paragraphs each will be looked at in turn.

a) Hedge Funds

Hedge funds have grown spectacularly. In 1989 they numbered about 1,000; there are now some 9,000.[32] The assets they manage amount to over $1,200 billion. But size is not the real issue. Hedge funds still represent a very small part of the market. The real issue is the high-volume of their trading activity. Hedge funds regularly account for a quarter to a third of equity trading volume in New York and London.[33] Hedge funds account for 5% of assets under management in US but for 30% of equity trading volume.[34]

What are hedge funds? 'There is no agreed definition', writes Kate Burgess in the *Financial Times*, '…in general, they are characterized as unconstrained, actively managed funds.'[35] So what do hedge funds do? They deal in risk. The reason they are called 'hedge' funds is that they seek to devise various mixes of risky ventures – which can make either huge gains or huge losses – with safer investments that provide a hedge in case of loss. Any sort of risk will do. Any sort of complex financial product will do (see 'Fuel' below) and any sort of strategy will do. The risks might be seen as related to factors as diverse as changes in interest rates, a shortage of commodities, a downturn in the markets, changes in government, natural disasters or wars. All such events cause prices of financial securities to rise or fall, often dramatically. And is it largely, though not exclusively, by their betting on the rise and fall of these prices that hedge funds make their money. And the riskiness of what they are doing incurred is compounded by the fact that they, like private equity funds (see feature 2: High Gearing and Leveraging) often play the game with borrowed money in the hope that they can repay it once they have made their gains.

Like good poker players, they have several cards and they know when to hold their cards, when to bluff, when to ask for new cards, and when to throw in their hand. The products are usually a very rich and mysterious mix. The strategies are varied. Hedge funds have too often been associated only with short-selling. This involves obtaining – often borrowing rather than purchasing – financial securities such as shares whose value the hedge fund manger suspects will go down (this may be based on privileged knowledge, good guesswork or action that the hedge fund manager will take to depress the price of that security). Their aim is to buy it back at a lower price and thus make a profit on the difference.

It all worked with dazzling success. Hedge funds outperformed other forms of investment and brought hedge fund managers astronomical rewards. It was so good that: a) more and more money poured into hedge funds – eventually with traditional institutions, such as pension funds, investing a part of their portfolio in hedge funds; and b) hedge fund managers, now in great demand, were able to charge hefty fees (performance fees range from 5% to as high as 20%). Edward Lampert, who controls ESL Investments, is reported to have taken home more than $1 billion in 2004 – that is one hundred times more than the mere $10 million earned by the chief executive of a typical top US company.[36] A recent *Sunday Times* survey found that more than a third of the City's 100 wealthiest business figures were hedge fund managers. Hedge fund managers world-wide earned $45 billion in fees in 2004 – down from 2003 when they made $57 billion but still more than 4 times more than they made in 2002.[37]

Initially hedge funds performed extremely well, outperforming the stock market as a whole. They enjoyed a 19.2% rate of return in 2003. Was it too good to last? In a word: yes. In 1990–95, return on investments averaged some 20%; by 1995–2000 this had slipped to 10% (with great fluctuations); and from 2000–2006 they were down to 7.7%. In 2004 the rate of return for hedge fund investment actually fell 8.9%.[38] This was partly because so many of the new drivers entering the race did not have the skill, experience, and inside knowledge of some of the star players, and partly because there is only so much risk around and faced with intense pressure to perform some drivers started to move into higher and higher areas of risk.

Poorer performance is causing a bit of a backlash and resentment that, as in many other areas of the new capitalism, the drivers are being overpaid for under performing. It is having two results. One is that investors can put pressure on hedge funds to lower their commissions, fees and charges. The other is to develop a system which does what hedge funds do, not by devising complex products and clever strategies, but simply by devising tracker hedge funds which track in minute detail the movements in hedge fund tactics. Towards the end of 2006, Goldman Sachs launched an Absolute Return Tracker indexed fund. As a tracker it does not so much devise investment strategies as identify the actual mix of strategies being pursued by hedge fund managers at any given moment. It has been working since 2004 on creating the technology and mathematical formulas that would enable it do this and claims to have reached a point where it can produce absolute returns but at only a fraction of the cost that would be demanded by a hedge fund.[39]

Does all this feverish activity really render a service? In some senses it does. If hedge funds offer to take on the riskier areas of investment, this can give more traditional investors the confidence they need to invest their capital rather than to sit on it or to look only for the safest, low-return outlets. Alan Greenspan, then Chairman of the US Federal Reserve Board, took a positive view: 'Hedge funds have become increasingly valuable in our financial markets….they often provide valuable liquidity to financial markets, both in normal market conditions and especially during periods of stress. They can ordinarily perform these functions more effectively than other types of financial intermediaries because their investors often have a greater appetite for risk and because they are largely free from regulatory constraints on investment strategies.'[40] Hedge funds are good at spotting where capital is being held back, for example from activities which are seen to involve too great a risk. In that sense they have an effect on the 'real economy'. Many institutions have deemed it prudent to invest a portion of their own resources in hedge funds. Even short-selling has been supported by the Securities and Exchange Commission because it is deemed to be providing the markets with more information and because it also gives scope for investors who have 'long' to generate some extra income by lending their shares to the shorts.[41]

b) Private Equity

Unlike hedge funds, private equity firms are about running a business. Their expansion in the past two decades and their move from the sidelines to the main arena represents a return of the capitalist as entrepreneur. Because they are not listed, private equity firms are free of many restrictions and reporting requirements. They can thus go about their business of generating value in ways that are more creative, more risky and often more questionable. They also seek to enhance profits by reducing tax liabilities and their encouragement of this practice has been seen as creating a threat to corporate governance by encouraging listed firms to follow suit in order to remain competitive.[42] The Chief Executives of private equity firms have a freer hand in awarding themselves a handsome share of the profits than they would if their actions were subject to changes in share prices to which listed equities are exposed. And unlike the Chief Executives of listed companies whose remuneration may include shares but which are not able to be sold for a certain number of years and which, when they are sold, are subject to 40% capital gains tax, Chief Executives of private equity firms can sell their shares whenever they wish and if they do hold onto them for two years, they can take advantage of taper relief regulations which reduce the rate of tax to only 10%.

Typical activities include venture capital (most often helping to encourage new businesses, especially those developing new products in, for example, biotechnology, information technology and environmental technology), leveraged buy-outs (taking out loans to get control of established businesses and then reshaping them) and distressed debt (salvaging businesses that have run aground). This has encouraged a new confidence that, if there is money to be made, one of the ways to do so is to take matters into one's own hand. And the aims are far from modest, particularly in the area of buy-outs. The value of announced such deals in 2006 was a record $700 billion – 20 times the level of such deals only ten years earlier. One group alone, the Texas-Pacific Group, was involved in seventeen deals with a total value of $101 billion.

Investors are pouring money into Private Equity funds which are performing well and this, in turn, is enabling these funds to use high leveraging to put together huge buy-out bids. In 2005 the Egyptian investor Naguib Sawiris bought control of Wind, the Italian communications company for €12.2 billion; in November 2006, Thomas H. Lee Partners and Bain Capital announced a bid of $28.6 billion to buy out Clear Channel, the US's largest radio network company; meanwhile the Blackstone Group was buying Equity Office Properties

Trust, the largest owner of office space in the United States after the federal government for $36 billion.

c) Shareholder Activists – Rebels, Raiders, Partners or Revolutionaries?

Shareholder Activism covers a very diverse range of activities by which shareholders – who may also be hedge funds and private equity firms – can assert their power to influence a company's practices. It can include anything from making representation to board members, to voting board members in or out of office, to disinvesting, etc.[43] What is even more significant than the type of action is the motive and purposes behind it. It is possible to distinguish four types of shareholder activists: rebels, raiders partners and revolutionaries.

Rebels

The rebels are those who are fed up with the way a company is being run, either because it is not providing high enough returns to shareholders or because relations between Boards and Chief Executives have become too cosy and are encouraging underserved rewards for poor performance. There have been some high-profile cases involving individuals. Jean-Pierre Garnier, Chief Executive of GlaxoSmithKline, had a lovely contract which entitled him to be awarded £22 million should he be sacked for poor performance. Dick Grasso, the former Chair of the New York Stock Exchange, arranged for himself to be given a $140 million remuneration package, the disclosure of which brought about his resignation in November 2003 and subsequent court action.[44] More worrying, because it is more widespread, is the practice of providing stock options in which Chief Executives are rewarded with stocks priced at below their actual value in a way which is not accurately reported in the official accounts. Hundreds of cases have been identified in the US, where 34 senior executives or directors in 17 corporations had stepped down or been fired as of October 2006.

Raiders

Corporate raiders, once thought to have passed from the scene after the scandals of the late 1980s, have once again been spotted. Their idea of activism is simply to get a controlling interest in a company and then to make as much personal profit from it as possible, either by asset-stripping (selling off the most profitable bits) or by re-writing the rules for the distribution of profits.

Partners

Not all shareholder activists need be seen as threats. Some companies are indeed under-performing and may have poor systems of corporate governance. They need help if they are to survive and to perform well. That is why at least some shareholder activists see their task as one of engaging with the managers to bring about improvements. That this can work may be seen from a recent study which found that the U.K. Focus Fund run by Hermes, the fund manager owned by the British Telecom Pension Scheme, had engaged with a number of firms and were able actually to enhance performance and returns.[45]

Revolutionaries

A fourth group of activists have as their particular concern the impact of company policies on society and the environment. The ethical investment movement has been going from strength to strength. In May 2003, a number of organizations which had, for some time, been active in the field, came together to form the 'Global Benchmarks' campaign as an international coalition of religious investors and campaign groups.[46] Added to this are encouraging signs that some powerful players, such as the public sector pension funds in California and trade union funds are beginning to use their power for social and environmental aims.[47] But they are often up against even bigger activists, each with their own particular interests – national and multi-national banks, insurance companies and industrial groups, pension funds and hedge funds.[48] On balance, the shift towards increased shareholder power may well prove to be less an opportunity for more socially responsible investment than a stimulus for capitalism to be even more ruthlessly competitive.

The resurgence of shareholder activity, of whatever type, reflects the inherent tension between shareholders and managers stemming from the fact that although both have an interest in a company, the nature of that interest can be very different. Shareholders tend to want a return on investment and will be happy to invest long-term if that is assured. Managers tend to look to the development of the company and will be happy to pay high dividends if that does not hurt the company's long-term interests.

For a good part of the past century, conventional wisdom had it that capitalism had moved beyond the entrepreneurial era and now depended for its success on what was subsequently described as a 'managerial revolution', classically diagnosed by Adolf A. Berle and Gardiner C. Means.[49] The essence of the revolution was not the introduction of more efficient *methods of production*, such as Taylorism and Fordism (which were adopted by communism and fascism as well as liberal capitalism). What made it a revolution was that it involved a *shift in the structure of power*. The entrepreneur had done his job. Now it was time for 'the organization man', as represented by the Chief Executives and Board, to do his. The sheer scale and complexity of what he had created needed different skills and different structures. Not everyone was happy with that revolution.

For example, Joseph Schumpeter warned: 'The capitalist process not only destroys its own institutional framework but it also creates the conditions for another. Destruction may not be the right word after all. Perhaps I should have spoken of transformation.' He discounts explanations which others have given for this trend, such as the 'Theory of Vanishing Investment Opportunity' (satiety) and the 'Evaporation of Industrial Property' (via the rise of the organization). At the heart of the problem, for Schumpeter, are issues to do with culture – a loss of faith and motivation on the part of the bourgeoisie: 'The modern corporation…socializes the bourgeois mind.' For James Burnham the transformation took on a much more sinister character. The managerial revolution posed a threat to liberal democracy itself, both by emasculating the power of capital and by containing the power of labour.[50]

Peter Drucker, on the other hand, saw the brighter side of this necessary transformation. Innovation, motivation and 'human capital' were becoming the key to productivity. The role of managers had to change. No longer mere 'bosses', they must become people responsible for the application and performance of knowledge: 'The shift from knowledge to knowledges [i.e. specialized] has given knowledge the power to create a new society. But this society has to be structured on the basis of knowledge being specialized and of knowledge people being specialists. This gives them their power. But it also raises questions – of values, of vision, of beliefs, that is of the things that hold society together and give meaning to life.'[51]

Shareholder activism, in whatever form, may be seen as part of a restoration of power that had shifted toward managers and executives in the course of the 20th century. The shift of power from manager to shareholder is far from complete. It is complicated by the fact that although most of the funding often comes from shareholders, it is the Board not the shareholders who legally own the company. Perhaps this is one reason why shareholders in the US have fewer rights in some areas than one might imagine. This led 16 mainly non-US investors, including private, public and pension fund managers, to write to the Chair of the Securities and Exchange Commission, arguing the case for shareholders to have access to the proxy so that they could have a say as to who is elected to company boards. Just how the new balance of rights will be enshrined in law is far from certain but what is certain is that shareholder activists will increasingly be making their presence felt.[52]

2. Lorries as Race Cars – High Gearing and Leveraging

Leveraging refers to the degree to which hedge funds play the markets with money they do not actually own but have borrowed. It rests on the hope that when it comes time to pay it back the fund will have made a profit, either because interest rates have fallen, inflation has risen or profits have been made.

The extraordinary levels of leveraging – particularly by hedge funds and private equity firms – has been the cause of growing concern on the financial markets. Freeport-McMoRan Copper and Gold, Inc. offered $26 billion to buy Phelps Dodge which is more than twice its size and Penn National Gaming Inc. entered into discussions to buy Harrah Entertainment whose market value is more than eight times its own. In June 2006, the exposure of just 13 banks to leveraged private equity buy-outs had risen to £45.5 billion.[53]

3. Highly Combustible Fuel – Derivatives

Derivatives are one of the favourite financial instruments used in the new capitalism. According to the Bank for International Settlements, the derivatives market quadrupled in size between 2000 and June 2006.[54] Derivatives are so-called because their value is derived from another 'underlying' financial security such as actual shares in a company, physical stocks of commodities, cash, credit notes, etc. They effectively involve the purchasing of rights and options to buy or sell under certain specified terms and conditions. Not only do derivatives operate at one remove from underlying securities, they also tend to be packaged into bundles of different types of derivatives. Governments have given a cautious approval. Ruth Kelly, then Financial Secretary to the Treasury noted that derivatives: '...have wrought a revolution in global financial markets through their contribution to price discovery mechanisms, the management of risk and the abundant market liquidity they can often provide'. She does not hesitate to acknowledge that 'the UK government is itself a significant player in the derivatives markets, for example in the management of foreign currency reserves and in the ability actively to use futures and foreign currency swaps, and in the ability to encourage National Savings and Investments with the introduction of a guaranteed equity bond.'[55]

There is good reason to be cautious for there are some inherent problems with derivatives. One is to do with the composition of this new fuel: it consists of a variable and complex mix in unknown quantities of a range of ingredients which themselves are not always fully understood. It could be highly combustible. These include such things as Contracts for Difference (CFDs) which, it is estimated, accounted for 40% of the trade in equities in London.[56] In CFDs the investor does not buy the shares/bonds/products but enters into a contract with the holder, usually an investment bank, based on a guess about how far the price of, for example, a share, will rise or fall by a particular date. It is in effect a sophisticated bet. As the trade is not in the purchase of actual shares, the trade is free of stamp duty. Concern has been expressed by the Association of Investment Trust Companies because this sort of betting on prices can actually affect the price of the share in ways which may bear little relation to its real value.

A second reason for caution stems from the way in which derivatives are traded. It has been estimated that 80% of derivatives are traded over the counter (OTC).[57] Derivatives, of course are not the only financial product that is traded OTC. Being traded over the counter means that they are not traded on the exchange, with the result that the actual prices being paid are not made public. The scope that this opens up for fraud, market manipulation and instability is obvious. The implications of this are particularly serious when it comes to trading in vital commodities. Yet perversely whilst trade in many commodities is subject, in the US, to the Commodity Futures Trading Commission, energy markets were exempted, due to lobbying by hedge funds and major energy groups such as Enron. No wonder the Commodity Futures Trading Commission has expressed concern.

4. Lightning Speed – Hypercapitalism

In 1965 US Pension funds held stocks on average for 46 months; by 2000, it was only 3.8 months, representing a ten-fold increase in rate of turnover.[58] When the Towards Social Transformation initiative was taking shape in 1989, trading on the world's financial markets amounted to some $600 billion per day. By 2004 it had more than trebled to $1,900 billion per day in 2004.[59] Why has the trade in both derivatives and their underlying securities speeded up so dramatically in recent years? For several reasons. Clearly there is an incentive for traders to make transactions as often as possible because they get a commission each time. But that is nothing new. One new factor is the development in information and communication technology, such as the introduction of electronic systems by Reuters and Electronic Broking Services in the early 1990s. As a result movements in the prices of shares and currencies can be traced immediately and transactions can be effected instantly and directly at the touch of a keyboard, and with less need for brokers. But that is only a precondition. The deeper reason is the new drivers, particularly hedge funds, which, as explained above, make their money by betting on the movement of share prices which tend to rise when buyers outpace sellers and fall when sellers outpace buyers and these movements occur from second to second. Fund managers have to know how to respond quickly and which of their wide range of financial instruments to employ. But this sets in motion what for them is a virtuous circle insofar as the rapidity of their responses itself makes prices move even faster. Hedge funds can turn over their portfolios twenty or thirty times faster than long-term investors normally would do.

5. Faulty Brakes – Turbocapitalism

The anarchic forces of capitalism have always needed a good set of brakes. Among the forces that once put a brake on capitalism were a strong labour movement, the banks, a welfare state, and, in the shadows, the spectre of communism. Some of these brakes are gone; others are not working as they should. Starting in the 1980s the brakes began to be loosened. Edward Luttwak – a true believer in capitalism – speaks of a shift from 'controlled capitalism' to 'turbo-capitalism'.[60] Internally, exchange controls have been relaxed, state enterprises have been privatised, and trade union power has been curtailed. Externally, the collapse of communism eased the pressure on capitalism to portray itself as being more socially responsible than it naturally is.

Luttwak scans the field for any remaining countervailing powers. Their shape and influence varies from place to place. The US is fortunate in having two such forces, he argues. One is the legal system; the other is the continuing 'pervasive influence of Calvinist values'. The former accounts for the increasing tendency towards litigation, class-action (against the tobacco industry and the food industry, for example) and anti-trust legislation. Calvinist values on the other hand provide the basis for three rules: a) becoming rich is a sign of divine favour; b) failing to prosper is a sign of divine disfavour; and c) refusing to accept rule number two merits punishment. The result is an 'insatiable demand for stricter laws [and] longer prison sentences.' But as soon as the laws are enacted, they are met with a mighty outcry.

As for the banks, it would seem to be in their interest to act as a restraining power insofar as they are normally very careful about to whom they lend their money. But what prompts banks to lend to the new breed of risk-takers – apart from the fact that many hedge funds have performed very well – is that the banks themselves are huge beneficiaries of hedge fund activities which bring in not only interest payments but also fees for advice, commissions for every transaction (which are many), and charges for clearing. In 2004, banks made $25 billion from hedge fund activity – representing one-eighth of their total banking investment revenues – earning $19 billion from trading with hedge funds plus a further $6 billion from prime brokerage services, such as lending, extending credit, clearing and settlement.[61] This sort of prime brokerage has been referred to as 'the crack cocaine of the financial system'.[62] To win the custom of hedge funds, individual banks are driven by competitive pressures to comply with what the hedge funds want, and are dropping their credit standards in order to attract this business.[63]

6. Poor Vision – Lack of Transparency

'Markets have become extremely unstable and historical measures of value at risk no longer apply,' observed George Soros as he felt led to make a major reorganization of his own huge funds.[64] Why are prices not reflecting the true value of shares, currencies and commodities? From what has been said already, the answer lies in a combination of facts: a) financial instruments themselves have become increasingly complex and obscure; b) many are traded over the counter (OTCs); and c) many are supported by debt. An added factor is that many are based off-shore and thus not covered by some of the standard regulations. The lack of transparency affects not only potential investors. It also affects those who hold shares since, increasingly, Chief Executive themselves are seeking to boost (apparent) profits and disguise (real) liabilities by engaging in financial activities which are conveniently kept off the balance sheet.

There have been repeated calls for more transparency, but, asking hedge funds to be more transparent is like asking poker players to be more transparent. How can they agree and still call it poker?

7. Cheating and Dirty Tricks

Any game has its cheats. And corruption and bribery, even on a grand scale, are hardly unique to capitalism. But with the financialization of capitalism the dangers are increased, both because the stakes are so high and because the means for covering one's tracks are so readily available. There are a number of forms of cheating that have raised concerns in recent years.

One is straightforward fraud. In the US there have been dozens of cases where people's expectations of making high returns from hedge funds have been exploited by inexperienced or unscrupulous hedge fund managers who make misleading offers. In the UK in the second half of 2005 the costs of fraud more than doubled (£900 million) compared with £329 million in the second half of 2004.[65]

Another is taking advantage of consumers' lack of technical knowledge. John Tiner, Chief Executive of the Financial Services Authority warned that benign financial markets could be providing a cover for malpractices which could lead to financial scandals, such as the previous misselling of faulty mortgage and pension products which has led to more than £2 billion having to be paid in compensation to consumers in the past 18 months.[66] Now the concern was about Venture Capital Trusts (VCTs) and payment protection insurance.[67]

A third is the abuse of insider knowledge about deals which are being put together. There is more insider knowledge partly because in constructing complex financial products such as derivatives so many different parties are involved, partly because of the conflicts of interest that arise from such deals, and partly because there has been a haemorrhage of knowledgeable staff from the banking industry to the hedge fund industry. In October 2006, France's stock market regulator, Autorité des Marchés Financiers, recommended imposing heavy fines on GLG Partners and Deutsche Bank for their involvement in a 2002 issue of convertible bonds by Alcatel, the French telecommunications equipment group. GLG and Deutsche Bank have been given an opportunity to respond.[68] In March 2006 the UK, Financial Services Authority identified unusual share price movements before 29% of takeover bids in 2000 and 2004, suggesting a high degree of misuse of insider knowledge. It is continuing to investigate the scale of such abuse.[69]

A fourth form of cheating is market manipulation. There are two versions of this. One is to try to make money by engaging in actions which depress the price of a share which is being targeted ('short and distort'). In August 2006, the Financial Services Authority fined Philippe Jabre, a highly successful, former managing director of GLG, one of Europe's largest hedge funds, £750,000 for short-selling which was alleged to have depressed the price, of 4,771 shares in Sumitomo Mitsui Financial Group in February 2003.[70] The other is to take measures which artificially boost the price of one's holding well beyond its true value and then to sell it ('pump and dump'). When prices are rising generally it creates a situation in which pumping and dumping are more tempting, as dramatised in the film *The Boiler Room*. But regardless of the overall conditions, investors wanting to increase their stake in a company may be tempted to resort to dirty tricks in order to affect the company's share price. Thus S&C Capital have been accused by Canada's Fairfax Financial of having used threats and of having spread misinformation so as to depress the price of the company's stocks. European firms are said to believe that similar dirty tricks have been used against them by other parties.[71]

8. Inadequate Policing

There are, of course, regulatory and supervisory boards set up to police all this. The problem is that they are having to deal with players (hedge funds), products (derivatives) and methods of trading (over the counter) that are new, complex, and lacking in transparency. Michael Snyder, Chairman of Policy and Resources for the Corporation of London, warned that Britain's lax approach to white collar crime risked turning the City into a honey-pot for fraudsters, and portrayed British authorities as being too soft in comparison with other countries and too lenient in sentencing.[72] But policing is not easy. How is it possible to establish the right kind of regulation for markets whose operations are not all that clear? And how is it possible to enforce unpopular regulations now that markets have become global since if investors do not like the approach being taken in one country they can simply pack their bags and do business elsewhere?

So although the need for more effective policing has been recognized, bringing it about will be a slow process. Before any major new regulations will be forthcoming, there appears to be a bit of groundwork to be done to make clear whether what is needed is more regulation – and if so what kind – or better enforcement – and if so, in what ways. The first task is simply to try to understand the system itself. The US Congress has begun to try to get a grasp of the role that hedge funds are actually playing. A second is to ensure greater transparency of financial values, liabilities and transactions. In September 2006, the US House of Representatives began debating a bill which would require the PWG (President's Working Group, which includes the Treasury, Securities and Exchange Commission, the Commodity Futures Trading Commission and others) to make recommendations on discloser-requirements for hedge funds. A third measure is to try to develop regional and international agreements that will begin to address the global dimensions of the new capitalism. Thus, in the autumn of 2005, top representatives of the US Securities and Exchange Commission, the Federal Reserve Bank of New York and the UK's Financial Services Authority began meeting, starting with work on the issue of credit derivatives. Their approach seems to be to work with leading investment funds in order to come up with a system that worked with rather than against the market.[73] In 2007, the G8 is planning to include hedge funds on its agenda.

Meanwhile, some more basic responsibilities appear to have been neglected. Criticisms have been made as to why a body like the Financial Services Authority has not been more vigilant in preventing wave after wave of financial scandals of the past decade and a half – the misselling of pensions, shares, insurance policies and endowment mortgages, collusion between auditing firms and their clients and between brokers and underwriters and the unfair advantages taken of their customer by retail banks.[74] In the view of the Fraud Advisory Panel: 'The Government is failing in its duty to protect the citizen from fraud because it refuses to spend the relatively small sum required'.[75]

9. Wrecks and Crashes – Destabilising the System?

The race is highly competitive. As the field grows, those who want to lead the pack are under pressure to take even greater risks – to move into more dangerous areas to devise new types of derivative, to take on more debt. But there is also danger for those who follow the herd since a drastic mistake by one is likely to affect all. It could even be argued that dramatic crashes involving one or two top drivers are not the main problem. True, that's not the way it once looked. In 1998, when the mighty so-called Long Term Capital Management hedge fund unexpectedly lost nearly 90% of its capital in the wake of the South East Asian and Russian crises, there were fears that it might have disastrous implications throughout the system, which is why 14 of the largest US and European financial institutions, encouraged by the US Federal Reserve Bank, took part in a major $3.6 billion rescue operation.[76] But since then, some claim, the system is better prepared to take such individual accidents in stride. In 2003, when Parmalat went bankrupt, with the 'disappearance' of as much as €10 billion, there were relatively few repercussions. The then Financial Secretary to the Treasury Ruth Kelly noted that this was at least in part due to the increasingly widespread use of default swaps.[77] More recently, in September 2006 when Amaranth Advisors made a wrong investment in natural gas and suffered a loss of $6 billion – the second largest loss ever seen in the sector – the system did not go into meltdown, nor did it a month later when Vega, whose assets under management had increased 5-fold in less than two years, lost its bet that Japanese, US and European bonds would not rally. Perhaps people are better prepared. In any case there have been entrepreneurs who make money out of wrecks and casualties since Dickens' time, and some have recognized that even in financialized capitalism, there is money to be made from failing companies and from 'distressed debt'.

Nevertheless the fear of instability is well-founded. It arises both from the possibility of unforeseen changes in the economic or political environment and from the fact there are extensive and complex networks of interdependencies throughout the system, particularly in the levels of highly leveraged unsecured debt which could affect every driver. One fear is that changes in the economic environment could cause some drivers to sit it out for a while or to pull out of the race. Thus, in 2004, when interest rates began to rise and when the hedge fund market was beginning to show lower rates of return, the Bank of England warned that too rapid an exodus from hedge funds could trigger problems in liquidity and stability.[78] A year later Alan Greenspan warned: 'One such concern is the potential for rapid outflows from the sector in the event that returns prove disappointing. Disappointments seem highly likely given the number of recent investors in this sector....[Furthermore] If institutional money proves to be 'hot money,' hedge funds could become subject to funding pressures that would impair their ability to supply liquidity to markets and might cause them to add to demands on market liquidity. Another circumstance in which hedge funds could negatively affect market liquidity is if they became so leveraged that adverse market movements could lead to their failure and force their counter parties to close out their positions and liquidate their collateral.'[79] In November 2006 the Financial Services Authority warned of the inevitability of a default of a large private-equity backed company, in the event, for example, that a downturn in the economy meant that such firms – several of which are each in the range of £5–13 billion – could not service their debts.[80]

But it is one thing to recognize the threat of instability, it is quite another to develop adequate defences. Neither the imposition of government controls nor simple faith in markets provide any firm guarantee. For some drivers have developed an ability to exploit whatever system happens to be in place. Thus when currency synchronization was attempted in the form of the European Exchange Rate Mechanism it proved a field day for speculators. The economies of the UK and Italy proved virtually defenceless as they tried vainly in 1992 to keep within the rules of the Exchange Rate Mechanism.[81] Ironically, one of the biggest beneficiaries of the fiasco, George Soros, has become one of the fiercest critics of purely deregulated global financial markets.[82] For, when the neo-liberal Washington Consensus held sway, once again speculators had a field day playing off one South East Asian currency against another and against the global markets.

Some look at the diversity of hedge funds and the sophistication of their instruments and strategies and take comfort from that. But others are more worried, precisely because the complexity and lack of transparency in the present situation means that no one knows for certain the interlocking pattern of financial instruments and institutions and how a collapse in a few could spread through the system.

There are indeed signs, at the time of writing, that many hedge funds are badly over-exposed and that a crisis may be brewing.[83] The European Union is preparing a Green Paper to look at ways in which scrutiny of fund activity can be improved.[84] In New York international regulators met financial industry leaders to identify what steps to take so as to ensure that a hedge fund collapse does not trigger a wider financial crisis. In London in November 2006 the Deputy Governor of the Bank of England, Sir John Gieve, noting that the Bank, the FSA and the Treasury regularly simulate crises and responses, warned that similar exercises needed to be undertaken at a global level to address possible crisis scenarios.[85]

10. Who Makes and Services the Lorries? Workers as an Afterthought?

Underlying the abstract money-value of share-prices, currencies and commodities is their real value. That is measured not by the stock market but by the usefulness of the things that are made and the services that are rendered. To use the image of the makers and servicers of the lorries that are being driven in this frantic race is to take them as a symbol for all those who make real things and render real services. It is an apt symbol in the sense that the automobile manufacturing industry is one where the effects of the 'new capitalism' are particularly evident.

To take the beneficial effects first, the theory is that hypercapitalism, by encouraging risk-taking and by stepping up the pressure on firms to perform well has helped workers in two ways. The first is by promoting growth that might not otherwise have occurred especially in today's very risky environment. And growth translates into jobs for workers not just into profits for capitalists. A further way in which the process has helped workers is that as consumers they can pay less for a wider range of goods, often of improved quality as prices are forced down.

But that is only part of the story. There are three very negative effects on workers as well – inequality, insecurity, and a scarcity of basic goods. First the unequal distribution of the benefits. In Britain in 2005 profits were the highest since records began in 1965, but real median earnings (after adjustment for inflation) actually fell by 0.4% and there is a connection. According to a memo from Goldman Sachs: 'Several factors have contributed to the rise in profit margins.

The most important is a decline in labour's share of national income.'[86] In 2000 the median earnings (including bonuses and incentive awards) of FTSE 100 Chief Executives was 39 times that of all full-time employees; by July 2006 it was 98 times more.[87] In 2005, some 3,000 employees in the London's financial centre each reaped bonuses of at least £1 million; in 2006 the number was likely to rise to 4,000 according to a forecast by the Centre for Economics and Business Research.[88] The picture is similar in the US, where average wages for non-managerial workers have fallen by 0.6% since the fourth quarter of 2001,[89] while between 1998 and 2005 real median family income (including wages) actually declined.[90] It is true even in China, where the degree of inequality was once one of the lowest in the world, but is now worse than that of Russia or even the US.[91]

At one end is a new class of hyper-rich. Investors, successful entrepreneurs and city dealers are doing obscenely-well. At the other end are those who are excluded from the game. They live – or struggle to survive – in both developed and developing countries. They comprise what Pope John Paul II and others have come to refer to as 'The Fourth World'.[92] In between, it is claimed that many of the poor have become less poor while many of the working class and lower middle class have become less well-off.[93]

But it is not just at the level of wages that workers are hit by the processes of contemporary capitalism. They are threatened with insecurity both in the present, in terms of jobs and in the future in terms of pensions. Even with company profits at record levels, company pension funds are running deficits and even closing down. The top 100 companies on the Financial Times Stock Exchange Index could be facing a funding gap of as much as £100 billion according to a report by Pension Capital Strategies on 16 October 2006. This is more than twice the official estimated deficit of £46 billion which, it is claimed, may have underestimated the effects of longevity.[94] And while occupational pension funds are capping benefits, or even closing down altogether, state pension benefits are kept low. Even private pension funds are too often found to be not what unsuspecting purchasers thought they were buying.

Meanwhile, work is increasingly being out-sourced to developing countries,[95] while labour is being recruited from developing countries, especially in the retail, catering and clothing trades, in health and personal care services. There is now an emerging global labour market. The fact that labour is cheap in the developing countries is used to keep wages down and jobs insecure in developed countries as well. And labour in developing countries is being deliberately kept cheap.Labour rights are restricted, trade union organisers are imprisoned and even assassinated, and slavery itself is rife. Transnationals often collude with local politicians to ensure that wages and conditions in these areas are kept low.[96] This in turn also creates pressure on workers in the more developed countries in that employers can keep a lid on wages whilst demanding more from ever smaller workforces by threatening to ship jobs abroad. As if that were not enough, many employers in the United States are taking positive measures to keep workers from joining unions.[97] The reality is, as Marx pointed out long ago, that capital is mobile (and is now more so than ever) while labour is far less so.

A third detrimental effect on workers is to do with their access to goods which meet the most fundamental of human needs such as health care, housing and leisure. This is being sharply felt in developed countries where such a premium is being put on labour-intensive industries (such as caring), on land (needed for housing) and on time. It is felt even more severely in developing countries. Medicines and drugs are being diverted from people and places where they are most needed to areas where they are most profitable. The rise in oil prices, brought on both by the heavy demand for it in developed countries and by the trading in commodities – as much as $8–10 of the increase per barrel has been attributed to speculative trading on future prices[98] – has negated many of the benefits which debt relief had brought to Heavily Indebted Poor Countries.[99]

Gradually, workers are attempting to join forces to address this new situation. In November 2006, the World Confederation of Labour (which originated in 1920 as a Christian trade union movement) and the International Confederation of Free Trade Unions (which split from the Communist-dominated World Federation of Trade Unions in 1949) merged to form the International Trade Union Confederation.[100]

In the US, the need to ensure that the benefits of globalization are more evenly distributed is being taken up on all sides. One sign that it is on the political agenda is the launching by the New Democratic Network in February 2006 of the Globalization Initiative led by former Under Secretary of Commerce Robert J. Shapiro.[101] A sign that it is on the economic agenda is the attention it was given at the meeting of the US Federal Reserve in August 2006 and by the insistence of its new Chair, Ben Bernanke, on the need to find ways of sharing benefits.[102]

So What's New?

The new capitalism is about the financialization of capital. There is no doubt that this is causing major transformations in the shape of capitalism. It is transforming the race so that smaller drivers, whether as managers of hedge funds or as private equity entrepreneurs are challenging the big boys, with a little bit of help from the new technology and a lot of help from banks and investors willing to lend. The pace and scale of private equity buy-outs has raised fears of the privatization of large sections of the global economy.[103] It is transforming the way the race is run – making it faster, more competitive and far riskier. Practices that were once thought of as dubious or as too risky are becoming respectable. It is transforming the landscape in both banking, which is becoming less local and more global, less linked to long-term investment industry and more geared up to help fund the frantic race for profit – indeed to join in the race themselves – and also in industry, with the emergence of new global firms being built up by entrepreneurs in India, Latin America and the Middle East which is beginning to challenge the traditional European- and North American- centred pattern of globalization.

But if the shape of contemporary capitalism is new the logic is certainly not. What is happening is fundamentally an acceleration and intensification of the basic processes of capitalism that have long been identified: a) codification as capital of assets, whether material, cultural, social or environmental; b) commodification into saleable items of goods, services, skills, etc; c) marketization of relations that might otherwise be voluntary, mutual or associational: and, behind it all, d) accumulation of ever greater and more productive capital – all processes which tend to generate not just inequality but class divisions. The working class, far from having been abolished, has now become globalized – and pitted against itself.

This is not a new capitalism. It is undiluted capitalism in a less inhibited, less disguised and less apologetic form. The answer is not a politics of envy. That is to mistake individuals (capitalists) for the system (capitalism). Nor is it crude class warfare (both because classes are more fragmented and because the benefits and losses have affected all classes albeit in greatly different ways). The real issue is about how far society, culture and the environment can withstand such inroads of capitalist forces and how far these are debasing our civilization and corrupting economic activity itself.

Luttwak sums up the result of what he calls turbo-capitalism: 'societies now serve economies rather than the other way around....'[104] It is, indeed, hard to escape the conclusion that what the new capitalism amounts to is a resumption, after an interval of two generations, of the sort of *Great Transformation*, which Karl Polanyi had seen slowly developing from the 16th to the 19th centuries and which had had such cataclysmic results. For Polanyi that transformation was an aberration in both anthropological and historical terms. The market society which had been allowed to develop was unnatural in that it involved the subordination and reconstruction of society according to the demands of the economy rather than ensuring that economic activity helped to enrich the life of society. Instead of being simply one mechanism of allocation, alongside exchanges based on reciprocity, mutuality and pure giving, the principles, values and dictates of the market were accorded the right to rule.

The transformations which capitalism has undergone have taken place, as always, within a wider social, cultural and political framework. It has penetrated and colonized those areas of life to an unprecedented degree. But that very process of transformation through a kind of dialectic generates its own trans-formative processes, and may, as Polanyi has shown, make possible and call forth reactions from society, state and culture which seek new ways to express and realize their proper character and place in human life. That is one possible scenario. But they also constitute a threat of unprecedented scale to humanity and the environment which gives an exceptional urgency to the need to explore the openings to a regime change. It demands a rethinking of our economic life, beginning with a concern for the common good – that which is good for humanity and for the environment – and going on to consider the sorts of insti-tutional changes which can help promote that re-orientation of our economic activity. That will be the task of the next sections.

2. Re-orientations: Transforming Economic Culture: Theological Perspectives

The direct effects of 'preaching' about economic relations and obligations are in general bad; and the kind of legislation which results from the clamor of idealistic preachers...is especially bad.
Frank Knight [105]

Time for a Rethink

It is time for a rethink not just in the sense that past economic systems have proved problematic but because time is running out. There is an urgency about our situation which makes the debate more than academic. Our social fabric is being undermined, and our eco-system is being assaulted. We are compet-ing for a limited and, in some cases, shrinking supply of natural resources, whether of oil and gas, minerals or even fish and water, and are thus setting the scene for desperate international struggles. We are creating ways of life that are simply unsustainable – socially, ecologically, aesthetically and ethically. So far the responses have consisted of a mixture of technological improvements in efficiency, pressure group protests, international agreements and laws, trading in 'permits to pollute', an increased sense of corporate responsibility and a dose of ecological asceticism. Will these be enough? The argument here is that they will not. Rather what is needed is a transformation of economic life so that it is grounded more firmly in a vision of the common good and thus becomes a 'good economy'.

Fortunately we are in a period when theologians and economists, workers and managers, consumers and shareholders are seriously rethinking the basis, structure and direction of economic life. The folly of 'market fundamentalism' has been mercilessly exposed not just by anti-capitalists but by the likes of Joseph Stiglitz, former Chief Economist at the World Bank, whose arguments can claim support from the United Nations Conference on Trade and Development, and by John Kay, former Professor of Economics at the London Business School and director of the Institute for Fiscal Studies. Kay is withering on the blinkered approach taken to markets by the dominant American business model: 'The countries that most closely resemble its prescriptions of unrestrained individualism with minimal government are among the poorest on the planet.'[106] But developed countries, too, have been burnt: 'No country has modelled its policies more deliberately on the American business model – applause for self-interest, market fundamentalism and the rolling back of the economic and redistributive functions of the state – than New Zealand after 1984, not even the United States....From 1984 to 1999 New Zealand followed policies of privatization and deregulation, and pursued labour market flexibility and reductions in social benefits. During this period, the country experienced the worst economic performance of any rich state.'

The United Nations Conference on Trade and Development, for its part, has found that excessive reliance on market forces was detrimental to countries with the least developed economies.[107] Narayan Ramachandran, Managing Director of the TD (Toronto Dominion) Emerging Markets Fund, argues that, in the changed economic environment following the bursting of the dotcom bubble, the emergence of excess demand and the trend towards disinflation, the best growth is being achieved by countries, such as Thailand, South Korea and China, which have refused to subscribe to the Washington Consensus.[108]

The move from market fundamentalism has generated a new openness to rethink the nature of economic life and to engage in dialogue so that different perspectives may be brought to bear. There are encouraging signs. People like George Soros and James Wolfensohn of the World Bank have been willing to enter into dialogue with critics, including the World Social Forum. Indeed, the World Social Forum itself is seeking to encourage dialogue amongst its participants. It is a golden moment for Christians to be engaged as well.

What goes into a rethink?

Economists have given us some clues. First, there is a growing consensus about the fact that economic systems depend on social institutions: 'The difference between rich and poor states is the result of differences in the quality of their economic institutions,' is Kay's message.[109] It is a theme echoed by de Soto, Stiglitz and Soros, as well as by Raymond Plant. It was the thesis of Karl Polanyi's classic study, *The Great Transformation*. Fortunately, it can draw on rich traditions of institutional and evolutionary economic theory, which have been enjoying a new burst of life in the past decade.[110]

A second part of the contemporary economic rethink is the recognition of the need to integrate economic growth with social and environmental welfare at every level. That is to say: a) at the level of output, so that what is produced is actually conducive to well-being; b) at the level of labour, so that in the process of production there is a saner balance between work and leisure, caring and producing; and c) at the level of material resources, renewable resources (such as water, air, the ozone, fish stocks, etc.) and waste products (such as pollutants), so that, as Michael Jacobs, leader of the 1997 Towards Social Transformation seminar stressed, these are no longer treated as mere 'externalities'.

Economic theory is well into its rethink. What about economic theology? What is its competence? And what is its added value? It is not that Christian faith has privileged access to better economic methods and models that will help create a 'Christian economic system'. But neither is it simply about motives and values. It is about not letting economics be defined as a purely technical or secular enterprise. It is about providing perspectives (different Christian traditions have different contributions to offer) in which economic activity and relationships may be interpreted, so that with the help of such perspectives: a) the purposes of economic life may be seen more clearly (the nature of a 'good economy'); and b) that a framework of meaning may be articulated so that judgments about economic relationships and priorities may not be made on the basis of power alone (the nature of a 'common culture').[111] Here that theological task will be approached on two fronts: a critical front, which asks hard questions about the existing economic regime, and then a constructive front, which suggests the sorts of things which might help bring into focus a more desirable economy. On the critical front are Ulrich Duchrow (the confessional mode) and David Jenkins (the interrogative mode); on the constructive front are attempts by Peter Heslam (the salvation history mode) and by the present writer (building on the notions of civil society and a common culture, as developed in the previous two chapters).

Criticism: The Confessional Mode

Capitalist religion, Capitalism and certainty of salvation are siblings nurtured
by the same milk. Both are a) seizures of property [and] b) seizures of God.
Therefore, with reason, protest by Bolshevism against the capitalist Christ.
Dietrich Bonhoeffer [112]

As John Atherton's historical review makes clear, the churches have tradition-ally viewed capitalism with suspicion – whether from a conservative, liberal or radical perspective.[113] Among contemporary theologians, few have applied a radical critique of capitalism with more persistence and theological vigour than Ulrich Duchrow in his work with the World Alliance of Reformed Churches and with Kairos Europa. For Duchrow, capitalism's totalizing logic, having been built from the beginning on exploitation and injustice, has now entered a stage where it is colonizing life itself – turning ecological life (water, climate), animal life, vegetative life (genetically modified foods), intellectual life (intellectual patents) into commodities, and threatening to destroy our very life support systems. So profound is the threat posed by capitalism to human and ecological life and so irredeemably is this connected with its system of values and struc-ture of capital, that it must be seen as a system totally in conflict with the will of God. Duchrow sees capitalism as connected with the wider system of imperialism 'global interconnected fascism' and weapons of mass destruction.[114] Tyrannical, totalitarian, idolatrous and death-dealing, the regime of capital-ism means: 'we are faced not simply with a question of ethics but with the choice between God and false god, between true worship and idolatry.'[115] It is a religious issue. It would be tempting – but mistaken – to conclude from the rhetoric that Duchrow is adopting a Manichean approach, as if capitalism were the incarnation of absolute evil. In fact, he is working contextually, arguing that the present state of affairs demands a confessional approach.

The challenge this poses to the church's integrity is, Duchrow argues, comparable to that posed by Nazism in Germany and by apartheid in South Africa. The only appropriate response is one similar to that of the 'Confessing Church' particularly as given a social dimension by Dietrich Bonhoeffer.[116] The call for confession is directed first and foremost to the church itself. It is a question of confessing both its complicity with a system that is effectively anti-Christ and of confessing the lordship of Christ over economic and political life. A 'confessional stance', such as that adopted by the South African churches in their Kairos Declaration, considers any churches which cooperate with radically anti-Christian systems guilty of practical heresy.

Duchrow formulated this argument nearly twenty years ago and has consistently urged the churches to develop a *'processus confessionis'*.[117] He views the subsequent development of capitalism as strengthening not weakening his case.[118] What that implies is that: 'The starting point for a confessing church is its own repentance, not the exclusion of others.'[119] Confessional words must be backed up by confessional practice, insists Duchrow. This means, among other things, that: 'The Churches must immediately withdraw their money from all commercial banks engaging in financial transactions for property accumulation on the international markets, and invest their money in their own cooperatives, local and regional banks that do not operate on the world market, or in alternative banks with interest rates not exceeding the growth rate of the real economy and which invest responsibly in social and ecological causes....Churches must sell all their stocks in companies that make their profits by the rules of the global market, i.e. without a commitment to society and life....'[120]

Criticism: The Interrogative Mode

...the earth, in turn, may not be able to afford to sustain capitalism much longer. Capitalism – that is – as currently practised and pursued.
David Jenkins [121]

John Atherton made it clear that markets should neither be rejected nor uncritically affirmed, but 'interrogated'.[122] David Jenkins, former Bishop of Durham, has taken up the challenge of interrogating the market economy with typical gusto. For all the talk about free markets and social markets, markets also represent structures of power that need to be challenged: 'Bankers run the world.... Where market processes threaten the money-making powers of the West, they are forcibly manipulated to preserve – or even to enhance – these powers.' For Jenkins, who had done such important work as Director of Humanum Studies for the World Council of Churches, the issue boils down to one of common humanity: 'This [the Free Market system] is not a decent way of being oneself or of treating one's fellow human beings. This corrupting falsity and indecency are endemic in the Free Market system as it is worked at present by the financial and business powers-that-be.' The answer is not so much an alternative system, argues Jenkins, but an alternative way of looking at the world and an alternative way of living. Jenkins does not categorically condemn capitalism, but he clearly points us in another direction: 'Our capacities for enterprise, innovation and trade have to be directed into a second wealth-creating system which corrects the excesses and nonsenses which the present one has arrived at.'[123]

His challenge is about a new sense of responsibility, expressed both at the personal level and through the development of democratic debate.

Constructive Dialogue: Salvation History

If there is to be new thinking about economics, then the point made by Peter Heslam, Director of Transforming Business at Cambridge University and co-ordinator of the London Institute of Contemporary Christianity's Capitalism Project, is important: 'There are other languages that need to be heard, and to be heard together, such as those of human dignity, the integrity of creation, justice and peace....People are able to understand each other again [after the fall and in the power of the Spirit] not because they return to a common language but because they are enabled to speak the language of others....'[124] It is the claim of markets to be the only valid economic language that needs to be challenged. Heslam is rightly insistent that distinctive Christian voices be heard, but as part of a wider dialogue.

Heslam then puts capitalism in perspective, employing the framework of salvation history. We live 'between the times,' Heslam comments. This will help Christians discern what to affirm and what to condemn about the process of globalization as well as to find ways of witnessing to better patterns of economic life. Thus, from the perspective of creation, economic activity is a way of glorifying God, expressing our relationships with one another, and of caring for creation. In this context, markets, competition, and economic growth all may be of service but also need to know their limits. From the perspective of the fall, however, come covetousness, strife and the transgressing of limits. Markets become flawed, economic interests dominate the state, poverty increases and the common good is lost. Economic activity takes on an element of the idolatrous and demonic. From the perspective of redemption, comes salvation not in the form of new technologies and new movements for reform but through the cross. A central dimension of the sort of liberation and redemption it brings is through the releasing of the debt which is borne, especially by the poor. The fourth stage is that of consummation. This implies that, whilst recognizing the imperfection of any reforms, Christians are also called to keep alive signs and anticipations of what is to come: and, therefore, to 'point to hopeful signs of change and seek imaginatively for alternatives.'

Constructive Dialogue: A Good Economy

Unlike material possessions, goodness is not diminished when it is shared, either momentarily or permanently, with others, but expands and, in fact, the more heartily each of the lovers of goodness enjoys the possession the more does goodness grow.

Augustine of Hippo [125]

Each of the three approaches just mentioned helps, in different ways, to stimulate the process of getting the economy in perspective in the light of Christian faith. The approach which will be developed next suggests that fundamental to any rethink is the need constantly to try to bring into focus what is meant by a 'good economy'. This approach, of course, needs to be understood within the framework of salvation history, as Heslam insists, and not on the basis of some abstract, purely philosophical notion of the good. The good is is not fully realized, but is, as Augustine's transformationist theology has it, participated in, partially and by way of analogy, by means of the healing of desire and of freedom from the *libido dominandi*.

From this perspective, the argument will draw on the themes discussed in Chapter Two (the scope for free association in civil society) and in Chapter Three (a common culture understood as equality of ability to participate in the 'articulation of meanings and values and in the consequent decisions between this meaning and that, this value and that'). As in any discussion, the key is to ask the right question. The argument here is that questions about exchange mechanisms (the market), distribution (justice), and even growth are secondary. The central question is about the production, sharing and enjoyment of the good – or, to put it in other words, about how economic activity can be part of the good life and can promote the common good. How the common good is discovered, it was argued in the previous chapter, was by way of participation – which means not just any sort of shared activity but precisely a participation in the good. That is why the first dimension to be explored here is that of participation.

The Good Economy: Participation in What?

...the purpose of a business firm is not simply to make a profit, but is to be found in its very existence as a community of persons who in various ways are endeavouring to satisfy their basic needs, and who form a particular group at the service of the whole of society....A business cannot be considered only as a 'society of capital goods'; it is also a 'society of persons' in which people participate in different ways.

John Paul II [126]

Whether participation is good or not depends on what one is participating in. Participation in the labour market has been the central plank of Western governments' recent attempts to transform and salvage the welfare state. Active labour policies are promoted as having moral and social value as well as economic advantage. Participation in economic life is being equated with being in paid employment. But what makes participation desirable is the extent to which it is a participation in the good. To participate in the making of products which are likely to be damaging to public health or environmental welfare, to participate in exploiting human labour, to participate in devising schemes for tax evasion are hardly aspects of good economic activity.

The sort of participation which Raymond Williams referred to, as seen in the previous chapter, was a more creative activity – participation in the articulation of meanings and values. Translated into economic life this would mean having some ability to influence what was being produced, how, for what purpose and for whom. It would begin not with concerns about profits and pay but with the intrinsic value of what was being done. That is to say that it would value – and therefore reward appropriately – not only participation in the formal economy but also participation in the informal economy of the household and neighbourhood. Within the formal economy, it would value – and therefore create opportunities for – participation both at micro-level, in a firm's research, planning, work-organization, investment, recruitment, equal opportunities policies, pension arrangements, etc., and, at macro-level, in decisions about the location of industries, environmental impacts, ethical investment, etc.

The Good Economy: True Wealth

Economic activity involves production, exchange and consumption. At each level, the presence of the good can exercise its own influence. At the level of production, the issue is about the production not simply of 'goods' (although the persistence of the term is significant) but about that which is good and which serves a good purpose. Current concern about 'quality control' is helpful. But quality can refer simply to serviceability. Current concern about wealth creation is important, so long as what is produced is not what John Ruskin described as 'illth'. The good is that which is characterized by an inherent desirability, beauty and ability to enrich life. Long before Duchrow developed his theology of the economy in the service of life, John Ruskin compared the bastard science of political economy of his time to witchcraft, being 'in the service of Death, the Lord of Waste and of eternal emptiness'. In contrast, the true science of political economy was like medicine in 'the service of Wisdom, the Lady of Saving, and of eternal fulness'.[127]

At the level of exchange, markets need to be seen as only one form of exchange. As Karl Polanyi in his anthropological studies has noted, societies have managed to provide more scope for reciprocity and pure giving than occurs in a 'market society'. To dismiss these as 'pre-modern' is, as has repeatedly been stressed, to succumb to the ideology of the present and to deny our radical historicity. It is also to deny the nature of the good, whose very nature tends towards outpouring ('*Bonum est diffusivum sui*' in the words of Thomas Aquinas[128]). Thus a perspective is offered which not only justifies but actually encourages the expansion of economic space for giving, sharing and for forgiving debts. This fundamental challenge to the ideology of 'possessive individualism' is rooted not in an argument for some other economic system but in ontology.

At the level of consumption, the emergence of the 'consumer society' has also brought with it its own critique, which focuses on the way desire itself has been colonized, and diverted from its true end by contemporary capitalism. Gilles Deleuze has portrayed capitalism as 'the discipline of desire'.[129] The centrality of desire and the need to heal it from the distortions of capitalist modernity has been a major preoccupation of the Radical Orthodoxy network, particularly in the work of Daniel M. Bell, Jr. and Graham Ward. According to Bell, the 'discipline of desire' was always part of capitalism's regime. But in the formative period of capitalism, that desire was suppressed, repressed and sublimated – with the help of the Protestant ethic – in an asceticism that stressed the need to work, to save, and to defer gratification. Today a consumer culture recasts rather than removes the discipline. Gratification now and payment deferred is the new rule – an arrangement which suits finance capital rather nicely by generating high rates of interest on credit. The ultimate answer to capitalism, argues Bell, is the development of the sort of alternative 'technologies of desire' that are offered by Christian spirituality, the chief of which is forgiveness, which makes possible the true 'liberation of desire' through a reorientation to the good.

From New Thinking to New Institutions

The preceding part of the rethink has been about the gaining of perspective, in the light of Christian faith. Another part has been about the recovering, with the help of economic theory, of the importance of the social dimensions of economic life. The next step is to see what bearing insights about the social might have on the institutional framework of economic life. If an economic system is to work efficiently, if people are to be participants and if economic activity is to contribute to a realization of the common good, then it also needs to be supported by the right sort of institutions.

There are many different institutional options on the path towards social transformation. In the following section, a range of different institutional patterns will be set out, adapting the grid which was used in Chapter Two to delineate the various understandings of civil society.

3. Transforming Economic Structures
– Societies, Markets and States

The social has been diminished; capitalism remains.
Richard Sennett on the demise of social capitalism [130]

There is no saving economic system. We need to develop institutions and organizations which will accept perpetual provisionality, monitoring and reordering, related to open experimentation and participation.
David Jenkins [131]

The purpose of the grid (see opposite), as explained in Chapter Two, is to show how different approaches give different weights to the roles of community and individuality, authority and spontaneity. There, the aim was to show the different projects for Civil Society. Here the aim is to show the different approaches to a good economy. As in Chapter Two, the point is to show that each of the different projects finds a place for individuality and community, just as each assigns a different role to authority and to spontaneity. All agree that economic activity needs some sort of co-ordination and that this involves a mix of what Grahame Thompson, joint leader of the 1992 Towards Social Transformation, has described as 'markets, hierarchies and networks'. [132]

The crisis of the 1970s led to a reaction against excessive reliance on the state. Increasingly this has become an over-reaction leading to an excessive reliance on markets. In both cases what has been neglected is the potential co-ordinating role of society. John Monks, former Secretary General the TUC recently described the current situation as: '…a yet further disintegration of the social nexus between worker and employer. This relationship, dating back to the industrial revolution and beyond, has produced… a culture containing broad social rights and obligations. The new capitalism wants none of it.'[133] That is why some have been calling for a global social contract.[134] But what is needed is more than just a new social contract. New institutional arrangements are needed as well so as not only to put the social back into social capitalism but also to prepare the ground for a proper harmony between markets, state and society. That means trying new models and creative ways of moving towards them. For that reason it was both encouraging and surprising that, just as the original manuscript for the present book was sent to the publisher, an approach strikingly similar to the one described below was published by Erik Olin Wright.[135] Surprising in that our two approaches had been arrived at completely independently with absolutely no contact, direct or indirect, between the two authors. Encouraging because both focus on the potential within civil society for moving towards new kinds of socialism, in which economic power is subordinated to social power enabling economic activity to meet social needs and overcoming the domination of society by one social class. Wright, who for over a decade has been hosting a 'Real Utopias' initiative, distinguishes three elements to such a project – the part that is desirable (the utopian element) and the parts that are viable and achievable (the 'real' parts). Viability refers to models that would actually work even if less than ideal. Achievability takes account of the

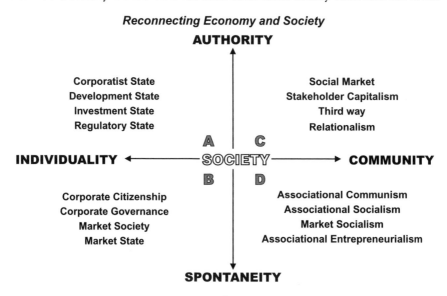

Reconnecting Economy and Society

AUTHORITY

Corporatist State	Social Market
Development State	Stakeholder Capitalism
Investment State	Third way
Regulatory State	Relationalism

A   C

INDIVIDUALITY ←———— **SOCIETY** ————→ **COMMUNITY**

B   D

Corporate Citizenship	Associational Communism
Corporate Governance	Associational Socialism
Market Society	Market Socialism
Market State	Associational Entrepreneurialism

SPONTANEITY

fact that we have to start from where we are, and that particular social and historical contexts offer both their own possibilities and limitations. That, he argues, is where a theory of transformation is needed, to help ensure that partial and imperfect measures are used not as mere compromises but as stages in a process.

Space does not permit a full exploration of all four quadrants. The focus here will be on Quadrants C (social market and stake-holding) and D (market socialism and associational economic activity). This is because both seek in their own ways to give fuller weight to the social dimensions of the economy. This is where alternatives to the present and recent past are most likely to emerge. The starting point, however, will be with a brief look at Quadrants B (market-led economies) and A (state-led economies).

Quadrant B: Markets with a Conscience?

> …it is very doubtful that markets can secure their own legitimacy. They do not necessarily protect liberty, they are indifferent to any distributional outcome, they may not be able to secure the echelon advance towards rising prosperity, and they may at some point begin to deplete the moral underpinnings upon which their own operations rest.
>
> Raymond Plant [136]

We start with quadrant B so as to acknowledge the genuine reforms that various promoters of 'free enterprise' have undertaken in recent years to contain some of the more scandalous and disruptive practices of the 1990's version of the new capitalism. It is impossible here to begin to do justice to the considerable range of initiatives for greater corporate social responsibility. What can be done is to point to two main types of reform – corporate governance and corporate citizenship. Corporate governance is about a firm's own efficiency and effectiveness, its financial integrity (transparency and accuracy of accounts) and management (clarity of roles, accountability, performance). Corporate citizenship is largely about the impact of the firm's activities on society and the environment.

Corporate Governance

Capitalism cannot function when investors suspect that firms are not giving them a true picture. Yet although the reform of Corporate Governance had been on the agenda for a decade, it did not prevent the debacles of Enron, WorldCom and Parmalat. [137] Reform is still needed to ensure that auditors do not have a vested interest in turning a blind eye to questionable practices, that board members are competent and genuinely independent, that accounts are designed to make transparent rather than to obscure the actual nature of financial transactions, profits and liabilities, that performance is improved, that poor managers are not rewarded with unjustified pay packages, that legal responsibilities are clearly stated and observed, etc. The approaches to corporate governance reform have varied. The US has, typically, resorted to rigid legislation,[138] while the UK has sought to encourage, as far as possible, flexible, voluntary compliance. In Europe the focal point has been the European Commission's development of International Accounting Standards. The OECD's *Principles of Corporate Governance* (1999; revised 2004) have been widely welcomed.[139] Adding to the pressure for reform have been the important campaigning activities of organizations such as Transparency International to combat corruption,[140] and the Pensions Investment Research Consultants, pressing for more responsible practices on the part of pension funds.[141]

The notion of corporate governance itself has begun to develop in ways that incorporate more democratic modes of action and that encourage shareholders to look to the longer term future of the firms in which they invest. Ira Millstein, a leading figure in the US world of corporate governance, has stressed the responsibilities, not just the rights, of investors. In April 2005, Sir John Sunderland, then President of the Confederation of British Industry called on shareholders to behave as owners not just rentiers. There is even a movement amongst shareholders themselves, notably Governance for Owners, to help ensure that their search for value includes a concern for the longer-term future and productivity of the companies in which they invest.[142]

Corporate Citizenship

'Corporate Citizenship' is a term used to cover a variety of activities ranging from treatment of a firm's own staff to its impact on social and environmental well-being. It has become a focal point for joint discussion between businesses, governments and non-governmental organizations and was given a huge boost at global level, in July 2002, with the UN Global Compact on Corporate Citizenship and its Principles for Responsible Investment Project (2005).[143]

Some initiatives have come from within the business community itself, such as Business in the Community to assist local projects,[144] and the International Finance Corporation's 'Equator Principles' aimed at fostering a global banking framework to help ensure that loans made for development meet certain conditions for sustainability.[145] Yet according to criteria devised by AccountAbility, the world's 100 largest corporations scored an average of just 24 out of 100 points in 2003.[146]

Other initiatives have come from governments. Besides including corporate responsibility amongst the tasks of a junior minister, the government has enacted legislation requiring company directors to: '[amongst other matters] have regard to ...the impact of the company's operations on the community and the environment...' and to include this as part of the business review in the directors' report.[147]

Some of the most significant initiatives have come from NGOs and other movements within civil society, which have been working effectively to make capitalist practice more responsible, by promoting fair trade (the Fairtrade Association)[148] and ethical trade (the Ethical Trading Initiative),[149] by exercising shareholder power, by pressing for more disclosure about transnational labour practices in developing countries, (the 'Publish What You Pay' Coalition),[150] by campaigning for a development tax on currency speculation (the Tobin Tax Campaign),[151] etc. In addition, consumer groups have organized to launch class-action law suits charging tobacco, fast food, asbestos-using and anti-depressant manufacturers with practices which have caused large-sale numbers of deaths and damage to health.[152]

It is important to start where we are and that means pricking the conscience of capitalism as well as letting powerful corporations see that it is in their own interest to clean up their act. But pressure-group activity does not fundamentally change the structures of capitalism. To do that means exploring the possibilities of the sorts of transformation which will ensure that social and environmental factors are fully represented within the structures of the economy rather than voices from the street. And that leads to a consideration of the other three quadrants depicted on the grid.

Quadrant A: Reversing the Retreat of the State

The continuing role and power of nation-states was a point made by several of the Towards Social Transformation seminar leaders. Grahame Thompson and Paul Hirst teamed up to show, on the basis of hard economic data, the continuing importance of national and regional economic activity.

After a period of flirtation with the idea that the retreat of the state would be the key to economic well-being, there has been 'a return of the state'. This by no means signals a revival of corporatism or of the command economy. Rather it is a matter of redefining the legitimate role of government. Principally this has been in order to enable economic activity to proceed in a more efficient manner.

But state action is also needed so as to ensure that economic activity is not allowed to create social chaos or political unrest. Here two types of state action will be looked at, using the broad headings of intervention and partnership.

Intervention

There are a number of areas where, for social or political reasons, governments are showing a new assertiveness – most dramatically in the 'energy nationalism' being pursued by socialist governments in Latin America. Other interventions are more defensive. These include limiting the impact of imports (tariffs), favouring certain domestic industries (subsidies), ensuring financial stability (support for exchange rates, blocking foreign takeovers), etc. To pin labels such as 'protectionism' on such activities begs the question. Most agree that 'protectionism' would be disastrous – the threat is real – but the controversies that are regularly brought to the World Trade Organization for adjudication often reflect quite legitimate and complex conflicts of interest. Fair trade simply cannot be equated with free trade. Account needs to be taken of the sheer power of transnational corporations and of global investment firms and their lack of commitment to the long-term well-being of particular countries. It is true that tariffs and subsidies often do encourage inefficient production and sometimes do give most to those who need them least, but they may also be designed in ways which protect independent farmers, small businesses and local communities.

Recent controversy over the Central American Free Trade Agreement (CAFTA-DR) illustrates the point. Opposition came on the one hand from powerful vested interests in the US and, on the other, from the weak small farmers and embattled workers' organizations in Central America.[153]

Certainly that supposed champion of globalization and of free markets, namely the United States, relies heavily on the state to provide huge subsidies to agriculture and key industries, to impose heavy tariffs to protect vulnerable domestic industries such as steel, to dump goods below market price, and to arrange dubiously legal tax breaks for US corporations working abroad. That is why it has been hit with a number of adverse rulings by the World Trade Organization and, for the first time in history, the passing of trade sanctions by the European Union in March 2004.[154] Nor have the EU states been passive. Of the $257 billion received by farmers in the OECD countries in 2003, nearly half was received by EU countries.[155] The collapse of the Doha round of negotiations which were intended to improve the terms of trade for the poorest countries shows how reluctant the wealthier countries can be to reduce tariffs (EU) and subsidies (US). As with external issues such as trade, so, too, with internal issues such as privatization, it makes no economic sense to ignore the role of the state. Although privatization may stimulate innovation, efficiency and responsiveness to consumer demand, it can also lead to near-oligarchic concentrations of economic power, intense pressures on staff (accompanied by reductions in benefits such as pensions), neglect of customers whose needs are more costly to meet and whose ability to pay is less, and vulnerability to take-over by asset-strippers. Privatization needs careful management, which is one reason why China, for example, has decided not to privatise those sectors of the economy which it deems – on grounds which are not always clear – to be 'strategic'.

Partnership

Reporting on the Inter-American Development Bank Board of Governors' annual conference in Okinawa, 10–12 April 2005, Richard Lapper of the *Financial Times* notes that: 'the state is back in fashion....private partner-ship is a watchword.'[156] The following month an IMF study of Latin America concluded that: 'An improved and more strategic role of the state is essential.'[157] The same point was made in March 2005 by the Africa Commission report, which concludes that '...the building of an effective state is vital for develop-ment....The attack on the role of government [by an excessive belief in the role of the private sector] and the neglect of the building of institutions not only had medium-term economic costs in many countries, but it has also severely damaged the long-term process of building an effective state.'[158] Or, to take once again the example of China, the government has insisted that if foreign multinationals want to set up shop in China they must agree to joint venture arrangements which will help ensure a transfer of technology and of managerial know-how.

State Action: Brake or Instrument of Capitalism?

Capitalism, like any other economic system, depends upon the state if it is to flourish. It needs state action to provide a legal, fiscal and administrative framework which will encourage investment. It needs a system of rights and responsibilities to govern the tensions between capital and labour and to impose the necessary disciplines. Indeed Marx went so far as to describe governments as simply the management committees of capitalism. Although that was never quite the case in the age of nation-states, given the current deficiencies in global governance (an issue to be treated in the next chapter), there is a real danger today that nation states have increasingly become tools of the actions of transnational corporations, global financial speculators and international organizations such as the IMF, the World Bank and the WTO.

Ian Gough, joint leader of the 1993 Towards Social Transformation seminar, has undertaken comparative research in an attempt to see empirically what kinds of state-economy relationships are most productive. On the basis of six procedural and substantive criteria, the winner turned out to be 'social corporatist capitalism'.[159] Bob Jessop leader of the 1996 Towards Social Transformation seminar, has analysed the process from a more theoretical point of view, having edited the five-volume standard work on regulation theory.[160] The question is not whether economic systems in general or capitalism in particular can do without the state. They cannot. The question is rather what role in this process the state should play. It is a question that is relevant to both types of state action that have been looked at here – intervention and partnership.

The development of global capitalism does not so much lessen the need for state action as change it. Left to their own devices, hypercapitalism and turbo-capitalism will pay little heed to national interests. The new capitalism has wings and will settle in any one place for as long or as short a time as it wishes, wherever actual or potential profits appear greatest. Industrial capital can pit nation-states against each other, forcing them to outbid one another with offers of tax concessions, lighter regulation, higher subsidies, a more disciplined and productive labour force, etc. in the competition to attract foreign investment.[161] And finance capital can bring nation states to their knees in its race to keep up with changes in foreign exchange markets.

But more fundamental than questions about whether particular state policies are promoting or stifling economic activity, is the question about the impact of economic power on state and society. On the one hand is the danger, not just from the formal structures of corporatism but also from the less formal practices of lobbying groups, that the state may be colonized by special interest groups of one sort or another. At the same time there is the related question as to how far economic powers, reinforced by the state, undermine society, by weakening the spirit of collaboration and autonomous collective economic activity or by creating dependent client groups. It is the importance of identifying and encouraging the economic role of 'society' that the next two sections will address.

Quadrant C: Representing Society

Quadrant C involves restructuring the state-society relationship so as to ensure that social interests are formally included in the making of economic policy but without seeking simply to rehabilitate the old corporatist models. Without suggesting that the lines can be drawn too sharply, the difference is that whereas the tendency of quadrant A is for the state to incorporate these interests into its agenda, the aim of quadrant C is to respect the integrity of social interests as such. There are various approaches to developing the social dimension of the economy. Two – relationalism and stakeholding – will only be touched on briefly here. More attention will be given to the Social Market model. This is because, a) it has a longer track record, b) it is enshrined in the European Union's draft constitution[162] and, c) it has received significant support from churches[163] (its achievements are acknowledged even by Ulrich Duchrow). The point is to illustrate that 'There Is An Alternative' and to illustrate how considerable is the scope for creative thinking.

Relationalism

The Relational Business Programme was set up in 1997 as part of Michael Schluter's Relationships Foundation. Its vision includes promoting congruence of interest between shareholders, managers and workforce, protecting rootedness for local communities and families, developing relational finance (regional banks, debt-free equity finance, reduction of government borrowing) and seeking parity in dealings between people who act as representatives of institutions whether public or private.[164] To date, most of the practical economic work of the Programme has been at micro-level, in the public, private and voluntary sectors – building up trust and appreciation of the work done by colleagues, developing a relational culture, measuring progress by a specially designed audit. The great obstacle faced by such an approach is precisely the way the 'new capitalism' is undermining the scope for relationships.

Stakeholder Capitalism

In the period leading up to the 1997 General Election, it began to look as though stakeholder capitalism might prove to be one of New Labour's 'big ideas'. Will Hutton, now Chief Executive of The Work Foundation, had been promoting the idea with considerable effect. He shone the spotlight on the financialization of capital, its short-termism and its lack of commitment to ensuring adequate industrial capital at a lower price and on a longer-term basis. The financial system, he argued, 'needs to be comprehensively republicanised. The first step would be made by establishing a republican-style central bank which understood that its role was to recast the financial system as a servant of business rather than its master.'[165] Stakeholding, Hutton insisted, must not be confused with corporatism. Nor, warns John Kay, should stakeholding be confused with employee share ownership, which he sees as a fair weather policy: 'A society in which everyone is having a punt on the stock market is not at all the same thing [as a shared commitment between investors and employees to satisfying customers and outperforming competitive products].'[166]

Hutton was able to draw on the work of Mark Goyder, who helped the Royal Society for the Encouragement of Arts, Manufactures and Commerce to set up the Tomorrow's Company Inquiry. Its report, published in 1995, deliberately avoided using the term 'stakeholding' so as not to divert attention from the substance of its argument. It spoke rather of an inclusive approach which would take proper account of the increasing overlap between customers, investors, suppliers and employees, which would appreciate their interdependence and which would reinforce their commonality of interest.[167]

Ten years on and things had moved backwards. Short-termism, which had traditionally created problems for investment in industry, was now wreaking havoc in the savings and pensions field as well. Financial advisers were making handsome commissions by encouraging people to invest in funds whose values they knew to be unrealistically high – not just because the market was already over-heated but because they themselves were actively pushing prices still higher by investing in one another's split trust funds and using borrowed money to do so. When the bubble burst, more than twenty such funds simply collapsed. Mis-advising became common as the system provided incentives, such as higher commissions for 'churning' (encouraging savers to move from one product to another), whilst making the real value of such funds increasingly obscure. This in turn prompted more intense competition amongst providers, which meant that savers were faced with a bewildering market of over 30,000 products and therefore the need to be even more dependent on advisers. As financial scandals began to multiply, conflicts of interests between investors, sales staff and other intermediaries began to emerge, with the result that trust was shattered. Once again there were fears that savings and investment would suffer.[168] Thus a further inquiry was set up by Tomorrow's Company, whose final and more radical report urged a transformation of the financial services industry, so that through greater transparency, closer collaboration between investors and companies and agreement on higher standards, longer-term and more productive investment practice could be encouraged.[169]

The Social Market: An Idea Whose Time Has Passed?

The continental social market that spawned German post-war prosperity will be among the first casualties of global free markets.
John Gray[170]

At the time of the launch of the Towards Social Transformation initiative, the social market model was being hailed as offering the saving path that would lead beyond neo-liberalism and socialism. Even in Britain, whose more individualistic traditions might have seemed to provide less fertile ground, a Social Market Foundation had just been established.[171] John Atherton was providing a theological argument in favour of the social market.[172] According to Charles Leadbeater, joint leader of the 1992 Towards Social Transformation seminar and later adviser to the Blair Government's Policy Unit: 'Now it is the language of the social market which is articulating the aspiration to move beyond Thatcherism...the new poles of debate will be about whether the economy is free market or social market....'[173] Writing at that time from a socialist perspective, Leadbeater, though not converted to the model, saw it as having the advantage of shifting the grounds of the debate: 'The idea of the social market is remarkably empty...it is not an economic theory. It is not a political ideology backed by distinctive values.' The real challenge, as Leadbeater saw it, was to use the social market as a means for extending citizenship, not just for modernizing the economy.

Now, even though the social market has been given a place of honour in the proposed new European Constitution, there are signs that John Gray's prophecy about the vulnerability of the social market model to the forces of global capitalism may indeed be coming true. Günter Grass, reflecting on the sixtieth anniversary of the defeat of Nazi German, asks: 'What has become of the freedom promised to us sixty years ago? Is it now no more than a stock market profit? ...what is paraded as neo-liberal proves to be on close scrutiny a return to disparaging practices of early capitalism. And the social market economy – formerly a successful model of economic and cohesive action – has degenerated into the free market economy....'[174] Even John Atherton, while still defending the model, is forced to admit: '...I have become much more aware of the dominant position of the global economy, instead of its being only one characteristic of the market economy. Yet much of what I argued for...at the beginning of the 1990s, still holds good....'[175] Others worry that, unless a way is found of containing the new capitalism, the social market may soon become an idea whose time has passed.

The German economy has been in deep trouble for over a decade. At first, the problems were ascribed to the huge economic costs arising from the re-integration of Eastern and Western Germany. It has since become painfully clear that the problem is deeper. By the beginning of 2005 the rate of unemployment in Germany was – ominously – the highest since the 1930s. More recently two events have occurred which dramatically underscore the vulnerability of the German social market economy to the forces of the new, global capitalism.

The first sign of the crisis of the social market comes from within Germany itself amid anger both at the growing penetration of German industrial and financial firms by global investors and by the gradual re-orientation of German firms themselves and even of the Social Democratic government towards more market-oriented, global economic realties. In February 2005, the Deutsche Bank decided to lay off almost 2,000 employees despite record profits – an action described by the Chair of the Social Democratic Party (SPD), Franz Müntefering, as 'immoral and irresponsible'.

In April 2005, in the run-up to crucial elections in North-Rhine Westphalia, leaders of the SPD began to adopt a strong 'anti-capitalist' rhetoric. The label may be somewhat misleading, the motives less than pure and the alternatives less than clear: was it directed only against hedge funds or against global private investors as such? But there was no mistaking the strength of feeling, expressed most graphically that month by Mr. Müntefering in his famous list of 'locusts' – large firms who, he claimed, were chewing up the profits for which Germans had worked hard and were than moving on to other fields.[176]

But the most dramatic event came on 9 May 2005 – symbolically, a day after the 60th anniversary of the defeat of Nazi Germany on 8 May 1945 – when large shareholders, not all of whom were hedge fund managers but who were led – again symbolically – by the British hedge fund TCI (The Children's Investment), forced the immediate resignation of the distinguished Chief Executive of Deutsche Börse, Werner Seifert and the deferred resignation of its Chair, Rolf Breuer, together with three other members of its supervisory board.[177] Ironically, the revolt was an angry response to Deutsche Börse's plan to take over the London Stock Exchange. From the perspective of global finance capital, the move could have been justified. For Germany, it was a devastating and humiliating blow.

The second sign of the crisis in the social market model arises from the way it is construed in the proposed new European Constitution. Although the social market model is endorsed in the Preamble, it is neo-liberalism which appears to call the tune in the specific provisions set out in Part Three.[178] Important as the lack of democratic consultation was, it was largely a sense of outrage: a) that the social market model should have been distorted in this way, and b) that so many detailed economic regulations should be enshrined in a constitution, which would be so difficult to change, that prompted trade unionists and socialists to lend their crucial support to the 'No' campaign in France leading to its overwhelming rejection on 29 May 2005.[179] The implications are profound, not just at the political level, where there is some unease about too integrated a Europe and too wide a democratic deficit, but even more at the economic level. There is the fear that the new Constitution's professed commitment to the social market may prove to be largely rhetorical, given that the sorts of social rights spelt out in the EU's Charter of Fundamental Rights lack full legal force and given the clear centre-right orientation of the European Commissioners who took office in November 2004. More fundamentally, there are those who argue that the social market model is a relic of the Old Europe and that if unemployment levels are to be brought down, it is the more neo-liberal path of the New Europe that must be followed.

What then is the Social Market?

The best way to understand the 'social market' is to see it in historical rather than abstract terms. Its central concern with social stability and social order is deeply rooted in German culture and history. It is reflected in 19th century centrist German Catholic social thought, with its stress on 'solidarism' – which, incidentally, had such a powerful influence on the first half century of papal social teaching.[180] It is reflected in Bismarck's proposal for a quasi-corporatist *Wirtschaftsrat* (Economic Council) heavily weighted toward landowners, merchants and artisans. It was reinforced by the late 19th century faith in sociology that was typical of Western Europe and which later had a strong impact even in the United States, and which, in the influential thought of Max Weber, Werner Sombart and others gave a prominent place to the social dimensions of economic and political systems. The idea of a social market, although not the term itself, began to take shape following the turbulence of the inter-war period as an attempt to avoid the extremes both of liberal capitalism on the one hand and Fascism on the other. In common with socialism and contrary to Hayek, it was teleocratic rather than nomocratic. That is to say, the market was seen as a means not an end. But unlike socialism the end in view was not equality but a harmonious, well-fashioned society – a '*formierte Gesellschaft*' in the words of Ludwig Erhard. This would be quite distinct both from a centrally planned economy but also from the purely spontaneous order championed by Hayek.[181] The actual institutions and policies might vary as historical contexts changed. The future of the social market, in other words, depends not on restoring and preserving forms that were appropriate in earlier periods but in seeing whether it is able to withstand the forces of the present period of global capitalism. Three such periods can be identified.

Social Market Thinking in the Inter-war Period

The gestation period began in the early 1930s. Perhaps the most conservative strain was represented by the development of 'Ordo-Liberalism'. It was liberalism in so far as it sought to promote competition as a means to productivity. It was 'ordo' in that it stressed the interdependence of social subsystems of family, agriculture, small businesses and workers. Ordo-Liberalism was conservative in two senses. In a romantic sense, its promotion of the role of *Handwerk* or small artisans was inspired by, though not modelled on, the medieval guild system. It was also conservative in a political sense, giving a crucial economic role to the *Mittelstand,* the core of small, often family-based business, independent farmers and professionals. By these means it sought to 'de-proletarianise' the working class – not so much by expanding their rights and power, as did the Social Democrats, but by providing security. Thus full-employment, wage agreements and the protection of workers were crucial elements.[182]

The most thoroughgoing exposition of what a social market economy might comprise was spelt out by Wilhelm Roepke. For Roepke, 'A satisfactory market…is an artistic construction and an artifice of civilization….'[183] Roepke's construction consisted, first, of an anti-monopoly policy, secondly, of an economic policy (subdivided into a framework policy to foster competition and a market policy) and, thirdly, of a 'structural' (or anthropological-sociological) policy. This last aspect was for Roepke: 'the most important…the one which gives the decisive form of our whole plan….The social and humanitarian principle…must balance the principle of individualism….A market economy is in the long term impossible in a society which has become engulfed by mass civilization, collectivised, proletarianised, uprooted, fundamentally dissatisfied and unstable…[What is needed is] a simultaneous decongestion of the population, de-proletarianization, de-collectivization, making countrymen and craftsmen as many as possible and a general decentralization of industry.'

The Social Market in the Last Half of the 20th Century

What made the social market approach acceptable across party lines after the Second World War was a shared commitment to combine enough stability to avoid the hyper-inflation of the 1920s with enough freedom to avoid the development of cartels and monopolies which had characterized pre-war Germany and which underpinned fascism. As a policy, it was adopted in the Christian Democratic Union's Dusseldorf Principles in 1949 at the insistence of Konrad Adenauer and Ludwig Erhard. The term social market itself seems to have been coined only in 1946 by Alfred Muller-Armack, a former member of the Nazi Party.[184] An added feature – *Mitbestimmung* (co-determination of business policy by labour and capital) – since seen as a distinctive part of the social market model, actually appears to have been added at the insistence of the Americans.[185] It became firmly entrenched in West Germany's political world in November 1959 when the SPD – without renouncing democratic socialism – embraced the social market approach at its conference in Bad Godesberg. And it has been adopted in various forms in 18 of the EU states but is most elaborate in Germany, where co-determination allows for a high degree of worker representation on boards, allowing for joint employer-employee decision-making in areas such as staffing, work organization, and collective bargaining. Its tendency to spill over into the formulation of strategy and policy has led some to warn of its becoming 'co-management'.

Phase Three: Social Market or Third Way?

The forces of global capitalism – even if they cannot simply be dismissed as a swarm of locusts – do nonetheless pose a major threat to the traditional institutional centrepieces of the German social market, namely the *Mittelstand* and *Mitbestimmung*, as well as the system of job security and generous pensions for workers. These institutions and policies, critics argue, simply lack the flexibility, responsiveness and innovative spirit necessary in a highly competitive global economy. The social market was in deep trouble.

Both the German trade unions' and employers' organizations have acknowledged the need to revise the structure of co-determination but the report in November 2004 of the employer-led Co-Determination Commission, was opposed by the unions as an attempt to strengthen the hand of business whilst posing as 'modernization'.[186] The uncovering of the way Volkswagen management is said to have turned a blind eye in allowing worker representatives to take luxury holidays, allegedly being supplied with prostitutes, has not only led to the resignation and subsequent conviction of Peter Hartz, VW's head of personnel (as well as a member of the influential IG Metall trade union and of the Social Democratic Party and also a key ally of Chancellor Schroeder's economic reform proposals). It has also created an opportunity for those who want to do away with *Mitbestimmung* altogether on the grounds that it creates too cosy a relationship between employers and workers – to the detriment of both. Defenders reply that, in a period of major economic reforms, *Mitbestimmung* is more useful than ever in helping the transition to occur peacefully.

Those reforms were then expressed in Agenda 2010, launched by the Social Democratic government, on 14 March 2003.[187] Agenda 2010 was a set of market-oriented measures designed to address the problems of persistent high unemployment and the flight of German capital to more profitable fields. Patterned on New Labour in many respects, Agenda 2010 was just as highly contentious. It built on the recommendations of the commission of modern labour services chaired by Peter Hartz. These were published in August 2002, and some have already become law.[188] But it went much further than labour market reform. It also envisioned fundamental changes to the health care and pensions systems and has enacted tax cuts, which took effect in January 2004, for both individuals and corporations.

Following the General Election of September 2005 the Social Democrats and Christian Democrats entered into coalition, with the Chancellorship going to Angela Merkel. Agenda 2010 had been a compromise and it has been slow to make an impact. Now pressure to move beyond Agenda 2010 is intensifying. Angela Merkel has declared: 'Globalization is now the context in which our ideas of democracy and the social market must prove themselves.'[189] Pressed by trade unions and many in his own party, Chancellor Schroeder had reportedly agreed to develop a plan to place new social standards on companies, to tighten controls on international financial movements and to resist attempts to undermine the German co-determination model of employer-employee decision-making. Ms Merkel has declared her wish to reduce the power of labour in the co-determination system, making it more like other European countries, and to let the minimum wage be set on a sector-by-sector basis.[190] But on her wider agenda she is meeting with strong resistance from within her own Party.

At the Heart of the Threat

Do these reforms signal the demise of the social market or its salvation? The question goes deeper than changes in policy and institutions. It goes to the moral heart of the social market approach. Will the Agenda 2010 stress on tax cuts, individual opportunity and individual responsibility, and the approach to encouraging entrepreneurship ('Me, plc') undermine the ethos necessary to sustain the sets of mutual commitment which make the social market meaningful? It is a big question.

Quadrant D: Re-mapping Socialism

It would be premature to dismiss the socialist option. The kind of socialism that was seen in the 20th century was actually too akin to rather than too different from capitalist modernity. John Milbank, taking an image from the Communist Manifesto in which Marx portrayed communism as the spectre that was haunting Europe, notes that socialism did indeed become spectral because it had been drained of the life-blood that only a vital ontology can provide.[191] The socialism of modernity cut itself off from a substantive nourishment that is offered by a recognition of a common good, based both on participation in the good and a participation that takes the form of mutual exchange (grace).

The answer to capitalism's destruction of community, argues Milbank, lies neither in left of centre liberalism, which remains infected with individualism, nor in left of centre communitarianism which relies on an alleged 'natural' organic community which is inherently constrictive and violently resistant to the other. What Milbank envisions is a 'socialism by grace' which flows from an ontology that sees Being as basically a process of giving, not one of self-sacrifice or even the kind of mutuality that is defined by contract or by law, but one which transcends the boundaries of status and contract, entitlement and retribution, and opens up a horizon of unknown variations in the rhythm of mutual giving: '...religious socialism insists like Augustine that only that which is common is truly good at all, or can be truly possessed, though only in the mode of reception of a gift, which must be relinquished and passed on.'

But how might a 'socialism by grace' be translated into institutional form? It would be foolish to be prescriptive. But some lines of exploration can be identified. It would have to take full account of the way that economic life today has developed. For it would be just as futile to seek to restore some medieval pre-industrial social economy as it would to remain stuck in a model that was rooted in the class conflicts of the industrial age. A post-industrial socialism would need to be more responsive to the purchasing power of consumers in a more affluent society and more able to draw on the ability of small producers to use new technologies to come up with innovations. It would have to work with new and changing networks of solidarity and focuses of common concern. That is why the explorations which follow will look particularly at market socialisms and associational socialism.

Market Socialisms

Market socialism is a term used to cover a variety of different schemes which have one thing in common: to use the market, rather than central planning, as a means of promoting the goal of equality. Raymond Plant, leader of the 1990 and 2001 Towards Social Transformation seminars, has observed: 'Socialism does require certain kinds of outcomes, not just those which emerge as the result of fair procedures....The central issues facing socialists in this context are, therefore, twofold. One is to argue the case for markets and explore forms of market provision in ways which may well upset many traditional socialist assumptions....The second is not to be seduced by those siren voices which assume that an advance towards socialism can be achieved without a powerful state. As socialists in Britain, we need to develop a theory about the role of the state as much as markets to meet the neo-liberal challenge....'[192]

Might market socialism provide an answer? And if so, which version of market socialism? Since the famous 1930s debates on the subject between Friedrich Hayek (against) and Oskar Lange (for), thinking about just what it might mean in practice has developed in several different directions.[193] First came the admission that setting the prices of goods on the basis of the estimated costs of input from labour, energy, etc. was inferior to letting prices be set by the market. Then, with the advent of computer technology, came the short-lived hope that perhaps some workable pricing systems could be devised after all. But then it was realized that the type of information used in the real world to set prices was not the sort of material which could be fed into and assessed by computers, because it was often held privately by a variety of agents and was subject to too many variable subjective factors. The opportunity to put some of these ideas into practice came with the more reform-minded socialist states in Central Europe, e.g. Yugoslavia, and to a lesser extent in Hungary. But this allowed only a modicum of price freedom and left the state in control. This prompted some to propose a more radical version of market socialism, under which public control would be abandoned and firms would be allowed to make profits. How this could still count as socialism was because it involved giving workers a stronger voice in the process of production as well as providing that profits would be socially distributed. Roemer's own vision is for a market socialism which would promote the socialist value of equality but not by means of equality of wages – which he sees as quite unjust. He opts for a stock-market run on the basis of a voucher system which would allow all adults to claim a share in the profits which would be distributed more or less equally. The fact that worker ownership would have to be abandoned on the grounds of inefficiency, and that a voucher system would be introduced would mean, Roemer concedes, that the other basic values of socialism, namely of community and cooperation, would indeed be downgraded. The debate is far from over.

Associational Economies: The Tradition

By an associational economy is meant not a multiplication of professional, producer and consumer associations each pressing their own interests, but a different structure of economic activity. Associational economic systems were popular in 19th century France and England. Often as not they were seen as part of a wider social and political project. A secular socialist version was propagated by followers of Robert Owen, especially by George Jacob Holyoake. A more conservative Christian socialist version was propagated by John Ludlow, who drew his inspiration from the even more conservative state-supported French *associations ouvrieres*. But with the development of monopoly capitalism and the consequent need for the state to play a more active role, in containing labour unrest and in mitigating the socially destructive consequences of capitalism, associational economies were seen as irrelevant.

Nonetheless, there were places where the tradition never died out. 'I came across free men first in 1946,' exclaimed Claire Huchet Bishop on discovering the 'Community of Work' founded by Marcel Barbu in Boimondau.[194] Drawing on the French tradition of fraternity, Barbu and his co-workers, referred to themselves as 'companions', and embarked upon 'the communitarian road'. There was no employer/employee relationship and decisions were to be taken by consensus. The aim was to develop a way of life not just a mode of production – working hours were gradually reduced. The experiment caught on after the war and gave rise both to some 200 centres of the '*Vie nouvelle*', with one of which, in the Paris suburb of Montreuil, the Abbe Depierre was linked.

The story of Boimondau and other examples of the 'Communities of

Work' movement in the Europe of the 1950s, including the proposals of Olivetti in Italy, are held up as models by Erich Fromm.[195] Fromm contrasts Marxist Socialism, which focuses on the question of ownership of the means of production with the approach of Robert Owen and others who focussed on the relationship of workers to their own work and to their fellow workers. The latter's communitarian socialism: 'was an industrial organization in which every working person would be an active and responsible participant, where work would be attractive and meaningful, where capital would not employ labor, but labor would employ capital.'[196]

Ulrich Duchrow, in his explorations of alternatives to capitalism, describes a similar communitarian initiative of La Poudriere set up in the late 1950s near Brussels. He also refers to the widely publicised co-operative system at Mondragon, set up in the early 1940s in the Basque country, and to some 12,000–15,000 self-managed firms in Germany alone. Eventually he notes, a crucial question had to be addressed: to what extent does the development of alternative models of living and working require political action as well? It is, notes Duchrow, a central question for the project of social transformation.[197]

Associational Economies: The Revival

Buried but not quite dead, associational economic activity is now back on the agenda. Why? Not so much because the idea has been rediscovered as because of changes in contemporary economic conditions, which, in some areas at least, mean that associational enterprises may be more feasible, but also cheaper and positively advantageous. They are feasible because of today's easy access to information and communications technology. They are cheaper because they tend to generate commitment, flexible working, innovation and reduced transaction costs due to the high level of trust. They are positively advantageous because they can draw on people's tacit knowledge, whether of reliable suppliers, advisers, and consumer preferences in the commercial context, or of local needs and resources in the context of regeneration schemes.

Associational economic enterprises are not tied to any one ideology. They can take the form of social enterprise (not-for-profit) or straightforward business enterprise.[198] An entrepreneurial approach is taken by Hernando de Soto, whose explanation of the nature of capital and property was described in Chapter One. De Soto challenges the view from Olympus that what developing countries need are macro-economic reforms in conformity with rules designed by the big players in global capitalism. The view from the ground is that only micro-economic reforms will let everyone play the game and more on their own terms.[199] In the developing countries, de Soto contends, the poor are not so much proletarians as entrepreneurs – genuine creators of (small-scale, insecure and under-capitalized) wealth. What makes them act extra-legally – squatting, seizing land, evading controls on migration, evading taxes, etc. – is not that they are lawless, much less criminal. It is the law that is at fault. The lack of adequate property law keeps the poor trapped on the extra-legal side of a dual economy. Good law, as de Soto has learned from his direct work with the poor of Peru from 1984–1994, is not law based on abstract principles or classical systems. Good law is law based on real life. De Soto reminds us that this was precisely the pattern which was followed in the development of the United States in the 19th century (to which he devotes an entire chapter). De Soto is impatient with the current fashion which claims that the secret of economic success lies with culture, whether this be the Protestant ethic in the West or the spirit of enterprise in South East Asia. The secret is not culture but institutions, above all the formalization of property law.

A more socialist version of associational economics, dedicated to promoting the goals of equality and collaboration, was proposed in the 1930's by Otto Neurath and has recently been advocated by John O'Neill.[200] Perhaps the most persistent advocate from a socialist perspective was Paul Hirst, co-leader of the 1992 Towards Social Transformation seminar.[201] Hirst was keen to dispel the idea that contemporary associational socialism needed to be linked solely with the working class as was once the case, or that it needed to be patterned on only one type of socialist model: 'It is compatible with complex forms of social ownership….By its very principle, it permits diversity in forms of organization and management of enterprises.'[202] Like market socialism, associational socialism takes the market seriously. But Hirst is wary of any 'uneasy synthesis of socialism in the enterprise and neo-classical market theory outside.' He warns of a certain naiveté in most forms of market socialism as if 'once the economic actors have been appropriately defined and have been socialized it is possible to rely on the competitive market…markets as media of interaction of enterprises require careful regulation if the associational basis of the social order is to be maintained.'[203]

Hirst's ambitious vision of associational socialism involves a three-stage process of development. At the most basic level of economic activity, Hirst's approach differs from that of market socialism by placing less weight on competition and by resisting the temptation to go for short-term gain, whilst not, however, advocating a return to central planning, nor the restraint of competition.

The next stage involves setting associational socialist economic activity in a framework of 'associative governance', which supplements, but does not supplant, the market. This means securing support from government in forms such as tax concessions to small businesses, incentives to co-operatives, and provision for ESOPS (employee-shared ownership plans).[204] All this is part of a much broader picture of social transformation according to Hirst. The next step would be to expand the scope and scale of associational enterprises in the economy as a whole: 'The aim of an associative reform process would be to move towards an economy in which small and medium-sized enterprises are more salient than at present, where ownership is firmly rooted within a locality, where capital is predominantly raised within the region and where collective services and economic regulation are provided by public-private partnerships between trade associations and the regional government.'[205]

Once having established and demonstrated the effectiveness of the principles of associational governance, the third stage of development of an associational socialist economic order is to seek ways of including within this framework even those firms which do not have an internal associational structure, including larger firms and even multi-national corporations. The structure of this wider regime of associative governance, suggests Hirst, might take the form of a two-tiered system of boards – a Supervisory Board, with shareholders, employees and the community each having one-third of the seats, and a Management Board, which would institute a Works Council and an ESOP scheme. This closer link between workers, managers and owners would not so much make trade unions redundant as transform them into associations which could have a wider role than unions, for example by taking on welfare functions, but which would be entirely voluntary.[206]

Hirst's vision was elaborated before capitalism had become globalized to the extent it is now. That clearly presents deeper challenges to such a project but does not make it redundant.

Conclusion

> To take property into state ownership does not socialize
> civil society, it negates it.
> Charlie Leadbeater[207]

The two books of John Keane's which inspired the Towards Social Transformation initiative offered hints at what a new type of socialism might look like if developed within the framework of civil society. Is such a socialism still possible? In one sense this question is irrelevant. The argument here is much broader, implying that what form the transformation of capitalism will take is still an open question and, indeed, one which will be determined as a result of collective human deliberation and unpredictable historical events. But to rule out the very idea of some new version of socialism would be to needlessly close off one possible path which the transformation of capitalism might usefully take. If one were to ask whether such a possibility still existed, one could find some support by drawing on the very different insights of two of the Towards Social Transformation seminar leaders: John Milbank and Charlie Leadbeater.

John Milbank – at least at one stage of his thinking – advocated a socialism which was genuinely Christian. He was not suggesting that this meant a particular set of institutional arrangements but that is was one which was based on participation in the good as revealed in Christ. It would have a strong aesthetic dimension which, by healing our desires, would enhance what we consume and produce. It would nurture practices of grace and generosity, forgiveness, sharing and mutuality. It would underscore the value of the informal and domestic economic sector, not just the formal and paid-employment economic sector. It would give rise to – rather than start from – a diversity of associational models of organization.

Charlie Leadbeater's reconstruction of socialism focussed more on the institutional aspects. 'Popular ownership' is crucial but not on the model of old-style socialism: The point of popular ownership is to develop a shift of power and a culture of responsibility that focuses on markets – how they are structured, who has access, how decisions are made, who is party to the decision-making process. Markets would be regulated democratically and locally, where possible. This would not mean planning outcomes, but of influencing outcomes. His approach had elements of stakeholding capitalism and market socialism but was not easily categorised as one or the other. Such ideas are worth revisiting.

All to Play for

To conclude from the preceding comments that the issue is about rehabilitating socialism would be to miss the point. The point is that the transformation of capitalism is far from complete and its outcome far from pre-ordained. Capitalism and its successors will always be products of particular configurations of forces, interests, values and choices, in the context of particular combinations of consensus, conflict and coercion. Neither the triumph nor the collapse of capitalism is inevitable; nor is the emergence of some new form of socialism inconceivable.

There are alternatives, but we are at a point where no *compelling* alternative has appeared and where no revolutionary opposition is waiting in the wings. There is all to play for. But whilst working to create space for alternatives to emerge, it is also important to keep the imagination alive and to envision, however tentatively, what it is we are looking for, be it social markets, market socialisms, associational economies. Simply being against capitalist globaliz-ation is not enough, although the protests have certainly helped to keep alive the justifiable anger and outrage about the bias of the present system. It is time for a rethink. That is why one of the aims of the World Social Forum is precisely to serve as '...a pedagogical and political space that enables listening, learning and political organizing'.[208]

Yet none of the ideas developed by such forums or in initiatives such as the Towards Social Transformation seminars will get anywhere unless they are trans-lated into political action. Visions of a 'good economy' will simply be marginal-ized, and the new economic institutions will simply be colonized – unless there is a renewal of democratic responsibility in both civil society and the state. What we have at present, however, is a staggering and growing 'global democratic deficit' in which unprecedented economic power is faced with weak and unrep-resentative political institutions which are themselves dominated by economic interests. Noreena Hertz puts it starkly: 'The final stage of the takeover is the end of politics itself, collapsing into cycles of protest, repression and despair.'[209] The statement is clearly meant more as a challenge than as a simple observation. It means that the final stage must not be reached and that a political renewal is imperative. That is why the next chapter will explore what capitalist modernity is doing to democracy and how a transformation might be possible.

Chapter Five

Transforming Politics
What Good is Democracy?

The 'nice' institutions like the UN are not efficient, and the 'nasty' ones like the World Trade Organization have no legitimacy. And that is our problem now.

Pascal Lamy[1]

By what right is the world run as it is?

Rowan Williams[2]

If democracy is to survive it must find a more adequate cultural basis than the philosophy which has informed the building of the bourgeois world.

Reinhold Niebuhr[3]

Précis

The gospel of democratization has been proclaimed with increasing vigour by Left, Centre and Right in recent decades. All the while, however, the processes of capitalist globalization are creating new problems for democracy. Increasingly the decisions about economic and political policy which most affect the shape of our world and the survival of our planet are being taken at levels which are ever more remote and inaccessible to most people. Meanwhile the demos itself is becoming de-politicized. This chapter will explore the transformations of democracy in both state and civil society that have occurred under the regime of capitalist modernity as well as the role of democracy in transforming that regime. It will proceed in five steps.

After a brief overview of the contradictory developments in contemporary democracy, the first section will examine the reasons why the focus has recently shifted from the structures of government to the process of governance.

This will be followed by a section examining the impact of capitalist modernity on the shape of present democratic structures and practice. It will discuss the role played by capitalist modernity in helping both to enshrine and to undermine the 'rule of law' and it will explore in detail its more recent influence in the emergence of the importance of governance.

Section three will ask questions about the goodness of democracy. It will insist that democracies be judged on the basis of the degree to which they represent good governance and good government, drawing on the arguments for a common culture and the common good developed in previous chapters. It will then identify three main perspectives from which the goodness of democracy may be assessed – democracy as a universal principle, democracy as a system for constraining and redistributing power and democracy as a way of life. It will offer theological reflection on each of these approaches.

Sections four and five will examine the main tasks involved in democratic transformation, in both state and civil society, first looking at the importance of developing the demos, and then suggesting some key practices which promise to lead towards that goal.

PREAMBLE: DEMOCRACY – FROM LEFT TO CENTRE TO RIGHT

When the Towards Social Transformation initiative was taking shape at the end of the 1980s, 'democratization' was the watchword of the Left. It was central to John Keane's challenge for the transformation of civil society. In Eastern Europe the movements for democracy seemed about to break through. In Italy and Britain, Communist parties were being transformed into parties of the Democratic Left. Keane went so far as to propose that: '…socialism be redefined as a synonym for the democratic maintenance and transformation of the division between civil society and the state.'[4] Paul Hirst, joint leader of the 1991 Towards Social Transformation seminar, summed it up: 'The intellectual Left in Europe and the United States has adopted democratization as the core of its political advocacy. This is more than fashion or happenstance. It is a response to the conjuncture in which representative democracy has become unchallengeable and unsurpassable.'[5]

But with the ending of the bi-polar world, the democratic agenda was taken over, first by the Centre in the 90s and then by the Right in the new millennium. Phillip Bobbitt, holder of posts with the US State Department and National Security Council in the Clinton administration, maps a development in policy from 'democratic engagement' under George Bush Senior, to 'democratic enlargement' under Bill Clinton, to 'democratic transformation' under George W. Bush, Junior.[6] The seriousness of the policy can be seen in the recent string of US-supported, professionally-managed and by no means spontaneous democratic uprisings: the Rose Revolution in Georgia (November 2003), the Orange Revolution in the Ukraine (December 2004), and the Tulip Revolution in Kyrgyzstan (March 2005). At the time of writing funding is being provided to support reform groups in Iran, Belarus and elsewhere. But anyone doubting that the policy of democratization is subordinate to the promotion of underlying US interests need only ask why it is being pursued so selectively and why only a few decades ago, in the bi-polar world, the US was actively working against democratization, by supporting coups against democratically elected governments (Chile, 1973), death squads (Central America in the 1980s), civil wars (Angola), and military dictatorships whilst indoctrinating allies in the ideology of the National Security State.

It is not just governments and civil society movements that have been promoting democratization. The private sector has been taking up the cause as well, none with greater passion and conviction than George Soros, who, as early as 1984, established foundations in Central and Eastern Europe to help prepare for the transition to democracy, and who, in 1993, set up the Open Society Institute, to support a range of initiatives for the development of civil society in over fifty countries, particularly in Eastern and Central Europe.[7]

But whose agenda was it? Why have all these efforts not led to some great flowering of democracy? Why was turnout in the historic European Union elections of June 2004 so shockingly low, even in the new democracies – 27% in Estonia, 21% in Poland, 17% in Slovakia? How is it that the United Nations could discover that a decade and more of progress of democracy in Latin America was followed by a period of disenchantment, with only 43% of the population being fully supportive of democracy, and a worrying 55% saying they would support an 'authoritarian' regime over 'democratic' government if authoritarian rule could resolve their economic problems?[8] One reason, suggests the UN Report, is that the first generation of Latin Americans to have come of age in functioning democracies has experienced world-record disparities in the distribution of national income, and virtually no *per capita* income growth – 225 million Latin Americans had incomes below the poverty line in 2003. As for Russia and China, its leaders are quite convinced that the best way to manage the transformation of their societies without unleashing social chaos on the one hand, or surrendering to the forces of global capitalism on the other, is to relegate democracy to second place.

Meanwhile, in the more established democracies, there are plenty of signs that all is not well on the democratic front. It is not just that people have become more apathetic, more disillusioned, and more cynical. There are structural factors which make them – and even their national governments – feel less able to influence the course of events. The globalization of economic activity, ecological processes and terrorism mean that key decisions are taken at levels higher than that of the nation-state. But there are also cultural reasons. People – at least in the more affluent nations – are tending to see politics as business, governments as managers and themselves as shareholders. A higher value is placed on effectiveness (delivery of services), efficiency (at the lowest possible level of taxes and of waste), and a climate conducive to private consumption and investment, while a lower value is placed on participation. In short, the less 'politics' the better.

1. Government and Governance

Why Governance?

Since the beginning of the Towards Social Transformation initiative at the end of the 1980s, the term 'governance' has come to overshadow that of 'government'. It is more than just a fad. In part it reflects a widespread crisis in government. More fundamentally it is a sign of the way the cultural, economic and technological transformations of our time have transformed the process and art of governing itself.

The kinds of crises which have given rise to a concern about governance are of two sorts. One is limited to 'rogue states', 'failing states' and 'outposts of tyranny'.[9] The other is far wider, affecting developed countries and long-standing democracies as well. It arises from the growing vulnerability of nation states in the face of global forces – economic, climatic, epidemiological, cultural – and their inability to contain these forces.[10] In the past century, the response has been to form international and regional political structures. This, however, has created its own problems by removing the processes of decision-making and even the language of political debate further from the lives of their own citizens. The sense of disillusion with national politics is thus compounded by a growing 'democratic deficit'.

Yet the current emphasis on governance represents much more than a response to crisis. Governance is here to stay. Why? Because we live in a world of innovation, of increasingly rapid transactions and of high mobility. The actions of individuals and institutions are no longer easily contained by rigid structures and there is a need for institutions to be more flexible, to adopt looser boundaries and to take a wider view of 'sovereignty'. In that rapidly changing, interdependent world, furthermore, power takes many forms. Governance is precisely about seeking to make power – especially economic power – accountable and to allow new forms of participation by the various forces in civil society. It focuses more on the processes and functions of governing than on the structures and forms of government.

What is Governance?

'The term "governance" is a very versatile one,' notes the European Union: '... it corresponds to the so-called post-modern form of economic and political organizations. According to the political scientist Roderick Rhodes, the concept of governance is currently used in contemporary social sciences with at least six different meanings: the minimal State, corporate governance, new public management, good governance, social-cybernetic systems and self-organized networks.'[11]

One of the crucial features that governance shares with government is that both claim the authority, not just the power, to govern. This, James Rosenau observes, is reflected in the recognition on the part of society of a duty of compliance with the rules and directives which are generated by processes of governance even though they are not limited to elected bodies nor is their remit constitutionally defined: 'While the rule systems of government can be thought of as structures, those of governance are social functions or processes that can be performed or implemented in a variety of ways at different times and places (or even at the same time) by a wide variety of organizations.'[12]

Governance and Democracy

Governance sets the context for democracy today, both globally and locally. But it is highly problematic. It is true that governance can create opportunities for new forms of participation. It is also true that such participation in political decision-making by non-elected actors may be useful and even imperative, but it can all get rather confusing. Rosenau observes: '...it is difficult to overestimate how crowded the global stage has become as the world undergoes a multiplication of all kinds of governance, from formal to multilevel governments, from formally sanctioned entities such as arbitration boards to informal SOAs [spheres of authority]...from transnational corporations to neighbourhood associations...from certifying agencies to social movements, and so on....'[13]

But crowd management is a relatively minor issue. The deeper questions are: Who makes the decisions and by what right? Who chooses these various 'representatives'? And to whom are they accountable? It was all so much simpler with the traditional one person – one vote type of democracy. Is the development of governance opening the way to new forms of democracy? Or is it taking us beyond democracy? And is democracy really a more important issue than good governance? It may help to look at some of the directions governance is taking, first at global level and then at local level.

Governance: Global

Global governance is in crisis....The economy is becoming increasingly global, while social and political institutions remain largely local, national or regional.
United Nations International Labour Organization [14]

There is an urgency about the need for global governance. Global epidemics or global climate change could each take a vastly higher toll of human life than global terrorism. Unless some system of legitimate order and justice is developed the alternative will be increased chaos, clashes of interest and the rule of power. As a recent UN report warns, the scarcity of water itself is becoming a cause of global insecurity. In the previous bi-polar world, the kind of 'order' that prevailed was not an order of peace and justice. At super-power level, it was a war of cold terror. At local level, while one super-power was promoting armed revolutionary struggles, the other was fostering brutal 'low-intensity conflicts' – all at the cost of millions of lives. With the ending of the bi-polar world, even that cruel 'order' has gone. The alternatives? Either American hegemony (the limits of whose authority and power have become increasingly apparent), or the rule of capital (whose limits have not yet become so apparent), or new processes of governance marked by a collaboration amongst states and between states and actors in civil society – business corporations, NGOs, local popular movements, churches and other faith communities.

Increasingly, over the past decade global governance has figured on the agendas of international bodies, including the churches. Since 1994, the United Nations has sponsored a programme for the Management of Social Transformations (MOST), among whose principal concerns have been 'Globalization and Governance'.[15]

For the past five years, the Commission of the Bishops' Conferences of the European Community (COMECE) has had a high-powered Group on Global Governance chaired by Michel Camdessus, Managing Director of the IMF from 1987–2000.[16]

What will the emerging framework of global government and global governance look like? What is the new context in which the question of democracy will be posed at global level? There are several different scenarios. Four of these are the new imperialism, a society of market states, the new medievalism and transnational democracy. What these mean and what implications each may have in helping determine the extent, mode and shape of democratic practice will be looked at next.

The New Imperialism

The 'new imperialism' was taking shape in both British and American circles long before 9/11 and is by no means limited to the invasions of Afghanistan and Iraq.[17] There are two senses in which 'the new imperialism' may be understood. One relates to the preservation and extension of Western interests This, in turn, has both a defensive and an offensive dimension. Defensive in that 'rogue states' (which may have weapons of mass destruction) and 'weak' states (which provide a safe haven for terrorists) are both perceived as constituting potential threats to national security.[18] Offensive, in that neo-conservatives in the US argue that America's exceptional global power brings with it an opportunity and a responsibility to develop a transformational foreign policy so as to spread the benefits of American-style democracy, free markets and freedoms. Both the practical mishandling of those agendas and some of the ideology behind them have generated a growing reaction in the United States, with the neo-cons in disarray.[19]

But there is also a new imperialism of a broader kind, which takes as its starting point a humanitarian concern about human rights. Here the argument focuses on states that are deemed to constitute a major threat to their own people – in terms of oppression or even genocide. The failure of the United Nations to intervene effectively in Rwanda and Srebrenica has given rise to an urgent attempt to rethink the 'right to protect' which already has a basis in Article 51 of the UN Charter. Thus there has been a growing recognition that the 'responsibility to protect' has not only a reactive dimension but a preventive and a rebuilding dimension as well. The argument seeks to move the boundaries of the traditional fixation on national sovereignty. But what becomes central in any such move is the question of legitimacy. By what authority can such action be taken?[20] And, what if, as in the crisis of Darfur, the parties involved refuse to recognize that authority?[21]

What of the implications for democracy in the new imperialism? The contradictions are obvious. Its professed aim is to promote democracy but yet it tends to do so by imposing from without a particular model of democracy on states which may not have the culture, social cohesion and institutions which can support any kind of democracy.

A Society of Market States?

...in a society dominated by the market, and therefore a society that
contains a radical divide between the rich and the poor, as in the USA, it is
financial resources which dominate the political process.
Church of England House of Bishops' Working Group[22]

Philip Bobbitt has no time for the new imperialists, whom he describes as 'the new evangelists'. These make the same mistake, he argues, as do the new internationalists and the new nationalists, the new realists and the new leaders. They all assume that nation-states will remain the central agents in the new global order. In fact, the dominant force, he argues, will be the market and the result will be a 'society of market states'. For Bobbitt: 'The market-state ceases to base its legitimacy on improving the welfare of its people, and begins instead to attempt to enable individuals to maximize the value of their talents by providing them with the opportunity to do so...it is up to the individual to avoid problems, not up to the state to fix them. If there are unsafe areas of town, the citizen is best advised not to go there, rather than expect the police to ensure a safe environment.'[23]

The market, while it is an anarchic force in some respects, is also an important co-ordinating force. In the new order access to markets rather than gaining territory is also the key to any nation's prosperity. But are markets a sufficient basis for democracy? A particular problem worth highlighting here has to do with Bobbitt's response to the likelihood that the market-state scenario contains a potential for internal divisions and for regional conflicts. The response is left to ad hoc 'coalitions of the willing' led by the United States. Part of the plan involves the increased co-option and the actual creation of NGOs as instruments of United States' and other great powers' strategies.[24] All this is done in a political vacuum as far as international structures are concerned and leaves unanswered serious questions about the legitimacy of such 'coalitions of the willing', however large or small they may happen to be.

A New Medievalism

To accept that the era of the nation-state may be coming to an end does not mean that it will be followed by a system of market-states. A quite different scenario that has been suggested is that of a 'new medievalism'. The concept was mooted at least a quarter of a century ago by Hedley Bull, who saw it as 'a modern and secular equivalent of the kind of universal political organization that existed in Western Christendom in the Middle Ages.'[25] But only in the past decade has the concept been given serious attention.[26] The development of information technology, the new patterns of economic activity, the dis-aggregation of many of the functions of the nation-state onto other bodies – all this has given rise to a world where supra-national regions, sub-national regions, and even cities are constituent parts of the new global political economy. Anthony Payne admits that the image of a new medievalism is best seen more as a metaphor than as a model. What is lacking today, of course, is the sort of overarching spiritual and political authority once represented by the Pope and the Emperor. But it does serve to highlight the fact that political authority is becoming increasingly over-lapping, multi-layered, and multi-centred.

Such a scenario could offer rich possibilities for more diverse and overlapping forms of democracy. It would obviously enhance subsidiarity at a practical level and would also provide greater scope for the formal representation of a wide range of corporate interests,

Transnational Democracy

All of the above scenarios have implications for the transformation of democracy at a global level, but none of them actually takes democracy as their point of departure. That is a task undertaken by Anthony McGrew, who in fact sets out four different models of 'transnational democracy'.[27] The first, Liberal Internationalism, accepts that the main international agencies of state and civil society will not be directly elected but presses for reforms that would make their operations more transparent, fairer and more accountable. McGrew sees this approach as characterising the approach of a range of bodies such as the World Health Organization and the Commission on Global Governance.[28] McGrew's second and third types call for new collective identities: Radical Democratic Pluralism builds from the bottom-up on solidarities of interest, particularly of oppressed and marginalized groups (Kairos Europa would be an example). Cosmopolitan Democracy seeks to develop a sense of universal citizenship. The fourth model, Deliberative (Discursive) Democracy works with stakeholders – whatever their official status – and involves the negotiation of interests. The four models are neither exhaustive nor mutually exclusive. They simply illustrate the different fronts on which the promotion of democracy in a global order is a very real possibility. But before this can happen, the debate needs to be opened up to a wider public debate as people like George Monbiot have been committed to doing.[29]

Civil Society in Action – Case Study:
Alternative Global Governance

Global governance is not, however, reducible simply to structures, for governance, as defined above by Rosenau, has to do with processes rather than structures. It is a process which is flexible, and may engage different agents in state and civil society, sometimes on a very temporary and highly focused basis. A striking example is the case of British American Tobacco. On 26 October, 2004 the internal memos, research reports and other documents comprising the British American Tobacco archive were made available on the internet.[30] The site currently contains more than a million pages of documents. It is primarily about transparency, which will lead to greater accountability. Ethical investors, government health offices and NGOs will be able to examine such activities as BAT's use of research or its tactics in encouraging smoking by women in Uzbekistan.

The example also illustrates the interaction of a range of actors. First, there is the power of the courts. The requirement to set up this website was due, not to legislation, but to a court ruling – not in Britain but in the United States, in a case brought by a statutory body (the State of Minnesota) and a private medical insurance firm (Minnesota Blue Cross and Blue Shield). Then the website itself was constructed by a consortium involving the educational sector – the London School of Hygiene and Tropical Medicine and the University of California at San Francisco – with the not-for-profit health sector – the Mayo Clinic in Minnesota – in what eventually came to be known as the Guildford Archiving Project (GAP) consortium (the BAT archives are deposited at Guildford). Each of the millions of pages had to be scanned separately – for which BAT charged 10p per page. Fortunately, a grant of £1 million from the Wellcome Trust and a $1 million grant from the Flight Attendant Medical Research Institute helped with the costs. The final global irony, however, was that, since the process of scanning was going to be very labour-intensive, most of this aspect of the work was outsourced to India.

Governance: Local

Local democracy in England has not been in a healthy state for some time. Some localities have been little more than one-party states. Some local councils have developed inefficient bureaucracies. In many local elections, far less than half those eligible bother to vote. Underlying it all, local authorities' power and discretion is severely restricted by central government. How to rekindle local democracy? Central government has adopted a two-pronged approach, aimed at strengthening both local government and local governance. The first involves the development of new structures (strong mayors, cabinet systems) whilst also holding out the promise of greater 'freedom and flexibility' in return for improved efficiency (as defined by the meeting of centrally-imposed targets). The second prong of the strategy – which is the focus here – has taken the form of new systems of local governance (partnerships, 'the new localism', regional assemblies). Each of these will be looked at briefly both in terms of how they are presented and the questions they raise.

Local Partnerships

The development of local partnerships – in regeneration, crime reduction, health promotion, education and training, etc. – has been a key plank of central government strategy for over a decade. Its fullest expression to date involves the requirement to develop Community Strategies, responsibility for which is normally undertaken by Local Strategic Partnerships (LSPs) – a 'partnership of partnerships.' The fact that LSPs are not statutory and have no executive power but nonetheless play a key political role illustrates the issue of governance. Members are not directly elected; some are indirectly elected (from the statutory and voluntary and community sectors), others are appointed or even hand-picked. Should churches be part of such structures? If so, is it as a matter of right (because of their importance in the community), by invitation (to lend legitimacy to the exercise) or by election (taking seriously the need to render an account of what they are doing in that role)?[31]

The New Localism

The 'new localism' is about more than partnership. In theory it represents an attempt to develop within local civil society an increased capacity to have people's voices heard, to have an influence over how public services are delivered and even to take over the running of public services by developing a range of not-for-profit local organizations. These would include mutuals (which benefit members, e.g. co-operatives and credit unions), social enterprises (not-for-profit but self-financing services) and public interest companies (such as NHS Foundation Trusts).[32] The new localism involves new systems of public accountability, new patterns of public participation, and a new commitment to the principles of community development. It seeks to develop and strengthen the role of neighbourhoods.[33] The approach has even been (over?-) sold by one government minister as a form of 'local socialism' and as 'part of a broader and deeper democratization of society'.[34] Local authority organizations, on the other hand, tend to suspect it as undermining electoral democracy.

Leaving aside the question of whether such initiatives would more likely prove to be vehicles for consumerism, managerialism, privatization and greater inequality of services, rather than for socialism, how realistic is it to see these as a 'broader and deeper democratization of society'? How much desire and how extensive a capacity do local communities have to take up such a challenge? Would it even be good governance? Alan Pike, formerly local government correspondent for the *Financial Times*, sees it as a recipe for the fragmentation of services. It is only local government, he argues, which has the comprehensive, long-term and inclusive view of the needs of the area.[35]

Regional Assemblies

The concept of regional assemblies stems from the recognition of the need for regional strategies and the desirability of finding appropriate ways of representing relevant interests and of ensuring accountability. English regional assemblies have considerable power over housing and planning. Were they to become fully elected assemblies, they would have additional powers in areas such as economic development. At present none of their members is directly elected, although normally a majority are indirectly elected, i.e. chosen from amongst elected local councillors. Take the East of England Regional Assembly as an example: for the year 2004/5 it comprised 74 local authority members and 32 'Community Stakeholder' members, including representatives of business, trade unions, the voluntary sector and the faiths forum. It is a classic example of the hybrid nature of local governance and of the complexity of making it properly democratic.

Governments, Governance and Social Transformation

The kind of government structures and governance processes we want and the kind of governments and governance that are possible are shaped by the regimes under which we live. Democracies take can take many forms – liberal democracy, social democracy, Christian democracy, to name three of the main versions. We may tend to take as normative the kind of democracy with we which are familiar. But it is only one kind of democracy. Classical republicanism placed citizenship and public duties at the centre. The democracy that has developed under the regime of capitalist modernity, by contrast, takes its stand on private property and individual rights. Just how good is that particular system of democracy and why should one wish to argue that it requires a transformation? That is the question which will be explored in the next section. In keeping with the analysis that has been suggested throughout this book, it will be suggested that capitalist modernity has introduced both improvements and distortions in governance. The point is not only to tell the difference; it is also to be able to know by what deeper criteria – if not the common good – one could make such judgments.

2. Democracy in the Regime of Capitalist Modernity

> The Abramoff case is…for US politics what the
> collapse of Enron was for US business.
> *Financial Times*[36]

If democracy as it has developed under capitalist modernity is only one particular kind of democracy, how would one describe its distinguishing characteristics? Here these distinguishing features will be looked at first in terms of influence of capitalism and then in terms of the influence of modernity. The features of capitalism relate to its transformations of class, of values (possessive individualism), and of the media. The features of modernity include the rule of law, individual rights, and technocracy.

Capitalism Transforming Democracy

Transformations of Class

The continuing process of capital accumulation generates continuing changes in the composition of classes and the shape of class relationships. In the industrial age, this meant the emergence of a powerful working-class. Faced with a choice between revolution or social democracy, the ruling classes (bourgeoisie and aristocracy) sensibly opted for the latter. In America, the spectre of plutocracy and the sheer power of the big corporations provoked widespread popular support for a 'New Democracy'.[37] By the time of the post-industrial age, however, capitalism has generated a much more fragmented class structure in which a rather comfortable majority, have a strong interest in retaining what they have got. The sizeable minority who desperately need a change of policies are viewed as financial burdens by 'taxpayers' (once known as citizens) and as electoral liabilities by politicians, so their voices can at last be safely ignored.

Colin Crouch portrays the rise and fall of social democracy as a parabola. It was on the upswing when the working class was strong, but is on the downside now that the class composition has changed. He argues that: '…the fundamental cause of democratic decline in contemporary politics is the major imbalance now developing between the role of corporate interests and those of virtually all other groups.'[38] The issue is not primarily that political 'representatives' and leaders are often people of significant personal wealth (a feature of American democracy). It is not even that powerful economic interest groups – oil, tobacco, pharmaceuticals, and arms manufacturers – have inordinate influence over legislation. It is that the relatively comfortable majority – including most of the working class – are co-opted. Crouch offers suggestions for democratic mobilization, but his sober verdict is: 'For much of the time, however, we must expect entropy of democracy.'

If we think of class at all under these conditions, it refers less to how we make our money than to how we spend it. We see ourselves first and foremost as consumers and property-owners. Does it matter as long as the state delivers on its promise of opportunity for all and wider choice? Yes, it does. And that is why the ethos of possessive individualism needs to be addressed.

Transformation of Values: Possessive Individualism

By the time the liberal bourgeois state was ready to be transformed into the liberal democratic state, argues C. B. Macpherson, the rules of the game had been established and the radical democratic impulse had been muted. By then 'the demand of the democratic forces was to get into the game, not to change the rules.'[39] Locke was no democrat, but the democracy which later followed was built on Lockean foundations which gave it its own particular shape and bias. Thus modern western democracy, argues Macpherson, was painted with the brush of possessive individualism. Clearly the extension of the right of property gave people more of a stake in the existing order (indeed it made them quite conservative). And the extension of the operation of the market enhanced people's sense of the right to choose. But this also transformed the *demos* into a mere collection of individuals, concerned to protect and enlarge their property (resentful of the state's extraction of taxes yet seeking the state's help to extend opportunities). It paved the way for viewing voters more like shareholders than citizens.

The state was supposed to be the force which would promote – and, in some theories, virtually incarnate – the common good by transcending factions and self-interest. Instead it consecrated self-interest. Appeals to the common good sound not just misguided but positively alien. They come from another world.

Transformations of the Public Sphere: Media Power

Common good requires public space. But public space is a
good deal more than a market.
Rowan Williams, Archbishop of Canterbury[40]

Of all the ways in which contemporary capitalism threatens democracy, however, the most pernicious must be its tendency to deform the public sphere by its immense – and largely unaccountable – power over the mass media. A free press is an essential part of democracy. And, indeed, much of the press remains free and continues to do an enormous service to democracy both by means of investigative journalism, by its non-deferential interrogation of political leaders, by its raising of controversial issues in ways which allow for genuine debate. But to credit that to capitalism would be ironic. It may have been a laddish boast to have claimed, after the unexpected victory of John Major in the 1992 elections that: 'It Was *The Sun* Wot Won It', but it can hardly be the sign of a healthy democracy when would-be leaders of the world's most powerful states desperately seek an audience at the court of the head of News International, for fear of what line may be taken on issues such as the Euro or immigration. Nonetheless, it is far too easy just to target media empires, serious though this development is. John Keane has rightly warned against '...slipping into the reductionist demonology of the evil media baron. The obsession with media magnates has little in common with a politics of maximizing freedom and equality of communication.'[41] Even more worrying than the concentration of media ownership is the way market forces, in the form of advertising revenue, determine the circulation, style and even content of the media. The effect of the pressure to sell newspapers and to attract TV audiences is degrading, fostering as it does an obsession with sex, sport, soap and scandal – a process which was described a century ago by George Gissing in *New Grub Street*. The corrosive effect is compounded, moreover, as sensationalism is accompanied by the filtering of information and the presentation of interpretation as fact. It becomes positively dangerous when it takes the path of inflaming populist passions in ways which may be designed to appeal to perceived prejudices, but which actually feed and nurture them.

The challenge, then, is about finding ways of promoting the sort of communication which Raymond Williams saw as central to the development of a common culture. In addition to conscientious journalism, there is also the need for institutional reform. If one task is to diversify ownership and control of the media, another is to ensure access, particularly to the voices of those who are exploited, marginalized and/or misrepresented, including minorities, trades unions, NGOs and faith communities. This might include a public service requirement, for example, within each mainstream TV channel or newspaper to provide a daily slot, at prime time, for the views of, say, trades unions as well as business (both clearly representing their own interests and views, not pretending they were speaking 'common sense' on behalf of all of society). So too with religion; it is not a question of moving the 'God-slot' into prime time, but rather of ensuring that the presentation of different religious views and social practices has a daily slot. And so with various minority voices as well. The point is not to create media ghettoes, but to facilitate genuine communication amongst the different voices. Rowan Williams has focussed on precisely this point: 'Serving democracy', he states, 'and nourishing the common good is, for the media, something that requires not only attacking corrupt secrecies in a society, but also defending non-corrupt communication.'[42]

David Edgar reinforces Rowan Williams' view which in turn echoes Raymond Williams. Edgar insists that 'public' means neither ghetto nor simply choice: 'The overwhelming case for the public sector (and the public service) is that it refuses to accept that we are all – inevitably and unarguably – one type of person. It provides a site for different kinds of relationship between us and that world....people understand that they are paying for a service that goes beyond their own wants to address other people's needs.'[43] It also provides conditions favourable to the development of critical autonomy whose importance was argued in Chapter Three.

Modernity Transforming Democracy: Governance as Management

Individual Rights

As with capitalism, so with modernity: it did not begin as a democratic movement but it did help prepare the ground by the development of a new consciousness. Among the features which modernity has stamped on democracy as we know it are three: individual rights, the rule of law and the tendency towards technocracy. As with Locke, so with Bacon and Descartes: it was not the intention but the implications of their thought that pointed in a democratic direction. Belief in individual autonomy, supported by the belief in each individual's capacity to reason (sometimes depicted as 'an inner light'), the recognition of the importance of experience, and the development of methods that made sound knowledge accessible to every person – all these created conditions favourable to the demand for democracy.

The Rule of Law

Modernity's reliance on the power of objective impersonal reason has helped provide a framework in which the rule of despots and tyrants, hereditary monarchs and schismatic leaders is overcome by basing legitimacy on the 'rule of law'. Though not inherently or even initially linked to democracy, this development has proved to be a crucial support for democracy, helping to curtail the arbitrary use of power, offering protection for the weak, and establishing, where the law is formulated on the basis of human nature rather than social status, a basic equality of all citizens before the law. The only question – and it is a big one when modernity links up with capitalism – is: who makes the law and in whose interests?

Technocracy

Modernity's passion for order and control has had its impact on political structures and practices – on the form of the state (the development of a bureaucratic civil service), on the notion of policing (the use of surveillance), on the organization of political forces (the co-option of social movements) and on the way the task of governing itself is conceived (the managing of social and economic conflict). The trend towards politics as administration, argues John Gray, leader of the 2002 Towards Social Transformation seminar, is one of the dangerous consequences of the universalizing tendency of Enlightenment modernity.

The more complex the world becomes, the more the mind-set of modernity leads in favour of technocracy rather than democracy. Issues such as the merits of GM crops, nuclear energy, the Euro – all major political issues of our time – are said to be too complex for anyone but experts to understand. The more 'ordinary people' try to get involved, the more they muddy the issues by introducing prejudice, particular interest and plain ignorance. Much better, so the argument goes, to entrust the complex political issues of our time to an independent central bank, or even a European central bank, to 'take the politics out' of social policy, and to let experts get on with the job.

The critique is also taken up, from a different angle, by Andrew Shanks: 'there is a certain sense in which totalitarianism arises, essentially, from a desire for the total abolition of politics, the total replacement of politics by administration, secret intrigue and violence.'[44] Underpinning this process of de-politicization are two fallacies. The first fallacy is that the experts themselves really do know what they are doing and that they are free of any self-interest or political ideology of their own. The second is that conflict, corruption, and simple misjudgements can somehow be banished from political life. Until these assumptions are challenged, the technocrats will continue to have the upper hand.

One suggestion for putting a check on the rule of experts is what Ulrich Beck has called 'sub-politics'. The distinctive feature of sub-politics, according to Beck, is the devising of institutional forms for self-criticism of the reign of science: 'things that until now have only been able to make their way with great difficulty against the dominance of professions or operational management must be *institutionally protected*: alternative evaluations, alternative professional practice, discussions within organizations and professions of the consequences of their own developments, and repressed scepticism....Only when medicine opposes medicine, nuclear physics opposes nuclear physics, human genetics opposes human genetics or information technology opposes information technology can the future that is being brewed up in the test-tube become meaningful and valuable for the outside world....This means that the *preserving, settling, discursive function of politics*...could become the core of its tasks.'[45]

3. Rethinking Democracy

Democracy is a 'bourgeois ideology' [which] cannot...be equated with freedom.
Reinhold Niebuhr [46]

What good is democracy? The argument to be developed in this section is that democracies must be judged on the basis of the degree to which they represent good governance and good government. The issue is not about 'democracy' in the abstract but about democracies. How good specifically is the kind of democracy which capitalist modernity fosters? What is it, in today's context, that makes democracies good forms of governance, globally and locally? Are some types of democracy likely to be better than others – and in what contexts? What makes for good democratic practice?

Such questions can only be answered in the light of some notion of 'the good'. But there is an essential supplementary question: 'What type of good governance is here and now possible?' In other words, systems of governance and government are to be judged not on the basis of an ideal but on the basis of the quality of human development, of social relationships and of practical constraints that obtain in any given historical context. Structures of government and processes of governance and their transformations need to be evaluated in terms of history and as part of a journey which, in keeping with the theological perspective adopted here, involves a calling to participate ever more fully in the common good.

Here, the question of how good democracy is will be explored in two stages. The first, brief stage will seek to set democracy in the broader framework of a common culture and the common good. The second stage will involve a more detailed look at the case for democracy from three different perspectives.

3.1 Good Governance

What might good governance look like? The question needs to be answered at three levels. The first is the very pragmatic level – 'what works?' This usually involves guidance by certain basic principles. The second level is to do with the ideological framework in the light of which those principles make sense. This level is about 'visions and values'. The third and deepest level is ontological. This relates to questions about human nature and destiny. It draws on the notion of the common good and a common culture which have been discussed in previous chapters.

The first-level answers to the question of what good governance might look like are the ones which are most familiar. For example, a European Union White Paper identifies five principles of good governance: openness, participation, accountability, effectiveness and coherence.[47] The Independent Commission for Good Governance in Public Services spells out six principles of good governance: focusing on the organization's purpose and outcomes for citizens and service users, performing effectively in clearly defined functions and roles, promoting values for the whole organization and demonstrating the values of good governance through behaviour, taking informed, transparent decisions and managing risk, developing the capacity and capability of the governing body to be effective, and engaging stakeholders and making accountability real.[48]

Both the examples just cited also move beyond the first level to a second-level insofar as they declare the value systems which support their pragmatic principles. The European Union locates its five principles within the wider framework of subsidiarity and proportionality. Similarly, the Independent Commission for Good Governance in Public Services places its six principles in a clear value-based context, which gives weight to things like the focus on citizens and consumers, the new organizational forms, choice and plurality, centralization and localism, regulation, targets and performance management and partnership working.[49] The Commission of Bishops' Conferences of the European Community list among their core values: respect for human dignity, the pursuit of solidarity and social justice, and the principles of subsidiarity, greater cohesion, truthfulness, transparency and accountability.[50]

But there is a third and deeper level. That is to do with the ontological reality of the good as set out in chapters one and three. Suppose that rather than starting with some particular form of polity, such as democracy, and then trying to find criteria either for justifying or condemning it, we were to try to start with an understanding of the good and then tried to see what kind of polity or polities it might entail? Would it lead to democracy? Does it matter? The fact that there are tensions between 'good governance' and democracy is not decisive since such tensions are likely to exist with any form of polity. In any case, 'good governance' itself has its own problems. Who defines what good governance is? For example, the term has become the central theme for the World Bank. But to imagine that what the Bank sees as 'good governance' is not part of the project of capitalist modernity would be naive in the extreme. The difficulties are not resolved simply by invoking the common good as the ultimate because most polities, especially the least democratic types, would claim that that is what they are seeking. How then is it possible to discern hints of some of the distinctive features of the kinds of polity that might be derived from an ontological understanding of the good and from an incorporation of the notion of grace?

One theologian who has attempted to do just that is John Milbank. For inspiration he draws on Augustine's vision of the City of God. More recently he has drawn more directly on the gospel stories of crucifixion and resurrection. The result is not a particular political model but rather a vision which combines radical pluralism with hierarchy, a mixture of democratic, aristocratic and monarchical elements, and a strong associational dynamic rooted in a theological notion of sovereignty. Whether the resulting vision is abundantly rich and fluid in a postmodern mode, or ultimately incoherent is, in a way, not the main question. More important is the challenge Milbank presents and the path he opens up for showing the powerful political implications of Christian doctrine but not in the ideological or literalistic ways that are far too common. It is worth looking at more closely.

At the heart of Milbank's vision – of what has here been called Civil Society – is a peaceful harmony of difference. Augustine, says Milbank, allows that: '…there should be, not a single imperium, but rather many cities, just as there are many households within a city….'[51] But Milbank's pluralism does not mean that difference implies equality, integration and social cohesion in the way these terms are often understood, for the hierarchical element runs through it so that: '…the view that religion concerns the relation of the "individual" to the "social" can be opposed in the name of "hierarchical" societies for which both individuality and collectivity are subordinate to a substantive organization of roles, purposes and values.'[52] His associational concern is not an argument simply for more associations of any sort whatsoever, but for a right ordering of associational life – with 'right' being understood not as being in accordance with a fixed rule but as expressing the good. In the realm of the good, judgements must be made about better and worse, about what reflects more or less clearly the reality of the good, And that, as both the philosophy of neo-Platonism and theology of Augustine illustrate, entails a hierarchy of goods and of desires.

Is that it, as far as democracy is concerned? On the contrary, the problem is not with democracy but with democracy as we now know it: 'We find ourselves in the midst of a debased, democratic politics….' Milbank argues that the Christian tradition of republican thought has been deformed into a largely negative system in the American tradition which has locked it into the uncreative condition of a 'sad deistic stasis', which actually fears rather than encourages genuine democracy, enshrining the privileges of the few and keeping at bay the mob with all its factions. To insist on the political relevance of goodness and truth – the hierarchical elements – can prevent democracy from being simply a matter of ruthless social power ('the tyranny of the majority') or cold legal power ('the rule of law').

Milbank is hardly original in his concern to find a way of bringing together democracy, good governance and truth. Pope John Paul II makes the point in typically strong terms: 'There are those who consider such relativism an essential condition of democracy, inasmuch as it alone is held to guarantee tolerance, mutual respect between people and acceptance of the decisions of the majority, whereas moral norms considered to be objective and binding are held to lead to authoritarianism and intolerance....It is true that history has known cases where crimes have been committed in the name of "truth". But equally grave crimes and radical denials of freedom have also been committed and are still being committed in the name of "ethical relativism"....Democracy cannot be idolized to the point of making it a substitute for morality or a panacea for immorality. Fundamentally, democracy is a "system" and as such is a means and not an end. Its "moral" value is not automatic....the value of democracy stands or falls with the values which it embodies and promotes.'[53]

The issue is not whether truth matters to democracy, but how it is best arrived at. Milbank would not put it quite the way Pope John Paul did. His approach is more analogical and thus more like that adopted by Rowan Williams for whom: '...the common good of a community is not a distinct end which can be invoked to overrule a specific perspective; it is rather the very capacity of the community to negotiate gifts and needs within an overall hope of growing into a relation with God analogical to that displayed in Christ'.[54] Put that way, it is surprisingly compatible with the approach taken by Raymond Williams, for whom, as was seen in Chapter Three, a common culture is one which allows people, on as equal a basis as possible, to 'participate in the articulation of meanings and values and in the consequent decisions'. One might speak of a gradation of democratic difference from Pope John Paul to John Milbank to Rowan Williams to Raymond Williams. The more democratic the approach, the more it will: a) give voice to those who might otherwise not be listened to; b) ensure access to information that has been compiled by those in government; and c) encourage public debate.

But how does this translate into the shape of a polity? For Milbank, it suggests a polity which is not purely democratic but which involves the harmonious interplay of three positive elements – the monarchical, the aristocratic and the democratic. The monarchical element (the one) reflects the harmony of life and our basic interconnectedness. The aristocratic (the few) recognizes the need for an ongoing initiation (*paideia* or discipleship) into wisdom and virtue in which teachers continually return to being disciples and vice versa. This shared attention to the good is the key to right ordering. It ensures that the third element, the democratic (the many) proceeds not by a process of levelling but by one of a continual pursuit of the good: 'So the point is not to question all formal mechanisms of democracy, but rather to insist on the priority of an educative culture which will sustain and extend them.'

Milbank puts his case in typical poetic style: 'The polis can only become a musical, worshipping realm, when it is at the hands of those…who understand how what is different can be combined, because they have a vision of their common, superordinate origin….' His attempt to ground the shape of the polity on the ontological and theological notion of the good does then find a place for the democratic element but it can hardly be said that democracy is central to the vision. The next section, therefore, will explore ways that have been attempted to make the case for democracy.

3.2 The Goodness of Democracy: Three Perspectives

How is it that democracy, which until well into the modern era was viewed as one of the most undesirable and indeed dangerous forms of government, is now implicitly accepted as the ideal?[55] Even leaving aside the naiveté of American neo-conservatives who thought that democracy in the Middle East and Latin America might turn out to be more sympathetic to liberal values and to American interests than it has, might the ideal of democracy blind us to the reality of what democracies are actually like? Here democracies will be explored as products of the interactions between three sets of factors: values (which inform a set of principles), power relations (which find expression in a set of institutions) and ways of life (which give rise to a set of practices). Just as democracy itself is not some pure ideal type, so each of these three dimensions of democracies are themselves diverse. In terms of values, democracies may, for example, be liberal, social, socialist or religious depending upon the different weight they give to civil liberties, solidarity, equality or revealed truth. So, too, with power relations. Democracies may be unicameral or bi-cameral. They may allow for formal representation of religious bodies, landed wealth, or even royalty as well as seeking to enshrine clear relations between capital and labour. The same holds true of the ways of life which underpin democracies. The role assigned to custom, to merit or virtue, to the will of the majority or to the desire for consensus reflects the way people seek to deal with one another in civic life generally. Furthermore, neither the content not the interaction of these factors is static. Democracies are living organisms with tendencies that can be either healthy or pathological, leading to the development of stability or crisis, of justice or tyranny.

The case for – and test of – democracy, as well as for the particular shape of democracies, rests on the way these three factors – values and principles, power relations and ways of life – combine to form a set of principles, a set of institutions and a set of practices that result in good governance. These provide complementary, not competing, criteria both for evaluating how well particular democracies may be working and for democracy itself. Each of these will be looked at next, with a theological comment.

Democracy as Value – A Set of Principles

> For really I think that the poorest he that is in England hath a life to live,
> as the greatest he; and therefore, truly, Sir, I think it's clear, that every man
> that is to live under a government ought first by his own consent to put
> himself under that government; and I do think that the poorest man in
> England is not at all bound in a strict sense to that government that he
> hath not had a voice to put himself under.
>
> Colonel Thomas Rainsborough, Leveller [56]

The words of Colonel Thomas Rainsborough, proclaimed two decades before the emergence of the philosophy of John Locke, have power to inspire even today. As the English Civil Wars continued, the King, whose fate had not yet been decided, began to be seen as the enemy of the people. But who then had the right to rule? 'All the Free-born people' according to the Levellers. Democracy was a matter of principle. It was with that sort of concern for principles that David Beetham, leader of the 1998 Towards Social Transformation seminar, developed his argument: 'It is important to start a discussion of democracy with its basic principles or "regulative ideals", rather than with a set of political institutions....'[57] It is a principle furthermore, which Beetham insists should be extended to civil society: '...democracy does not just belong to the sphere of the state or of government, as we usually tend to think of it. Democratic principles are relevant to collective decision-making in any kind of association. Indeed, there is an important relation between democracy at the level of the state and democracy in the other institutions of society.'[58] Beetham bases his approach on certain principles and two of the most fundamental of these are developed in a booklet he helped produce on behalf of the United Nations: 'Democracy… entails the twin principles of *popular control* over collective decision-making and *equality of rights* in the exercise of that control.' Elsewhere he elaborates on the principle of popular control, which implies 'the ability and willingness to play a part in common affairs…and to acknowledge some responsibility for them'; and on the principle of equal rights, which entails 'a respect for the rights of other citizens, an acknowledgment of their equal dignity, and the recognition of their right to an opinion, especially when it differs from one's own.'[59]

The sorts of ideals and principles that are associated with Beetham's approach are so familiar that we tend to take them for granted, without necessarily thinking through their implications. But being a political Subject is about more than demanding one's rights. Beetham's definition is as demanding as it is simple. 'Ability', 'willingness', 'responsibility', 'popular control', 'equality of rights in the exercise of that control' – these imply more than casting a ballot every few years. They imply that democracy depends on the attitudes and maturity of the demos – the common people, ourselves.

But how much do 'The People' want democracy? For John Dunn, the defeat of the more egalitarian democratic Conspiracy of Gracchus Babeuf in 1796 led to an historic choice. Thereafter people would settle for a trade off, hanging onto the word democracy to sustain hope and to suggest an agenda of inclusion, decency and ultimate political authority but letting go of the dream of equality in favour of having a share in what was on offer: 'The market is the most powerful mechanism for dismantling equality that humans have ever fashioned. But it is not simply equality's enemy….' It is not that the people were manipulated or were labouring under some sort of false consciousness, argues Dunn: 'Had it [democracy] really been rule by the people…it would assuredly not have triumphed, but dissolved instead, immediately and irreversibly, into chaos.' Dunn sees their historic choice as reflecting the wisdom of Aristotle. But must it be the end of the story?[60]

Christian Theology and the Democratic Principle

When he [Jesus] took God by the hand and called him 'our Father', he democratised the conception of God....He not only saved humanity; he saved God. He gave God his first chance of being loved and of escaping from the worst misunderstandings conceivable.

Walter Rauschenbusch[61]

That was how, a century ago, Walter Rauschenbusch, the leading theologian of the American Social Gospel movement saw it. Such a view represents, to use the typology of H. Richard Niebuhr, the 'Christ of Culture' type of Christian social theology.[62] It is not possible here to explore all the approaches to democracy that might stem from each of Niebuhr's five types, much less to open up a discussion on different theological methods. It may, however be helpful to identify four broad approaches that have been taken by the churches. The first amounts to a celebration of democracy in and of itself. The second, looks upon democracy as simply an historical fact whose justification took time to develop. The third starts with theological vision and attempts to develop a distinctive type of 'Christian Democracy'. The fourth explores the interaction between political concepts and the changing social, economic and cultural context.

The first tendency, the celebration of democracy in and of itself is represented by Rauschenbusch. The second tendency, that of gradual acceptance and justification, was represented in the stance enshrined in official Catholic social teaching until the mid-twentieth century.[63] It was expressed classically by Leo XIII: 'Again, it is not of itself wrong to prefer a democratic form of government, if only the Catholic doctrine be maintained as to the origin and exercise of power. Of the various forms of government, the Church does not reject any that are fitted to procure the welfare of the subject; she wishes only – and this nature itself requires – that they should be constituted without involving wrong to any one, and especially without violating the rights of the Church....'[64] Today Roman Catholic social teaching has developed a more philosophical rationale, drawing on a personalist reading of natural law.[65]

The third stance is represented by the attempt to develop a distinctive type of Christian Democracy. The label has been used to cover a very wide and different set of ideologies. Continental Christian Democracy is a far cry from some of the 19th century versions which tended to see it as part of a project of developing a new Christendom.[66]

A more heuristic approach was taken by David Nicholls, joint leader of the 1991 Towards Social Transformation seminar. He interprets historical experience in a more critical, one might say dialectical, manner. Nicholls' fascinating insights build on the notion that there is an interaction between the shape of power in any given period and our ideas of God. He is careful, however, not to reduce one to the other. Rather, employing a method that has similarities with Raymond Williams' approach to the idea of culture, Nicholls explored these issues in two insightful volumes, part of a planned trilogy which was never realized due to his premature death. Nicholls sees an affinity – but not a simple cause and effect – in the 18th century between the concern for government of the 'rule of law' and the need of the age for a cosmological system based on natural and divine law after the upheavals of the 17th century, which were based on the rule of a person, i.e. the king. Applying it to our own times, Nicholls does not go so far as to advocate replacing the language of 'the Kingdom of God' with 'God's federal republic', because it risks making the constitution into a type of god and turning government into rule not by people but by lawyers.[67] If our idea of God is deeply Trinitarian, argues Nicholls, then this too will tell us something about the context and style of governing.

Democracy as Power Relations – A Set of Institutions

Liberal-democracy is a fairly late product of the market society; the first
need of the market society was for the liberal state, not a democratic one.
C. B. Macpherson[68]

Conceiving democracy as an ideal needs to be complemented with a realistic appreciation of democracy as a set of power relations. There is nothing morally wrong about power relations. On the contrary, democracy thrives on a sound understanding of how power is best used and how legitimate interests can be represented.

Power is one of the three components of democracy, serving to ensure the institutional arrangements which incorporate values and principles, which recognize the importance of social practices, and which provide forums where intelligent debate about issues of common concern can be held. It is as much about empowering those who, in theory, have an abstract right to participate in governance as it is about checking concentrations of economic, political or cultural power. Democracy came to be not because everyone thought what a splendid idea it was, but because they struggled both to put a halt to the abuse of power and also to obtain a share in the exercise of power.

The problem comes when power and self-interest try to hide behind the rhetoric of democratic ideals. This gives the green light to the *libido dominandi*, allowing projects of 'democratization' to be invoked as a cover for the promotion of national, class or cultural interests. But the holders of power, whoever they may be, tend to want to exercise that power as they see fit. They do not like to lose it and may often be tempted to extend it. When Lord Acton observed: 'Power tends to corrupt, and absolute power corrupts absolutely,' he was not thinking of democracy. But the tendency for power to seek more power is just as evident in democratic polities as in any other kind of political system. In theory, the great advantage of democracy, however, is that it is inherently better designed to contain the exercise of power by diffusing it and by calling it to account. Democracy, in other words, depends crucially upon the way the certain key relations of power are delimited in a written or unwritten constitution.[69] The need to contain power has played an important part in the Whig theory of democracy, made all the more necessary by reason of its assumption of the centrality of private property and self-interest. The first constraint had to do with the separation of powers within government, the second with the rights of individuals and groups in relation to the government. Neither was entirely original.

The importance of the separation of powers predates modernity. It also can take at least three different forms.[70] It may point to a separation of functions – Aristotle distinguished the deliberative, the executive and the judicial.[71] Or, secondly, it may refer to a separation of organs or departments – the Roman Republic, argued Niccolo Machiavelli, owed its stability not to the harmony between the patrician (the Senate) and the plebeian (the People) elements, but precisely to the useful contention between them.[72] Thirdly, it may indicate a separation of constituencies or estates – William Blackstone (1723–1780) lauded the 'true excellence of the English government, that all parts of it form a mutual check upon each other. In the legislature the people are a check upon the nobility and the nobility a check upon the people…while the King is a check upon both.'[73]

The second crucial constraint on power in the Whig approach to democracy was the protection of the freedom of individuals and groups in relation to the government, increasingly spelt out in Declarations, Charters and Bills of Rights. Again, this was neither new nor peculiar to democracy. Both Roman Law and English common law recognized liberties, rights, and powers – as well as privileges – which people were not prepared to sacrifice simply because there was a change in the form of government. Enshrining such insights in the democratic constitutions is essential in order to prevent democracies from becoming simply 'the will of the people' or the tyranny of the majority.

One of the questions confronting contemporary democracies is whether these sorts of constitutional arrangements are sufficient to address the sort of power relations which have developed under capitalist modernity. This is not to suggest that the answer lies in more authoritarian structures. It is to ask, first, to what extent constraints similar to those traditionally placed on political power need to be placed on economic power and secondly, how far the sort of empowerment provided by political rights needs to be extended to economic rights and freedoms.

Long before America became democratic, its English colonists harboured a deep mistrust of the concentration of power, whether in the hands of the state or the church. That same mistrust of power was expressed in later centuries in the face of the growth of economic monopolies. The American socialist movement – such as it was – was able to appeal to this sentiment and was, for a while at least, in no way perceived as 'un-American'. It finds echoes still in the response to the films of Michael Moore, which resonate with those who love America, not, as outsiders might suspect, with those who despise it. It characterized the Progressivist and Social Gospel movements and has particularly been part of the heritage of the Democratic Party.

But, if democracy is to flourish, a deeper sort of questioning may now be needed. Democracy and the holding of property were once thought to be essentially linked. In one sense, that link is weaker than it was in that the right to vote, to participate in public debate, and to hold office is now recognized as rooted more in human dignity than in property. Controversially, links remain. On one side, are the proponents of a property-owning democracy, arguing that if people have a stake in the status quo, whether through home-ownership, shares or pension rights they are less likely to seek radical change. On the other are those who argue that such property-based stability does not necessarily promote either social justice or environmental well-being and that what needs to be challenged is the proprietary notion itself of democracy.

The tradition of 'possessive individualism', argues C. B. Macpherson, had even found its way into the thinking of the Levellers. For they conceived independence in terms of a person's proprietorship of their personhood and capacities. The reason that they did not deny the vote to labourers, as they did to women, servants, and beggars was precisely their view that one's labour was a 'property' which they were able to sell and which, consequently, provided a material basis for freedom and for the right to have a voice.[74]

Christian Realism

Christian realism (lower case) here refers to describes theologies that engage with realities such as self-interest and social conflict which are resistant to appeals to reason, justice and the common good and which, therefore, justify courses of action which may involve the use of force. Christian Realism (upper case) refers to one version of this which was associated with Reinhold Niebuhr: 'Man's capacity for justice makes democracy possible; but man's inclination to injustice makes democracy necessary.'[75] There is clearly a strong dose here of Reformation theology ('Christ and Culture in Paradox', to use the typology of Niebuhr's brother), with a strong reliance on a particular reading of Augustine. Niebuhr takes seriously the *libido dominandi*, the operation of self-interest and the reality of power. This did not make him a cynic or a pessimist. For all his insistence on the need to take power seriously, he warned that to define the task as merely achieving an effective balance of power was to consign democracy to being little more than 'managed anarchy'. Government operates, for Niebuhr, within the framework of power, but it is also about love, justice and shared values. At the heart of Niebuhr's realism was a sense of human limitation, which he applied to democracy itself. It enabled him to avoid overstating the importance of democracy. Democracy was useful. It was: '...a method of finding proximate solutions for insoluble problems [but]....To make a democratic society the end of human existence....is dangerous.'

A second, more antagonistic approach, takes inspiration from Hegel's view of the dialectic of opposition between Master-Slave, which seeks resolution in mutual recognition. In the Hegelian-Marxist tradition, which has had an important, though not determining influence on liberation theology, struggle is built into the script. It has an ontological basis. For Milbank, this is a sign that liberation theology has not broken radically enough with the 'agonistic' character of secular reason.

There is a third kind of 'realism', which is more radically historical in nature and is able to savour the irony this brings into the story of democracy. What better irony than to detect ways in which undemocratic churches have actually contributed unintentionally to democracy. Figgis, for example, observes: 'Political liberty is the fruit of ecclesiastical animosities.'[76] But not as the myth of religious minorities fighting and ultimately winning the battle for religious liberty would have it: '...political liberty, *as such*, never was and never will be an ideal of Puritanism.'[77] David Nicholls, who has done more than anyone to resurrect Figgis' views, adds: 'Toleration, then, was not achieved by any single group, but by the failure of any group to predominate sufficiently to crush the rest.'[78] It is interesting to note that the American political philosopher John Rawls picks up this theme, but with a more muted sense of irony: 'Political liberalism is not a form of Enlightenment liberalism....the historical origin of political liberalism (and of liberalism more generally) is the Reformation and its aftermath....'[79]

Democracy as a Part of a Way of Life – A Set of Practices

Democracy is a form of government only because
it is a form of moral and spiritual association.
John Dewey[80]

Current attempts by the West to export democracy could be in danger of repeating the same mistake made in its attempt to export markets in the 1990s. It should be obvious: democracy grows from the bottom up, not from the top down. The weighting given to particular democratic values and principles, the particular shape of constitutional arrangements, the bases of legitimacy, and the understandings of what it means to be a Subject do in fact vary from culture to culture. This is because democracies contain a third dimension – the way of life and a set of practices in which they happen to be embedded. Such a claim does not imply a simple endorsement of 'the way we do things here'. If that were the case slavery and patriarchy would still be with us. It involves taking a critical view of actual practice in the light of the professed values of a people. Rainsborough himself provided a splendid example when he clinched his eloquent argument for the right of 'the poorest he' to have a say in government with his evocation of the traditions and identity of his hearers with this body-blow: 'I should doubt whether he was an Englishman...that should doubt of these things.'[81]

One might call this third approach to democracy 'communitarian', provided the term is understood not in substantive terms, as if it entailed giving a privileged place to 'community', solidarity, cohesion, etc., but in a formal sense as a reminder that often the most persuasive arguments come from inside particular traditions with an appeal to the identity which a particular people are proud to own.

The American political philosopher, Richard Rorty (the grandson of Walter Rauschenbusch) relies on a sort of 'liberal communitarianism' in his pragmatic defence of democracy.[82] That is to say, the acid test of democracy for Americans is that Americans see themselves as democrats and see democracy as being woven into their way of life, to the extent that it has become not simply a philosophy but almost a creed, among whose greatest prophets was John Dewey.

The communitarian argument is not inherently aggressive or reactionary. It calls both government and fellow citizens to account by challenging them to act consistently with their own professed principles. That, argues Michael Walzer, is what the prophets did with kings and what Jesus did with the religious leaders of his times. And that is why Rorty distances himself from those intellectuals who, in their criticism of the US policies have either marginalized themselves or reverted to a Kantian-style universal principle approach: '…their long-run effect has been to separate the intellectuals from the moral consensus of the nation rather than to alter that consensus.'[83]

But just as American democracy is grounded in and reflects its way of life, so other nations with other ways of life provide the elements for other styles of democracy. Amartya Sen has invoked the much older traditions of his native India to challenge the notion that democracy is a mainly Western idea. The Indian experience enables him to argue that 'Democracy is best seen as the opportunity of participatory reasoning and public decision making – as "government by discussion".' Sen, a secularist himself, argues further that while we may tend to see 'public reasoning' as a part of a secular Greek legacy, it was also practised in Hindu, Buddhist and Muslim contexts as well. Indeed in the 1590s, notes Sen, under Akbar, the great Moghul emperor of India, inter-faith meetings were set up between Hindus, Muslims, Christians, Jews, Parsees and atheists.[84]

Christian Communitarianism

The difficulty faced by Christians with democracy as a way of life is precisely that for most churches democracy is not 'how we do things'. There have, of course, been instances where the churches have adopted less hierarchical patterns of polity. Some of the orders of religious communities in the later Middle Ages did move from a paternal model of authority to a more fraternal model. Then, at the time of the Reformation, some of the free churches which themselves had suffered greatly at the hands of ecclesiastical authority, began to develop more congregational systems of polity. And there has been, throughout the history of the church, the emergence of more radical Christian communities – some admittedly far from democratic – which have developed their own form of communism. In the wake of the Second Vatican Council, the notion of the church as 'the people of God' began to gain favour in Catholic circles, particularly under the influence of Liberation Theology; but more hierarchically-minded forces soon acted to neutralize such a dangerous development.

By and large, the churches, whether their polity is papal, episcopal or presbyterian are far from democratic, whilst even those with a more congregational structure do not always operate within the structures of rights and accountability that is commonly associated with democracy. Certainly neither Augustine's own approach nor his vision of the City of God was democratic. Whether the churches will become more democratic, must depend not on imitating secular democracy but on developing, as a result of historical experience, fresh insights into the way in which such practices may actually resonate better with the Gospel.

Stanley Hauerwas abhors the label communitarian but, in the sense that the term is used here, it does not seem unfair to cite him as an important example of this approach. His community has a narrative which leads him to take an almost aggressive stance towards liberalism, whether in its idealist, realist or communitarian modes and to question whether democracy is necessarily entailed by a Christian vision of politics: 'The problem with our society is not that democracy has not worked, but that it has, and the results are less than good'.[85] By democracy, Hauerwas means that democracy which is based on the christening of self-interest from vice to virtue, has exalted freedom of the individual as an end in itself, and has helped produce a society which is based on collective mistrust and competition, where people are strangers to one another and where in place of common bonds there are procedures, regulations, covert coercion and theological self-policing. Hauerwas sees the problem as due to the fact that Western democracy is underpinned by secular liberalism. The argument here is that it is also a reflection of capitalist modernity.

Hauerwas laments the fact that 'Christians have learned to police their convictions in the name of sustaining such orders'. Seeking to expose their reasons for doing so, he levels the accusation that the praise of democracy by Protestant Christians in the past has been only a justification for why *we* should rule.[86] Instead, he argues that a key part of the church's social task is to provide a 'contrast model', an 'alternative polity', in which, under the right form of authority and discipline, a new type of freedom would be realized – a freedom from mutual fear – founded in the virtuous practice of mutual forgiveness, which in turn would create space for trust, and replace the rule of violence with the peaceable kingdom of reconciliation.[87] This approach does not succeed or fail on the basis of actual church practice. If it did, it would surely fail. In many ways the church has often provided a pretty appalling example of how to use power. Non-transparent power and unaccountable power have frequently been the rule – often in the noble and genuine name of seeking to operate on the basis of love alone – as if power was an unmentionable, unclean aspect of common life. The communitarian argument relies rather on the possibility of calling communities to be faithful in practice to the tradition which gave rise to them. If the church is to represent an alternative polity, it has a lot of work – and a lot of repenting – to do.

Making Democracy good

The three rationales offered for democracy – that it represents a universal set of principles, that it provides a check against the abuse of power, and that it develops the collective identity of a people – together help to strengthen the argument that democracy promotes good governance and fits well within the basic framework of the common good and a common culture. They also provide valuable insights by which the state of health of existing democracies may be assessed. As for the health of democracy under the regime of capitalist modernity, its strengths and weaknesses were explored earlier in this chapter. The questions that remain to be addressed in the following sections are: what can be done to improve the health of the democratic system under which we live and what sorts of transformations are needed to allow a healthier form of democracy to flourish? The answer may lie within the democratic practice itself. That is to say, the point is not to try to promote one specific model of democracy but to suggest that a development of democratic practice, in both state and civil society, is the way in which social transformation will take place. This involves two main tasks: building up the demos, and identifying creative forms of democratic practice. Those are the two tasks which will be looked at separately in the next two sections.

4. Transforming Democracy: We The People

When the founding fathers said 'we the people', they didn't mean me.
Condoleezza Rice [88]

At the heart of the question of democracy is not the question of structures but the more fundamental question of the 'demos' itself. Who exactly is the demos and on what grounds does it claim a share in government? The *demos*, the *'populus'*, *'the people'*, is not simply another name for the population as a whole. It is a political concept, best understood as 'the citizenry'. Its focus was the public sphere of life – *res publica res populi* – which is one reason why those whose lives were restricted to the private sphere of the household, i.e. women and slaves, were not considered to be part of 'the people'. There was an element of class as well, insofar as the plebs and the aristocracy occupied different roles within the republican life. But it is the link between demos and citizenship that is essential. Without it there is good reason to be wary of democracy, for without a demos democracy can degenerate into factions, into racial, nationalistic or religious tribalism or into the populism.

The fears of populism remain real. The World Bank has warned of its rise both in countries in Eastern Europe, which are struggling to adjust to capitalism, and countries in Latin America which are seeking alternatives to capitalism.[89] Nor has Western Europe left it behind. According to one unnamed senior European Union diplomat: 'The kinds of things some of these central European politicians say are far worse than anything Haider [of Austria's far right Freedom Party] ever said.'[90]

A people does not become a demos naturally. The natural tendency was to view the people as subjects not as Subjects. Oliver Cromwell was not a democrat. Nor was John Locke. Nor was Adam Smith. Nor was Edmund Burke. Nor were the authors of the American Constitution. The First Continental Congress in November 1775 might urge delegates from each colony to 'call a full and free representation of the People', just as the Virginia Declaration of Rights of June 1776 might also declare '[t]hat all power is vested in, and consequently derived from the people' and 'that magistrates are their trustees and servants, and at all times amenable to them' – but these were republican not democratic refrains. True, there did arise in the American colonies, incipient democratic movements, challenging the domination of the mainly Anglican, gentlemanly, property-owning class that had developed over the preceding 150 years, but alliances between the 'mechanics and small farmers of the West and the radicals and proletariat of the East' were still rare.[91] The US Constitution eventually drafted in 1787 might begin 'We the people...', but it actually represented the ascendancy of Whig over democratic forces, which were assigned their proper place, which generally meant a lower house.

The demos, with its consciousness of being a political Subject rather than simply a subject, emerged, as a rule, out of the need to challenge those who claimed an exclusive right to rule but who were using that power for private advantage rather than public good. It required a struggle. Underpinning the struggle, however, was sometimes a commitment to the common good, but sometimes simply a desire for a share of the action. Even so, the struggle of the demos was typically a struggle not for power but for freedom, that entailed a transformation both in the structures of power and in the fundamental attitude to power and authority. It was, as Hazlitt insisted, a struggle between the idol of Legitimacy and the call to freedom. 'For a people to be free, it is sufficient that they will to be free', he wrote. 'But,' he lamented, 'the love of liberty is less strong than the love of power....'[92]

Power does not let go easily. The Levellers struggled for a share of power in the late 1640s – but lost. A century and a half later, radical groups like the London Corresponding Society organized to take up the case for universal manhood suffrage and annual parliaments – and found their meetings infiltrated with government spies and their leaders charged with treason. The Chartist movement of the 1840s faced stiff resistance from the established powers. And women had to struggle for almost another century until they too were allowed to vote. But although these struggles were eventually successful, victory often meant less the creation of a new game than entry into a game which was already well under way and whose rules had been set. The democracies which resulted did not end in a draw, but they do tend to bear the marks of a compromise between the demands of those who are struggling for a share of power and the terms on which those who had power but were prepared – or forced – to share it.

The specific requirements for citizenship – age, wealth, residence, even religious affiliation – might vary as do the specific rights and duties connected with that status. What does not vary is the fact that they arose out of a desire for freedom and for a voice in the decisions which affect one's life.

The development of this sense of being a Subject, occupied, interestingly enough, a central place in the social teaching of the late Pope John Paul II. 'Authentic democracy,' he declared, '...requires that the necessary conditions be present for the advancement both of the individual through education and formation in true ideals, and of the "subjectivity" of society, through the creation of structures of participation and shared responsibility.'[93]

Thus subjects have become Subjects and those who exercise the role of governing do so as representatives and 'ministers', i.e. public servants. It is a remarkable transformation. How can it be justified?

From 'Subject' to Citizen

The first transformation involved becoming Subjects; the second is about becoming Citizens. The first is about gaining voice and identity, the second about accepting rights and responsibilities. The traditional contempt for democracy was based on prejudice against and fear of the demos. It was a view articulated by the ruling classes in defence of the ruling classes. It was, in short, ideology. Like all ideologies, it owed its persuasive power to the fact that it was able to resonate with peoples' experiences. The demos was neither well educated nor did it always subscribe to the civic virtues to which the ruling classes at the very least paid lip service. Now that the majority of most populations are educated, have access to information, have had some religious and moral training and have their own interest to defend, there is less justification for such arrogant dismissals of democracy. But how deep are the roots which incline us to transcend tribal loyalties of ethnicity, religion and nationality, to respect the rights of minorities, and to accept personal responsibility for the life of our polis?

In some parts of the world, the answer is not very encouraging. And the attempt to impose a nominal democracy where there is no demos may be simply mischievous, threatening a country with instability (the Cedar Revolution in the Lebanon) or plunging it into civil war (what President Bush dubbed 'the Purple Revolution' in Iraq after the dye used on index fingers for voting). But even in areas where democracy appears to have taken root, it is unwise to take the health of the demos for granted. The tendency to put basic needs such as security ahead of freedom must not be underestimated. It is easy to forget that the country which is now pushing democratization across the globe was, only a few decades ago, pushing the National Security State. Indeed the continuing subordination of 'democratization' to the defence of strategic political and economic interests was clearly revealed by American willingness to allow popular movements in Uzbekistan, Chechnya and Burma to be brutally suppressed. So, too, with the tendency to put material benefits and even entertainment ahead of responsibility. The more the demos becomes a collection of consumers rather than an active citizenry, the more liable it is to elect governments which promise more for less and which refuse to elicit the sacrifices needed to create a more just world.

The demos is no more or less virtuous than the aristocracy, and no more or less wise than the technocrats. The *libido dominandi* is at work in the demos just as much as in the ruling class, only in a different way. Machiavelli saw this as being at the heart of the useful struggle between the Senate, fearful of losing the power they had, and the People, intent on enlarging their power: '...the first have a great desire to dominate, whilst the latter have only the wish not to be dominated.'[94] For Hazlitt, the problem was rather the opposite: the People wanted to worship power. The People, he lamented, did not love freedom enough. They preferred to enjoy vicariously the power and glory of those who were above them: 'All we want is to aggrandize our own vain-glory at second-hand....' And again: 'Man is a toad-eating animal. The admiration of power in others is as common to man as the love of it in himself.'[95]

Hazlitt referred to the need to 'serve out our apprenticeship to liberty'.[96] The same might be said about our apprenticeships as Subjects of democratic responsibility.

We are, rightly, no longer prepared to hand government over to philosopher-kings or to the rule of the saints. Why then should we hand power to transnational corporations or to hedge funds? Have we any basis for assuming that democratic structures will automatically lead to good governance? It is important, but not sufficient, to recognize that people are the best judges of their own interests. But politics is also about the common good and the common good is more than an accumulation of private goods or a temporary resolution of the conflict between interest groups. How can we move, with Augustine, from the *libido dominandi* to the love of the good? The answer may lie in learning through practice. And that is what will be explored in the final section of this chapter.

5. PRACTICING DEMOCRACY: CIVIL SOCIETY AND THE STATE

We overestimated the power of movements and underestimated the need
for lasting new democratic institutions. Now many of us are working
on such institutions: for a participatory democracy, for a socially owned
economy, for ending international financial speculation and breaking up
corporate power. And we are not working in a political vacuum...
Hilary Wainwright [97]

In arguing for the need to give pride of place to civil society, Gellner was not expressing an antipathy to democracy but simply warning against the naïve notion that the shape of society depends upon our choices. The context into which we are born, the values of our culture, its institutions and structures are to a large measure antecedent to such choices. That does not mean that these cannot be changed. Indeed, in some cases, they must be. It does mean that we need to take them into account.

That is why for John Keane the task involves the democratization of both state and civil society, as well as the democratization of the right relationship between the two. That relationship is not a zero-sum game as if the strengthening of civil society entailed the weakening of the state. In fact the reverse is the case. But how, at the institutional level, to get the relationship right so that new possibilities of social transformation may emerge? Here the question will be looked at in five of its aspects. Firstly, the practices of everyday life – does democracy begin at home? Secondly, new social movements – what is so 'new' about them? Thirdly, the integrity of associations and groups in civil society – what is the source of their authority? Fourthly, associative democracy – should associations be accorded quasi-public status? And fifthly, reclaiming the state – how might the state/civil society relationship be redefined?

Everyday Life: The Re-grounding of Democracy

...to be effective, international networks and campaigns need to be rooted in people's everyday lives.
Hilary Wainwright[98]

To suggest the importance of everyday life for the grounding of democratic practice does not mean that everyday life should be 'politicized', colonized by ideology, inhibited by 'political correctness' or subjected to the logic of rights. On the contrary, the movement is precisely in the opposite direction: the experiences of everyday life can help reshape politics in a more democratic direction. And this in three ways. First, it can help ensure that the content of political debate reflects the needs of everyday life. Secondly, it can legitimise the right of those whose experience is mainly in this realm to be listened to. Thirdly, it can allow the practice of politics to change so that space is created for the scope of love, forgiveness and mutuality.

Support for such an approach comes from a range of very different perspectives. From Tom Paine comes the appeal to 'common sense': politics is not some mysterious world. From Charles Taylor comes the reminder that Judaism and Christianity, in contrast to classical Greek and Roman thought, have insisted that 'ordinary life' – the family, labour, commerce – be included as essential components of 'the good life'.[99]

But the issue is more than simply validating the experience of everyday life. It is also about the way in which everyday life offers the potential for the transformation of political life. From John Milbank, leader of the 1995 Towards Social Transformation seminar, come insights, drawn from the early Pauline household churches and from the vision of Augustine about a new type of 'City', which suggest that the practices of the household (*oikos*) and neighbourhood (*paroikia*) should be allowed to have greater impact on the politics of the state (*polis*).[100] By reason of baptism, a new kind of community is formed, affording each person – female or male, slave or free, child or adult – full membership, and giving rise to a new set of practices, love, forgiveness and reconciliation. The performance of these practices offers signs as to what life in a polis can be and enlarges the scope for their application. At the same time the diversity and flexibility of household patterns suggest the viability of a diversity of political units and associations within the wider, global political community. This is why, argues Milbank, Augustine, although not presenting the City of God as wholly coterminous with the church, can nonetheless see in the church and apply to the church the image of a city, the City of God,

From Hilary Wainwright leader of the 1994 Towards Social Transformation seminar comes the attempt to take the insights of the anti-socialist Friedrich Hayek, about the uncodifiable aspects of everyday practical knowledge, and turn them on their head. Wainwright argues that such knowledge can be seen as power, offering new ways of calling power to account and providing new forms of participation, thus preparing the ground for new models of democratic socialism.[101] Wainwright pays tribute to Paulo Freire (1921–1997) whose method – a 'pedagogy of the oppressed' – systematically enabled even the experiences of crushing poverty to be transformed into political empowerment through a process of 'conscientization'. In describing the democratic experiment in Porto Alegre, the site of the first three World Social Forum meetings, Wainwright acknowledges: 'It is impossible to understand the participatory methods of the PT [Workers' Party of President Lula da Silva and main party in Porto Alegre] without recognizing the contribution made by Paulo Freire's ideas on education.'[102]

For both Wainwright and Milbank, an important dimension of the validation of the experience of everyday life and of the sphere of the household/neighbourhood is that it gives greater scope for participation by women. This, in turn, provides further impetus for the transformation of politics, not only in terms of the shaping of its agenda but also – and ultimately more importantly – in the style of wider political organization and action. It was some twenty-five years ago that Wainwright, with her colleagues Sheila Rowbotham and Lynne Segal, made a significant impact on the Left with their argument about socialism's need of a feminist perspective to get beyond the very male – and often adolescent – way of organizing socialist activity, such as she had experienced in her brief involvement with the International Marxist Group and the Socialist Workers Party.[103] The women's movement brought a more flexible and open approach – a new type of democratic culture, which grounds itself on the real, though fragmentary, experiences of exploited groups, and makes possible creative interaction and common and experienced-based action.

New Social Movements – The Practice of Self-Limitation

It is about time socialists abandoned this futile claim to hegemony.
Paul Hirst[104]

What is so 'new' about new social movements? After all, social movements have a long history. As long ago as the 18th century, Quakers and others were the leading spirits behind movements for the abolition of slavery and for prison reform, and Hannah More was spearheading the movement for popular education and moral reform. And all through the 19th century there were movements for better working conditions, for temperance, for moral welfare, for pensions, for women's suffrage and for a host of other important causes. What, then, is so new about 'new' social movements? The concept of new social movements has been developed by Jean Cohen and Andrew Arato and, in a very different way, by Andrew Shanks. For them it is not a matter of new issues or new tactics but a new role. Whereas the role of traditional social movements – which are still needed – is to achieve particular changes in policy – the role of new social movements is to nurture a transformation in the political process itself. It is about encouraging the practice of critical political discourse – an approach which is consistent with Raymond Williams' notion of communication as developed in Chapter Three.

Cohen and Arato base their approach on the endorsement of modernity as developed especially by Jurgen Habermas. The task is to renegotiate the relationship between civil society, the economy and the state but in a way which respects the autonomy of each of the different spheres of action. It relies on the principle of self-limitation, which both refuses to see their issues in isolation and refuses to be co-opted by the state as some NGOs and social movements have been.[105]

For Andrew Shanks, on the other hand, the basis for new social movements is not so much modernity as the 'solidarity of the shaken'. New social movements aim to challenge the attitude that any authority, secular or religious, in state or civil society, is in full possession of the truth. The mission of the new social movements is 'to transform the general conduct of public affairs' by opening up the public space for unhindered conversation among the 'shaken'. The new social movements are not crusades. They work for a considerable degree of mutual respect on all sides.[106] New social movements should become 'licensed agencies of antipolitics' argues Shanks.[107] This does not mean refusing all co-operation with the state. Such agencies would have to be independent of any political party and not engaged in propaganda, even religious, but they would receive state funding. This would come through an independent commission, on which religious and other civic groups would be represented. Their whole purpose would be to explore new ideas, to think in the longer term. A condition for receiving funding might be: '…that it helped give a public hearing to voices which would otherwise tend not to be heard: the voices of the poor, the discriminated against, the excluded, the inarticulate – voices from abroad, voices representing the interests of future generations.'

Challenging State Sovereignty: The Personality of Social Groups

This is the true meaning of our word Commons; not the mass of the common people, but the community of communities.
John Neville Figgis[108]

The 'demolition of the notion of state sovereignty': that is the mission of the radical pluralist tradition, which David Nicholls, joint leader of the 1991 Towards Social Transformation seminar sought to revive.[109] This challenge to the very existence of state sovereignty is not to be confused with the current debates about the diffusion of state sovereignty below the nation-state, as for example the Scottish Parliament or above the nation-state, as with the European Union, where a sharing of sovereignty has long since occurred. Such blurring of the edges of sovereignty, however, relate only to the sphere of statutory authority. Nicholls stepped outside that box altogether, arguing against the notion of state sovereignty as such, and seeking to reclaim the inherent and inalienable authority of the groups, communities and associations which make up civil society. The notion of sovereignty is demythologized and seen as a product of historical circumstances. This approach goes by the name 'Political pluralism' in the sense given it in a tradition which Nicholls traces from Figgis to G. D. H. Cole to Harold Laski. It is not to be confused with the way the term 'political pluralism' is understood in the United States, where it refers to interest groups competing for a share of power and influence over existing state structures.

The key figure behind this tradition is John Neville Figgis.[110] What prompted Figgis' more radical challenge to state sovereignty was the way the state – as represented in Germany by Bismarck's *Kulturkampf* and in France by the secularist policies of the Third Republic under Émile Combes – was asserting the right to interfere with the autonomy of the church. As a friend of Lord Acton's, Figgis shared the traditional Whig fear of excessive state power, but Figgis went further. If such interference was being justified in the name of state sovereignty, then it was against the principle of state sovereignty that the counter-attack must be launched. The challenge to state political sovereignty included a challenge to its claim to legal sovereignty.[111] The state was not the ultimate legal authority, argued Figgis. It was subject to a higher law – not a theoretical, 'natural' law, but the living law emanating from associational life. As Nicholls puts it: '...the state is not the offspring of law...any more than the law is the child of the state.'[112]

The aim was to establish the fact that associations and groups had a life and personality of their own. From such a premiss flow two crucial implications. First, the state is denied the right to impose rules and restrictions on associations which violate their identities. Secondly, because associations are living and evolving, they are not legalistically bound by the strict letter of their own original constitutions. Figgis takes the church as an example: 'Belief in the Catholic Church is a belief in development; and this means a creative evolution.'[113]

As an historian, Figgis was able to base his argument for the moral personality of the group on the work of his revered tutor William Maitland.[114] It was through Maitland, furthermore, that Figgis was introduced to the works of the German historian Otto von Gierke and was able to develop his argument based on the political role played by associations under Germanic, as distinct from Roman, law. The notion of state sovereignty, as Figgis saw it, was rooted in Roman law and baptised by the Church when, under Constantine, it was made the state religion. Until 1495, Figgis claims, there existed alongside this a Teutonic model, but then this, too, was subsumed under the Roman model. Drawing on the Germanic tradition, Maitland and Figgis see the state rather as a 'community of communities' (*communitas communitatum*).[115] The system of multiple and overlapping jurisdictions was typical in imperial rule, whether religious or secular, Persian, Roman, Ottoman, Habsburg, Spanish or British. It could be developed now, argued Figgis, who had sympathies with the federal system. As an historian, he saw it exemplified in the system of 'states' rights' which prevailed in the United States until the Civil War, after which it was gradually being subsumed into the state sovereignty model.[116]

The challenge to state sovereignty was not a plea for anarchy. The pluralists saw a value in the state's granting recognition to associations. They also accepted that some degree of regulation would be needed. Cole acknowledges the state's right to regulate religious associations, mainly in the sense of co-ordinating their interaction, whilst appearing to acknowledge the right of state intervention where a religion is part of the establishment.[117] But, as Nicholls argues: 'When Laski and Cole moved away from a belief in group personality they moved away from pluralism.'[118] At the heart of the 'political pluralism' of Figgis and Nicholls are the claims that: a) freedom is primarily realized in associational life; b) associations have a public character and a real personality; c) personality is not derived from the state and hence the state must not be seen as sovereign; and d) democracy is enhanced as associations acquire a proper political role.

Associative Democracy

> The pluralist state will be a minimal one but one whose primary task is
> to create the conditions for associations, and through them individual
> citizens, to be free to pursue their purposes.
>
> Paul Q. Hirst[119]

The project of associative democracy goes well beyond anything envisioned by Figgis and is wholly incompatible with the self-limiting approach of the new social movements. For it proposes that associations should not remain purely in the sphere of civil society. Their potential contribution to democracy is so significant and so necessary that they should be accorded 'quasi-public status'. The case for 'associative democracy' is argued by Paul Hirst,[120] joint leader of the 1991 Towards Social Transformation, and by his colleagues in the 'Real Utopias' project, Joshua Cohen and Paul Rogers.[121] To a limited extent the proposal draws on the tradition of functional democracy as developed in the early part of the last century by G. D. H. Cole and Harold Laski.[122]

Cohen and Rogers are keen to dispel any suggestion that associative democracy is a sort of 'postmodern corporatism', as though the void left by break-up of the old united working class should now be filled by a 'rainbow coalition' of disadvantaged groups. The main contribution of associative democracy would be not to develop new power blocs but to create an associational environment. This would open the way for a more radical form of democracy, characterized by equality-through-empowerment (by giving people an effective voice in policy) than can be achieved by equality-through-redistribution (by tax and benefit reform).

It is true that one objective of associative democracy would be to accord associations a more direct and formal governance role at national, regional and local levels. Extending the realm of participation in public policy and developing the democratic competency of those who participate are part of the project. But the governance role is secondary and in any case it would only complement territorial-based democracy. The key is to develop a democratic associational framework.

But there's the rub. How to ensure that the 'right kind of secondary association' exists – by which they mean not just those which play by democratic rules but also those which enable currently underrepresented and excluded groups to be included? The problem arises because the real world of associations is marked by huge disparities of size, status and money – and therefore power. To base associative democracy on the pattern of existing associational life would be a recipe for factionalism, not for the common good, and for more domination by the most powerful economic, charitable or religious groups. This could result in the corruption of the state by interest groups to an even greater degree than anything seen in the past. This is hardly what democracy is meant to be about.

To address such issues, Cohen and Rogers advocate more positive involvement on the part of the state. This would justify, they argue, a degree of 'artifactuality' in the state's role of empowering and even helping to establish associations. Such action would be taken only where necessary. It would neither apply to all associations nor would it involve creating new associations to replace existing ones. Here Hirst takes issue with Cohen and Rogers. Hirst would be more inclined to work from the bottom up.

How might faith communities fare under associative democracy? Paul Hirst chides Cohen and Rogers for neglecting to acknowledge the important contribution which churches can make.[123] Phillipe C. Schmitter, however, asks 'how they would propose dealing with the demands for participation of, say, religious sects or patriotic groups on the grounds that they have an overriding ethical concern with virtually all substantive issue areas.'[124] Figgis, for example, had argued fervently in favour of denominational schools. But what if denominational schools promote un-democratic and even anti-democratic cultures? The suspected role of certain radical Islamic schools in contributing to the upheavals in Afghanistan, for example, has prompted the government of Pakistan to seek to curtail their influence.

The problems connected with associative democracy are not ducked by their advocates. But they remain unresolved nonetheless.

Reclaiming the State:
Redefining the Contract between State and Civil Society

In the past, socialism has been seen either as a protest or an alternative programme; now it must be about building cooperation between different movements for social justice.

Hilary Wainwright [125]

Associative democracy would have to tread carefully in seeking to respect the integrity of civil society and the state. Rowan Williams has described this relationship nicely: 'The challenge is for a state apparatus to become a reliable and creative "broker" of the concerns of the communities that make it up – not simply a dependable tribunal before which rights may be argued, but a legal and (in the broadest sense) moral framework within which communities may interact without the fear that any one may gain an unjust or disproportionate power. This "interactive pluralism", rooted in the liberalism of thinkers like Acton, Maitland and Figgis, would see the healthy state neither as a group of suspiciously coexisting groups, nor as a neutral legal unit whose citizens all possessed abstractly equal rights, but as a space in which distinctive styles and convictions could challenge each other and affect each other, but on the basis that they first had the freedom to be themselves.'[126] The danger is perhaps less acute in the partnership model suggested by Hilary Wainwright. Wainwright's vision is inspired both by her work with the Greater London Council in the early 1980s as one of the co-ordinators of its Popular Planning Unit, and, more recently by her contact with the democratic experiment in Porto Alegre.[127] What is involved is a sort of conversion on the part both of the new social movements and of political parties. If new social movements must take on a new role, so too must political parties: '...an increasing number of parties are emerging that are in effect the electoral voice of coalitions of social movements.'

Wainwright dedicates a full chapter to the story of Porto Alegre. The mentality of the new kind of party is reflected in the comment of a Brazilian Workers Party activist, who declares that its aim is to 'share power with those movements to whom we owe our success' – a comment which would inspire some and terrify others. It is more a question, therefore, of learning from rather than trying to replicate the Porto Alegre experience – which, in any case, has its own flaws. Wainwright sets that experience alongside a handful of other, less spectacular struggles in Britain. She also relates this to similar movements in Western Europe, notably the 'Laboratory for Democracy' initiative in Italy.[128]

The important point is to realize that such experiments themselves do not simply emerge from nowhere. Behind the experiment in Porto Alegre lay an important preparatory period: a spirit of resistance to military government, the development of strong, highly politicized neighbourhood associations, and a Workers Party whose participatory methods had been shaped by the educational methods of Paulo Freire, with his emphasis on cultural as well as political and economic transformation. What is needed is an experimental approach, often on a very small, local scale. Of course the success of such experiments cannot be guaranteed. But, provided they are conducted in a transparent manner and according to clear rules, their real value may lie in being signs of the new world which is possible.

Conclusion

Modern ethical thought has wreaked untold damage in its false assumption
that love is first of all a personal affair rather than a political one.
Terry Eagleton [129]

Democracy is not something fixed and static. It can take many forms, forms which go beyond existing models – as this chapter has tried to show. It is both shaped by culture and by economic structures, and is able, in turn, to help transform such cultures and economic structures by enlarging the scope for participation in discourse and action about the kind of civil society that is worth developing. It requires calling power to account, not in the name of abstract principles but for the realization of the common good. Democracy is problematic for capitalist modernity, with the green light it gives to the *libido dominandi*. But it is also problematic for the church, with its emphasis on hierarchy and the authority of revealed truth. This can lead to exercises in power-politics whereby Christians are mobilized simply to use democratic structures to elect Christian representatives who will then pass Christian legislation – a tactic which not only weakens democracy, but more importantly, makes Christians a faction and turns the church into a power bloc. Instead, might not the hope for a different kind of politics be nurtured with the help of the resources of Christian tradition? Might Augustine's vision of the two cities, animated by the two loves provide the framework for the promotion of a 'civilization of love'? That will be the note on which these explorations towards social transformation will conclude.

Conclusion

Church, Civil Society, Social Transformation

God, in your grace, transform the world.
Theme for the 9th Assembly of the World Council of Churches,
Porto Alegre, Brazil, February 2006

Précis

The Towards Social Transformation initiative began by looking for hope in civil society. Has the failure of those hopes meant that the focus on civil society was misguided and that, all along, attention should have been centred on installing new economic and political systems? That is not the case that has been argued here. Regime change? Certainly. But if the regime of capitalist modernity is to be changed it will require a much deeper renewal of both civil society (the sphere distinct from the state) and Civil Society (a civilization's overall culture, institutions and regime). And it is in that context that the transforming mission of the Church needs to be looked at afresh.

This concluding chapter will look explicitly at the relation of the church both to civil society (lower case) and Civil Society (upper case) as spelt out in Chapter Two. In its relationship with civil society the church simultaneously plays three different roles. First and fundamentally its status is that of an association, which, as discussed in Chapter Five, implies limits to the right of the state to impose regulations which might alter its identity or frustrate its mission. Secondly, insofar as the church accepts state funding for the performance of certain social or civic services, it may legitimately be expected to accept the conditions to which all Third Sector organizations are subject. Thirdly, the church can act as an interest group within civil society and is perfectly entitled to press for changes in public policy, such as tax exemptions, which promote its own well-being. More important than all these, however, is the church's relationship to Civil Society. This involves two different roles. The one about which it must be most careful precisely because it appeals to the *libido dominandi*, concerns the functions traditionally associated with 'civil religion', i.e. those which uniquely reinforce the legitimacy of the state. The role which is more central, because it relies more on transformation by grace might best be described in terms of its civilizing mission. And that is what will be the focus of attention here.

The church's civilizing mission means a recognition that the Gospel has profound implications for the transformation of cultural, economic and political values and institutions. It is not without its own set of problems. It has sometimes been equated with the establishment of Christendom in Europe, or the extension of Western Christianity to the rest of the world. But there is plenty of unfinished business as far as the civilizing of the West is concerned, centred, it has been argued here, in the taming and conversion of capitalist modernity through a transformation by grace.

A transformation by grace, however, entails not domination but, literally, a give-and-take – a mutual learning from other cultures, the promotion of collaboration in economic life, the sharing of power in political affairs. It includes both a prophetic (working for justice) and a pastoral (working for healing and reconciliation) dimension globally. It is about the emergence of what some have called 'a civilization of love'. It involves, in Augustine's imagery, a struggle between two civilizations based not on two different faiths but on two different loves.

TRANSFORMING MISSION: A CIVILIZATION OF LOVE

Are we dreaming when we speak of a civilization of love?
No, we are not just dreaming.
Pope Paul VI [1]

The Resurgence of Faith Communities – Regime Change or Regime Consolidation?

One of the most remarkable changes that has occurred since the first local Towards Social Transformation gathering in September 1989 is the new appreciation of the political and social role played by religion and by faith communities. This is true at both the level of Civil Society (the overall polity) and civil society (the sphere distinct from the state). At each level, however, critical questions need to be asked as to how to ensure that the church is being true to its authentic mission and is playing its proper role.

For example, at the level of Civil Society, it is certainly true that 'religion' and faith communities have become forces to reckon with in the political arena. This is as true of the so-called 'Religious Right' in the United States as it is of the growing influence of Islamic parties in Turkey, the Middle East[2] and in Central and Southern Asia. Even in France, that most avowedly secularist of states, the growth of the Muslim population has re-opened the thinking amongst the political elite about the role of religion.[3] In the Philippines, it was Cardinal Sin who inspired the people's power which brought about regime change not once but twice – in 1986 (Ferdinand Marcos) and in 2001 (Joseph Estrada). And, when asked to name 'The Most Influential European of the Past 25 Years', readers of the *Financial Times*, chose not Mikhail Gorbachev, Margaret Thatcher, Gro Harlem Brundtland, Helmut Kohl, Tim Berners-Lee or Jacques Delors, but Pope John Paul II.[4] At the same time, however, such developments do pose serious questions about the way religious power should be used. When Christians act as a political pressure group or a power bloc as has been the case in the US, when the Orthodox church colludes in the suppression of dissent as it did in the former Soviet Union and when papal power is brought to bear on the suppression of liberation theologians as was the case in Latin America, it is hardly surprising that some see the church as more concerned with enjoying alliances with the state than with promoting Civil Society.

At the level of civil society, too, questions arise about the new roles which faith communities are being invited by governments to play. In Britain an important sign of this new thinking came in 1993 with the setting up, under the Conservative government, of an Inner Cities Religious Council, followed by periodic attempts to relocate 'faith communities' depending on whether they are seen in terms of regeneration, community cohesion, delivery of public services, civil renewal or equalities.[5] In the US, a White House Office of Faith-Based and Community Initiatives was launched in January 2001 – eight months before 9/11. It now has Centers for Faith-Based and Community Initiatives in the Departments of Education, Health and Human Services, Housing and Urban Development, Justice, and Labor.[6] Faith communities have now come to be recognized as important players in the shaping and delivery of policy, especially at regional and local levels, as many Regional Assemblies and Local Strategic Partnerships have set aside places on their boards for faith community representatives – even if there is still plenty of healthy debate about what precisely are the most appropriate roles for faith communities to play.

Such recognition must, of course, be welcomed. It would be irresponsible for faith communities not to respond. But it also requires of faith communities a duty to interpret these new developments critically. To what extent are policies of social cohesion and social inclusion about genuine social transformation as distinct from social control? To what extent are the new policies, even though promoted under the heading of civil renewal, actually being run by and in the interests of the established political and economic powers? Whose agenda is being promoted? The Church's primary mission in society consists not in setting up projects, joining campaigns, or sitting on partnership boards. But if the church is primarily intent on pursuing its own mission, should it expect to receive funding and other support from the state to further that mission? In short, how does it all relate to the transforming mission of the church? The answer, it will be argued, is that above all the church's mission is about being the church.

Rethinking the Church's Civilizing Mission

One way of trying to clarify the role of the church today in Civil Society and in civil society is to place it in the context of the history of the church's civilizing mission. It is a mission rooted in the commission to preach the gospel to all peoples. The 'civilizing' bit emerged gradually and has always been understood in very different ways. Here the attempt will be made to draw on insights largely from the European chapter of the history of that civilizing mission.

Although Christianity developed in the cities, it broke with the classical understanding of civilization by reaching out, first to the people of the country-side, and later to the barbarian tribes as well.[7] The church was inclusive. Nor was it elitist. Even though hierarchical, it offered a faith to be embraced and practiced by the uneducated as well as the educated, and it accommodated itself to the roles undertaken by lay people. The church's civilizing mission, which had begun well before the Constantinian era, was not a blueprint for society, a pre-ordained economic system, a divinely-sanctioned political structure.

For several centuries this civilizing mission took the shape of Christendom. But, already weakened by the internecine battles that marked the Reformation, it was unable to withstand the challenge of capitalism with its insistence that faith was a matter of individual choice and of modernity with its relegating of religion to a separate sphere. It could speak to but not challenge the autonomy of the economic and political spheres.

But the civilization of capitalist modernity itself was torn apart by the indus-trial strife of the 19th century and by the catastrophe of the First World War. Thus began a struggle for the soul of the West. The civilizing mission of Christianity was looked at afresh. Faced with an emerging plutocracy at turn of the century America, Walter Rauschenbusch's social gospel aimed at 'Christianizing the social order' in a socialist and democratic direction. In Europe, traumatized by the First World War, some Christians were supporting the 'New Order' offered by Fascism. Others were seeking to reshape socialism. And others, both in Britain and in France exploring the possibilities of a 'new Christendom'.[8] Echoes of that can still be seen in recent debate between the leaders of two of the Towards Social Transformation seminars, John Milbank and Ian Markham.[9] The latest challenge to the idea of the church's civilizing mission arises from what some call a 'clash of civilizations'. All this makes the issue of civil society more, not less, important than it was when the Towards Social Transformation initiative was launched. What does this mean for the Church's civilizing mission today?

Here the argument is that it may mean developing the notion of 'a civilization of love', bravely enunciated by Pope Paul VI at the height of the threats to Europe's democratic civilization from the armed 'autonomous' movements of the far Left and the preparations for military coups and a National Security State by those on the far Right.[10] His appeal for a civilization of love was later picked up by Pope John Paul II and is captured in the concluding words of the recent Roman Catholic Compendium of Social Doctrine. It can be enriched by drawing on the Augustinian tradition, in which the task is not about invoking love but about healing perverted love by grace. It is the actual conflict between the two loves that animates the earthly and heavenly cities. The belief that the world is being transformed by the grace of God was adopted by the World Council of Churches as the theme for its 9th Assembly in February 2006.

Love as grace. Could this provide the key to a vision in which political power would open up, which promotes mutuality in economic life, and stimulates genuine communication in civil society? Love has in the past been placed at the heart of social theology, but it has been understood differently in different traditions. In the American Protestant tradition, the perspective has tended to be more redemption-oriented, focusing more on the power of the Spirit at work in the lives of those who have been justified. Even in pre-Civil War America revivalists drew on the Calvinist tradition of 'disinterested benevolence' and the Methodist tradition of 'perfect love'. This current affected some of the 'Social Gospel' theology half a century later, and could be found in the great Baptist theologian of the social gospel Walter Rauschenbusch. By contrast, in the Catholic tradition, particularly as developed by Aquinas, as well as in the theology of

Milbank, love is seen as grounded in creation, focusing on God's love at the heart of all being. Both traditions can, of course, draw on Augustine, albeit in different ways. And both have something to contribute to social transformations. Reinhold Niebuhr's reorientation of social theology after the carnage and disillusionment of the First World War is best seen not as a rejection of the role of love but rather as a rejection of the deep-seated perfectionist current in American thought.[10a] This does not invalidate the criticism made of Reinhold Niebuhr by John Milbank. Niebuhr's concept of love as 'heroic individual self-sacrifice' enters, says Milbank, as 'a *secondary* intrusion upon a pattern fundamentally governed by pure power relations. Thus the more original drama of love as mutuality is here relegated to the domain of purely "natural" (familial) and therefore ambiguous, relationships.'[11] Nonetheless, Niebuhr's view of the interaction of love, power and justice was effectively employed by Martin Luther King in a way which did not diminish the primacy of love.[12] What light then might the vision of a 'civilization of love' cast upon the role of the Church in Civil Society and in civil society?

The Church, Civil Society and Political Power

> We cannot have our cake and eat it.
> We cannot claim liberty for ourselves,
> while at the same time denying it to others.
> John Neville Figgis[13]

What is remarkable about the development of the Christian civilization of Europe was not how much, but how little it depended upon the state. The church refused to be a 'civil religion' in the traditional sense. There were many reasons for this. One was theological, as reflected in Augustine's vision of the two cities. Other factors included the weakness of Western imperial power (part of which has been attributed precisely to the church's refusal to support the Empire), but also the fact that even in its healthier days the Empire allowed a degree of religious tolerance and cultural pluralism, provided a system of law and established a certain security of private property. A further factor was the system of local autonomy both in the countryside – with baronial and ecclesiastical autonomy, aided by the fact that the church at one time owned nearly one-third of the land – and in the commercial urban centres. For these reasons, Christian civilization provided the unifying core to Europe but at the level of society not of the state. In short, Christendom was not a theocracy.[14]

Clearly this did not mean that the church had no collaboration with the state. It benefited enormously from the patronage of Constantine and many of his imperial successors. Emperors such as Theodosius, encouraged by Ambrose, Bishop of Milan and tutor to Augustine, adopted an aggressive policy of stamping out not just paganism but Christian 'heresies' as well. Augustine's celebrated biographer Peter Brown goes so far as to call Augustine 'the first theorist of the Inquisition'.[15] Nonetheless, the church did exert a restraining and healing influence on the state. This is not the place to examine in detail where the church got its relationship with the state right and where – as for example in its support for dictatorships and even fascism – it got it shamefully wrong. The issue here is whether and how the church's civilizing mission can fittingly be expressed under today's conditions. Three examples might illustrate what a civilizing mission vis-à-vis political power entails.

First, the church has offered both individuals and society protection from the abuse of state power. Both the World Council of Churches and the Vatican, since the time of Pope John's XXIII's encyclical *Pacem in Terris* (1963) have been strong advocates of human rights. The work of the churches with movements for peace and human rights in places like east Germany and Poland, enabled it to play a key role in the transformation of the political order. Admittedly, other theological traditions still find great difficulties with the very notion of human rights. Nowhere were the contradictions more dramatically exemplified than in the person of Pope John Paul II, who played such an historic role, on the one hand, in the undoing of Communist regimes in eastern Europe, by supporting civil society movements such as Solidarity, whilst on the other undermining Church support for liberation movements in Latin America.

A second means of healing of political power involves seeking to limit that power through constitutional means. That is precisely one of the contributions Christianity is argued to have made to the development of the Western liberal tradition according to Oliver O' Donovan.[16]

A third means of healing political power is by participation in the exercise of political power but in ways that transform the way such power is understood and used. The recent focus on governance and on participatory democracy which was discussed in Chapter Five provides an ideal context. The mission would involve making political power more inclusive by ensuring that the voices of the least powerful and most vulnerable were heard. This would undoubtedly entail a blurring of the edges between the state and other bodies in society. But this sort of blurring can be justified theologically. John Milbank describes the whole church/state question as a matter of secondary, albeit real, importance. The state is neither purely secular nor is the church simply religious: 'Better, then, that the bounds between Church and state be extremely hazy', Milbank argues, 'so that a "social" existence of many complex and interlocking powers may emerge, and forestall either a sovereign state, or a hierarchical Church.'[17] Such blurring would allow, in exceptional cases, for churches and faith communities to play a more direct political role. For example, in Africa faith communities, Christian, Islamic and syncretistic, have been singled out as key factors in the desperate quest for good governance.[18] In so doing, the church can show how true power derives intimately not from force or domination but from a present and enduring love centred on the cross and resurrection of Christ.

The argument here, as developed especially in Chapters Two and Five, is that the state is of secondary not primary importance. This is partly for the sort of theological reason articulated in Augustine's contrast between the earthly city and the other city which he designated 'heavenly' not only because it included the angels and the souls of the just, but also because it was present in the world, pointing to that more perfect commonwealth which represented the fulfilment of our desires.[19] It is also because of the particular history of Europe, out of which, argues John A. Hill, an organic relationship between state and society emerged: 'The European state evolved slowly and doggedly in the midst of a pre-existent civil society.'[20] It is that 'pre-existent civil society' and the continuing civilizing mission of the church in that sphere which will be looked at next.

The Church, civil society and Associational Life

The greatest danger to our civilization is not selfishness nor self-interest. It is the combination of intense loyalty and selfless behaviour towards one's own group with the utmost neglect and cruelty to those outside.

Samuel Brittan[21]

In his assessment as to the reason why the emperors Decian, Valerian and Diocletian reversed a long standing imperial tradition of religious toleration and launched their determined persecution of Christians, Hall suggests that the reasons were social rather than religious: 'Something further was important to the State...a deep suspicion of secondary organizations.'[22] Indeed something had been happening. Christianity had long since ceased being a sect and had become a church. It was now threatening to become a new extensive body which gathered people of every class and nation, female as well as male. It was acquiring wealth and status and was organizing its life according to a different set of laws. Gibbon, famously, blamed this development for the decline and fall of the Roman Empire. To the extent that this accusation is true – and it is of course an oversimplification – the church ought to be congratulated. More recent historical assessments have made the point that: 'Ironically, then, Europe's great good fortune lay in the fall of Rome and the weakness and division that ensued.'[23] Or, as Hall puts it, following Gellner, what emerged was the miracle of civil society – that sphere of free activity which is more than the family and less than the state. The miracle was a product of the interplay of a host of factors in European history. But Hall attributes to the church a far more positive role for that miracle than does Gellner. In that development, the contribution of the church had both a negative and a positive dimension.

Negatively, the church refused to give religious sanction to the Roman empire or even to give priority to participation in its civic life. That was none of its business. In that sense Gibbon may have had a point in saying that part of the reason why the (Western) empire proved unable to resist the barbarian invasions was because it was weakened from within. The disappearance of a strong central power opened up a space which facilitated the development even under the 'Holy' Roman Empire of a kind of plurality of largely autonomous and overlapping political jurisdictions as well as scope for parliaments, civil liberties, markets and checks on power. This was part of the story. But the church played a positive role as well. 'The market was made possible because people felt themselves part of a single community,' argues Hall, making a similar point about the social as well as the theological reasons why the medieval church called for a pause in hostilities through such institutions as the Peace of God and the Truce of God.[24]

This provides an important historical background for the more theological argument made by John Milbank, whose portrait of 'gothic space' was described in Chapter Two. The 'sublime indeterminacy' of Milbank's 'social ontology' sees society not as some all embracing 'body' of which individuals are a part, nor a tightly defined 'community' which is neatly bounded, but a rich associational mixture which opens up space for multiple and overlapping groupings. 'Only in this way,' argues Milbank, 'can one sustain a non-resignation to liberal capitalism without lapsing into the dangerous illusions of state socialism, fascism and social democracy.'[25] Associational life becomes more than a matter of utilitarian cooperation. It becomes a sign and a partial realization of the rich, overlapping, multi-layered, baroque superabundance of grace, giving and communion which results from a participation in divine life.

Yet associationalism can be used in very different ways. Milbank detects in Catholic social teaching a worrying tendency to interpret the essentially rich, pluralistic and associational concept of gothic space in a right wing way: 'Where this is done, I want to argue, one has incipient fascism....It is of course clear that Pope John Paul II has not returned to a full-scale endorsement of corporatism, but exactly the same misapprehension and sickly false consciousness informs also the vaguely social market philosophy he seems to espouse, and is capable of engendering a kind of "soft fascism"....Thus Catholic social teaching is engulfed in a kind of tragedy....'[26]

Both because of its history and because of its theology, the church is well-placed to help civil society flourish with a rich associational life. It does so not because it sees some advantages in hopping onto an associational bandwagon, but because that is part of its own true character. It can fulfil this aspect of its civilizing mission, however, only if it cultivates richness and diversity in its own life and resists the temptation to impose uniformity and to become monolithic and monocultural. Figgis praised the Anglican Church in standing for: 'a conception of the religious society which is organic and federalized, as against one which is merely unitary and absolutist.'[27] For this reason, he did not hesitate to make the case for the dispersal of power within the church. By creating openings for association, for conversation and for collaboration, the church not only presents a more appealing vision of what church life is like, it also witnesses to the transforming power of grace in the refashioning of civil society.[28]

From the Global to the Local and Back Again

From the Global to the Local

Being the church means being part of a global community in and through its engagement in any particular place. The global/local interaction runs in both directions. It is essential that the church at local level should try to trace the global implications of what it does. But a fuller appreciation of what it means for the church to be church implies starting at the other end, and seeing how its global character helps shape its mission at local level. We are part of a common humanity, with debts to one another and responsibilities for one another. In witnessing to the City of God, the church offers a sign of a global Civil Society. As John Atherton has recognized in his discussion of the importance of local civil society, few organizations in civil society are better placed to do this than are faith communities with their historic world-wide vision and their continuing vital links with members of their community across the world.[29]

The churches' role in campaigns for debt relief, in campaigns for peace, for truth and reconciliation, for human rights and for world development are central, not peripheral, to the church's mission. To make them real, however, it is important to see how they impinge on the local community.

For example, in a world steeped not only in weapons of mass destruction, but in sophisticated weapons equipped for long-distance killing, local churches have a mission in relation to the ways in which industrial and scientific activity in their area may be contributing to the arms race. It cannot duck the difficult issue that, just as mining and steel communities have had to adapt to a new economy, so towns which have been dependent on the military-industrial complex may also have to adapt and make the transition to creating products, services, and jobs that are more oriented to global peace and development.

Or, to take another example, in a world of global upheavals and migration, local churches have a mission to ensure that their communities do not become enclaves but may help provide a refuge for those who have been uprooted. In a world where people have been impoverished by the influx or the withdrawal of global capital, local churches have a mission of solidarity with those who must migrate to earn a living for themselves and for their families. It should explore the possibility of fair-trade link-ups with particular initiatives in particular developing countries.

In a world where global and local identities are being reforged, local churches should welcome initiatives around community cohesion which give it a radical meaning, working to ensure that these become not simply a means of stabilising the existing system but of transforming it, as was discussed in Chapter Three. In a world where the demands of the formal economy and paid employment are claiming priority over the quality of family life, local churches can help develop a more integrated vision of life, by promoting new forms of local social enterprise and alternative economic activity, as was discussed in Chapter Four, and new models of public life which connect the domestic (*oikos*), neighbourhood (*paroikia*) and civic (*polis*) spheres, as was discussed in Chapter Five.

From the Local to the Global

Although it is important to start with a sense of being a global community, it is also helpful to be reminded that the 'global' is not something out there but that it is also right here and can be realized by taking seriously the agenda of the local community. For the local is not merely the link with the global. The local *is* the global. John Keane points to the strategic importance of local initiatives. This is not only because participation in local action can serve as schools for democracy whether by critical engagement with local government, as in 'the new localism' (including an enhanced role for local people in the shaping and delivering of public services), or by taking sides with local people through community-action initiatives such as the Citizen Organising Foundation.[30] It is also because today 'large-scale organizations, such as state bureaucracies and capitalist corporations, rest upon complex, molecular networks of everyday power relations…and that the transformation of these molecular powers necessarily induces effects upon these large-scale organizations.'[31] In a similar vein, Bob Jessop, leader of the 1996 Towards Social Transformation seminar, has spoken of 'glurbalization' to suggest that in a knowledge and information economy, local economies have a new potential. They can literally relocate themselves by defining themselves and their key relationship not with their nation or capital city but with producers in other parts of the world for whom their contribution in terms of technological skills and access to markets may be vital. The redefinition of the relationship between market, state and network does not take place in a vacuum. The local is one of the key fields where it is being played out.[32] It is a point illustrated in several case studies by Hilary Wainwright.[33]

It is in this interaction between the global and the local that the full richness of Civil Society can be developed. Here Milbank meets Keane: Keane's observation that 'global civil society consists of a vast mosaic of socio-economic groups, organizations and initiatives that are variously related to government structures'[34] ties in nicely with Milbank's suggestive image of gothic space.

Nurturing a Transformative Culture

The development of a transformative culture is not something which happens automatically. It needs to be nurtured. The nurturing offered by the church is a nurturing in grace, rooted in the creative love of God. It brings freedom from both the personal and collective bondage in which we find ourselves and which is reinforced by the regime of capitalist modernity. It makes possible a healing transformation because it places us in touch with a realm of abundant life which expresses itself in ever new ways and relationships. But it needs nurturing. Among the key pastoral tasks that this involves, and in which the church has a unique contribution to make, are the following: the practice of forgiveness, the promotion of civic virtue, the commitment to communication and the rekindling of hope.

The Practice of Forgiveness

The churches are made up of human beings and are ordered in ways which give plenty of scope for the *libido dominandi* – whether in its more blatant forms of ambition and aggression, or in its less honourable forms of timidity to challenge abuses of power and vicarious identification with the trappings of glory.[35] The church's witness consists not in showing what it is like to be sinless but in showing how to deal with sin. The City of God is really – but only partially – reflected in the life of the church. The secret of that City as well as the crucial opening to transformation is through the practice of mutual forgiveness.[36] Forgiveness not as mere indulgence in human foibles as if life were but a comedy. Nor forgiveness as merely saying sorry. It is not something that one party can give or receive unilaterally. It must be reciprocal. It is through this sort of exchange that the *libido dominandi* is put to rest. The assurance of mutual forgiveness frees us from the fear of failing, of being destroyed by or destroying one another and enables us to dare to hope and to act in hope.

So great is the need for forgiveness that social transformation requires atonement, the bearing of one another's sins. The full horror of sin and evil far surpasses human ability to bear it and yet the possibility of bearing it is what is revealed in the crucifixion of God incarnate. For Milbank this 'ensures that we can be drawn back to the cross as the very consummation of the preaching of the kingdom....[which] means (speculatively), and illustrates (practically) bearing the burdens of others, even of our accusers. Thus, it is Jesus's end as well as his life that we are to imitate.'[37]

The Promotion of Civic Virtue

Andrew Shanks argues for 'the transformation of the church into an agency of anti-politics'. He suggests that the way the churches responded, spontaneously and accidentally, in the former East Germany, might offer a glimpse of the sort of role which the church should deliberately cultivate.[38] The church's true place would be in the area of what the Hungarian civil society activist George

Konrad called 'anti-politics' – 'the political activity of those who don't want to be politicians and who refuse to share in power.' The church's central contribution to civil society would consist in acting as an effective truthful witness both against recent historical experiences of totalitarianism, genocide and domination and for the historical possibilities of pluralism, peace and freedom. Far from shutting the door on politics, Shanks sees such 'anti-politics' precisely as the way to 'reopen the possibility of politics'.

Shanks grounds such practices in a 'civil theology' which, for him, rests on a sense of responsibility which combines three virtues. The first, inspired by Nietzsche, is 'free-spiritedness' – freedom from the need to regulate, order and contain all thinking and acting. The second, inspired by Hegel and Gadamer, is a 'flair for tradition' – a rooted creativity, which fully appreciates the possibilities for the future which the past makes available in the present. The third, inspired by Levinas, is 'transcendent generosity' – a readiness to surrender the privileges of citizenship by recognizing the immediate claim that arises from the sheer proximity of 'the Other' as represented in one's neighbour.

A Commitment to Communication

Stanley Hauerwas praises A. D. Lindsay's insight into the merits of discussing genuinely different points of view: 'Perhaps the most significant thing the church can do for any society,' Hauerwas suggests, 'is to be a community capable of sustaining the kind of discussion necessary for the formation of good and truthful arguments and lives.'[39] Colin Gunton, developing the implications of Trinitarian theology, sees 'being in communion' as forming the heart of the church itself. He cites Edward Farley's picture of the church as a place where interpersonal relationships and reciprocities are central and which themselves depend upon an 'intersubjective structure in which participants constitute each other as believers'.[40]

This brings us back to the argument advanced in Chapter Three by Raymond Williams, who noted that: 'It is very difficult to think clearly about communication, because the pattern of our thinking about community is, normally, dominative.' The alternative is not to turn down the volume but rather to acknowledge that 'a transmission [of ideas] is always an offering...not an attempt to dominate, but to communicate to achieve reception...and living response.'[41] Part of his vision was to ensure that 'in a socialist society, the basic cultural skills are made widely available, and the channels of communication widened and cleared, as much as possible has been done in the way of preparation, and what then emerges will be an actual response to the whole reality....' It is encouraging to hear John Gray, leader of the 2002 Towards Social Transformation seminar observe: 'One cannot engage in dialogue with religious thinkers in Britain today without quickly discovering that they are, on the whole, more intelligent, better educated and strikingly more freethinking than unbelievers (as evangelical atheists still incongruously describe themselves).'[42]

The Rekindling of Hope

What the Towards Social Transformation initiative sought to do above all was to expand the horizon of hope – a mission that has become more, not less, import-ant, as so many hopes proved fallacious. The source of our hope lies in being true to the Christian narrative. It is a big narrative, with a transforming power that is at work in history. Being faithful to it means two things. First, that there is no point in being overly possessive or controlling about it. On the contrary, precisely because it is so rich and so sublime, it needs always to be re-interpreted in the light of changes in history and of the insights – and even criticisms – of those who inhabit other traditions. Secondly, it means that our voices matter, however small we may feel either as individuals or as a minority in an alien city and however fallacious the hopes we may have entertained. Recently a number of Americans – many of whom were, in the hopeful 1960s, prominent activists in movements for peace, social justice, community action and political reform – were interviewed about hope. Many had clearly been inspired by their Christian beliefs. Most had seen their hopes unfulfilled. But virtually none had stopped hoping or translating those hopes into action.[43] What they showed in the past and what they continue to show in the present is that what matters is not the smallness of the voice but the bigness of the narrative.

Epilogue
No Alternative or Many Alternatives?

We can imagine a future in which each country would be free to find its own version of modernity....Though we can imagine such a world, it is hard to imagine anything resembling it coming about by design.
John Gray[44]

...since there are many peoples and cultures, there will be many socialisms.
Raymond Williams[45]

Other Worlds Are Possible

The 'Other City' to which the church is called to bear witness is not simply a possibility. It is a reality which is taking shape. That is what Christians believe. A social transformation is under way. The church's civilizing mission prevents her from colluding in efforts to restrict that mission to a separate 'religious' sphere, or to civil society. The heart of her mission is captured by the vision of a far broader, richer and freer Civil Society. It is a city which prizes otherness and is rich in diversity. The church's mission is to create openings for that Other City to emerge. It can do so by offering a mirror, in which society, especially the state, can recognize its flaws and injustice. But the real challenge of mission is to offer visible and credible signs not just of 'an alternative' but of many and ever different alternatives, offering reminders that there are alternative ways of ordering social life.

One sign may be the fact that the World Council of Churches decided to hold its 9th Assembly in Porto Alegre, Brazil, the venue for the first three World Social Forums, with their slogan 'Another World Is Possible'.[46] The reason why the forums began in Porto Alegre was because of that city's practical experiment in participatory local democracy.[47] Whether or not the World Social Forum continues, whether participatory democracy bears fruit and whether or not the socialist regimes in Latin America open up new paths, there remains 'another city', a new form of politics, a new way of arranging our economic, political and social lives.

The possibilities for social transformation are many. The lesson of radical historicity is that we are not embarked on any predetermined path, whether towards (post-) modernity, the market state, the clash of civilizations or the land of cyborgs, but that history is open – open to recovery as well as to discovery. Capitalism and modernity, as well as the notion of social transformation and the paths towards that end – associationalism, social rights, the common good, etc – are all historical realities, all needing continually to be rethought.

Only a few decades ago the proponents of capitalist modernity were proclaiming that 'There Is No Alternative'. Not so. We live in a world where there are many alternatives – many capitalisms, many socialisms, many modernities, many fundamentalisms, many democracies, many types of state, many types of Civil Society, many faiths. For Christians the response is neither simply to celebrate pluralism or to seek to establish a new Christendom. It is rather to tell the difference between alternatives which reinforce the earthly city, ruled by the *libido dominandi* and alternatives which partially reflect and provisionally capture the otherness of the heavenly Civil Society, animated by grace. The issue is not so much whether another world is possible It is about how deeply we *desire* that other world and whether we are prepared to persevere in the face of fallacious hope.

Towards Social Transformation
Seminars and Seminar Leaders

The Spark – *Civil Society* 1988

John Keane is Professor of Politics at the University of Westminster. He was one of the founders of the Centre for the Study of Democracy in 1989. With the Centre for the Study of Democracy, Keane is one of the lead partners of the European governance project of the European Civil Society Network. He is also a member of the American-based Institutions of Democracy Commission, as well as being active in dialogue with groups in Iran and the Middle East and has lectured in Japan and Taiwan. He is currently Director of the History of Democracy Project, attempting a critical survey of the history of democratic ideas and institutions.

It was Keane's two influential books, *Civil Society and the State: New European Perspectives* and *Democracy and Civil Society* (both Verso, 1988), which sparked off the Towards Social Transformation initiative. While the annual national seminars were in the course of preparation, a few smaller half-day seminars were held in London, one of which was led by John Keane. Ten years on, looking back on the mountain of literature on the subject, which his works had helped generate, Keane notes, in *Civil Society: Old Images, New Visions* (Polity, 1998), that civil society had by then become a central focus of political theory. He has written a biography of Tom Paine, *Tom Paine: A Political Life* (Bloomsbury, 1995) and also of Vaclav Havel, *Vaclav Havel: A Political Tragedy in Six Acts* (Bloomsbury, 1999), having previously edited Havel's *The Power of the Powerless: Citizens against the State in Central-Eastern Europe* (Hutchinson, 1985). He has also written about the global dimensions of civil society in *Global Civil Society?* (Cambridge University Press, 2003) and *Violence and Democracy* (Cambridge University Press, June 2004), and has edited *Civil Society: Berlin Perspectives* (Berghahn Books, 2006).

The Seminars

○ 1990: In Search of a Common Purpose
Leader: Raymond Plant

Raymond (Lord) Plant led both the first and twelfth seminars, in 1990 and 2001. He was Professor of Politics at the University of Southampton, then Master of St. Catherine's College, Oxford and is Professor of Jurisprudence at King's College London. He was Home Affairs spokesperson for the Labour Party from 1992–1996. He chaired the Labour Party's Working Party on Electoral Reform (*The Plant Report: Democratic Representation and Elections,* Labour Party, 1993) and the Fabian Society Commission on Taxation and Citizenship (*Paying for Progress: A New Politics of Tax for Public Spending,* Fabian Society, 2000). He was President of the National Council for Voluntary Organizations from 1998–2002. He has combined his academic work with frequent contributions to dialogue both with Christian social ethicists and with various centres, left and right wing think-tanks, serving as a member of the Advisory Board of the Social Market Foundation.

He has written extensively, including (with Kenneth Hoover) *Conservative Capitalism in Britain and the United States: A Critical Approach* (Routledge, 1989), *Modern Political Thought* (Basil Blackwell, 1991) and *Politics, Theology and History* (Cambridge University Press, 2001). He has edited, with Matt Beech and Kevin Hickson, *The Struggle for Labour's Soul: Labour's Political Thought since 1945* (Routledge, 2004).

○ 1991: Patterns of Power – Social Transformation in a Pluralist and Associationalist Mode
Co-Leaders: David Nicholls and Paul Hirst (both since deceased)

David Nicholls died in 1996 at the age of 60. He was Vicar of Littlemore and was closely involved with the work of the Christendom Trust. A former lecturer in Politics at the University of the West Indies, he also served on the board of the Latin America Bureau. His stimulating and scholarly works include *From Dessalines to Duvalier: Race, Colour and Independence in Haiti* (Macmillan1979), *Three Varieties of Pluralism* (Macmillan, 1974), *The Pluralist State* (Macmillan, 1975), *Deity and Domination: Images of God and the State in the 19th and 20th Centuries* (Routledge, 1989) and *God and Government in an 'Age of Reason'* (Routledge, 1995).

Paul Hirst died in 2003 at the age of 57. He was Professor of Social Theory at Birkbeck School of Politics and Sociology at the University of London. He chaired the Executive of Charter 88 and played a prominent part in the Open Democracy initiative and in the Real Utopias project. Among his many writings are *Asssociative Democracy: New Forms of Economic and Social Governance* (Polity, 1994), (with Sunil Khilnani) *Reinventing Democracy* (Blackwell, 1996) and as editor (with Veit Biders), *Associative Democracy: The Real Third Way* (Frank Cass, 2001). For an account of Paul Hirst's intellectual journey see Gregory Eliot, 'The Odyssey of Paul Hirst', *New Left Review* 159 (1986), pp. 81–103.

○ 1992: The Market in Context – Agenda for a Social Economy
Co-Leaders: Grahame Thompson and Charles Leadbeater

Grahame Thompson, co-leader of the 1992 TST seminar, is Professor of Political Economy at the Open University. Formerly editor of the journal *Theoretical Practice* (1971–1973), he is managing editor of the journal *Economy and Society* and has played a prominent role in the European Association for Evolutionary Political Economy. He is currently continuing research into the process of 'globalization' with reference to issues of corporate responsibility.

His works include *The Political Economy of the New Right* (Pinter, 1990), *Markets, Hierarchies and Networks: The Coordination of Social Life*, edited jointly with Jennifer Frances, Rosalind Levacic and Jeremy Mitchell (Sage, 1991), *The Economic Emergence of a New Europe?* (Edward Elgar, 1993), (with Paul Hirst) *Globalisation in Question: The International Economy and the Possibilities of Governance* (Polity Press, 1996) and *Between Hierarchies and Markets: The Logic and Limits of Network Forms of Organization* (Oxford University Press, 2003). He has also edited *Governing the European Economy* (Sage, 2001).

Charles Leadbeater was, at the time of the 1992 seminar, writing for *The Financial Times*, where he spent ten years working as Labour Editor, Industrial Editor and Tokyo Bureau Chief before becoming the paper's Features Editor, whilst at the same time contributing frequently to *Marxism Today*. In 1994 he became Assistant Editor at *The Independent*. He has also served as adviser to the Downing Street Policy Unit, the Department of Trade and Industry and the Department of Education. He was rated by Accenture in 2005 as one of the world's top management thinkers. He has recently been working, with the Foreign Office and others on a two-year project, 'China India, Korea and the Geography of Science'.

His publications include *The Politics of Prosperity* (Fabian Society, 1987), *Living on Thin Air: The New Economy* (Viking, 1999), *New Measures for the New Economy* (Institute of Chartered Accountants, 2000), *The Weightless Society: Living in the New Economy Bubble* (Texere, 2000), and *Up the Down Escalator: Why the Global Pessimists Are Wrong* (Viking, 2002). He is Senior Research Associate for the think-tank Demos, for whom he has written a regular series of booklets, including *The Self-policing Society* (1996), *The Rise of the Social Entrepreneur* (1997), (with Kate Oakley) *The Rise of the Knowledge Entrepreneur* (1999), *Innovate from Within: An Open Letter to the New Cabinet Secretary* (2002), *Personalisation through Participation: A New Script for Public Services* (2004) and *The Pro-Am Revolution: how Enthusiasts are Changing Our Society and Economy* (2004).

○ 1993: All Shall Be Well – A New Future for Social Welfare
Co-Leaders: Anna Coote and Ian Gough

Anna Coote was Deputy Editor of the *New Statesman* (1978–82) and Deputy Director of the Institute for Public Policy Research (1993–1997), having been Senior Lecturer in Media Studies at Goldsmiths College before serving as Director of the Public Health Programme at the King's Fund. She then served as a member of the London Health Commission and of the Government's advisory Sustainable Development Commission and as Head of 'Engaging Patients and the Public' at the Healthcare Commission.

She has written or edited numerous policy reports over the years, including *Prevention rather than Cure: Making the Case for Choosing Health* (King's Fund, 2004) and (with Jessica Allen and David Woodhead) *Finding out What Works: Understanding Complex Community-based Initiatives* (King's Fund, 1994) as well as *The Welfare of Citizens: Developing New Social Rights* (IPPR, 1992).

Ian Gough was senior lecturer in Social Policy at the University of Manchester at the time of the TST seminar. He is currently Professor of Social Policy at the University of Bath, Deputy Director of Economic and Social Research Council's Research Group on Wellbeing in Developing Countries and is on the Editorial Advisory Board for the journal *Global Social Policy*.

His works include the influential *The Political Economy of the Welfare State* (Macmillan, 1979), and (with Len Doyal) the prize-winning *A Theory of Human Need* (Macmillan, 1991). Gough has brought together his more recent writings in *Global Capital, Human Needs and Social Policies: Selected Essays 1994–99* (Palgrave, 2000). He has also edited (with G.Olafsson), *Capitalism and Social Cohesion: Essays on Exclusion and Integration* (Macmillan Press, 1999) and written (with Geoff Wood and Armando Barrientos) *Insecurity and Welfare Regimes in Asia, Africa and Latin America* (Cambridge University Press, 2004).

○ 1994: It Needn't Be Like This – The Politics of Practical Knowledge
Leader: Hilary Wainwright

Hilary Wainwright was from 1982–1986 one of the co-ordinators of the Popular Planning Unit of the Greater London Council. She is a fellow of the International Labour Studies Centre at Manchester University, of the Centre for Global Governance of the London School of Economics and of the Transnational Institute in Amsterdam. She was a founding member of Charter 88 and is on the editorial board of the political think tank, The Catalyst Trust. She has kept the flag flying as editor of *Red Pepper*.

Her works include, with Sheila Rowbotham and Lynne Segal, *Beyond the Fragments: Feminism and the Making of Socialism* (Merlin Press, 1979), *Arguments for a New Left: Answering the Free Market* (Blackwell, 1994) and *Reclaiming the State: Experiments in Popular Democracy* (Verso, 2003).

○ 1995: Policing the Sublime – Tradition and Transformation
Leader: John Milbank

John Milbank has been Maurice B. Reckitt Teaching Fellow in Modern Christian Social and Political Thought at the University of Lancaster, Lecturer in Philosophical Theology at Cambridge University, and Francis Gall Professor of Philosophical Theology at the University of Virginia. He is currently Director of the Centre of Theology and Philosophy at the University of Nottingham.

His work *Theology and Social Theory: Beyond Secular Reason* (Blackwell, 1990) is a landmark in Christian social theology and has led to the gathering around Milbank of the 'Radical Orthodoxy' network, described in a work he co-edited with Catherine Pickstock and Graham Ward, *Radical Orthodoxy: A New Theology* (Routledge, 1999). A collection of Milbank's essays has been published under the title *The Word Made Strange: Theology, Language, Culture* (Blackwell, 1997). He has also written (with Catherine Pickstock) *Truth in Aquinas*, (with Graham Ward and Edith Wyschogood, Routledge, 2000) *Theological Perspectives on God and Beauty* (Trinity Press International, 2003) and *Being Reconciled: Ontology and Pardon* (Routledge, 2003).

○ 1996: Local Economies – Sites of Struggle
Leader: Bob Jessop

Bob Jessop is Director of the Institute of Advanced Studies at the University of Lancaster. Jessop's special interest has long been in state theory but always with an interdisciplinary approach, stressing the links between sociology, economics and politics. He has been an active member of the European Association of Evolutionary Political Economy. He is currently beginning a new research project on the cultural political economy of the knowledge-based economy.

His numerous publications include: *Nicos Poulantzas: Marxist Theory and Political Strategy* (Macmillan, 1985), *Thatcherism: A Tale of Two Nations* (Polity 1988), *State Theory: Putting the Capitalist State in its Place* (Polity, 1990), (with Charlie Malcolm-Brown) *Karl Marx's Social and Political Thought: Critical Assessments* (Routledge, 1990), *Fordism and Post-Fordism* (Lancaster Regionalism Group, 1991), *The Politics of flexibility: restructuring state and industry in Britain, Germany and Scandinavia,* (Edward Elgar, 1991), (with Russell Wheatley) *The State, Politics and Civil Society* (Routledge, 1999), the 5 volume series *Regulation Theory and the Crisis of Capitalism* (Edward Elgar, 2001), *The Future of the Capitalist State* (Polity, 2002), and (with Ngai-Ling Sum) *Beyond the Regulated Approach: Putting Capitalist Economies in Their Place* (Edward Elgar, 2006).

○ 1997: Environmental Politics for the Real World
Leader: Michael Jacobs

Michael Jacobs is an environmental economist. Shortly after giving his seminar on ecology in 1997 he was appointed general secretary of the Fabian Society, as well as serving as one of the many advisers to the Cabinet Office. In that position he wrote *Environmental Modernisation: The new Labour agenda* (Fabian Pamphlet 591, October 1999), and (with Adam Lent and Kevin Watkins) *Progressive Globalization* (2003), as well as the provocative article 'Reason to Believe' (*Prospect*, September 2002). In February 2004 he became a member of Council of Economic Advisers at the Treasury. He is also Honorary Senior Research Fellow at the Institute for Environment, Philosophy and Public Policy.

His earlier works include *The Green Economy: Environment, Sustainable Development and the Politics of the Future* (Pluto Press, 1991), and *The Politics of the Real World: Meeting the New Century* (Earthscan, 1996).

○ 1998: Democracy Revitalized – Time of Renewal
Leader: David Beetham

David Beetham was, prior to his retirement in 2002, Professor of Politics and Director of the Centre for Democratisation Studies at Leeds University, where he holds the position of Professor Emeritus. He has recently directed a comparative programme of democracy and human rights assessment for the International Institute for Democracy and Electoral Assistance, Stockholm. A leading expert on human rights, with a focus on economic and social rights, he has acted as consultant on democracy to UNESCO and the Council of Europe. Beetham initiated the 'Democratic Audit', described in his own words as 'the simple but ambitious project of assessing the state of democracy in a single country'. He has travelled throughout the world extending the application of the democratic audit, and acting as consultant on issues of good governance. He is currently Fellow of the Human Rights Centre at the University of Essex.

His many books include *Max Weber and the Theory of Modern Politics* (Allen and Unwin, 1974), *The Legitimation of Power* (Macmillan, 1991), *Politics and Human Rights* (Blackwell, 1995), (with Christopher Lord) *Legitimacy and the EU* (Longman, 1998), (with Kevin Boyle) *Introducing Democracy, 80 Questions and Answers* (UNESCO, 1995), (with Stuart Weir) *Political Power and Democratic Control in Britain: the Democratic Audit of the United Kingdom* (Routledge, 1999). He edited *Democracy under Blair: A Democratic Audit of the United Kingdom* (Politico's, 2002).

○ 1999: Beyond the Brave New World
– Science, Technology and the Reshaping of Humanity
Leader: Michio Kaku

Michio Kaku is Professor of Theoretical Physics at the City University of New York as well as acting as host of a weekly, syndicated radio science programme. He is one of the co-founders of 'string-theory' and has long been in pursuit of the 'theory of everything', i.e. reconciling Einstein's theory of relativity with Bohr's quantum physics. He has also explored the human, political and cosmological impact of the accelerating technological revolutions.

His publications include: *To Win a Nuclear War* (with Daniel Axelrod, South End Press, 1987), *Quantum Field Theory: A Modern Introduction* (Oxford University Press, 1992), *Hyperspace: A Scientific Odyssey through Parallel Universes* (Oxford University Press, 1995), *Beyond Einstein: The Cosmic Quest for the Theory of the Universe* (Anchor Books, 1995), *Introduction to Superstrings* (Springer-Verlag, 1998) the popular *Visions: How Science Will Revolutionize the 21st Century* (Oxford University Press, 1998), *Einstein's Cosmos: How Albert Einstein's Vision Transformed Our Understanding of Space and Time* (Great Discoveries, 2004) and *Parallel Worlds: A Journey Through Creation, Higher Dimensions, and the Future of the Cosmos* (Allen Lane, 2004).

○ 2000: Transforming Discourse – The Theology of Public Engagement
Leader: Ian Markham

Ian Markham was Chair of Theology and Public Life in the Department of Theology, Liverpool Hope University College, and has also served as Chair of the Christian Theology Trust, editor of the *Theological Book Review,* associate editor of *Teaching Religion and Theology* and as a committee member of the Interfaith Foundation. He was one of the leading spirits behind 'The Liverpool Statement: A Call to Join the Forum for Religion and Theology' in November 1997. He is currently Dean of Hartford Seminary (Connecticut) where he is also Professor of Theology and Ethics.

His publications include *Truth and the Reality of God: An Essay in Natural Theology* (T&T Clark, 1998), *Plurality and Christian Ethics* (Seven Bridges Press, revised edition, 1999), and *A Theology of Engagement* (Blackwell, 2003). He has also edited *A World Religion Reader* (Basil Blackwell, 1996), with J'annine Jobling, *Theological Liberalism: Creative and Critical* (SPCK, 2000) and, with R. John Elford, *The Middle Way: Theology, Politics and Economics in the Later Thought of R. H. Preston* (SCM Press, 2000).

○ 2001: Civil Society – Past, Present and Future
Leader: Raymond Plant

Raymond Plant (see above, 1990), in his return visit as leader of a TST seminar explored a range of issues central to the development of civil society, including the role of the voluntary sector, the limits of markets, and the debates between liberal and communitarian approaches, and between universalism and postmodernism.

O 2002: The New Liberal Empire
– How Should Christians Respond?

Leader: John Gray

John Gray, Professor of European Thought at the London School of Economics, who led the seminar in 2002, is acclaimed as one of the most stimulating and provocative contemporary political thinkers. Gray's critique of the Enlighten-ment universalism includes laying some of the blame at the door of historic Christianity.

His works include *Post-liberalism: Studies in Political Thought* (Routledge, 1993), *Liberalism* (Open University Press, rev. ed. 1995), *Isaiah Berlin* (Harper Collins, 1995), *False Dawn: The Delusions of Global Capitalism* (Granta, 1998 and 2002), *Two Faces of Liberalism* (Polity, 2000), *Hume on Liberty and the Market: A Twenty-First Century Perspective* (David Hume Institute, 2002), *Straw Dogs* (Granta, 2002), and *Al Qaeda: What It Means to Be Modern* (Faber, 2003). For accounts of Gray's intellectual journey see Robert Colls, 'Ethics Man: John Gray's New Moral World' in *Political Quarterly* 69 (1998–1): 59–71 and Andrew Gamble 'The Last Utopia' in *New Left Review* 236 (July/August 1999).

O 2003: The Politics of the Common Good

Leader: Fr. Patrick Riordan, S. J.

Patrick Riordan was formerly Dean of Philosophy at the Milltown Institute in Dublin. He is currently Lecturer in Political Philosophy at Heythrop College, University of London, and is an Associate Director of the Heythrop Institute for Religion, Ethics and Public Life. He has also lectured in the United States and in the Philippines, where he wrote *People Power* (Ateneo de Nag University, 2001).

His writings include *A Politics of the Common Good* (Institute of Public Affairs, 1996), and various essays on liberalism, pluralism and the common good in the Irish Jesuit quarterly, *Studies*.

O 2004: Mapping the Mundi Afresh:
Globalization, Development and Citizenship

Leader: Ian Linden

Ian Linden is Associate Professor in the Department for the Study of Religions in the School of Oriental and African Studies at the University of London, having served as Director of the Catholic Institute for International Relations from 1986 to 2001. His writings include *Church and State in Rhodesia, 1959–1979* (Kaiser, 1979), (with Peter B. Clarke) *Islam in Modern Nigeria: A Study of a Muslim Community in a Post-independence State 1960–1983* (Grunewald, 1984), *Liberation Theology: Coming of Age?* (Catholic Institute for International Relations, 1997) and *A New Map of the World* (Darton, Longman & Todd, 2003).

Notes

Preface: The Towards Social Transformation Initiative

[1] Pontifical Council for Justice and Peace, (Libreria Editrice Vaticana, 25 October 2004), presentation by Cardinal Renato Raffaele Martino, p. xxv.

[2] The name 'Helsinki Citizens Assembly' was chosen to signal the importance of 'détente from below' paralleling the 'détente from above', which was then taking place under the aegis of the Helsinki process and the inter-governmental Conference on Security and Cooperation in Europe. An official, joint appeal for the HCA was issued in Budapest in February 1990 by Vaclav Havel, then president of Czechoslovakia, and Lech Walesa, then president of Poland. Two further HCA Assemblies were held – at Bratislava in March 1992 (which I attended along with over a thousand others) and at Ankara in 1994; for an account see *From Bratislava to Ankara: 1992–93* (HCA, 1993).

[3] The Kairos Europa Declaration was a call 'to work for the liberation of society from the stranglehold of the deregulated globalized economy and its competitive culture... [for a] *fundamental change in our economic, political and value system* is necessary today...[and a] call on the churches to take a clear stance, to identify the structures and mechanisms which destroy life and to support those forces which promote justice': www.c3.hu/~bocs/kairos-a.htm.

[4] See Annex for a fuller description of the impressive scope of Keane's international involvement in initiatives for democratic renewal in the past fifteen years as well as his major writings: www.johnkeane.net.

[5] 'There is a constant search for something that is neither a society of atomized individuals nor a bureaucratic state. History has shown innumerable times that no path leads there.... This conviction has driven my four-year polemic in favour of the market alone [and]...has also directed my actions to create a society of free citizens rather than the misleading idea of a so-called "civil society".' Vaclav Klaus, former Czech Prime Minister, as cited by Nicholas Deakin, *In Search of Civil Society* (Palgrave, 2001), p. 112.

[6] See Annex for further details of the seminar leaders.

[7] Aart Nicolaus van der Berg, *God and the Economy: Analysis and Typology of Roman Catholic Protestant Orthodox and Evangelical Documents on the Economy 1979–1992*, (Eburon, 1998), p. 2. It was also a time, as signalled in the Ecumenical Symposium held at Princeton Seminary two months after the first Towards Social Transformation seminar, 'for the churches to attend to the spirit of society and to seek to nourish and to vitalize spiritual resources for social transformation....'; Dana Wilbanks, 'The Church as Sign and Agent of Transformation' in Dieter T. Hessel, *The Church's Public Role: Retrospect and Prospect* (Wm. B. Eerdmans, Grand Rapids, Michigan, 1993), pp. 22, 34.

Introduction: A World Transformed

[1] The transformation of civil society was central to the strategy of Antonio Gramsci (1891–1937), Secretary of the Italian Communist Party. Among other influences on Gramsci's thought was the example of the Italian Catholic Church and the way it managed to exercise a

kind of hegemony even in the face of an anti-clerical state. Both the church and the communist movement relied heavily on a strategy of an extensive development of associations – popular but centrally-directed, social but with a definite political orientation – a strategy which became all the more relevant with the advent of totalitarianism. Gramsci's strategy dictated that the working class should rely less on the traditional 'war of manoeuvre' (full frontal attack, involving strikes, seizures of power, etc.) and more on a 'war of position' (occupying key strongholds). Once having become dominant in civil society, the party would then be in a position to bring about the ultimate goal of the replacement of the state by a self-regulating society. The writings of Gramsci, who spent the last decade of his life as a prisoner of Mussolini, were rediscovered in the 1960s and had an enormous influence on Western European socialists for the next two decades. Keane explains his reservations in *Civil Society and the State: New European Perspectives* (Verso, 1988), pp. 20–25.

[2] Keane, *Democracy and Civil Society*, p. 15.

[3] Ian Linden, *A New Map of the World* (Darton, Longman & Todd. 2003), p. 140. John Keane, whose writings on civil society were the biggest single factor prompting the 'Towards Social Transformation' initiative made a 'ten-years-on' assessment of thinking about civil society since his twin volumes in 1988. He describes the way civil society has come to play a central role in contemporary political thought. John Keane, *Civil Society: Old Images, New Visions*, (Polity, 1998). Keane has continued actively to promote dialogue, taking on the added role as the Centre for the Study of Democracy's co-ordinator of the European Civil Society Network, and incorporating a global perspective, both in his recent writing and in his engagement with groups in Iran and the Middle East. John Keane, *Global Civil Society?* (Cambridge University Press, 2003). For information about the European Civil Society Network see: http://cisonet. wz-berlin.de. For further information about the developments of global civil society see *Civicus*, a world alliance which is dedicated to strengthening citizen action and civil society, founded in 1993 and convenor of biennial World Assemblies: www.civicus.org, and the Global Civil Society Project of the London School of Economics: www.lse.ac.uk/collection/CCS.

[4] The Archbishop of Canterbury, Rowan Williams, has warned: '…its [America's] influence is so vast and its recent military initiatives so forceful that it is naïve to think that it does or even can act as a benevolent elder sibling or a helpful and disinterested guest.' *The Worlds We Live in: Dialogues with Rowan Williams on Global Economic and Politics (*Darton, Longman and Todd, 2005; originally a series of discussions at St. Paul's Cathedral in September 2004), p. 125.

[5] By 2006 Abramovich, though richer, had slipped to third place. *Sunday Times* annual 'Rich List' compiled by Philip Beresford, 23 April 2006.

[6] United Nations *Human Development Programme Report 2003* (8 July 2003): www.undp. org/hdr2003.

[7] Male life expectancy declined between 1990–2000 by 7 years in Malawi, 10 in Kenya, 11 in Zambia, 14 in Botswana, and 15 in Zimbabwe; T. Jamison, Jeffrey D. Sachs and Jia Wang, *The Effect of the AIDS Epidemic on Economic Welfare in Sub-Saharan Africa*, WHO Commission on Macroeconomic and Health Working Paper Series – Paper No. WG1:13 (December 2001). See also *Working Together for Health* (WHO, April 2006).

[8] Among the goals to be achieved by 2015 were: halving the number of people who suffer from hunger, halving the proportion of people who are unable to reach or to afford safe drinking water, ensuring that children everywhere, boys and girls alike, will be able to complete a full course of primary schooling and that girls and boys will have equal access to all levels of education, reducing maternal mortality by three quarters, and under-five child mortality by two thirds. Special measures were to be taken to address the challenges of poverty eradication and sustainable development in Africa, including debt cancellation; United Nations General Assembly, 8th Plenary Meeting (8 September 2000): ww.un.org/millenniumgoals.

[9] United Nations Conference on Trade and Development, *Least Developed Countries Report 2004*, (27 May 2004): www.unctad.org.

[10] United Nations, *AIDS Report 2006* (May 2006): www.unaids.org.

[11] See the account by Bernard Cassen of the highly sophisticated campaign for a 'No' vote in France by the ATTAC movement for democratic renewal, 'ATTAC against the Treaty', *New Left Review* 33 (May/June 2005):27–33.

[12] 'The outlines of an Asian employment crisis are already taking shape,' says the Asian Development Bank's Chief Economist, Ifzal Ali. 'Strong economic growth alone will not solve the problem.' Jesus Felipe and Rana Hasan, eds., *Asian Development Bank, Labor Markets in Asia: Issues and Perspectives* (Asian Development Bank and Palgrave, April 2006): www.adb.org/media/Articles/2006/9757-Asia-job-creation.

[13] The fall in income is from unpublished preliminary research for the World Bank as reported in the *Financial Times*, 22 November 2006. In the communiqué on state television announcing the 11th Five Year Plan for National Economy and Social Development (2006–10) the Central Committee of the Communist Party of China acknowledged: 'We have to...put more emphasis on social equity, enhance efforts in adjusting income distribution and try hard to alleviate the tendency of the widening income gap between regions and some members of society.' (October 2005.)

[14] http://www.newscientist.com/channel/earth/dn10507-carbon-emissions-rising-faster-than-ever.html; World Meteorological Organisation, *Greenhouse Gas Bulletin* (November 2006): http://www.wmo.int/web/arep/gaw/ghg/ghgbull06.html. *Climate Data: Insights and Observations*, Pew Centre on Global Climate Change (December 2004), p. 4.

[15] See the reports of the International Panel on Climate Control, *Climate Change 2001: Impacts, Adaptation and Vulnerability* (United Nations World Meteorological Office and United Nations Environmental Panel) Chapter 10, 'Africa': www.grida.no/climate/ipcc_tar/wg2/379.htm.

[16] The Global Commission on International Migration was launched by the United Nations Secretary-General and a number of governments on 9 December 2003. Its report, *Migration in an Interconnected World: New directions for action*, was published on 5 October 2005: www.gcim.org/en.

[17] Such were the threats experienced at the first American performance of John Adams' controversial *The Death of Klinghoffer* in San Francisco in 1992 – nearly a decade before 9/11 – that never again have American companies dared stage a full performance. In the legal sphere, the growth of The Federalist Society (which also contains a libertarian strand) has 180 chapters in US law schools and 20,000 members – still small compared with the American Bar Association's 400,000 members – not all of whom, of course, are 'liberal'; (*Financial Times*, 21 June 2005): www.fed-soc.org. Universities, generally, have seen the growth of College Republicans, whose membership has tripled in the last few years to 120,000; (*Financial Times*, 12 July 2005): www.crnc.org. A key figure in the development of college Republicans was none other than Karl Rove, who played such an effective role in mobilising the moral Christian right in organizing G. W. Bush's electoral campaign. As for the media, not only have liberal papers such as the *New York Times*, felt the need to project a less 'liberal' image, but newspapers generally have found their impact on public opinion lessened as the influence of often ultra-conservative radio talk shows has grown.

[18] The 1997 Chemical Weapons Convention gave an impetus to the de-constituting of these weapons, and to that end, nearly $2 billion has been contributed by a number of donor nations to develop a chemical weapons destruction plant in the Russian city of Shchuchye (*Financial Times*, 15 November 2005). See the work of Green Cross Switzerland (www.greencross.ch/en/index.html) and the more recently established Green Cross International (www.gci.ch/index.htm).

[19] For the work of the Institute for Environment and Human Security see: www.ehs.unu.edu/PDF/051004_final_EHSreleaseENG.pdf.

[20] Report by a Working Group of the Church of England's House of Bishops Report, *Countering Terrorism: Power, Violence and Democracy post 9/11* (September 2005), p.7: www.cofe.anglican.org/info/socialpublic/international/foreignpolicy/terrorism.pdf. *Hazards of Nature, Risks to Development* (World Bank, April 2006). The report does not mention the role of

developed countries in causing climate change.

²¹ See, for example, the report *United States of America / Yemen: Secret Detention in CIA 'Black Sites'* (Amnesty International, 8 November 2005): http://web.amnesty.org/library/Index/ENG AMR511772005?open&of=ENG-USA.

²² The leaked report of the June 2005 UK intelligence agencies' Joint Terrorist Analysis Centre *Young Muslims and Extremism*, states: 'Events in Iraq are continuing to act as motivation and a focus of a range of terrorist related activity in the U.K.'; *New York Times*, 19 July 2005. The same point was made a month later in a report by Chatham House: 'There is no doubt that the situation over Iraq….gave a boost to the Al-Qaeda network's propaganda, recruitment and fundraising….Riding pillion with a powerful ally has proved costly in terms of British and US military lives, Iraqi lives, military expenditure, and the damage caused to the counter-terrorism campaign'; Frank Gregory and Paul Wilkinson, *Security, Terrorism and the UK*, Royal Institute of International Affairs ISP/NSC Briefing Paper 05/01 (18 July 2005), p. 2.

²³ National Security Council, *The National Security Strategy of the United States of America* (16 March 2006), pp. 2, 43: www.whitehouse.gov/nsc/nss/2006/nss2006.pdf. National Intelligence Council, *Mapping the Global Future: Report of the National Intelligence Council's 2020 Project* (US Central Intelligence Agency, December 2004), pp. 18, 94, 113: www.foia.cia. gov/2020/2020.pdf.

²⁴ 'Climate Change Science: Adapt, Mitigate, or Ignore?' (*Science*, 9 January 2004). Sir David King is also Head of the Department of Trade and Industry's Office of Science and Technology. Speaking to the American Association for the Advancement of Science in February 2004, King stated: 'We estimate that in Europe something like 30,000 people died prematurely during this summer arising from this extreme event.' Lord Rees, Joseph Rotblat Memorial Lecture, Guardian Hay Festival, 28 May 2006: http://comeclean.org.uk/articles.php?articleID=234

²⁵ Irene Kahn, General Secretary of Amnesty International, launching their *Annual Report,* 26 May 2004.

²⁶ Turner attached these words to his horrific painting, *Slavers throwing overboard the Dead and Dying – Typhon coming on* (1840). See prelimary Note on the Cover.

²⁷ *The Hero of a Hundred Fights* (1810?), *Snowstorm: Hannibal and his Army crossing the Alps* (1812), *The Battle of Fort Rock: Val d' Aouste, Piedmont, 1796* (1815), *The Eruption of the Souffrier Mountains in the Island of St. Vincent, at Midnight, on the 30th of April 1812* (1815), *The Decline of the Carthaginian Empire* (1817), *Vision of Medea* (1828), *Caligula's Palace and Bridge* (1831), *The Fates and the Golden Bough* (1834), *The Fountain of Fallacy* (1839), *Slavers throwing overboard the Dead and Dying – Typhon coming on* (1840), *Shade and Darkness – the Evening of the Deluge* (1843), *Light and Colour – the Morning after the Deluge – Moses writing the Book of Genesis* (1843), *The Sun of Venice going to the Sea* (1843) and *The Visit to the Tomb* (1850).

²⁸ Initially it may have been occasioned by John Langhorne's *Visions of Fancy: Elegy IV*: Turner had done a watercolour in 1799 called precisely *Dr. Langhorne's Visions of Fancy*. The term 'Fallacious Hope' appears in the popular poem of James Thomson (1700–1748*) Seasons: Autumn* (1730)), to whose sections on Summer and Winter Turner referred in his paintings. Turner is thought also to have been influenced by the poem *The Pleasures of Hope, composed* in 1799 by Thomas Campbell (1777–1844) and *The Pleasures of the Imagination*, composed in 1744 by Mark Akenside (1721–1770).

²⁹ Andrew Wilton, *Turner and the Sublime* (British Museum Publications, 1981), p. 68. The sublime had been the subject of fascination, for most of the previous century, for essayists such as Joseph Addison, philosophers such as Immanuel Kant, and political figures such as Edmund Burke. Terry Eagleton suggests that the theme of the sublime had an ideological dimension, functioning as part of the bourgeoisie's struggle for political hegemony. Their aesthetics of the beautiful, he suggests – expressed in the bourgeois cultivation of sentiments, affections and manners – represented their attempt to make their order attractive; their aesthetics of the sublime – expressed in the fascination with the awesome, the powerful, the incomprehensible

– represented the desire for submission to power; Terry Eagleton, *The Ideology of the Aesthetic* (Blackwell, 1990), especially pp. 3, 8, 23, 52–53, 58, 90.

[30] See Shanes, p. 25 and Jack Lindsay, *Turner: His Life and Work* (Nicholls and Co., 1966).

[31] See, for example, Chapter Five: 'Policing the Sublime: A Critique of the Sociology of Religion', in John Milbank, *Theology and Social Theory: Beyond Secular Reason* (Blackwell, 1990).

[32] One has only to contrast the theologies of Reinhold Niebuhr, Oliver O'Donovan and John Milbank, to see what very different paths and insights Augustine can open up.

[33] Samuel Beckett 'Duthuit Dialogues', *transition* (December 1949) translated by John C. Calder, *The Philosophy of Samuel Beckett* (Calder Publications, 2000), pp. 82–83.

[34] Eagleton, *Ideology of the Aesthetic*, p. 229.

[35] John Milbank, 'On Complex Space', in *The Word Made Strange: Theology, Language, Culture* (Blackwell, 1997), p. 276. Milbank is referring specifically to Ruskin's *Stones of Venice*, which celebrates the gothic as demanding respect for deficiencies and irregularities which are 'wild and wayward' and which resist totalization.

[36] Reinhold Niebuhr, *The Irony of American History* (originally given as lectures in May 1949 and in January 1951; Charles Scribner's Sons, 1962), pp. 145–147.

[37] 'We envisage Rapid Dominance as the possible military expression, vanguard, and extension of this potential for revolutionary change. The strategic centers of gravity on which Rapid Dominance concentrates, modified by the uniquely American ability to integrate all this, are these junctures of strategy, technology, and innovation which are focused on the goal of affecting and shaping the will of the adversary. The goal of Rapid Dominance will be to destroy or so confound the will to resist that an adversary will have no alternative except to accept our strategic aims and military objectives. To achieve this outcome, Rapid Dominance must control the operational environment and through that dominance, control what the adversary perceives, understands, and knows, as well as control or regulate what is not perceived, understood, or known.' Harlan K. Ullman and James P. Wade, *Shock and Awe: Achieving Rapid Dominance* (National Defense University Press, 1996), Prologue.

[38] Paul Mendes-Flohr, 'Lament's Hope' in Moishe Postone and Eric Santner, *Catastrophe and Meaning: The Holocaust and the Twentieth Century* (University of Chicago, 2003), p. 251.

[39] Reinhold Niebuhr, *The Nature and Destiny of Man*, (originally given as The Gifford Lectures, Edinburgh, April, May and October 1939; Charles Scribner's Sons, 1948); the passages cited here are from Volume II, pp. 56, 212.

[40] Milbank, *Theology and Social Theory*, p. 397.

[41] Willem A. Visser t'Hooft, 'An Act of Penitence', in Ronald Gregor-Smith and Wolf-Dieter Zimmermann, eds. *I Knew Dietrich Bonhoeffer: Reminiscences by His Friends* (Harper, 1966), p. 194 as cited by Larry L. Rasmussen, *Dietrich Bonhoeffer: Reality and Resistance* (Abingdon Press, 1972), p. 56.

[42] Samuel Beckett 1961, as quoted by John Keane in *The Media and Democracy* (Polity Press, 1991), p. 173.

[43] Church of England Mission and Public Affairs Council, *Facing the Challenge of Terrorism: A Report to General Synod* (GS 1593, 15 November 2005), para. 22: www.cofe.anglican.org/about/gensynod/agendas/nov05.html.

[44] Mission and Public Affairs Council, *Facing the Challenge of Terrorism*, para. 20.

[45] House of Bishops, *Countering Terrorism*, p. 38.

[46] Report by Mercer Human Resource Consulting, based on a survey of more than 600 companies in India and China (*Financial Times*, 15 November 2005).

[47] House of Bishops, *Countering Terrorism*; the passages cited here are from pp. 36–39 and pp. 46–47.

[48] The folly of the argument that international law is so imperfect that it is right to disregard it is exposed by Philippe Sands, *Lawless World: America and the Making and Breaking of Global Rules* (Allen Lane, 2005).

[49] Arrighi does not merely describe the unravelling of American hegemony; he offers an explanation, drawing heavily on an analysis of the dynamics of capitalism. The phenomenon of 20th century American hegemony is placed in the context of the need generated by capital accumulation for a 'spatial fix'. He compares the 20th century cycle of capital accumulation, led by America, with previous cycles which he identifies as the Genoese-Iberian (15th- early 17th century), Dutch (late 16th – late 18th century), British (mid 18th- early 20th century); Giovanni Arrighi, Hegemony Unravelling', a two-part essay in *New Left Review* 32 (March/April 2005):23–80 and 33 (May/June 2005):83–116.

[50] Stanley Hoffman, 'American Exceptionalism: The New Version' in Michael Ignatieff, ed., *American Exceptionalism and Human Rights* (Princeton University Press, 2005), p. 228.

[51] John Williamson, of the Institute for International Economics, has vigorously defended himself against charges that the Consensus was about market fundamentalism or 'Reaganomics'. He reminds critics that he actually prepared the policy for the administration which would follow Reagan, aiming precisely at something on which consensus might be achievable; *Center for Strategic & International Studies* (6 November, 2002). He repeats the ten principles of the 'Washington Consensus': 1. Fiscal Discipline; 2. Reordering Public Expenditure Priorities; 3. Tax reform; 4. Liberalizing Interest Rates; 5. A Competitive Exchange Rate; 6. Trade Liberalization; 7. Liberalization of Inward Foreign Direct Investment; 8. Privatization; 9. Deregulation; 10. Property Rights. John Williamson, *A Guide to the Writings of John Williamson* (Institute for International Economics). Williamson: www.iie.com/staff/jwguide.htm.

[52] *Forbes Magazine*, The Year in Scandals (December 2003): www.forbes.com/2003/12/09/cx_aw_timeline.html.

[53] Arthur Andersen, one of the most prestigious accounting firms was wiped out as a result of its failure to spot the irregularities of Enron.

[54] In 1995 Barings, Britain's oldest merchant bank collapsed due to the huge losses of some £830 million, through unauthorised, and unsupervised speculative trading by its agent in Singapore, Nick Leeson.

[55] Citigroup has been plagued by a number of scandals including charges of providing biased research to investors. It was criticized by European and American financial regulators for appearing to manipulate markets when, within a few minutes on 2 August 2004, it rapidly sold €11 billion worth of bonds, driving down the price, and then bought some €4 billion back at cheaper prices. An investigation is pending. It was also accused of helping Enron cover potential loan losses. It has paid out over $1.5 billion to settle these cases, without necessarily admitting guilt.

[56] Raymond Baker Senior Fellow at the Center for International Policy and Guest Scholar at the Brookings Institution, was always shocked throughout his 40 years in business, in both developed and developing countries, at the scale of 'dirty money' used by local and transnational corporations, and is now leading a crusade to curtail it. His conservative and carefully documented estimate is that the flow of 'dirty money' amounts to some $1,000 billion a year, of which more than two-thirds takes the form of 'commercial tax-evading money' through mispricing of goods, and services, abusive transfer pricing and false transactions such as billing for goods and services never delivered. Raymond W. Baker, *Capitalism's Achilles Heel: Dirty Money and How to Renew the Free-Market System* (Wiley and Sons, 2005), p.172. The US Government Accountability Office estimated that some $129 billion had been lost in tax receipts as a result of the use of tax shelters, of which nearly half was in the five year period 1998–2003 (Tax Shelters; Services provided by External Auditors, February 2005): http://www.gao.gov/new.items/d05171.pdf.

[57] In 2001 the giant energy firm Enron faced bankruptcy, and charges of fraudulent dealing and of having hidden hundreds of millions of losses from its balance sheet, thus encouraging investors to pay excessive prices for shares. 50,000 investors filed a class action suit and received some compensation; 25,000 employees lost their jobs; and, five years later, former Chief Executives Ken Lay and Jeffrey Skilling were convicted of fraud.

[58] Jean-Pierre Garnier, Chief Executive of GlaxoSmithKline, enjoyed a contract which provided for him to be awarded £22 million should he be sacked for poor performance. Dick Grasso, former Chair of the New York Stock Exchange, arranged for himself to be given a $140 million remuneration package, the disclosure of which brought about his resignation in November 2003 and subsequent court action.

[59] In November 2005 Conrad Black (Lord Black of Crossharbour) – already deposed as Chairman and Chief Executive of Hollinger International, which owned over 400 newspapers world wide, was indicted by a federal grand jury on eight counts of fraud, subsequently doubled to sixteen – all of which he denies – including the fraudulent use of corporation funds and the diversion for the use of himself and other executives of some $84 million.

[60] In 1998 the powerful, so-called Long Term Capital Management hedge fund lost nearly 90% of its capital in the wake of the South East Asian and Russian crises. It could have resulted in a global financial disaster had not 14 of the largest US and European financial institutions taken part in a dramatic $3.6 billion rescue operation mounted by the US Federal Reserve Bank.

[61] In 2003 it was discovered that as much as €10bn had 'gone missing' from the accounts of Italy's food and beverage giant, Parmalat.

[62] In 2005 Refco, the world's largest futures trading firm was charged with keeping over $430 million in bad debts off of the company's books so as to inflate earnings and bolster Refco's share price. The discovery wiped out more than $1 billion in shareholder value.

[63] On 25 July 2005 Sony BMG agreed to pay $10 million to settle charges of 'pay to play' to radio stations to promote the music it sells.

[64] In 2002 the former chief executive and the former chief financial officer of Tyco International Ltd. were indicted yesterday on charges that they reaped $600 million through a racketeering scheme involving stock fraud, unauthorized bonuses and falsified expense accounts.

[65] The All China Federation of Trade Unions has protested about the concerted attempts of transnationals to circumvent Chinese laws which oblige them to establish unions (*Financial Times*, 5 January 2005).

[66] In 2002 the spotlight shone on WorldCom, which was found to have inflated its assets by more than $12 billion.

[67] For more information on corporate scandals in the US see the website of The Corporate Crime Reporter: www.corporatecrimereporter.com.

[68] *Financial Times*, 24 December 2004.

[69] Baker, *Capitalism's Achilles Heel*, p. 53.

[70] To take one example, Janos Bogardi, Director of the Institute for Environment and Human Security at the UN University of Bonn has warned that the number of ' environmental refugees' – not just from sudden emergencies such as hurricanes and earthquakes but also from longer terms processes such as desertification or coastal erosion – could reach 50 million by 2010: www.ehs.unu.edu/index.php?lang=en.

[71] Martin Wolf, *Financial Times*, 13 July 2005.

[72] House of Bishops, *Countering Terrorism*, p. 38. The bishops draw on Anatol Lieven's analysis of the 'thesis' and 'antithesis' in America's view of its relationship to the wider world. In this view, the 'American thesis' of civic nationalism (its civic commitment to liberty, democracy, individualism and the rule of law – but which has become a sort of American Creed with a liability to religious messianism and moral crusading) is in tension with 'the American antithesis...a chauvinist and bellicose type of "Jacksonian nationalism", consisting of conservative populism at home and aggressive nationalism abroad....[which] reflects a view of America as a closed cultural community at risk from a hostile and treacherous world'; p. 37. The Working Group also express particular concern about the recent increase of influence by the more apocalyptic, fundamentalist side of evangelical Christianity.

[73] Nicholas Lash, *The Beginning and the End of 'Religion'* (Cambridge University Press, 1996), p. 219.

[74] Keith Clements, *Faith on the Frontier: A Life of J. H. Oldham* (T&T Clark, 1999), p. 135. Clements describes the work of 'The Moot'(1938–1947), that astonishing think tank set up by Oldham (1874–1969), which captured a spirit shared by Liberals (Beveridge), Labour and Communists alike that post-war Britain had to be radically different from the Britain of the past: 'The subjects dealt with by the Moot continued to focus on social transformation and the necessary tensions between planning and freedom.' p. 383.

[75] www.progressive-governance.net.

[76] The World Social Forum first met in January 2001 in Porto Alegre, Brazil as a counter-witness to the World Economic Forum. It has attracted as many as 100,000 participants. See the account of the World Social Forum by William F. Fisher and Thomas Ponniah, *Another World Is Possible: Popular Alternatives to Globalization at the World Social Forum* (Zed Books, 2003). It has also convened regional forums, whose growing importance was highlighted at the January 2004 Forum in Mumbai, India. See Achin Vanaik, 'Rendezvous in Mumbai', *New Left Review* 26 (March/April 2004): 53–65. At the Forum of January 2005, held once again in Porto Alegre, a mood of impatience and a desire not to be only a talk-shop led, for the first time, to the drafting of a 'Consensus', with a set of specific demands. In January 2006 it was held simultaneously in three continents: Africa (Bamako), South America (Caracas) and Asia (Karachi). For details of the Forum's global and regional events see: www.forumsocialmundial.org.br/home.asp or www.wsf2007.org.

[77] CivWorld is a project of the Democracy Collaborative at the University of Maryland: http://civworld.org/about.htm.

[78] Citizens for Tax Justice: www.ctj.org.

[79] The Citizen Organising Foundation is committed to the development of civil society through engaging people in public action, focussing around issues relevant to particular neighbourhoods, whilst at the same time acknowledging that many local issues require broader, strategic solutions: www.cof.org.uk.

[80] Citizen Works, founded by Ralph Nader in April 2001, seeks to advance justice by strengthening citizen participation in power and to give people the tools and opportunities to build democracy: www.citizenworks.org/admin/about.php.

[81] Edward Said acknowledges his debt to Williams: 'I need hardly say that many parts of this book are suffused with the ideas and the human soul and moral example of Raymond Williams, a good friend and a great critic'. *Culture and Imperialism* (Vintage edition, 1994; originally published by Chatto and Windus in 1993), p. xxxi. The Williams-Hall approach is, of course, only one current in contemporary cultural studies. For the debate about putting this approach in context, see David Simpson, 'Politics as Such?', *New Left Review* Second Series 30 (Nov/Dec 2004): 69–82.

[82] As cited by Lawrence Lessig, 'Do you Floss?', *London Review of Books*, 18 August 2005.

[83] Berners Lee's original proposal may be found on his website at: www.w3.org/History/1989/proposal.html.

[84] Scott Atran, 'The "Virtual Hand" of Jihad', The Jamestown Foundation, *Terrorism Monitor* 3:10 (May 19, 2005): www.jamestown.org/terrorism/news/article.php?search=1&articleid=2369701. The Al-Qaeda-linked network is diffuse and loosely organized, sustained by a complex mixture of causes – ideology (the Wahabi version of Sunni Islam in Saudi Arabia) and a sense of outrage against the decades of injustice perpetrated by the West in the Middle East, and desperation.

[85] The One Laptop per Child (OLPC) project, first announced at the World Economic Forum at Davos, Switzerland in January 2005 is an initiative of Nicholas Negroponte of the MIT Media Laboratory: http://web.media.mit.edu/~nicholas. Ndiyo (*Ndiyo*, the Swahili word for 'yes') is a Cambridge-based project which was set up to foster an approach to networked computing that is simple, affordable, open, less environmentally-hostile, and less dependent on intensive technical support than conventional PC-based networking technology: http://www.ndiyo.org.

Chapter One: Transforming Mission – Regime Change

[1] Lady Thatcher, at the annual conference of the Institute of Directors, as quoted in the *Financial Times*, 1 May, 2003.

[2] Opening Remarks as delivered before the Senate Appropriations Committee, Washington, DC, February 17, 2005: www.state.gov/secretary/rm/2005/42419.htm.

[3] From 'The Life of Blessed Paul' by St. Jerome, as cited by Helen Waddell, *The Desert Fathers* (Fontana Library, 1962, orig. 1936), p. 24.

[4] Rowan Williams, *The Kingdom Is Theirs: Five Reflections on the Beatitudes* (Christian Socialist Movement, 1996), p. 4.

[5] David J. Bosch, *Transforming Mission: Paradigm Shifts in Theology of Mission* (Orbis Books, 1991), p. xv.

[6] Fernand Braudel, *Civilization and Capitalism: 15th–18th Century*, Volume II: *The Wheels of Commerce* (original French 1979; English translation by Sian Reynolds, Collins, 1982) pp. 455–457.

[7] Chesterton was president of the Distributist League, founded in 1926. Seven years later, in the midst of the Depression, the movement also launched a Distributist Party.

[8] de Soto develops the insight spelt out by Marx, namely that capital is not simply assets – raw materials, commodities, property or even money. These become transformed into capital only to the extent that they generate value by commercial, financial or productive activity. This process of transformation involves a sort of codification, which is a way of identifying and representing those particular qualities which make a thing or an activity capable of generating more value in any particular social and historical context. In the same way, property, for de Soto, is not simple ownership. It is a process by which aspects of physical realities are transformed into virtual realities through incorporation into a representational world: '...it allows assets to become fungible by representing them to our minds so that we can easily combine, divide and mobilize them to produce higher-valued mixtures. This capacity of property...is the mainspring of economic growth.' Hernando de Soto, *The Mystery of Capital: Why Capitalism Triumphs in the West and Fails Everywhere Else* (Bantam Press, 2000), pp. 39–42; 201–204.

[9] The World Health Organization notes that tobacco is the second leading cause of death, being responsible for nearly 5 million deaths per year at present, a figure which, on present trends, could rise to 10 million per year by 2024 – with as many as 70% of these in developing countries. To try to contain this it has developed a Framework Convention on Tobacco, which has been ratified by 57 countries and which came into effect on 27 February 2005: www.who.int/tobacco/framework/en.

[10] A World Bank report in February 2004 concluded that sugar was the 'most policy distorted of all commodities' and that multilateral reform of sugar policy could produce global welfare gains of $4.7 billion per year. In the United States sugar is becoming far and away the country's most protectionist regime, according to a lengthy report by Edward Alden and Neil Buckley in the *Financial Times* (27 February 2004). Thus, when a bilateral free-trade agreement was concluded between the US and Australia in January 2004, sugar was specifically excluded. In April 2003 The World Health Organization and the United Nations produced a joint report, *Diet, Nutrition and the Prevention of Chronic Diseases*, which called, among other things, for a campaign to reduce sugar consumption. In response, Andrew Briscoe, President of the US Sugar Association, informed the Director General of the WHO that his association would be 'asking congressional appropriators to challenge future funding of the US's $480m contribution to the WHO' – a quarter of the annual total. In May 2004, American and European sugar interests persuaded African and Caribbean countries to join their campaign against this aspect of the WHO anti-obesity campaign, even though in purely economic terms, this would keep these countries locked into a system of dependency, from which Europe and the US benefit most.

[11] Ulrich Duchrow, *Alternatives to Global Capitalism: Drawn from Biblical History and Designed for Political Action* (International Books and Kairos Europa, 1995).

[12] Robert Putnam, *Bowling Alone: The Collapse and Revival of American Community* (Simon and Schuster, 2000), p. 20.

[13] Richard Sennett, *The Culture of the New Capitalism* (Yale University Press, 2006; Castle Lectures in Ethics, Politics and Economics given at Yale University in 2004).

[14] Karl Polanyi, *Origins of Our Time: The Great Transformation* (Gollancz, 1945; later published – and better known – as *The Great Transformation: The Political and Economic Origins of Our Time* (Beacon, 1957).

[15] Philip Bobbitt, *The Shield of Achilles: War, Peace and the Course of History* (Allen Lane, 2002), Part III: 'The Society of Market States', pp. 667– 809.

[16] Bobbitt, *Shield,* pp. 230, 701.

[17] Rodney Hilton, Introduction, *The Transition from Feudalism to Capitalism,* (Verso, 1978). See especially Hilton's own chapter, 'Capitalism – What's in a Name?', pp. 145–158.

[18] Kevin J. Vanhoozer, ed., *The Cambridge Companion to Postmodern Theology* (Cambridge University Press, 2003), p. xiv.

[19] Amitai Etzioni, *The Active Society: A Theory of Societal and Political Processes* (Free Press, 1968). Etzioni speaks of 'the post-modern period, the onset of which may be set at 1945', pp. vii–viii, 7.

[20] John Milbank, 'Culture: The Gospel of Affinity' in *Being Reconciled: Ontology and Pardon* (Routledge, 2003; originally in Ethical Perspectives 7:4 [December 2000]), pp. 194–209.

[21] Atherton, *Christianity and the Market: Christian Social Thought for Our Times* (SPCK, 1992), p. 217.

[22] Atherton, *Public Theology for Changing Times* (SPCK, 2000), p. 83.

[23] Philip Sampson, Vinay Samuel and Chris Sugden, eds. *Faith and Modernity* (Regnum Books International, 1994).

[24] 'If Europeans were to avoid falling into a sceptical morass, they had, it seemed, to find *something* to be "certain" about'; Stephen Toulmin, *Cosmopolis: The Hidden Agenda of Modernity* (Macmillan, Free Press, 1990), p. 55. Toulmin's is an essay in retrieval, seeking to recover an earlier, more humanistic and even sceptical version of modernity, as represented by the Renaissance. Toulmin believes that that sort of humanistic modernity is precisely what is needed in our own times.

[25] R. H. Tawney, *Religion and the Rise of Capitalism,* (original edition 1925, Penguin, 1937).

[26] Francis Bacon, as cited By Norman Hampson, *The Enlightenment: An Evaluation of Its Assumptions, Attitudes and Values,* 1968 (Penguin edition, 1982), pp. 36–37.

[27] René Descartes, *Philosophical Writings,* as cited by John Cottingham, *Descartes* (Basil Blackwell, 1986), p. 7.

[28] Cottingham, *Descartes,* p. 19.

[29] The Institute for Social Research, to give it its proper name, was lodged in New York during the Second World War. Its most prominent figures were Theodor Adorno, Max Horkheimer, Herbert Marcuse and Erich Fromm.

[30] Theodor W. Adorno and Max Horkheimer, *Dialectic of Enlightenment* (Verso 1979, written originally in German in 1944), p. 16.

[31] John Milbank, 'Policing the Sublime', *Theology and Social Theory,* Chapter 5.

[32] Alasdair MacIntyre has played a central role in calling attention to how, in the construction and government of the modern self, the concern for character and virtue has given way to the realm of experts, managers and therapists. *After Virtue: A Study in Moral Theory* (Duckworth, 1981), pp. 25–31; 73–77.

[33] Norbert Elias, *The Society of Individuals* (edited by Michael Schroeter, Basil Blackwell, 1991), p. 87.

[34] Anthony Giddens, *The Consequences of Modernity* (Polity Press, 1990), pp. 4–5.

[35] Etzioni, *Active Society*; Etzioni sees reflexivity as the hallmark of 'the post-modern period', pp. vii–viii, 7.

[36] Anthony Giddens. See especially his *The Consequences of Modernity,* pp. 138, 142.

[37] Ulrich Beck, 'Misunderstanding Reflexivity: The Controversy on Reflexive Modernization', in Ulrich Beck, *Democracy without Enemies* (Polity Press, 1998), pp. 84–102.

[38] Jurgen Habermas, 'The Entwinement of Myth and Enlightenment: Horkheimer and Adorno', in *The Philosophical Discourse of Modernity: Twelve Lectures* (Polity Press, 1987, original German edition, 1985), pp. 106–130.

[39] Jurgen Habermas, *Contributions to a Discourse Theory of Law and Democracy* (Polity Press, 1996), pp. xli, xliii.

[40] Charles Taylor, *Sources of the Self: The Making of Modern Identity* (Cambridge University Press, 1989), pp. 93, 502–513.

[41] Niebuhr, *Christ and Culture*, pp. 190–191.

[42] H. Richard Niebuhr (1894–1962), brother of the influential social theologian Reinhold Niebuhr (1892–1971), was both a church historian and a theologian. The continuing fruitfulness of his approach is indicated by the recent reassessment of this classic on the occasion of its 50th anniversary reprint (see the discussion in *Journal of the Society of Christian Ethics* 23:1 (Spring/Summer 2003): 99–165.

[43] This recently discovered manuscript comprises the Prologue of the reassessment of Niebuhr made by Glen H. Stassen, Dianne M. Yeager and John Howard Yoder, *Authentic Transformation: A New Vision of Christ and Culture* (Abingdon, 1996), p. 10. There is a warmth, generosity and catholicity in Gilson's term 'families', that may well be worth recovering. Gilson's book, *Reason and Revelation in the Middle Ages* (Charles Scribner's and Sons, 1939) focuses only on the medieval period.

[44] 'Culture', as will be discussed in Chapter Three, can be understood in several different senses. Niebuhr, taking as his guide Bronislav Malinowski, uses it in the anthropological sense as referring to the 'artificial secondary environment which man superimposes on the natural. It comprises language, habits, ideas, beliefs, customs, social organization, inherited artifacts, technical processes and values.' H. Richard Niebuhr, *Christ and Culture* (Harper and Row, 1951), p. 32.

[45] H. Richard Niebuhr, *Christ and Culture* (Harper and Row, 1951); the passages cited here are from pp. 190–229.

[46] *Constitutio Pastoralis de Ecclesia in Mundo Huius Temporis – Gaudium et Spes* (7 December 1965); the passages cited here are from paras 4, 38 and 40.

[47] Paul VI: 'Going beyond every system, without however failing to commit himself concretely to serving his brothers, he will assert, in the very midst of his options, the specific character of the Christian contribution for a positive transformation of society;' Apostolic Letter *Octogesima Adveniens* (14 May 1971), para. 36. Paul insists that transformative action is an integral part of evangelization: 'For the Church, evangelizing means bringing the Good News into all the strata of humanity, and through its influence transforming humanity from within and making it new.' Apostolic Exhortation *Evangelii Nuntiandi* (8 December 1975), para. 18.

[48] The Synod of Bishops, describing the 'network of domination' which is oppressing the greater part of humanity, declares: 'Action on behalf of justice and participation in the transformation of the world fully appear to us as a constitutive dimension of the preaching of the Gospel…'. Referring to the developing countries where '…the principal aim of this education for justice consists in an attempt to awaken consciences to a knowledge of the concrete situation and in a call to secure a total improvement' [it is inconceivable that they did not have in mind Paulo Freire's 'Pedagogy of the Oppressed'], the Bishops go so far as to state that: '…by these means the transformation of the world has already begun.' *Justice in the World* (November 1971), Introduction and Chapter III.

[49] Oliver O'Donovan *The Desire of the Nations: Rediscovering the Roots of Biblical Theology* (Cambridge University Press, 1996), p. 143.

[50] Stanley Hauerwas, 'The Church and Liberal Democracy: The Moral Limits of a Secular Polity', in *A Community of Character: Towards a Constructive Christian Ethic* (University of Notre Dame Press, 1981); the passages cited here are from pp. 73, 246–247.

[51] Stassen et al., *Authentic Transformation: A New Vision of Christ and Culture.*

[52] Yoder, in *Authentic Transformation*; the passages here are from pp. 34, 40, 42–43, 69–70, 72, 75–76.

[53] Timothy J. Gorringe, *Furthering Humanity: A Theology of Culture* (Ashgate, 2004); the passages cited here are from pp. 4, 15–16, 43, 75, 102, 120.

[54] Richard Niebuhr, in his preparatory manuscript for Christ and Culture places Reinhold in the 'Oscillatory Type (Christ and Culture in Paradox)'; Stassen, et al., *Authentic Transformation* while in *Christ and Culture* itself he appears to qualify this, applying it to Reinhold's earlier work *Moral Man and Immoral Society*; *Christ and Culture*, pp. 183n, 230n.

[55] Niebuhr, *Christ and Culture*; the passages in this section are from pp. 138, 172, 176, 178–179, 185–186.

[56] David Goodhart, editor of *Prospect*, writing in the *Financial Times*, 29 September 2004. Every year the British public affairs magazine *Prospect* gives an award to what it deems to be the best British think tank. Although think tanks have grown in number, observes Goodhart, the market for 'big ideas' has got smaller. This does not mean that think tanks are useless, concludes Goodhart. What it means, as he sees it, is simply that times have changed and that, unlike the 1970s, our times are not times for 'big transforming ideas'.

[57] Michio Kaku has helped popularize the challenges of technology in the United States by his work in the media and in his many writings. The development of microchips, nano-technology, lasers, robots, genetics, etc., as they take effect particularly via new systems of information and communication, are reshaping our patterns of work and leisure, our social relationships, our ability to replace diseased body parts, to clone human life, and to modify human personality. One of his best known works is *Visions: How Science Will Revolutionize the 21st Century and Beyond* (Oxford University Press, 1998).

[58] John Atherton concludes that transformationist theology, as represented by the Christian socialism of F. D. Maurice, the incarnational theology of Charles Gore and, across the Atlantic, the 'Social Gospel' theology of Walter Rauschenbusch belongs firmly back in the 19th and early 20th centuries, when the state was accorded a central role. Atherton does, however, allow scope for more local and more reflexive forms of transformational activity noting that even these will demand 'a major change in our thinking and practice as a response to continuing change, in order to affect change....It can only emerge...out of a prolonged process of cultural self re-examination and philosophical re-evaluation....It will therefore provide essentially provisional but workable frameworks for interpreting and engaging the emerging context.' Atherton, *Public Theology*, the passages cited here are from pp. 75–82, 84, 86, 93–109.

[59] Evangelical Alliance: *Annual Review 2005–2006* (September 2006): www.eauk.org/about/review/upload/annual_review_2005_2006.pdf;*Compendium*, para. 55.

[60] Augustine of Hippo, *The City of God* (edited by Vernon J. Bourke, Doubleday Image Books, 1958 edition), Book XIV, Chapter 28, p. 321.

[61] Edward Said describes how, after the period of 'primary resistance' against outside intrusion, there follows a period of 'secondary, that is, ideological resistance'; *Culture and Imperialism*, pp. 252ff. It is in this latter stage that the struggle becomes even more bitter, when it is waged between those for whom a new identity consists in a particular identity (nationalism, tribalism) as against those who seek a more universal, collective identity (pp. 323ff).

[62] Peter Brown, *Augustine of Hippo: A Biography* (Faber and Faber, 1967), p. 312.

[63] Brown, *Augustine*, p. 336.

[64] In *De catechizandis rudibus* (c.399–400AD) XIX–XX, the two cities are intermingled in body but separate in will; Jerusalem is seen as the sign of the heavenly city. In *De Genesi ad litteram* (401 AD) XV, the two cities are described as prompted by two loves, one social the other private. Shortly after the sack of Rome, in *Sermo 105*: 9–10 (410/411 AD) Augustine, contrasts the changing of earthly regimes with the lasting heavenly kingdom, referring to the holy city, rooted in heaven and a resident alien on earth. Later (415 AD) in *Enarratio in Psalmum 64: Sermo ad plebem*, Augustine again writes of two loves at the heart of the two cities and, holding

up the vision of the heavenly city, exclaims: 'Already in longing we are there.'

⁶⁵ The theme is developed particularly in Book III, Chapter 14; Book XIV, Chapters 14–23, 28, Book XV Chapters 4, 7, and Book XIX, Chapter 15.

⁶⁶ Tom Paine, letter to a female correspondent in New York (1787), quoted by Paine in his letter to George Washington (1795), in *The Thomas Paine Reader* (edited by Michael Foot and Isaac Kramnick, Penguin Books, 1987), p. 493.

⁶⁷ Augustine, *City of God*, Book IV, Chapter 7.

⁶⁸ 'Where justice is lacking, what is sovereignty but organized brigandage? For what are bands of brigands but petty kingdoms, groups of men, under the rule of a leader, bound together by a common agreement, dividing their booty according to a settled principle. If this band of criminals, by recruiting more criminals, acquires enough power to occupy regions, to capture cities, and to subdue whole populations, then it enhances its claim to the title of kingdom, conferred upon it by the populace, not as a result of the renunciation of greed but by the increase of impunity.' Augustine, *City of God,* Book IV, Chapter 4. See also all of Book XIX.

⁶⁹ Augustine, *City of God*, Book III, Chapter 14.

⁷⁰ Heidegger's philosophy is fundamentally shaped by the German experience of pre-war decline and then of Fascism, which he briefly supported, but which leads to his later spirit of renunciation. See the sympathetic interpretation of the later (post-1934) Heidegger given by Fred Dallmayr, *The Other Heidegger* (Cornell University Press, 1993). This presents emancipation as a leaving behind of the need for power and violence, which then opens up a return home through reticence (*Scheu*), reserve (*Verhaltenheit*), and awe (*Erschrecken*) and letting Being be (*Gelassenheit*).

⁷¹ Taylor, *Sources of the Self,* p. 21.

⁷² The European Kairos Declaration states: 'Deeply rooted in *European culture* is the *violent desire for domination and possession.* The roots of this can be traced back to the origins of patriarchy.' The document traces its further development in the form of imperialism (from Aristotle through the Constantinian Christianity) and finds that in '*the last five or six centuries,* the tradition of cultural violence has been connected with the *violence of the capitalist monetary economy.*': www.kairoseuropa.org.

⁷³ Reinhold Niebuhr, *The Nature and Destiny of Man,* vol. I, p. 96.

⁷⁴ Niebuhr, *The Nature and Destiny of Man,* vol. I, p. 183.

⁷⁵ R. A. Markus, *The End of Ancient Christianity* (Cambridge University Press, Canto edition, 1998, first published in 1990), p. 78. In *De Genesi as litteram* XV Augustine contrasts two loves, one holy and social, the other unclean and private, the first seeking what is of common benefit for the sake of the supreme society, the second seeking to boost one's power for the sake of arrogant domination. In *The City of God*, Book XV, Chapter 17 Augustine defines in similar terms the struggle between Abel and Cain, whose very name for Augustine signified ownership: '..."Ownership" was the originator of the city of earth.'

⁷⁶ Brown, *Augustine,* p. 327.

⁷⁷ Oliver O'Donovan. 'The Political Thought of the City of God 19', in Oliver O'Donovan and Joan Lockwood O'Donovan, *Bonds of Perfection: Christian Politics, Past and Present* (William B. Eerdmans, 2004); the passages here are from pp. 65 and 68.

⁷⁸ Brown, *Augustine,* p. 240.

⁷⁹ Pope John Paul II, Letter to Artists (4 April 1999), quoting Dostoevsky, *The Idiot*, Part III, chap. 5.

⁸⁰ David J. Bosch, *Transforming Mission: Paradigm Shifts in Theology of Mission* (Orbis, Books 1999), pp. 431, 483.

⁸¹ Milbank, "The Poverty of Niebuhrianism," in *The Word Made Strange*, p.238.

⁸² The references here are to Lewis Hyde, *The Gift: How the Creative Spirit Transforms the World* (Canongate 2006; originally 1979), p.152–153; John Milbank, "Culture: The Gospel of Affinity" in *Being Reconciled: Ontology and Pardon* (Routledge, 2003; originally in Ethical Perspectives 7:4 [December 2000]), pp. 187–211; Rowan Williams, *Grace and Necessity:*

Reflections on Art and Love (Continuum, 2005), pp. 37, 53, 150.

[83] Rowan Williams, *Grace and Necessity*, p. 156.

[84] Milbank, 'A Critique of the Theology of Right', in *The Word Made Strange*, pp. 28–29

[85] Niebuhr, *Children of Light*, pp. 10, 63.

[86] Anthony Giddens, *The Consequences of Modernity*, p. 165.

[87] Augustine of Hippo, *The Confessions of St. Augustine* (translated by John K. Ryan, Doubleday, Image Books, 1960), Book 10, Chapter 6, p. 234.

[88] John Milbank, *Theology and Social Theory: Beyond Secular Reason* (Basil Blackwell, 1990), pp. 206–255.

[89] Marx's criticism of 'utopian socialism' is often misrepresented. He was not so much dismissive of the vision of the 'utopian socialists'. On the contrary, he acknowledged: '...they are full of the most valuable materials for the enlightenment of the working class. The practical measures proposed in them – such as the abolition of the distinction between town and country, of the family, of the carrying on of industries for the account of private individuals, and of the wage system, the proclamation of social harmony, the conversion of the functions of the state into a mere superintendence of production – all these proposals point solely to the disappearance of class antagonisms which were, at the time, only just cropping up.' (*The Communist Manifesto*, 1848.) Why this fell short of his 'scientific socialism' was because it was proposed without a recognition that certain stages of capitalist development and class warfare had first to be arrived at before any such visions could be implemented.

[90] Jurgen Habermas, 'The New Obscurity: The Crisis of the Welfare State and the Exhaustion of Utopian Energies' in *The New Conservatism: Cultural Criticism and the Historians' Debate* (Polity Press, 1989), pp. 48–70.

[91] Mill, *On Liberty*, pp. 76, 80, 103–108.

[92] Hilary Wainwright, *Reclaim the State: Experiments in Popular Democracy* (Verso, 2003), p. 28.

[93] *Centesimus Annus* (I May, 1991), para. 38. The notion of 'structures of sin' is developed more fully in the encyclical *Sollicitudo rei socialis* (30 December 1987), para. 36–37 where Pope John Paul states that '...a world which is divided into blocs, sustained by rigid ideologies, and in which instead of interdependence and solidarity different forms of imperialism hold sway, can only be a world subject to structures of sin.' In this context he repeats the point made in his apostolic exhortation *Reconciliatio et Paenitentia* (2 December 1984) that structures of sin are rooted in personal sin, and thus always linked to the concrete acts of individuals who introduce these structures, consolidate them and make them difficult to remove.

[94] Markus, *End of Ancient Christianity*, p. 134; Markus defines the secular '...as that sector of life which is not considered to be of direct religious significance', p. 15. Markus argues that it was not until a century after Augustine that Christian theology abandoned its sacred/secular world view and that from then on a process of 'de-secularization' sets in, in which all institutions were subject to 'religious or ecclesiastical domination or influence'; p. 16.

[95] Brown, *Augustine*, p. 266.

[96] Milbank, *Theology and Social Theory*, pp. 406–408.

[97] Brown, *Augustine*, p. 289.

[98] Giddens, *Consequences of Modernity*, pp. 165–173.

[99] The 'Real Utopias Project' (begun in 1991) has been running for roughly the same time as the Towards Social Transformation initiative. It has taken the form of workshop conferences focussing on a provocative manuscript that lays out the basic outlines of a radical institutional proposal and then inviting 15–20 scholars to write essays that in one way or another address this document. Collections are published in the Real Utopias Project Series by Verso publishers, London. It is co-ordinated by Erik Olin Wright at the University of Wisconsin: www.ssc.wisc.edu/~wright.

[100] The call for the churches to adopt the kind of 'confessional' stance which some courageously did in the face of Nazism and apartheid has long been sounded by Ulrich Duchrow in his

work with the World Council of Churches and more recently with Kairos Europa. Clearly there are significant elements of idolatry in the worship of wealth and of the demonic in what Schumpeter called the 'creative destruction' wrought by capitalism. But the enormous rise in living standards which have accompanied it cannot simply be dismissed as by-products.

[101] John Gray, *Al Qaeda and What It Means to Be Modern* (Faber and Faber, 2003), pp. 104–105.

[102] Ernest Gellner, 'The Importance of Being Modular', in John A Hall, ed, *Civil Society: Theory, History Comparison* (Polity Press, 1995), p. 39.

[103] Milbank, *Theology and Social Theory*, pp. 12, 14, 16.

[104] Brown, *Augustine*, p. 348.

[105] *Enarratio in Psalmum 64, 2* as cited by Brown, *Augustine*, p. 323. Brown observes: 'What was at stake, in the City of God and in Augustine's sermons, was the capacity of men to long for something different...' (p. 322).

Notes to Chapter Two: Transforming Relations – What Kind of Civil Society?

[1] Francis Fukuyama, speaking at Reuters HQ, London, July 2004, as quoted by Hal Weitzman, *Financial Times Magazine,* 7 August 2004.

[2] See the fascinating study of the period by Paul Langford, *A Polite and Commercial People: England 1727–1783*, Oxford University Press, 1989; paperback edition, 1992): 'Politeness conveyed upper-class gentility, enlightenment and sociability to a much wider elite whose only qualification was money, but who were glad to spend it on acquiring the status of gentleman.... This debasement of gentility was one of the clearest signs of social change in the eighteenth century'; pp. 4, 66.

[3] John Keane, *Democracy and Civil Society*, pp. 15–19.

[4] Mary Kaldor, *Global Civil Society: An Answer to War* (Polity, 2003), p. 76.

[5] Margaret Thatcher, *Woman's Own*, (October 1987). The observation was subsequently qualified: 'Society is not an abstraction but a living structure of individuals, families, neighbours and voluntary associations. And no government can do anything except through people, and people must look to themselves first. It's our duty to look after ourselves and then to look after our neighbour.' Margaret Thatcher, *The Downing Street Years* (Harper Collins, 1993), p. 626.

[6] The same observations apply to the pressing issue of global peace-making. See the insightful essay by Paul W. Schroeder, 'International Order and Its Current Enemies', *Journal of the Society of Christian Ethics* 24:2 (Fall/Winter 2004): 193–211.

[7] Ernest Gellner, *Conditions of Liberty: Civil Society and Its Rivals* (Hamish Hamilton, 1994); the passages cited here are from pp. 32, 86, 99, 119,140, 145, 207.

[8] For an intricate journey through the confused and contradictory meanings of 'civil society' see Jean L. Cohen and Andrew Arato, *Civil Society and Political Theory* (MIT, 1992).

[9] Kaldor, *Global Civil Society*, p. 2.

[10] John Keane, *Global Civil Society?* (Cambridge University Press, 2003), p. 186.

[11] The *Compendium of the Social Doctrine of the Church* states: 'This is the realm of *civil society,* understood as the sum of the relationships between individuals and intermediate social groupings, which are the first relationships to arise and which come about thanks to "the creative subjectivity of the citizen".' (para. 185). And again: 'The political community and civil society, although mutually connected and interdependent, are not equal in the hierarchy of ends. The political community is essentially at the service of civil society and, in the final analysis, the persons and groups of which civil society is composed. Civil society, therefore, cannot be considered an extension or a changing component of the political community; rather, it has priority because it is in civil society itself that the political community finds it justification....Civil society is in fact multifaceted and irregular; it does not lack its ambiguities and contradictions. It is also the arena where different interests clash with one another, with the risk that the stronger will prevail over the weaker' (para. 418).

[12] Adam Ferguson, *An Essay on the History of Civil Society*, (originally 1767; as in the 7th edition, Basil, 1814). Ferguson extols the 'civil arts' – the pursuit of improvement, literature, ease, commerce, polity and war – and the civil virtues – industry, respect for property, lawfulness as opposed to the more primitive state of indolence, rapacity and violence. Civil Society for Ferguson is a glorious achievement, combining utility and self-interest with benevolence and the natural affections, establishing through the artifice of law, a wondrous harmony between the two: 'It shall seem, therefore, to be the happiness of man, to make his social dispositions the ruling spring of his occupations; to state himself as a member of a community for whose general good his heart may glow with an ardent zeal.' pp. 31, 60, 62, 64, 89, 92, 95, 181.

[13] Surprisingly, the *Compendium of the Social Doctrine of the Church* also distinguishes civil society from the economic, not just the political sphere: '*Civil society is the sum of relationships and resources, cultural and associative, that are relatively independent from the political sphere and the economic sector*'; para. 417.

[14] Gellner, *Conditions of Liberty*; the passages cited here are from pp. 56, 89–90, 137, 143, 163, 193, 206–207, 212.

[15] Gellner, *Conditions of Liberty*, pp. 213–214.

[16] C. B. Macpherson, 'Hobbes's Bourgeois Man', in Macpherson, *Democratic Theory: Essays in Retrieval* (Oxford University Press, 1973), pp. 240, 244.

[17] C. B. Macpherson, *The Political Theory of Possessive Individualism: Hobbes to Locke* (Clarendon Press, 1962), p. 65.

[18] John Locke, *An Essay Concerning the True Original Extent and End of Civil Government* (1690); the passages cited here are from Book II, Chapter 5. 33.

[19] 'Locke: The Political Theory of Appropriation', in Macpherson, *Political Theory*, pp. 195–262.

[20] Jurgen Habermas, *The Structural Transformation of the Public Sphere* (Polity Press, 1989); the passages cited here are from pp. 26–27, 160.

[21] Alexander Pope, 'Moral Essay III: Of The Use of Riches: An Epistle To the Right Honourable Allen Lord Bathurst', 1733.

[22] Ferguson, *Essay on the History of Civil Society*, pp. 31, 89, 93, 171, 310–312, 402–403.

[23] John Keane, *Tom Paine: A Political Life* (Bloomsbury, 1995). Yet, for all his preoccupation with the abuses of political power, Paine began to be concerned about the rise of monopoly power in the new American union. Writing to George Washington, he is typically combative: 'Monopolies of every kind marked your administration almost in the moment of its commencement. The lands obtained by the Revolution were lavished upon partisans...the chief of the army became the patron of fraud. From such a beginning what else could be expected than what has happened?' Tom Paine, *Letter to George Washington* (1795), *Thomas Paine Reader*, p. 492.

[24] Tom Paine, *Common Sense* (1776) in *The Thomas Paine Reader*, p. 66.

[25] Tom Paine, *Rights of Man, Part II* (1792), *The Thomas Paine Reader*; the passages quoted here are from pp. 266–268, 276, 297–298.

[26] Tom Paine, *Rights of Man, Part I* (1791), *The Thomas Paine Reader*, p. 217.

[27] Tom Paine, *Agrarian Justice* (1795), *Thomas Paine Reader;* the passages quoted from this essay are on pp. 472, 475–476, 482, 485–486.

[28] David G. Green, *Civil Society: The Guiding Philosophy and Research Agenda of the Institute for the Study of Civil Society* (Institute for the Study of Civil Society, 2000); the passages cited here are from pp. 2, 11, 33.

[29] Stuart Hall, 'The New Challenge of the Right' in Stuart Hall, ed., *The Hard Road to Renewal: Thatcherism and the Crisis of the Left* (Verso, 1988), p. 48.

[30] Ulrich Beck. 'Living Your Own Life in a Runaway World: Individualization, Globalization and Politics'; in Will Hutton and Anthony Giddens, eds., *On the Edge: Living with Global Capitalism* (Vintage, 2001), p. 165.

[31] Ulrich Beck, *Risk Society: Towards a New Modernity* (Sage, 1992), p. 99.

[32] Beck, *Risk Society*, p. 135.

[33] Ulrich Beck, 'Living Your Own Life', p. 171.

[34] The Communitarian Network – www.communitariannetwork.org.

[35] The Civil Renewal Unit states its aim as to promote awareness and practices that will help to increase citizens' active and democratic engagement in decisions or activities which affect their lives. Its work includes Community Development – developing policy proposals to increase citizen participation in the governance of their communities, by working with networks and partnerships of community groups, local authorities, public service providers, and civil society organizations, the establishment of a Centre for Active Citizenship, and the development of policy ideas in support of Neighbourhood Governance.

[36] Henry Tam, *Communitarianism: A New Agenda for Politics and Citizenship* (Macmillan, 1998), p. 29.

[37] Tom Paine, *Rights of Man: Part One*, in *The Thomas Paine Reader*, p. 245.

[38] Robert N. Bellah, Richard Madsen, William M. Sullivan, Ann Swidler and Steven M. Tipton, *Habits of the Heart: Individualism and Commitment in American Life* (Harper and Row, 1985), pp. 72–74.

[39] Francis Fukuyama, *The Great Disruption: Human Nature and the Reconstitution of the Social Order* (Profile Books, 1999). Fukuyama remains sanguine, however, interpreting 'the Great Disruption' of 1960–1990 as simply the sign of a period of economic transition. Just as the early 19th century marked the transition *to* an industrial society, so the end of the 20th century marked a transition *from* an industrial society. We have already turned the corner, he claims, witness the return to 'values' in the 1990s, with an increase in religiosity thrown in for good measure; pp. 87–91, 271–279.

[40] Schluter, 'The Relational Market Economy', in Michael Schluter and David Lee, *The R Factor* (Hodder and Stoughton, 1993), pp. 193–229.

[41] Michael Schluter, 'Making Relationships a Priority for Public Policy' in Nicola Baker, ed., *Building a Relational Society: New Priorities for Public Policy* (Arena, 1996), pp. 3–16. The Relationships Foundation has developed diagnostic tools to help assess and evaluate the quality of relationships within and between organizations. For an update on the work of the Relationships Foundation, see their web-site: www.relationshipsfoundation.org.

[42] The Relationships Foundation was set up under the wing of the Jubilee Centre in 1993. Michael Schluter tells the story of his path to Relationalism, starting with his years of Bible study sessions with Roy Clements, in 'Relationalism – Pursuing a Biblical Vision for Society', in Michael Schluter and the Cambridge Papers Group, *Christianity in a Changing World: Biblical Insight on Contemporary Issues* (Marshall Pickering, 2000), pp. 51–62.

[43] Schluter, 'Relationalism – Pursuing a Biblical Vision for Society' p. 59. Schluter acknowledges that his understanding of the various uses of the theme of law owes a great debt to Christopher Wright's *Living as the People of God: The Relevance of Old Testament Ethics* (Inter-varsity Press, 1983).

[44] Michael Ovey and Christopher Townsend in Michael Schluter and the Cambridge Papers Group, *Christianity in a Changing World*.

[45] For the study of the interpretation and significance of Althusius' thought see the Johannes-Althusius-Gesellschaft: www.tu-dresden.de/jfoeffl6/althusius2eng.htm.

[46] Johannes Althusius, *Politica Methodice Digesta (1603): 'Politica est ars homines ad vitam socialem inter se constituendam, colendam et conservandam consociendi, unde συμβιωτικη vocatur'.*

[47] The federal/covenantal aspects of Althusius' thought have been developed by Professor Daniel J. Elazar (1934–1999), formerly head of the Center for the Study of Federalism at Temple University (USA) and of the Jerusalem Center for Public Affairs.

[48] Carl Joachim Friedrich: 'What Althusius is setting forth is the theory of a corporative state…characterized by the fact that in the last analysis it devours the entire community [and] becomes one with it.' *Politica Methodice Digesta of Johannes Althusius (Althaus)* (Harvard University Press, 1932), p. lxxxvi.

[49] In Italy, the issue was complicated by the bitter conflict between the secular state and the economic and political power of the papacy. The fact that Catholics were forbidden to participate in political life by the decree of Pius IX *Non expedit* (29 February 1868) left them with only the 'social space' in which to organize, even though the decree was moderated by Leo XII and Pius IX. Papal control over Catholic associational life was reasserted in an ever more forceful way when Pius X disbanded the *Opera dei Congressi*, replacing them with the Catholic Unions. The influence of the hierarchy remained powerful in the later form of Catholic Action. See Paul Misner, *Social Catholicism in Europe: From the Onset of Industrialization to the First World War* (Darton, Longman and Todd, 1991), pp. 201, 241–246, 252–258, 288–293.

[50] Papal emphasis on associational life took on greater urgency in the 1930s with the development of totalitarianism. It is in this context that the highlighting of the principle of subsidiarity by Pius XI may be understood. In the late 1940s, with the very real possibility that the Italian Communist Party might be elected, there was a new campaign to develop church-sponsored civic associations under Pius XII.

[51] Alexis de Tocqueville, *Democracy in America: Volume I* (original edition, 1835, edited by J.P. Mayer, Anchor Books, 1969, based on 13th edition of 1850), pp. 246–276.

[52] Alexis de Tocqueville, *Democracy in America: Volume II* (original edition 1840; edited by J.P. Mayer, Anchor Books, 1969, based on 13th edition of 1850); pp. 511–524.

[53] This was also true of France, where its Law of Associations (1901) actually served as a means of suppressing religious orders.

[54] G. D. H. Cole, *The Social Theory* (Methuen, 1920) as cited in Paul Q. Hirst, *The Pluralist Theory of the State: Selected Writings of G. D. H. Cole, J. N. Figgis and H. J. Laski* (Routledge, 1989); the passages cited here are from pp. 55, 102.

[55] Temple, clearly echoing Figgis, complains: '...most political theories...tend to ignore the intermediate groupings. But that makes any understanding of actual liberty impossible; for it exists for the most part in and through those intermediate groups – the family, the Church or congregation, the guild, the Trade Union, the school, the university, the Mutual Improvement Society'; William Temple, *Community and Social Order* (Penguin, 1942), p. 70; as quoted by Atherton, *Public Theology*, p. 96.

[56] See especially David Nicholls, *The Pluralist State* (Macmillan Press, 1975).

[57] Robert Nisbet, *Community and Power* (Galaxy Book, 1962). Nisbet altered the original title, *The Quest for Community* (Oxford University Press, 1953), perhaps to make it clear that he was not indulging in mere nostalgia (p.73). Nisbet seeks to claim associationalism for conservatism, placing great store on traditional associations, including the church and the small social group (p. 25), and advocating a new form of *laissez-faire* (p. 278).

[58] *To Empower People: The Role of Mediating Structures in Public Policy* (American Enterprise Institute, 1977; reproduced by the American Enterprise Institute in 1996, in a collection of essays by Michael Novak et al. with subtly changed subtitle, *To Empower People: From State to Civil Society*). Berger and Neuhaus worked together from 1976–79, advocating, among other things, the development of 'Neighbourhood Enterprise'; the passages cited here are from the 1996 edition, pp. 158, 176, 187, 189, reprinted with the permission of the American Enterprise Institute for Public Policy Research, Washington, D.C.

[59] Paul Q. Hirst, *Representative Democracy and Its Limits* (Polity Press, 1990), pp. 92–93.

[60] Hirst's proposals are similar to those later suggested by Philippe C. Schmitter, 'The Irony of Modern Democracy and the Viability of Efforts to Reform its Practice', in Erik Olin Wright, ed., *Associations and Democracy* (Verso, 1995), pp. 167–183. Schmitter also suggests that contributions to the national fund should be obligatory, but at a low level, for all tax payers.

[61] Hirst, *Representative Democracy*, pp. 73, 79.

[62] When the French sociologist, Hippolyte Taine, undertook his tour of mid-Victorian England he could scarcely contain his amazement: 'There are swarms of societies engaged in good works: societies for the saving of drowning persons, for the conversion of the Jews, for the propagation of the Bible, for the advancement of science, for the protection of animals, for

the suppression of vice, for the abolition of tithes, for helping working people to own their own homes...for emigration...for Sabbath-day observance...for funding schools to train girls as schoolteachers, etc.' Sir James Stephen made a similar observation: 'Ours is the age of societies. For the redress of every oppression...For the cure of every sorrow....For the diffusion of every blessing'); "The Clapham Sect", in *Essays in Ecclesiastical Biography* (Longman, Brown, Green and Longmans, 3rd edition, 1853), p, 384.

[63] Tocqueville, *Democracy in America: Volume I*: the passages cited here are from pp. 317, 321.

[64] As reported in the *Manchester Guardian*, 1 June 1844.

[65] See the sobering analysis by Gary Younge, 'A Promise not Kept', *The Guardian Weekend*, 25 May 2004.

[66] John Donne, 'Meditation 5: *Solus Adest*' *Devotions upon Emergent Occasions*, p. 25. Donne is writing during his convalescence, probably from the serious epidemic which struck London in the winter of 1623–24. It was the isolation associated with this highly contagious illness rather than the fear of death itself which Donne found so unbearable: 'As sicknesse is the greatest misery, so the greatest misery of sickness is solitude....and it is an Outlawry, an Excommunication upon the patient....A long sickness will weary friends at last, but a pestilential sicknes averts them from the beginning.'

[67] Nicholls comments on the Trinitarian theology of Conrad Noel, Nicolas Berdyaev, Eric Peterson, David Brown and Jurgen Moltmann. Significant contributions have also been made by John Zizioulas, and Colin Gunton. Half a century previously, Jacques Maritain drew on the doctrine of the Trinity as the basis for his Christian personalism: '...the idea of the person is an analogical idea which is realized fully and absolutely only in its supreme analogy, God....There in its full sense, this expression leads us directly to the society of the Divine Persons for the idea of society is also an analogical idea...the Three who compose the Trinitarian society are by no means parts....They are three wholes who are the Whole.' Jacques Maritain, *The Person and the Common Good* (Geoffrey Bliss, 1947), pp. 40–41.

[68] David Nicholls, *God and Government in an 'Age of Reason'* (Routledge, 1995), p. 220.

[69] Nicholls, *Deity and Domination: Images of God and the State in the Nineteenth and Twentieth Centuries* (Routledge, 1989); the passages cited here are from pp. 118–127, 235–241, and *God and Government*, pp. 195, 215–222.

[70] Colin Gunton, *The Promise of Trinitarian Theology* (T & T Clark, 1991); the passages cited here are from pp. ix, 39, 150.

[71] John Zizioulas, *Being as Communion: Studies in Personhood and the Church* (Darton, Longman and Todd, 1985), p. 17, as cited in Gunton, p. 9.

[72] Gunton claims: 'In Augustine we are near the beginning of the era in which the church is conceived essentially as an institution mediating grace to the individual rather than of the community formed on the analogy of the Trinity's *interpersonal* relationships.' Gunton contrasts 'the Cappadocian and Augustinian conceptions of the Trinity. The latter is modalist in direction, if not actually modalist....the Cappadocian development, which Augustine so signally failed to appropriate, is that there is no being anterior to that of the persons. The being of God is the persons in relation to each other....The being of God is not now understood in the way characteristic of Greek metaphysics, but in terms of communion.' *The Promise*, pp. 50–51, 74. 96, 150.

[73] Milbank, *Theology and Social Theory*; the passages here are from pp. 5, 392, 405–406, 428.

Chapter Three: Transforming Meanings – Common Culture, Common Good

[1] Raymond Williams, *Culture and Society 1780–1950* (Penguin books 1961; original edition Chatto and Windus, 1958), p. 304.

[2] Raymond Plant, *Politics, Theology and History* (Cambridge University Press, 2001), p. 356.

[3] R.H. Tawney, having cited Figgis on the secularization of political theory; *Religion and the Rise of Capitalism: A Historical Study* (given as the Holland Memorial Lectures 1922; Pelican edition 1938), pp. 23, 25.

[4] John Ruskin, *Unto This Last: Four Essays on the First Principles of Political Economy* (George Allen and Unwin, 1862), p. 126.

[5] Michael Walzer, *Spheres of Justice: A Defence of Pluralism and Equality* (Martin Robertson, 1983).

[6] Maarten A. Hajer argues that environmental issues are fundamentally cultural both in the way they are defined and in the way they need to be addressed through the tracing back of different environmental discourses to different narratives; 'Ecological Modernisation as Cultural Politics', in Scott Lash, Bronislaw Szerszynski and Brian Wynne, et al., *Risk, Environment & Modernity: Towards a New Ecology* (Sage, 1996), pp. 246–268.

[7] Williams, *Culture and Society*, pp. 311, 16.

[8] See the analysis of the excesses of 'the cultural turn' and the attempt to re-conceptualize the social in Victoria E. Bonnell and Lynn Hart, eds. *Beyond the Cultural Turn: New Directions in the Study of Society and Culture* (University of California, 1999).

[9] The Working Men's College was founded by the first Christian Socialists in 1852. The founder of the Workers' Education Association, founded in 1903, was Albert Mansbridge, whose mentor was Charles Gore. Its first president was William Temple.

[10] Karl Polanyi, during his time in Britain, 'argued passionately that the adult education movement in Britain was mired in a futile debate which did not confront the essential problem, the absence or denial of a working-class culture. Workers first had to recognize their capacity to transform the social order before the 'crude pessimism' which governed their lives could be reversed. Adult education was not perceived as a way out'; Marguerite Mendell, 'Karl Polanyi and Socialist Education', in Kenneth McRobbie ed., *Humanity, Society and Commitment: on Karl Polanyi* (Black Rose Books: Critical Perspectives on Historic Issues Series, Volume 4, 1994), p. 39.

[11] Business for Diplomatic Action was launched in January 2004. It is precisely because of globalization that its Chairperson and President, Keith Reinhard, sees promoting the image of America as even more crucial than in the time of the Vietnam War; *Financial Times*, 24 June, 2004.

[12] Williams, *Culture and Society*, pp. 17–18.

[13] Williams' 1953 essay 'The Idea of Culture' arose partly as a response to T. S. Eliot in his 1948 *Notes towards the Definition of Culture*. Williams applies to Eliot the tribute that John Stuart Mill paid to Coleridge: 'an enlightened Radical or Liberal ought to rejoice over such a Conservative'; pp. 224, 230, 236.

[14] Williams, *Culture and Society*, p. 274.

[15] Reinhold Niebuhr, *The Children of Light and the Children of Darkness: A Vindication of Democracy and a Critique of Its Traditional Defense* (Charles Scribner's Sons, 1944), p. 102.

[16] This is true, argues Eagleton, both of the aesthetics of the beautiful – expressed in the bourgeois cultivation of sentiments, affections and manners – and of the aesthetics of the sublime – representing the desire for submission to power: 'The beautiful and the sublime are in fact essential dimensions of ideology'. Eagleton depicts the emergence of the aesthetic in dialectical terms, enabling it not only to bolster bourgeois ideology but also to play a crucial role in the transformation of that ideology: Terry Eagleton, *The Ideology of the Aesthetic* (Blackwell, 1990), pp. 8–9, 23.

[17] Porter, *Enlightenment*, especially pp. 72–95.

[18] 'The best way to govern a society, and to engage everyone to conduct himself according to a plan', suggests Sir James Steuart, 'is for the statesman to form a system of administration, the most consistent possible with the interest of every individual, and never to flatter himself that his people will be brought to act…from any other principle than private interest.'; as quoted by Stephen Copley, ed., *Literature and the Social Order in Eighteenth-century England* (Croom

Helm, 1984) as cited in Roy Porter, *Enlightenment: Britain and the Creation of the Modern World* (Penguin – Allen Lane, 2000), p. 263.

[19] See Nicholls, *God and Government*.

[20] John Milbank, 'Policing the Sublime: A Critique of the Sociology of Religion', in *Theology and Social Theory*, Chapter 5.

[21] David Hume, *Dialogues concerning Natural Religion*, as cited in Porter, p. 127.

[22] Fichte's 1804 lecture 'On the Essential Characteristics of the Present Age' is held up as an early sign of Europe's sense of decline by Karl Lowith, *Martin Heidegger and European Nihilism* (trans. Richard Wolin, Columbia University Press, 1995), p. 192.

[23] Unlike Spengler, however, Heidegger suggests that the experience of dissolution may be a stage on the way towards a homecoming: 'Sheltered in apartness, the evening land [*Abendland*, occident] does not go down in decay'; instead it 'remains in wait for its inhabitants as the land of going under into spiritual night….The spirit of home yearns itself for otherness from where alone a return home is possible.' Even in his early writings, however, Heidegger acknowledged 'the existential openness of *Dasein* as co-being for the Other, particularly for the 'voice of the friend that every *Dasein* carries with it.' Fred Dallmayr, *The Other Heidegger* (Cornell University Press, 1993), pp. 110–111, 155, 175, 182.

[24] Hampson, p. 201.

[25] Oswald Spengler, *The Decline of the West: Volume I: Form and Actuality* (original German edition, 1932; George Allen and Unwin, translated by Charles Francis Atkinson, 1971) pp. 32–33. Spengler insisted: '*No, I am not a pessimist!*'; 'Pessimism' (1921), in Oswald Spengler, *Selected Essays* (translated by Donald O. White, Henry Regnery, 1967), p. 148.

[26] Williams, *Culture and Society*, pp. 272–3.

[27] T. S. Eliot, *The Idea of a Christian Society* (Faber and Faber, 1939), pp. 76–8.

[28] Williams, *Culture and Society*, pp. 308, 313.

[29] John Gray, 'The laptop fascists', *New Statesman*, 27 May 2002.

[30] The Defense of Marriage Act, enacted on 21 September 1996, under President Bill Clinton, provides that no U.S. state shall be required to give effect to a law of any other U.S. state with respect to a same-sex 'marriage'. It does not challenge the right of any US state to recognize such unions. President George W. Bush repeatedly referred to the need for an amendment to the US Constitution to prevent the Act's being undermined by 'activist courts': 'Today I call upon the Congress to promptly pass, and to send to the states for ratification, an amendment to our Constitution….The amendment should fully protect marriage, while leaving the state legislatures free to make their own choices in defining legal arrangements other than marriage.' 24 February 2005: www.whitehouse.gov/news/releases/2004/02/20040224-2.html.

[31] Trevor Phillips, *The Guardian*, 28 May 2004.

[32] Matthew Waggoner, 'On Why I Missed the "Religious Turn"', *Bulletin of the Council of Societies for the Study of Religion* 33:1 (February, 2004):14–19.

[33] Gordon Brown, *British Council Annual Lecture*, 7 July 2004. Brown later amplified his concept of 'Britishness' as including the qualities of 'creativity, inventiveness, enterprise and our internationalism, our central beliefs are a commitment to – liberty for all, responsibility by all and fairness to all….'. He also repeated that 'our commitment to the future is the creation of British national community service' and stressed the importance of the British tradition of associational and mutualist activity. Address to Fabian Society '*Who do we want to be? The future of Britishness*', 14th January 2006: www.fabian-society.org.uk/press_office/news_latest_all.asp?pressid=520.

[34] The story is told poignantly by Amos Elon, *The Pity of It All: Portrait of Jews in Germany 1743–1933* (Allen Lane, 2000).

[35] Amartya Sen, 'Multiculturalism: an unfolding tragedy of two confusions', *Financial Times*, 22 August 2006.

[36] Raymond Williams, 'The Idea of a Common Culture', in Brian Wicker, ed. *From Culture to Revolution: The Slant Symposium 1967* (Sheed and Ward, 1968), p. 35.

[37] Raymond Williams makes incisive comments about this distorted version of a socialist approach to culture; *Culture and Society*, pp. 268–273.

[38] Williams, 'The Idea of a Common Culture', p. 35.

[39] Williams, *Culture and Society*; the passages in this section are from pp. 219, 274, 301, 304, 310.

[40] Williams, *Culture and Society*, p. 304.

[41] Nicholls, *God and Government*, p. 221.

[42] Milbank, *Theology and Social Theory*, pp. 339– 347.

[43] Jonathan Sacks, *The Dignity of Difference: How to Avoid the Clash of Civilizations* (Continuum, 2002).

[44] 'What Is Religious Education For: Getting the National Framework Right' (20 January 2004: http://www.ippr.org/research/files/team23/project164/RE%20Event%20Report%20.PDF.

[45] Faith Communities Unit, *Working Together: Cooperation between Government and Faith Communities* (Home Office, 29 March 2004): www.communities.gov.uk/index.asp?id=1502 454.

[46] Reinhold Niebuhr, 'The Idolatry of America', *Christianity and Society* (Spring 1950), as reproduced in *Love and Justice: Selections from the Shorter Writings of Reinhold Niebuhr* (edited by D. B. Robertson, World Publishing Company, 1967), pp. 94–97.

[47] Len Doyal and Ian Gough, *A Theory of Human Need* (Macmillan, 1991), pp. 187–188.

[48] Jurgen Habermas, 'Discourse Ethics, Law and *Sittlichkeit*' in Peter Dews, ed., *Autonomy and Solidarity: Interviews with Jurgen Habermas* (Verso, 1992), esp. pp. 248–249, 252, 260–261.

[49] Jurgen Habermas, 'The Dialectics of Rationalization', in Dews, p. 100.

[50] Rorty, 'Introduction', *Objectivity*, pp. 13–14.

[51] For an elaboration of the ethics of the Kingdom of God in terms of 'parabolic action' see Bruce Chilton and J. I. H. McDonald, *Jesus and the Ethics of the Kingdom* (SPCK, 1987); the passages cited here are from pp. 30–31, 36, and 42.

[52] For more on Jan Patocka see Shanks, *Civil Society*, pp. 115–127, and *The Philosophical Work of Jan Patocka: Research and Publication*, a project established in 1984 at the Institut für die Wissenschaften vom Menschen, Vienna: www.iwm.at/i-patarc.htm. At one level Patocka presents shakenness as the normal third stage of human ethical and religious development, marked by the realization that one must transcend the first stage – acceptance and love of one's roots – and the second stage – active struggle for survival – and assume responsibility for history. At another level, however, there is the shakenness arising from specific historical events in 20th century Czech history – the crushing of the Prague Spring in 1967, the Communist takeover in 1948, the betrayal by Chamberlain in 1938 and the general sense of crisis of European culture, which Patocka imbibed early on under the influence of Heidegger and Husserl.

[53] In the Munich Agreement of 29 September 1938, Britain's Prime Minister, Neville Chamberlain, gave Hitler the green light to seize Sudetenland from Czechoslovakia. It profoundly shook T. S. Eliot: 'I believe that there must be many persons who, like myself, were deeply shaken by the events of September 1938, in a way from which one does not recover; persons to whom that month brought a profounder realization of a general plight....The feeling which was new and unexpected was a feeling of humiliation, which seemed to demand an act of personal contrition, of humility, repentance, and amendment....It was not, I repeat, a criticism of the government, but a doubt of the validity of a civilization.' *The Idea of a Christian Society*, pp. 63–64.

[54] Vaclav Havel: 'When a person chooses to take a certain stand, when he breathes some meaning into his life, it gives him perspective, hope, and purpose. When he arrives at a certain truth and decides to "live in it" it is his act and his alone; it is an existential, moral and ultimately a metaphysical act.' Letter from Prison, 22 January 1983, in Vaclav Havel, *Open Letters: Selected Prose 1965–1990* (Faber and Faber, 1991), p. 231.

[55] T. H. Marshall, the annual (Alfred) Marshall lecture in 1949, as republished in T. H. Marshall and Tom Bottomore, *Citizenship and Social Class* (Pluto Press, 1992); the passages

cited here are from pp. 16, 18, 28, 33, 46.

[56] Amartya Sen, *Development as Freedom* (Oxford University Press, 1999), p. 75. Sen identifies five key freedoms: political freedoms, economic facilities, social opportunities, transparency guarantees and protective security, pp. 10, 75.

[57] Anna Coote, *The Welfare of Citizens: Developing New Social Rights* (Institute for Public Policy Research, 1992), Acknowledgements.

[58] Doyal and Gough, *Human Need*; the passages cited here are from pp. 93–111, 122–123, 188–189.

[59] Raymond Plant, 'Social Rights and the Reconstruction of Welfare' in Geoff Andrews, ed., *Citizenship* (Lawrence and Wishart, 1991), pp. 50, 63.

[60] Richard Titmuss, 'Welfare State and Welfare Society', in *Philosophy of Welfare*, p. 153. Titmuss, 'The Role of Redistribution in Social Policy'; lecture given in December 1964 as reproduced in Brian Abel-Smith and Kay Titmuss, eds. *The Philosophy of Welfare: Selected Writings of Richard M. Titmuss* (Allen and Unwin, 1987), p. 211.

[61] Titmuss, 'Social Welfare and the Art of Giving'; first published in Erich Fromm, ed., *Socialist Humanism* (Doubleday and Company, 1965), as reproduced in Abel-Smith and Titmuss, p. 126.

[62] Doyal and Gough, *Human Need*; the passages cited here are from pp. 93, 100, 102–104, 106, 111.

[63] Ruskin, *Time and Tide* (1867), p. 99.

[64] John J. Rodger, 'Social Solidarity, Welfare and Post-Emotionalism', *Journal of Social Policy* 32:3 (July 2003): 414–415.

[65] In America considerable pressure is applied in American universities and in some businesses and neighbourhoods, to undertake some form of 'voluntary' service as a condition for promotion and even of full acceptance. On 17th May 2004, the British government's Active Community Unit set up the Russell Commission to draft a set of proposals for a National Youth Volunteering Strategy. Two months later, in delivering the *British Council Annual Lecture*, Gordon Brown appeared to take it further: 'I am sure that following the Russell Commission on young people, we will wish to consider establishing a national youth community service. If America has its Peace Corps and now its Americorps, South Africa its National Youth Service, France its "Unis-Cité", the Netherlands its "Groundbreakers Initiative", Canada its Katimavik programme, should not Britain.... be doing far more to provide nationally and locally the means by which young people find it easy to participate?' The Commission issued its report, *A National Framework for Youth Action and Volunteering* on 16 March 2005, proposing four possible models for a national implementation body. The proposals have been supported by the Treasury and by the Department for Education and Skills: www.russellcommission.org.

[66] Williams, *Culture and Society*, p. 315.

[67] Rowan Williams, 'Christian Resources for the Renewal of Vision', in Alison J. Elliot and Ian Swanson, eds., *The Renewal of Social Vision* (Centre for Theology and Pubic Issues: Occasional Paper No. 17, 1989), p. 4.

[68] Nicholls, *The Pluralist State*, p. 10.

[69] Atherton, *Christianity and the Market*, p. 256. This abandonment of the idea of the common good represents a radical departure from Atherton's position of only four years earlier where he suggested that the notion of the common good could provide a useful basis for social discourse; *Faith in the Nation* (SPCK, 1988), pp. 31–47.

[70] Enrique Dussel, *Ethics and Community* (originally published in 1986; translated by Robert R. Barr, Burns and Oates, 1988), pp. 41, 42, 48, 50.

[71] Protestants for the Common Good is a Chicago-based network founded in 1995: 'The organization was founded out of a concern that organizations from the Christian political right, such as the Christian Coalition, mistakenly portray themselves as speaking on behalf of all Protestant Christians on a wide range of public issues'. www.thecommongood.org/historyandmission.

[72] M. S. Kempshall, *The Common Good in Late Medieval Political Thought* (Clarendon Press, 1999).

[73] *Catechism of the Catholic Church* (Bantam [Doubleday], April 1995).

[74] Riordan's work on this arose out of the debates in the Republic of Ireland as to whether, in updating the very Catholic constitution of 1937, references to 'the common good' were still appropriate. Patrick Riordan, *A Politics of the Common Good* (Institute of Public Administration, 1996). Further evidence of the political relevance of the notion of the common good can be seen in the attention that was given to the statement of the Catholic Bishops of England and Wales in the run-up to the 1997 General Election. Catholic Bishops' Conference of England and Wales, *The Common Good and the Catholic Church's Social Teaching* (October 1996).

[75] Milbank, 'On Complex Space', pp. 218–282.

[76] Fredric Jameson notes that although these themes were already expressed over a century ago in modernism, they have in postmodernism become dominant according to some, and domesticated according to others; in Hal Foster, ed., *Postmodern Culture* (Pluto Press, 1985), p. 123.

[77] A 'potent mixture of Christian tradition, political radicalism and postmodernism....' is how Catherine Pickstock describes Radical Orthodoxy. 'It [Radical Orthodoxy] is both with postmodernism in viewing reality as full of differences and diversity which are best known through the surface of signs and symbols which are continually shifting and needing to be deciphered; it is against postmodernism in that it sees this world of difference and indeterminacy as opening out not onto nihilism but onto an incomprehensible plenitude of being. The watchword of radical orthodoxy, beyond postmodernism, is participation.' Catherine Pickstock, 'Is Orthodoxy Radical?', *Affirming Catholicism Paper*: www.radicalorthodoxy.org.

[78] Jean-Francois Lyotard, 'Answering the Question: What Is Postmodernism?; originally in *Critique* (April 1982):357–367, in *The Post Modern Condition: A Report on Knowledge* (Manchester University Press, 1984), p. 82. In the same collection Lyotard states: 'I define postmodern as incredulity towards meta-narratives....The narrative function is losing its functions, its great hero, its great dangers, its great voyage, its great goal...little narratives [are] the quintessential form of imaginative invention'; p. 166.

[79] Milbank, *Theology and Social Theory*, p. 335.

[80] Milbank, 'On Complex Space', p. 280.

[81] Richard Titmuss has particularly been singled out for placing an excessive stress on altruism and for not fully recognizing the destructive effects of 'the culture of poverty'. See the debate and the – only partially convincing – defence of this aspect of Titmuss by John Welshman 'The Unknown Titmuss', *Journal of Social Policy* 33:2 (April 2004): 225–247.

Chapter Four: Transforming Economies – Life After Capitalism

[1] Peter Drucker, *Post-capitalist Society* (Heinemann, 1993), p. 1.

[2] Eric Hobsbawm, *The New Century* (Abacus, 2000; trans. Allan Cameron from the original Italian, 1999), p. 58.

[3] David Jenkins, *Market Whys and Human Wherefores: Thinking Again about Markets, Politics and People* (Cassell, 2000), p. 268.

[4] Atherton, *Christianity and the Market*, p. 74.

[5] J. K. Galbraith, *The Economics of Innocent Fraud: Truth for Our Time* (Allen Lane, 2004), pp. 19–20.

[6] Andrew Britton and Peter Sedgwick, *Economic Theory and Christian Belief* (Peter Lang, 2003). Britton explains: 'The market system is compatible with a wide variety of different patterns of ownership and control....Capitalism, as described by Marx, is just one possible variant of the market economy among many.' p. 177.

[7] The report itself actually builds a very strong moral case against mere consumerism and for greater justice in areas such as taxation, trade, international finance and debt, consistently

developing its argument from the central notion of the common good. It stresses the need for a 'transformation of consciousness [as] an aspect of conversion to the common good…'. *Prosperity with a Purpose: Christians and the Ethics of Affluence* (Churches Together in Britain and Ireland, February 2005), pp. 21, 54. The Commission uses the term 'secular capitalism' to designate 'the current narrow value base of capitalism (power, profit and status)'. *Faithful Cities: A Call for Celebration, Vision and Justice* (Methodist Publishing House and Church House Publishing, May 2006), p. 94.

[8] The kind of socialism foreseen but by no means welcomed by Joseph Schumpeter (1883–1950): '…excludes guild socialism, syndicalism and other types. This is because what we have termed "Centralist Socialism" seems to me to hold the field so clearly that it would be a waste of space to consider other forms.' For Schumpeter Centralist Socialism does not entail some 'Central Board or Ministry of Production' nor is it equated with central planning and rationing; much less with state control: '…it seems best to say that the state, the product of the clashes and compromises between feudal lords and bourgeoisie, will form part of the ashes from which the socialist phoenix is to rise.' Schumpeter sees socialism as having to take much the same rationalist approach as capitalism. Joseph A. Schumpeter, *Capitalism, Socialism and Democracy* (Third edition, Harper Torchbacks, 1950); the passages cited in this section are from pp. 134, 156, 162, 168–169, 174, 179–180, 182. For the continuing development of Schumpeter's insights see the International Joseph A. Schumpeter Society: http://www.wiwi.uni-augsburg.de/vwl/hanusch/iss.

[9] The features of the present post-capitalist economy according to Dahrendorf included: the dissolution of capital (the separation of owners/shareholders from controllers/managers), and the dissolution of labour (the emergence of a two types of salariat as well as a greater differentiation amongst wage labourers). He also perceived a post-capitalist society, marked by the mitigation of class conflict (aided by the spread of social rights), the more civilized resolution of class conflict (by institutionalized rules and procedures for dispute resolution) and even a degree of 'industrial democracy'. Ralf Dahrendorf, *Class and Class Conflict in Industrial Society* (Stanford University Press, 1959); especially pp. 35–61 and 246–269.

[10] One of the latest attempts to bring together the business community, NGOs and the government is the London-based consortium, The Climate Group, launched on 27th April 2004, whose umbrella is big enough to include oil giants such as BP and Shell: www.theclimategroup.org.

[11] George Soros, *Open Society: Reforming Global Capitalism* (Little, Brown and Co., 2000), p. xxvii, commenting on the gloom-and-doom analysis he had provided only two years earlier in *The Crisis of Global Capitalism: Open Society Endangered* (Little, Brown and Co., 1998).

[12] 'In the mid 1970s I called it "Pension-fund Socialism"; might not "Employee Capitalism" be a better term?' Drucker, *Post-capitalist Society*, p. 74.

[13] Soros, *Open Society*, p. xxviii. For Soros, who is heavily indebted to the philosophy of Karl Popper, fallibility is a positive not a negative quality, enabling knowledge to develop not simply on the basis of what is known but on the basis of openness to experience, and therefore by trial and error.

[14] Soros, *Open Society*, p. 345.

[15] A report in the *Financial Times*, 30 August 2004, describes a typical programme lasting for 100 hours and costing $20,000. The founder, Steven Oberfest, claims to have had thirteen clients a year. Mr. Oberfest may have some higher profile 'customers' than he dared dream of if the current trend continues in the American courts of harsh (exemplary?) sentencing for fraud. On 17 June 2005, Dennis Kozlowski, former Chief Executive of Tyco, was sentenced to 25 years in jail. Two days later the 80-year old founder of Adelphia Communications, John Rigas, was sentenced to 15 years in jail. On 13 July 2005, Bernie Ebbers, former Chief Executive of WorldCom, was sentenced to 25 years in jail. In October 2006 Jeffrey Skilling former Chief Executive of Enron was sentenced to 24 years in prison: www.iop-nyc.com/index.html.

[16] Anthony Giddens, in Will Hutton and Anthony Giddens, eds., *On the Edge: Living with*

Global Capitalism (Vintage, 2001), p. 10.

[17] On the basis of criteria used by the global management consulting firm A. T. Kearney – economic integration, technological connectivity, personal contact and political engagement – the most globalized country in the world in 2005 was Singapore – hardly the world's freest state – with Ireland slipping to second, with the UK in twelfth place. A. T. Kearney/*Foreign Policy Magazine*, *Globalization Index 2005*: www.atkearney.com/shared_res/pdf/2005G-index.pdf.

[18] The Commission was set up in February 2002. Its report notes that one reason social goals such as employment fail to receive priority at the global level is because international organizations with different mandates do not work together sufficiently well. It also stresses the importance of making the IMF, the World Bank and World Trade Organization more democratic and accountable; *A Fair Globalization – Creating opportunities for all* (International Labour Organization, 24 February 2004): www.ilo.org.

[19] A. T. Kearney, *Globalization Ledger* (Global Business Policy Council, April 2000).

[20] Hutton and Giddens, *On the Edge.*

[21] Philip Augur, *The Greed Merchants: How the Investment Banks Played the Free Market Game* (Penguin, May 2005) as cited in a review by John Gapper (*Financial Times*, 25 April 2005). Augur was head of Schroders Securities. He notes that investment bankers are on the inside of most financial transactions as advisers, brokers, underwriters and even as co-investors. This illustrates the point made by Fernand Braudel, cited in Chapter One, about capitalism being 'anti-market'.

[22] Richard Sennett, *The Culture of the New Capitalism*, p. 40.

[23] Jean and John Comaroff, eds., *Millennial Capitalism and the Culture of Neoliberalism* (Duke University, 2001).

[24] Edward N. Luttwak, *Turbo-Capitalism: Winners and Losers in the Global Economy* (Weidenfeld and Nicolson, 1998).

[25] Jeremy Rifkin, *Age Of Access: The New Culture Of Hypercapitalism, Where All Of Life Is a Paid-For Experience* (2001, Penguin Putnam, 2001).

[26] Attributed to Franz J. Hinkelammert by Daniel M. Bell, Jr., *Liberation Theology after the End of History: The refusal to cease suffering* (Routledge, 2001), pp. 9–12.

[27] Attributed to Michel Albert, *Capitalism against Capitalism* (trans. Paul Haviland, Whurr Publishers, 1995; original French edition, 1991) by John Plender in *Going Off the Rails: Global Capital and the Crisis of Legitimacy* (Wiley, 2003), p. 4.

[28] According to the Office of National Statistics, the gross value added comes primarily from lettings and dwellings (£45.3 billion) and secondly from banking & finance (£35.5 billion; as cited by the *Financial Times*, 21 August 2006.

[29] London Stock Exchange: www.londonstockexchange.com/en-gb/about.

[30] *Financial Times,* 24 November 2006.

[31] Sennett, *The Culture of the New Capitalism*, pp. 37–38.

[32] Casey, Quirk & Acito, as cited in the *Financial Times*, 16 October 2004.

[33] *Financial Times*, 12 May 2005.

[34] *Financial Times*, 28 September 2006.

[35] *Financial Times*, 11 March 2005.

[36] Institutional Investors Alpha survey, as reported in the *Financial Times*, 28 May 2005. The same survey found that the top 25 hedge fund managers made an average of $251 million, with George Soros having made 'only' $305 million, down from $750 million in 2003: www.institutionalinvestor.com/default.asp?page=1&SID=513177&ISS=14977&type=10.

[37] Report by Swiss-based UBS, 22 March 2005, based on data from Hedge Fund Research; *Financial Times*, 23 March 2005.

[38] CFSB-Tremont Index, as cited in the *Financial Times*, 28 February 2005. The report adds that hedge funds are coming to dominate the field of distressed debt since conventional institutions are barred from holding debt that falls below investment standard.

[39] *Financial Times*, 4 December 2006.

[40] Alan Greenspan, '*Risk Transfer and Financial Stability*' Remarks to the Federal Reserve Bank of Chicago's Forty-first Annual Conference (5 May 2005): www.federalreserve.gov/boarddocs/speeches/2005/20050505/default.htm.

[41] *Financial Times,* 3 November 2006.

[42] *Financial Times,* 12 October 2005.

[43] For a useful description see European Corporate Governance Institute: www.ecgi.org/activism/index.php.

[44] An internal investigation, conducted in 2003 by the New York Stock Exchange's lawyer Daniel Webb, and released by the Exchange on 2 February 2005 in compliance with a court order, found that Mr. Grasso was overpaid by $156 million; *Financial Times,* 3 February 2005.

[45] Marco Becht, Julian R. Franks, Colin Mayer and Stefano Rossi, *Returns to Shareholder Activism Evidence from a Clinical Study of the Hermes U.K. Focus Fund* (European Corporate Governance Institute, 4 December 2006)

[46] Members of the Global Benchmarks campaign include the Ecumenical Council for Corporate Responsibility (UK), the Interfaith Center on Corporate Responsibility (USA) and the Taskforce on the Churches and Corporate Responsibility (Canada): www.bench-marks.org. Some religious bodies are also using their investor power to change company policy on issues such as abortion and planned parenthood and the distribution of violent or indecent videos. For a listing, see the *Green Money Journal* 14:2 (Winter 2005/06): No. 57: www.greenmoneyjournal.com/article.mpl?newsletterid=10&articleid=68. For its reports and a useful list of links to similar initiatives: www.earthsummit2002.org/es/issues/susfin/susfin.htm.

[47] The UNEP's Responsible Investment Initiative was launched on 15 July 2004 after a 14-month study: www.unepfi.net/stocks. See also the Earth Summit Sustainable Finance programme. For its reports and a useful list of links to similar initiatives: www.earthsummit2002.org/es/issues/susfin/susfin.htm.

[48] See the analysis by John Plender 'Shareholder activism chips away at vested interests', *Financial Times,* 6 March 2004.

[49] Adolf A. Berle and Gardiner C. Means, *The Modern Corporation and Private Property* (Corporation Trust Company, 1932). This is considered a landmark in the American institutionalist approach to economics.

[50] James Burnham (1905–1987) underwent his own personal transformation from 1930s Trotskyist to 1940s CIA collaborator and champion of American imperialism. The most thorough-going material revolution, in Burnham's view, was to be found in the Soviet Union, with Nazi Germany a close second, but with the tendency emerging in the US as well; James Burnham, *The Managerial Revolution* (John Day, 1941).

[51] Peter Drucker, *Post-capitalist Society,* pp. 6, 25–42, 74.

[52] Attempts by outgoing members of US Securities and Exchange Commission to promote legislation that would have strengthened the role of shareholders were frustrated by fierce opposition from the chief executives' organization, the Business Roundtable, and by scepticism from the government; *Financial Times* 4 August 2005.

[53] Financial Services Authority survey as cited in *The Guardian,* 7 November 2006.

[54] Bank for International Settlements, *OTC Market Derivatives Activity in the First Half of 2006* (17 November 2006) as cited in the *Financial Times,* 18 November 2006.

[55] Ruth Kelly, Speech at the International Derivatives Conference, 28 June 2004.

[56] *Financial Times,* 27 September 2006.

[57] Benin Steil Director of Economics at the Council on Foreign Relations, *Financial Times,* 28 November 2006.

[58] Sennett, *Culture of the New Capitalism,* p. 40.

[59] Bank for International Settlements, as reported in the *Financial Times,* 29 September 2004.

[60] Edward N. Luttwak, *Turbo-Capitalism: Winners and Losers in the Global Economy*

(Weidenfeld and Nicolson, 1998). 'Privatization + Deregulation + Globalization = Turbo-capitalism'; p. 25; the other passages cited here are from pp. ix, 12, 69.

[61] Study of hedge funds by Credit Suisse First Boston as reported in the *Financial Times*, 11 March 2005.

[62] Anonymous respondent to the survey conducted by the Centre for the Study of Financial Institutions as quoted by John Plender in the *Financial Times*, 16 February 2005.

[63] However, Tim Geithner, President of the New York Federal Reserve Bank, dismisses the claim that this is a general practice; *Financial Times*, 19 November 2004.

[64] Soros' Quantum Fund, set up in 1969, suffered more than one jolt in the 1990s, leading him in April 2000 to split the Fund into a Quantum Endowment Fund to provide a more reliable flow of income to support his charitable work and a Quantum Emerging Growth to carry on with the riskier end of the business.

[65] *Financial Times*, Comment, 31 July 2006.

[66] The mortgage industry has so far dealt with 1.8 million claims of misselling of endowment mortgages – most of which were sold in the late 1980s and early 1990s – and has paid out £2.7 million; *Mortgage Endowments: Delivering Higher Standards* (Financial Services Authority, December 2006): www.fsa.gov.uk/pages/Library/Communication/PR/2006/133.shtml

[67] *Financial Times*, 28 July 2006.

[68] *Financial Times*, 18 October 2006.

[69] Given the increasing number of parties involved in putting deals together and taking them forward, it is impossible to know for certain how many people have access to insider knowledge much less how they are using that knowledge. One approach is to use, as an indirect indicator of possible abuse, any IPMs (Informal Price Movements) that may have preceded significant announcements. See Ben Dubow and Nuno Monteiro, *Measuring Market Cleanliness* (Financial Services Authority, March 2006): www.fsa.gov.uk/pubs/occpapers/op23.pdf.

[70] Financial Service Authority, Final Notice to Philippe Jabre, 1 August 2006: www.fsa.gov.uk/pubs/final/jabre.pdf.

[71] *Financial Times*, 3 November 2006.

[72] Michael Snyder, essay in the *Financial Times*, 31 July 2006.

[73] *Financial Times*, 28 September 2006.

[74] A list of abuses were identified by Don Cruickshank, Chairman of the London Stock Exchange in his *Competition in UK Banking: A Report to the Chancellor of the Exchequer* (March 2000): www.hm-treasury.gov.uk/documents/financial_services/banking/bankreview/fin_bank_reviewfinal.cfm. Five years on, Cruickshank can barely contain his anger at the 'outrageous' way in which the Government has diluted his recommendations. 'Banks are earning between 25 and 30 per cent return on equity on their retail and small business banking in the UK,' he charges. 'This is where banks actually make their money, not from lending'; interview for the *Financial Times*, 19 February 2005.

[75] Fraud Advisory Panel, Statement, 27 October 2006.

[76] The scale of LTCM's exposure is indicated by the value of its derivatives, put at $1,400 billion in August 1998; see the report of the US General Auditing Office: *Long Term Capital Management: Regulators Need to Focus Greater Attention on System Risk* (October 1999).

[77] Ruth Kelly, Speech at the International Derivatives Conference, 28 June 2004.

[78] Bank of England, *Financial Stability Review* (June 2004), as reported in the *Financial Times*, 28 June 2004.

[79] Greenspan, 'Risk Transfer and Financial Stability'.

[80] Financial Service Authority, *Private equity: a discussion of risk and regulatory engagement: A Discussion Paper* (6 November 2006): http://www.fsa.gov.uk/pages/library/policy/dp/2006/06_06.shtml.

[81] 'Black Wednesday' – 16th September, 1992 – was the day when the government decided to leave the European Exchange Rate Mechanism, after the Bank of England had poured in some £10 billion to sustain the pound in the face of massive currency speculation. The dilemma

was that the German economy was fighting inflation and needed high interest rates, while the UK economy was in recession and could not increase interest rates in the direction required. Later some re-christened it 'White Wednesday', because the decision, humiliating as it was, did enable the UK to adopt the sort of economic policies which eventually made for more sustained growth than most of its EU partners. For a bitter interpretation of the real versus the professed motives of the EU proponents of currency convergence, see the account of the former head of the European Commission's National and Community Monetary Policies Unit, Bernard Connolly, *The Rotten Heart of Europe: The Dirty War for Europe's Money* (Faber and Faber, 1995). The (selective) release of official papers on 9 February 2005, made possible by the Freedom of Information Act 2000, which came into effect on 1 January 2005, has served only to open rather than close the debate: Labour blames Conservatives, politicians blame Treasury, the Treasury blames other contemporary analysts, free-marketers blame exchange controls in principle, etc.

[82] The most unhelpful response to global financial deregulation, according to Soros, would be for countries to re-impose national controls on the movement of capital. The temptation is all the greater, he warns, because such a 'solution' actually worked for Malaysia. If followed by everyone, however, it would result in a cutting off of the very resources needed to help poorer countries develop. The solution has to be international. Soros has developed a range of proposals including 'International Credit Insurance Corporation' and the use of the IMF's Special Drawing Rights, all aimed at enabling countries to play the global currency game but with better rules and surer protection: www.soros.org.

[83] Timothy Geithner, President of the New York Federal Reserve has warned that: 'Changes in the structure of the financial system and an increase in product complexity could make a crisis more difficult to manage and perhaps more destructive.'; *Financial Times*, 12 May 2005.

[84] Charlie McCreevy, European Commissioner for Internal Market and Services, Address to the annual Global Funds Conference, Dublin (20 May 1005) www.finfacts.com/irelandbusinessnews/publish/article_10001888.shtml.

[85] Sir John Gieve, 'Practical Issues in Preparing for Cross-border Financial Crises', Speech to the Financial Stability Forum Workshop, 13 November 2006: www.bankofengland.co.uk/publications/speeches/2006/speech290.pdf.

[86] As cited by Richard Tomkins, 'Profits of doom', *Financial Times Magazine* (14 October 2006, p. 22.

[87] Incomes Data Services *Executive Compensation Review*, November 2006, as cited in the *Financial Times*, 6 November 2006.

[88] *Financial Times*, 30 October 2006.

[89] Brookings Institute – Hamilton Project (25 July, 2006): http://www1.hamiltonproject.org/es/hamilton/hamilton_hp.htm.

[90] US Census Bureau, Income, *Poverty and Health Insurance Cover in the United States 2005* (August 2006).

[91] *Financial Times*, 12 December 2006.

[92] John Paul II, *Sollicitudo Rei Socialis,* para.14 and *Centesimus Annus*, para. 33. See the impressive work at grass roots level of the Christian organization ATD Fourth World: www.atd-fourthworld.org/accueil-uk.html.

[93] The debate about the effects of NAFTA (North American Free Trade Agreement) illustrates the point. The results look positive when one looks simply at the overall statistics for its first ten years (1993–2003). Trade within the NAFTA region doubled, and trade between NAFTA and the rest of the world increased by 42%. The fact that a significant number of jobs were shifted out of the US to Mexico does not appear to have led to massive job losses in the US, where jobs were created in other sectors. It also meant cheaper goods for consumers, including the poor and low-paid. But when one looks at the social and human side, the picture is less rosy. Many of the new jobs created in the US are insecure and low paid. Particular communities have been hit extremely hard: 'The problem for advocates of the pact is that the losers from free trade

are easy to identify and have faces, whereas those who have benefits are invisible and unaware they have been helped. The costs are highly concentrated and the gains are large but diverse', according to Gary Hufbauer of the Institute for International Economics; *Financial Times,* 24 February, 2004.

[94] *Financial Times,* 16 October 2006.

[95] Forrester Research has predicted that 100,000 UK jobs will have gone abroad by 2005, rising to 760,000 by 2015; as reported in the *Financial Times,* 16 August 2004.

[96] The All China Federation of Trade Unions – which is the only legal union body and whose brief, unlike Western unions, is actually to promote harmony on the shop floor and prevent confrontations over pay and conditions – has told local media that transnationals, such as Wal-Mart, Kodak and Samsung, are refusing to comply with Chinese laws which oblige them to establish unions. The companies deny this. Yet US business associations have held seminars in Shanghai and Beijing advising members how to respond to union campaigns; *Financial Times,* 5 January 2005.

[97] A study of American company behaviour found that more than half of all employers made threats to close all or part of their plant in the event of a trade union organising drive; Kate Bronfenbrenner, *Uneasy Terrain: The Impact of Capital Mobility on Workers, Wages and Union Organizing* (Cornell University, September 2000) the study, by the Cornell University: www.citizenstrade.org/pdf/nafta_uneasy_terrain.pdf.

[98] The estimate was made by the chief energy strategist at Merrill Lynch; *Financial Times,* 26 May, 2004.

[99] *Financial Times,* 11 June 2004. Why high oil prices have such a disproportionate effect on developing countries is that such countries are heavily dependent on energy-intensive activities, including transport, but are relatively inefficient in their use of energy.

[100] International Trade Union Confederation (ITUC): www.ituc-csi.org.

[101] NDN: www.ndn.org/advocacy/globalization.

[102] *Financial Times,* 26 August 2006.

[103] *Financial Times,* 7 November 2006.

[104] Luttwak, *Turbo-capitalism*; the passages cited here are from pp. 46, 236.

[105] Frank H. Knight, 'Ethics and Economic Reform', 1939 as reproduced in vol. II *Laissez-Faire: Pro and Con,* p. 61, in the collection edited by Ross B. Emmett, *Selected Essays by Frank H. Knight* (University of Chicago, 1999). Knight was the dominant influence in the economic department at the University of Chicago during the interwar period.

[106] John Kay, *The Truth about Markets: Their Genius, Their Limits, Their Follies* (Allen Lane, 2003); the passages cited here are from pp. 10, 45.

[107] *Least Developed Countries Report 2004* (27 May 2004): www.unctad.org.

[108] *Financial Times,* 4 August 2003.

[109] Kay, *Markets*, p. 378.

[110] The European Association for Evolutionary Political Economy – some of whose annual conferences I have attended – is a good example. Other networks include the International Society for New Institutional Economics, the International Confederation of Associations for Pluralism in Economics and the Post-Autistic Economics Network, although the theoretical frameworks employed are quite diverse. A good way into this is through Post-Autistic Economics Network – whose website contains *Global Economic News*, an invaluable daily review of media articles on economic issues: www.paecon.net.

[111] For a thoughtful attempt at showing how theology and economics might engage in meaningful dialogue see Britton and Sedgwick, *Economic Theory.* A more accurate title, however, would have been 'Neo-classical economic theory and Christian belief', since there is no exploration of other theories, such as Keynesian and Marxist theory (an omission which is acknowledged) or of evolutionary economics, institutional economics, or environmental economics or political economy (which are simply not mentioned). The result is that the entire dialogue is conducted within a highly individualistic framework, confining itself to a

psychological rather than a social anthropological framework whilst ignoring ecology altogether. It is refreshing to read the conclusion that 'Neo-classical economic theory in the form that we have discussed it in this book is coming to look a little out-of-date as are many of the attempts to modernise theology.' p. 213.

[112] Dietrich Bonhoeffer '*Vorlesung*', 1932–33, p. 159 (as cited by Duchrow with Franz J. Hinkelammert in *Property for People*, pp. 214–215. Elsewhere Duchrow gives a slightly different translation: 'Capitalism and assurance of salvation are foster brothers. The grasping for goods is a grasping for God. Election finds expression in economic success of a worldly kind. This throws light on the Russian revolution. It is a protest against a capitalist Christ, not against Christ as such. But the West has known him and still knows him only as the capitalist Christ. Protest against this Christ is more than justified'; *Global Economy: A Confessional Issue for the Churches* (World Council of Churches, 1986), p. 52. Duchrow makes clear that Bonhoeffer is not pushing politicians towards socialism but is calling the church to repentance and discipleship.

[113] Atherton, *Christianity and the Market*.

[114] Duchrow, *Global Economy*, pp. 104–105, 115– 117.

[115] Duchrow, *Global Economy*, p. 177; here Duchrow draws on the work of his subsequent collaborator, the Latin American Franz Hinkelammert.

[116] Bonhoeffer was not actually present in May 1934 for the famous Barmen Declaration drafted by Karl Barth for the Confessing Church (which had existed even before Hitler's seizure of power). There the emphasis was on the integrity of the church: '…it was essentially a struggle of the Church against itself for itself' in the words of Arthur C. Cochrane, *The Church's Confession under Hitler* (Pickwick Press 1976; first published by Westminster Press in 1962), p. 11. Bonhoeffer supported it but grew increasingly concerned about its lack of emphasis on the mission of the church as 'being-for-others'. In his unfinished *Ethics* (Macmillan 1955; first published in German by Kaiser Verlag in 1949), Bonhoeffer gives his own version of the kind of confession that is demanded of the Church:'The Church confesses that she has witnessed the lawless application of brutal force, the physical and spiritual suffering of countless innocent people, oppression, hatred and murder, and that she has not raised her voice on behalf of the victims.…The Church confesses that she has witnessed in silence the spoliation and exploitation of the poor, and the enrichment and corruption of the strong.…The Church confesses that she has desired security, peace and quiet, possessions and honour, to which she had no right, and that in this way she has not bridled the desires of men but has stimulated them still further. The Church confesses herself guilty of breaking all ten commandments.…By her own silence she has rendered herself guilty of the decline in responsible action.…'(pp. 113–115).

[117] Ulrich Duchrow, *Economy in the Service of Life: Churches in the Ecumenical Process for Globalizing Justice* (Kairos Europa, Short and to the Point series, 2003).

[118] Duchrow, *Global Economy*. Duchrow has consistently developed his appeal for a confessional stance. See *Alternatives to Global Capitalism*, where Duchrow outlines the 'totalitarian structure of the world economy' (pp. 230–239); and, with Franz J. Hinkelammert, in *Property for People*.

[119] Duchrow, *Global Economy*, p. 126.

[120] Duchrow, *Property*, pp. 216–217. Here, too, Bonhoeffer can be called in support, although he appears to be referring specifically to the German National Church, indeed possibly drawing on a theological demand for atonement: 'To make a start it [the National Church] should give away all its property to those in need. The clergy must live solely on the free-will offerings of their congregations, or possibly engage in some secular calling. The Church must share in the secular problems of ordinary life, not dominating but helping and serving....' *Letters from Prison* (enlarged edition, SCM, 1971), p. 382, as quoted in Eberhard Bethge, *Bonhoeffer: An Illustrated Introduction* (Collins, 1979), p. 167.

[121] Jenkins, *Market Whys and Wherefores*; the passages cited here are from pp. 168, 225, 230, and 242.

[122] Atherton, *Christianity and the Market*, pp. 232–261. The notion of 'interrogation' implies

more than simply asking questions. It has been developed as part of a cross-referential model of theology by Kenneth Cragg: 'Theology's first task…is to interrogate this diversity of self-legitimation, its own and that of others, and seek what might establish between us the sort of *bona fide* relationship which does not exempt its own credentials from engagement with the other.' *The Christ and the Faiths* (SPCK, 1986), pp. 10–11, as quoted by David Wood, *Poet, priest and prophet: The life and thought of Bishop John V. Taylor* (Church House, 2002), p. 223.

[123] Jenkins, *Market Whys*, pp. 265–266.

[124] Peter S. Heslam, *Globalization: Unravelling the New Capitalism* (Grove Books, Ethics Series, 2002); the passages cited here are from pp. 20–21, 24.

[125] Augustine, *City of God*, Book XV, Chapter 5.

[126] John Paul II, *Centesimus Annus*, paras. 35, 43.

[127] Ruskin, *Unto This Last* (originally published as a series of essays for *Cornhill Magazine* in 1860–61, George Allen & Sons, facsimile production 2000); especially the chapter '*Ad Valorem*', where Ruskin paints a picture of true value and wealth; pp. 119–120.

[128] Thomas Aquinas, *Summa Theologica*, I q.5, a.4, ad 2.

[129] As cited by Daniel M. Bell, Jr., *Liberation Theology after the End of History: The Refusal to Cease Suffering* (Routledge, 2001), pp. 12–19.

[130] Sennett, *The Culture of the New Capitalism*, p. 82.

[131] Jenkins, *Market Whys*, p. 249.

[132] Grahame Thompson, Jennifer Frances, Rosalind Levacic and Jeremy Mitchell, *Markets, Hierarchies and Networks: The Coordination of Social Life* (Sage, 1991).

[133] John Monks, Bevan Memorial lecture: 'The Challenge of the New Capitalism' (14 November 2006, European Trade Union Confederation: www.etuc.org/a/3052).

[134] The case for developing a global social contract, region by region, has been argued by Jeff Faux, who worked as an economist with the U.S. Office of Economic Opportunity and the U.S. Departments of State, Commerce, and Labor and founder of the Economic Policy Institute which is about sharing the prosperity created by globalization, in Washington D.C: www.epi. org/author_details.cfm?author_id=162.

[135] Wright suggests five paths of 'social empowerment' which would transform the relationships of state, market and civil society. One path – which might find a home in Quadrant C – continues to develop the elements of 'social capitalism' (for example developing worker participation in industry, stakeholder power in the ownership and use of pension funds). A second – which might be placed in Quadrant A – accepts selected features of 'state socialism' (state provision of certain services). A third – which might also best fit in Quadrant A – takes elements of social democratic regulation (for example, setting minimum wages, environmental standards, etc.). The fourth, which involves the development of 'associative democracy' is exactly what is being explored here under Quadrant D. The fifth – which would also come best under Quadrant D – is characterized as a 'social economy' where economic activity, including health and care, is actually run by various associations from civil society (as an example of progress along this path, Wright cites Quebec's Chantier de l'economie sociale). He does not discuss the social market or some of the other options identified here but that is a matter of detail. Erik Olin Wright, 'Compass Points: Towards a Socialist Alternative', *New Left Review* 41 (September/October 2006): 93-124).

[136] Raymond Plant, *Equality, Markets and the State* (Fabian Society, Tract No. 494, January 1984), p. 14. Nearly twenty years on, Plant develops the same insight at greater length, stressing that markets require both moral underpinnings (to facilitate the operations of trust) and moral constraints (to place a curb on self-interest). Raymond Plant, 'Markets, Morality and Theology' in *Politics, Theology and History* (Cambridge University Press, 2001), pp. 177–195.

[137] One of the main factors leading to the formation of the Global Corporate Governance Forum was the financial crisis of 1997-98: www.gcgf.org/index.htm.

[138] The focal point in the US is the Sarbanes-Oxley (Public Company Accounting and Investor Protection) Act, passed in July 2002, which has provoked a growing backlash.

[139] The focal point in the UK is the Report by Sir Derek Higgs, *Review of the Role and Effectiveness of Non-Executive Directors* (Department of Trade and Industry, 20 January 2003). This, in turn, is part of a series of independent reports, most notably the committee set up by the Financial Reporting Council, and the London Stock Exchange which produced the Cadbury Report, *The Financial Aspects of Corporate Governance* (1 December 1992) and a series of independent reports commissioned by the Treasury, such as that by Paul Myners, who produced his *Myners Principles for Institutional Investment Decision-making* (6 March 2001) which challenged bodies such as pension fund trustees not simply to be market followers but to develop their own ability to take wise and informed decisions about investment. Myners has argued, along with John Sunderland, of the Confederation of British Industry, that similar reforms are urgently needed in the financial sector; *Financial Times*, 13 May 2005. For the OECD *Principles of Corporate Governance* see: www.oecd.org/document/49/0,2340,en_2649_37439_31530865_1_1_1_37439,00.html. The Transatlantic Corporate Governance Dialogue was launched in July 2004 as a joint effort of the European Corporate Governance Institute and the American law Institute: www.ecgi.org/tcgd/index.php.

[140] The World Bank put the cost of corruption globally at $1,500 billion. Although Transparency International produces an annual Corruption Report, it basically leaves the job of exposing corruption to investigative journalism. Its distinctive role is to work with governments to introduce reforms whether these have to do with multi-national oil companies, local businesses or even the police: www.transparency.org.

[141] Information about PIRC and about the various services it offers to investors is available on their website: www.pirc.co.uk.

[142] Governance for Owners: http://www.auhd73.dsl.pipex.com/g4owners/About.htm.

[143] The United Nations Global Compact on Corporate Citizenship is a personal initiative of Kofi Annan, UN Secretary General, proposed at the World Economic Forum in January 1999 and launched on 26 July 2000. Corporate citizenship in this context involves a commitment to nine principles, covering areas such as human rights, labour rights and environmental protection. The Global Compact – which is a voluntary scheme – includes over 1,000 businesses, NGOs, and several UN agencies. It was followed by a Global Corporate Governance Pact as part of the 'Monterrey Consensus' in 2002. On 17 April 2006, the 'Principles for Responsible Investment' were signed by the leading investment institutions from 16 countries, representing more than $2 trillion in assets. The principles involve incorporating environmental and social issues into investment analysis and decision-making processes but are, in the UN's own words only 'voluntary and inspirational': www.unpri.org/principles.

[144] Business in the Community has, for many years, been one of the more sustained attempts by the business community to encourage business support for local needs.

[145] The 'Equator Principles', like the UN's 'Principles for Responsible Investment', are only aspirational nor do they even require subscribing institutions to sign an agreement to abide by them: www.equator-principles.com.

[146] *The Accountability Rating* ® – *New tool for modelling corporate accountability* was launched by AccountAbility (22 June 2004) to coincide with the meeting of the UN Global Compact Leaders' Summit. The criteria include corporate governance, stakeholder involvement as well as social and environmental impact measures. But the data used are from the companies' own public reporting: www.accountability.org.uk.

[147] Companies Act 2006: Chapter 46 paragraphs 172 (1) and 417(5). The Explanatory Notes repeatedly give the assurance that the proposed incorporation of such duties into statutory law is not wholly new but is based on and should be interpreted in the light of existing principles of common law and equity.

[148] The Fairtrade Association was set up in 1994 by CAFOD, Christian Aid, New Consumer, Oxfam, Traidcraft and the World Development Movement. By 2004, Fairtrade turnover had reached the £100 million mark in Britain alone and had 18% of the UK roast and ground coffee market: www.fairtrade.org.uk.

[149] The Ethical Trading Initiative is an alliance of companies, trade union organizations and NGOs, including Anti-Slavery International, Christian Aid, CAFOD and Oxfam formed in 1998 to ensure that the working conditions of workers producing for the UK market meet or exceed international labour standards: www.ethicaltrade.org.

[150] The 'Publish What You Pay' coalition of over 170 NGOs calls for international regulations requiring the disclosure of net taxes, fees, royalties and other payments made by companies to developing country governments in all countries where they operate. The campaign includes Global Witness, CAFOD, Oxfam, Save the Children UK, Transparency International UK, and the George Soros Open Society Institute: www.publishwhatyoupay.org.

[151] The Tobin Tax was first proposed in 1972, by the American Nobel Prize winner James Tobin, who died two days before the launch of the Tobin Tax Network on 13 March 2002. The campaign builds on work undertaken by War on Want and ATTAC, and is supported by Christian Aid, CAFOD, the United Reformed Church, Oxfam and others. Some $1,900 billion is traded each day on foreign exchange markets. It has been estimated that up to 80% is not for purposes of investment or saving but purely for short term gain, i.e. speculation: www.tobintax.org.uk. However, Tobin himself, was reported to have said, in an interview with the German news-magazine *Der Spiegel*: 'I have absolutely nothing in common with those anti-globalization rebels....the loudest applause is coming from the wrong side'; as cited by Helmut Reisen, 'The Tobin tax: could it work?' (*OECD Observer*, March 29 2002). Support for such a tax, however, has come from some surprising sources. French President Jacques Chirac has long been sympathetic to the idea of a tax on currency speculation. The then German Chancellor, Gerhard Schroeder, caused some surprise at the World Economic Forum in Davos, in January 2005, by appearing to announce his conversion: 'We should have taxation on purely speculative financial transactions' he stated, but qualified it as a personal opinion, suggesting that it would be difficult to get international agreement on this because of US opposition; *Financial Times*, 29 January 2005.

[152] The Association of British Insurers produced Social, Ethical and Environmental Guidelines in 2002, pressing firms to disclose to investors the scale of risks they face from possible bad publicity and legal action arising from their labour policies, or the impact of their operations on health and environment. Two years on, they were able to report modest progress on the part of the larger firms but minimal progress among second-tier firms; *Risks, Returns and Responsibility* (Association of British Insurers, 25 February 2004).

[153] George Bush had pressed for the establishment of CAFTA-DR since January 2002 as part of his transformational agenda: 'By transforming our hemisphere into a powerful free trade area', he declared at a meeting with six Central American presidents on 12 May 2005, 'we will promote democratic governance, human rights, and economic liberty for everyone.' On 27th July 2005, Congress finally gave its backing.

[154] The US Foreign Sales Corporation tax scheme was judged illegal by the WTO in 2002. The United States' reluctance to bring its Anti-Dumping Act of 1916 into conformity with the World Trade Organization led the WTO's Arbitrators to conclude in February 2004 that the European Communities may suspend obligations under GATT 1994 and the Anti-Dumping Agreement against imports from the United States Decision (WT/DS136/ARB) issued by the WTO on 24 February 2004. From the 1st of March 2004, European Union customs officials were able to levy an additional 5% on a range of American products from roller skates, to nuclear reactors, from steel and textiles, to natural honey and toys; *Financial Times*, 1 March 2004.

[155] OECD report (10 June 2004). The report expresses disappointment that the level of subsidies to US farmers has actually increased since the mid 1990s. It commends the EU, however, for its 2003 reforms to the Common Agricultural Policy, which will help to reduce trade distortions which hurt developing countries most. The EU, however, has itself been charged by Australia, Brazil and Thailand with exporting two types of sugar which are allegedly subsidised contrary to the WTO Agreement. When, on 15 October 2004, the World Trade Organization publicised its interim report supporting the complainants, the EU decided

immediately to appeal.

[156] *Financial Times*, 14 April 2005. Lapper says that this is 'partly because the growth record of the more liberal laissez-faire 1990s – which came to be known as the Washington consensus – was so mediocre.' For the official conference report see: www.iadb.org.

[157] Central to the IMF's concern was the need to develop a framework which would reduce Latin America's chronic vulnerability to economic crises. 'The state has a crucial role in improving regulatory governance', the authors argue. Specific issues included more secure property rights, labour market reforms, action against corruption, greater accountability in the public sector, and a stronger judiciary: Anoop Singh et al., *Stabilization and Reform in Latin America: A Macroeconomic Perspective on the Experience since the Early 1990s* (IMF Occasional Paper 238, May 2005), Chapter 8: http://www.imf.org/external/pubs/ft/op/238.

[158] *Our Common Interest,* Report of the Africa Commission (11 March 2005), Executive Summary, para. 20: www.commissionforafrica.org/english/home/newsstories.html.

[159] Ian Gough, 'Economic Institutions and the Satisfaction of Human Needs', reprinted in Ian Gough, *Global Capital, Human Needs and Social Policies: Selected Essays 1994–99* (Palgrave, 2000), pp. 33–64. Gough takes into account several key studies in this line of enquiry, notably W. Streeck and P. Schmitter, *Private Interest Government: Beyond Market and State* (Sage, 1985) and Jonathan Boswell, *Community and the Economy: The Theory of Public Co-operation* (Routledge, 1990).

[160] Bob Jessop, editor, *Regulation Theory and the Crisis of Capitalism* (Edward Elgar, 2001). See also Jessop, *The Future of the Capitalist State* (Polity, 2002), p. 19.

[161] European states have recently been warned that unless they make more legal, administrative and fiscal reforms, investors will begin to drift away from Europe towards emerging economies; European Private Equity and Venture Capital Association, *Benchmarking European Tax and Legal Environment*, 24 May 2004: www.evca.com.

[162] 'The Union shall work for the sustainable development of Europe based on balanced economic growth, a social market economy, highly competitive and aiming at full employment and social progress, and with a high level of protection and improvement of the quality of the environment.' *Treaty Establishing a Constitution for Europe*, Part I, Title I: Preamble: Definition and Objectives, Article 1–3.3 (presented to the President of the European Council by the European Convention, 18 July. 2003): http://europa.eu.int/constitution/en/ptoc2_en.htm#a3.

[163] See the sympathetic treatment, but not formal endorsement, of the social market model by the Conference of European Churches in the discussion paper. 'European social market economy – An alternative model for globalization?' prepared by the North-South Working Group of the Church and Society Commission of the Conference of European Churches for the consultation organized at Soesterberg in the Netherlands in June 2002: http://www.warc.ch/pc/soester/05.html.

[164] 'The Relational Market Economy', in Michael Schluter and David Lee, *The R Factor* (Hodder and Stoughton, 1993), pp. 193–229.

[165] Will Hutton, *The State We're In* (Jonathan Cape, 1995), p. 298. For a development from 'republican' to 'democratic' capitalism see Marjorie Kelly in *The Divine Right of Capital: Dethroning Corporate Aristocracy* (Berrett-Koehler, 2001).

[166] John Kay, 'Stakeholding misconceived', *Financial Times*, 12 February 2002.

[167] Mark Goyder is Director of the Centre for Tomorrow's Company: www.tomorrowscompany.com.

[168] *Financial Times* report, 19 June 2004.

[169] *Restoring Trust: Investment in the Twenty-First Century* (Tomorrow's Company, 15 June 2004).

[170] John Gray, *False Dawn: The Delusions of Global Capital* (Granta, 1998) as cited in Robert J. Antonio, ed. *Marx and Modernity: Key Readings and Commentary* (Blackwell, 2003), p. 340.

[171] To mark its 10th anniversary in 1999, the Social Market Foundation published *Social*

Market and the State: www.smf.co.uk.

172 Atherton. *Christianity and the Market*, especially pp. 256–258.

173 Charles Leadbeater, 'Whose Line Is It Anyway?' *Marxism Today* (July 1991).

174 Günter Grass, 'The high price of freedom', *The Guardian,* 7 May 2005.

175 Atherton, *Public Theology,* p. 123.

176 On Müntefering's locust list were Deutsche Bank itself, Goldman Sachs,, WCM, KKR, Apax, Carlyle, BC Partners, Advent International, CVC Capital, Permira, Saban Capital, and Blackstone. The locust image had been employed five months earlier by Chancellor Schroeder himself when he urged: 'We must help guard those entrepreneurs who fight for the sustainability of their companies and the interests of their workers against the irresponsible swarms of locusts that measure success on a quarterly basis and let companies die once they have sucked them dry'; Speech to the Friedrich Ebert Foundation, November 2004; as quoted in the *Financial Times,* 19 May 2005.

177 Two weeks later, Mr. Breuer actually reassured the Börse's annual meeting: 'I am in favour of hedge funds'; *Financial Times,* 26 May 2005.

178 *Treaty Establishing a Constitution for Europe,* Part III, 'The Policies and Functioning of the Union' Title III 'Internal Policies and Action: http://europa.eu.int/constitution/en/ptoc24_en.htm#a158.

179 The European No Campaign is a EU-wide cross party network of organizations and individuals covering the spectrum from right to centre to left, which have a common aim of opposing the proposed new European Constitution: www.europeannocampaign.com.

180 For an account of the development of a 'social metaphysic' by the German Social Catholics, see Joseph N. Moody, ed, *Church and Society: Catholic Social and Political Thought and Movements 1789–1950* (Arts, Inc., 1953), esp. pp. 508–535. Somewhat less influential was the corporatist motif, as developed by Catholic social thinkers in the Fribourg Union (1885–1891), although it found support in the 1930s in the papacy of Pius XI, and was applied in Austria and Portugal and to a lesser extent in Ireland and Brazil. See Norman J. Paulhus, 'Social Catholicism and the Fribourg Union', *Selected Papers* (The Society of Christian Ethics, 1980): 63–88.

181 Maurice Glasman, *Unnecessary Suffering: Managing Market Utopia* (Verso, 1996), p. 51. Even Hayek, according to Amartya Sen, supported markets not for their own sake or unconditionally or even primarily for their role in promoting economic prosperity, but to the extent which they promoted human freedom and liberty, unlike Milton Friedman whose criteria are more about prosperity and utility; *Financial Times,* 21 September 2004.

182 'The labour market is the area in which the differences between a market economy organized in accordance with neo-liberal principles and a social market economy are most clearly revealed.' Detlef Radke, *The German Social Market Economy: An Option for the Transforming and Developing Countries?* (German Development Institute, 1995), p. 34.

183 Wilhelm Roepke, *Civitas Humana: A Humane Order of Society* (translated by Cyril Spencer Fox, William Hodge and Co., 1948); the passages cited here are from pp. 28–33.

184 A. J. Nicholls, *Freedom with Responsibility: The Social Market in Germany 1918–1963* (Clarendon Press, 1994), p. 121.

185 Nicholls, *Freedom with Responsibility,* p. 338. Indeed, Glasman claims that Erhard once sought to make co-determination illegal; *Unnecessary Suffering,* p. 136.

186 See the report by European Industrial Relations Observatory: www.eiro.eurofound.eu.int/2004/12/feature/de0412103f.html.

187 *Agenda 2010 Deutschland bewegt sich* (Press and Information Office of the Federal Government, February 2004): www.german-embassy.org.uk/Agenda_2010_brochureengl.pdf.

188 Hartz I creates new employment opportunities with the help of Personnel Services Agencies; Hartz II encourages mini-jobs, Ich- AG ('Me plc') and Job Centres; Hartz III calls for the restructuring of employment agencies; Hartz IV – the most bitterly fought by unions

– is about reducing unemployment benefits and social welfare benefits to create Basic Income for Job Seekers.

[189] *Financial Times*, 31 May 2005.

[190] Speech to DGB Trade Union Federation Congress, 24 May 2006.

[191] Milbank "Socialism by Grace", in *Being Reconciled*, pp. 162–186 but first published a in *New Blackfriars* (December 1996); the passages cited here are from pp. 162, 176 and 178.

[192] Raymond Plant, 'Socialism, Markets and End States', in Julian Le Grand and Saul Estrin, eds., *Market Socialism* (Clarendon Press, 1989), pp. 74–77.

[193] For a good survey of the state of the debate see Pranab K. Bardhan and John E. Roemer, *Market Socialism: The Current Debate* (Oxford University Press, 1993).

[194] 'Boimondau', near Valence in France, was a name contrived so as not to be identified on any map which the Nazis might read: '*boitier*' (watch-case), '*montre*' (watch) and '*Dauphine*' (the area). The community was set up in occupied France in 1943. Barbu himself survived confinement in Buchenwald, where he had been sent for refusing to co-operate with the Nazis. Bishop was later led to discover other, earlier communitarian schemes: the Essertines (Reformed), Bouron (Quaker), Syesses (Evangelical) and L'Aurore (communist); Claire Huchet Bishop, *All Things Common* (Harper and Brothers, 1950).

[195] Erich Fromm, *The Sane Society* (Fawcett, 1955), pp. 247–294.

[196] Bishop, p. 248.

[197] Duchrow, *Alternatives to Global Capitalism*, p. 246.

[198] Impressive work has been done on all these fronts by the New Economic Foundation: www.neweconomics.org.

[199] de Soto, *The Mystery of Capital*, pp. 82, 73–78, 93–116.

[200] John O'Neill, *The Market: Ethics, Knowledge and Politics* (Routledge, 1998).

[201] Paul Q. Hirst, *Representative Democracy: and Its Limits* (Polity, 1990) and especially, *Associative Democracy: New Forms of Economic and Social Governance* (Polity, 1994).

[202] Hirst, *Representative Democracy*, p. 73.

[203] Hirst, *Representative Democracy*, p. 75.

[204] Hirst, *Associative Democracy*, pp. 135–136.

[205] Hirst, *Associative Democracy*, p. 128.

[206] Hirst, *Associative Democracy*, p. 151.

[207] Charlie Leadbeater, 'Popular Social Ownership', in Peter Alcock et al., *The Social Economy and the Democratic State* (Lawrence and Wishart, 1989), p. 95.

[208] The World Social Forum – a counter to the World Economic Forum – is a network of activists first convened in January 2001 in Porto Alegre, Brazil; William F. Fisher and Thomas Ponniah, eds., *Another World Is Possible: Popular Alternatives to Globalization at the World Social Forum* (Zed Books, 2003), p. 4.

[209] Noreena Hertz, *The Silent Takeover: Global Capitalism and the Death of Democracy* (Heinemann, 2001), p. 270.

Chapter Five: Transforming Politics – What Good is Democracy?

[1] Pascal Lamy, Director-designate of the World Trade Organization, then European Union Trade Commissioner, speaking at the International Progressive Governance Conference, London, 11–13 July 2003.

[2] Rowan Williams, *The Worlds We Live in: Dialogues with Rowan Williams on Global Economic and Politics* (Darton, Longman and Todd, 2005), Afterword, p. 128.

[3] Reinhold Niebuhr, *The Children of Light and the Children of Darkness* (Charles Scribner's Sons, 1944), pp. 5–6.

[4] John Keane, *Democracy and Civil Society*, p. 33.

[5] Paul Hirst, *Representative Democracy*, p. 2.

[6] Phillip Bobbitt seeks to combine the 'Idealism' of the era of Woodrow Wilson, who took America into the First World War in order to make the world safe for democracy, with the 'Realism' that has been a consistent thread in American foreign policy thereafter; interview in *Financial Times Magazine*, 13 March 2004.

[7] Soros, acknowledging Karl Popper as his inspiration, describes the open society as 'characterized by a reliance on the rule of law, the existence of a democratically elected government, a diverse and vigorous civil society, and respect for minorities and minority opinions': www. soros.org.

[8] *Democracy in Latin America: Towards a Citizens' Democracy* (United Nations Development Programme, 21 April 2004). The report argues for a deepening of democracy, with a significant expansion of 'social citizenship', aided by an exchange of ideas around an Extended Agenda for Democratic Development. On the other hand, there has been significant mobilization of workers and indigenous peoples to elect left-wing governments in Brazil, Venezuela, Bolivia, Ecuador, Nicaragua, Argentina, Uruguay, and nearly in Peru and Mexico as well. Democratization at a regional level might also be said to have received a boost when, on 2 May 2005, the Organization of American States elected Jose Miguel Insulza, Chile's Interior Minister, as their Secretary General, as part of the deal negotiated with Condoleezza Rice. Mr. Insulza promised to hold accountable governments that failed to govern democratically. 'It's a turning point in relations between the US and Latin America,' according to Julia Sweig of the Council for Foreign Relations (*Financial Times*, 3 May 2005).

[9] Small Governance Teams have been set up in 15 non-Kurdish areas in Iraq by the Coalition Provisional Authority. 'In the future, the United States will be involved in assisting other nations establish or strengthen democratic governance. Success will be more likely if we are able to "operationalize" what we learned in Iraq.' Celeste J. Ward, *The Coalition Provisional Authority's Experience with Governance in Iraq: Lessons Identified* (United States Institute of Peace, Special Report 139, May 2005) www.usip.org/pubs/specialreports/sr139.html.

[10] See, for example, the Progressive Governance Network, which emerged under former President Clinton in Washington 1999. It has since held regional and global meetings with heads of state and other key parties (Berlin, June 2000; Stockholm, February 2002; London, July 2003; Budapest, October 2004; Johannesburg, July 2005; Selsdon Park, May 2006). It is served by a Policy Network chaired by Peter Mandelson. Describing itself as 'centre-left', its agenda is about 'modernization', which translated appears to mean the redefining of social justice and the reshaping of social welfare in accordance with the requirements of a more efficient capitalist economy: http://progressive-governance.net.

[11] European Union 'Governance in the EU': http://europa.eu.int/comm/governance/index _en.htm.

[12] James N. Rosenau, 'Governance in a New Global Order', in David Held and Anthony McGrew, eds., *The Global Transformations Reader: An Introduction to the Globalization Debate* (Polity Press, second revised edition, 2003), p. 225.

[13] Rosenau, 'Governance in a New Global Order', p. 230.

[14] *A Fair Globalization – Creating opportunities for all* (International Labour Organization, 24 February 2004): www.ilo.org; *Beyond Scarcity: Power, Poverty and the Global Water Crisis* (United National Development Project, 9 November 2006), p. 48.

[15] MOST is part of UNESCO. Its Globalization and Governance work has included policy analyses in areas such as development, sustainability, and regional coping strategies in the fight against drug-trafficking: http://portal.unesco.org/shs/en/ev.php-URL_ID=3724&URL_DO =DO_TOPIC&URL_SECTION=201.html. The United Nations is exploring reforms on a whole range of structures (including the General Assembly and the Security Council) and activities (ranging from internal management and finance to work on its economic and social programmes: www.una-uk.org/reform/topics.html.

[16] The Group has produced regular reports, and has called for a stronger system of global governance, *Global Governance: Assessment 2003* (COMECE, December 2003). It has also

argued the case for participation at churches and other faith communities in the process of global governance: www.comece.org/upload/pdf/pub_GGassmt_031202_en.pdf.

[17] Five years before 9/11 Robert Cooper, of the Foreign Policy Centre and one of Tony Blair's key advisers, was already arguing the case for 'a new kind of imperialism'. In contrast to the 'old imperialism' it was no longer to be about conquest. This is because for Cooper we are gradually moving towards a postmodern political order, in which rigid boundaries between nation states no longer make sense. Issues of global insecurity as well as global prosperity deepen our common interests. Thus between post-modern states, such as the European Union, the new imperialism takes a cooperative form which entails adopting, where appropriate, common systems and procedures, administered by a controlled 'imperial bureaucracy'. Clearly the world is far from being wholly postmodern. Therefore in their relations with 'premodern' states (where order has broken down) and modern states (which still pursue national interests by coercive and military means), the new imperialism may take the form of intervention either for the sake of nation-building or for 'defensive imperialism'. Robert Cooper, *The Postmodern State and the World Order* (Demos, 1996, reprinted 2000; updated with Foreign Policy Centre, 2002): http://fpc.org.uk/publications/postmodern-state.

[18] George W. Bush singled out 'weak states' as a focal point for terrorism in his National Security Strategy (2002). Subsequently, the Commission on Weak States and US National Security recommended that: 'Prevention should be the overriding goal of US policy.' *On the Brink: Weak States and US National Security* (Center for Global Development, 8 June 2004): www.cgdev.org. Tony Blair reaffirmed his new stance, first articulated following NATO's intervention in Kosovo, where he called for 'a doctrine of international community', justifying military intervention on the grounds that 'our self-interest was allied to the interests of others; and seldom did conflict in one region of the world not contaminate another.' Tony Blair, *'On the Threat of Global Terrorism'*, 5 March 2004.

[19] Fukuyama seems to feel that it is the third wave of neo-cons who have drifted from the basic neo-conservative principles. Francis Fukuyama, *After the Neo-Cons: America at the Crossroads* (Profile, 2006).

[20] The Canadian sponsored International Commission on Intervention and State Sovereignty concluded: 'The task is not to find alternatives to the Security Council as a source of authority, but to make the Security Council work much better than it has.'; *The Responsibility to Protect* (December 2001), para. 6.14: www.iciss.ca/menu-en.asp.

[21] Alex de Waal, " 'I will not sign'," London Review of Books, vol. 28: no. 23 (30 November 2006): 17–20.

[22] *Countering Terrorism, Power Violence and Democracy post 9/11: A Report by a Working Group of The Church of England's House of Bishops* (September 2005), p.67: www.cofe.anglican.org/info/socialpublic/terrorism.pdf.

[23] Bobbitt envisions three possible ideal types of market state. Whilst acknowledging that in the real world no state will completely embody any of these, he points to the predominance of certain types in particular states: 'The mercantile type (Japan and China) seeks market share in order to gain relative dominance in international affairs.' The managerial (France and Germany) seeks power through its hegemony within a regional economic zone, even at the cost of sharing some of its sovereignty. The entrepreneurial (United States – with Britain likely to follow) 'seeks leadership through the production and marketing of collective goods that the world's states want.' Bobbitt, *Shield of Achilles*, pp. 243–290.

[24] Bobbitt, *Shield of Achilles*, p. 338.

[25] Hedley Bull, *The Anarchical Society: A Study of Culture in World Politics* (Columbia University Press, 1977), p. 254, as cited by Anthony Payne, 'Globalization and Models of Regionalist Governance', in Held and McGrew, *Global Transformations Reader*, p. 214.

[26] Grahame Thompson, joint leader of the 1992 Towards Social Transformation seminar, sees as a possible model for future global authority, something resembling a secular version of the Holy Roman Empire, with a range of lesser and overlapping sovereignties: 'Toleration and

the Art of International Governance: How Is It Possible to "Live Together" in a Fragmenting International System', in Jean Hiller and Emma Rookeby, eds., *Habitus: A Sense of Place* (Ashgate, 2002).

[27] Anthony McGrew, 'Models of Transnational Democracy', from A. Carter and G. Stokes, eds., *Democratic Theory Today* (Polity Press, 2002) as reprinted in Held and McGrew, *Global Transformations Reader,* pp. 500–513.

[28] The international commission, comprising twenty-eight members, all serving in a personal capacity, arose from the Stockholm Initiative on Global Security and Governance. It began work in September 1992 and published its report, *Our Global Neighbourhood* in 1995. It called for global taxation, a standing UN army, an Economic Security Council, UN authority over the global commons, an end to the veto power of permanent members of the Security Council, a new parliamentary body of *'civil society'* representatives (NGOs), a new *'Petitions Council'*, a new Court of Criminal Justice, binding verdicts of the International Court of Justice and expanded authority for the Secretary General. It resolved that: 'Military force is not a legitimate political instrument except in self-defense or under UN auspices' and that 'The production and trade in arms should be controlled by the international community': www.eldis.org/static/DOC2163.htm.

[29] Monbiot proposes: a) transforming the World Trade Organization into a *Fair* Trade Organization; b) replacing the IMF and the World Bank with an International Clearing Union, which would establish new norms and rules for international lending and investment (his account of how Maynard Keynes' proposal for an International Clearing Union was sidelined at Bretton Woods makes fascinating reading); and c) setting up, alongside a reformed United Nations, a World Parliament. Such a Parliament would not be a World Government. It would not represent nations since this would give the edge to the wealthier nations – but would be a parliament of people, arranged in constituencies of 10 million people each. This would ensure that, for example, more Chinese and Indian voices would be heard but not as representatives of China or India. George Monbiot, *The Age of Consent: A Manifesto for a New World Order* (Flamingo, 2003), especially pp. 158–174.

[30] The collection will continue to grow by 200,000 pages each month. It will take until 2007 for all six–seven million pages to be made available. The Minnesota settlement also required continued public disclosure of tobacco company documents produced in subsequent smoking and health litigation in the U.S. for ten years, i.e. until 2009. BAT is withholding some documents on unchallengeable grounds of privilege and some 181 files have unaccountably gone missing from the Guildford Depository: http://bat.library.ucsf.edu.

[31] See the recent reports, Nigel Berkeley et al., *Faithful Representation: Faith Representatives on Local Public Partnerships* (Church Urban Fund, September 2006) and Phillip Escott and Pat Logan, *Faith in LSPs? The experience of faith community representatives on local strategic partnerships* (Churches Regional Network, December 2006).

[32] Much of the thinking on 'the new localism' is being promoted by the New Local Government Network: www.nlgn.org.uk.

[33] See the discussion document *Citizen Engagement and Public Services: Why Neighbourhoods Matter* (Office of the Deputy Prime Minister, 31 January 2005).

[34] Hazel Blears, then Minister for Public Health, *Communities in Control: Public Services and Local Socialism* (Fabian Society: Fabian Ideas 607, June 2003), p. 45.

[35] Alan Pike, *The Disintegration of Local Government: dangers of single-service elected bodies* (Association of London Government: Discussion Booklet, October 2003).

[36] Abramoff was sentenced to prison for his multi-million business of lobbying members of congress. The *Financial Times'* concern was that the basic practice is systemic in US politics: 'Nowhere else in the civilized world is it so widely accepted that money buys access and influence over policy and that interest groups must "pay to play". The problem is less the crimes that Mr Abramoff committed than the corrupting practices he employed were not illegal…'(*Financial Times*, 7 January 2006).

[37] Walter E. Weyl, *The New Democracy: An Essay on Certain Political and Economic Tendencies in the United States* (Macmillan Company, 1912). The need for reform was stressed by Republican and Democratic presidents, notably by Teddy Roosevelt and Woodrow Wilson.

[38] Colin Crouch, *Coping with Post-democracy*, (Fabian Society: Fabian Ideas No. 598, December 2000); the passages cited here are from pp. 6, 56.

[39] C. B. Macpherson, *The Real World of Democracy*, (originally given as a series of broadcasts on Canadian Broadcasting Corporation in January and February 1965; Clarendon Press, 1966); p. 57.

[40] Rowan Williams, 'The Media, Public Interest and the Common Good'. Lecture to media professionals, politicians, and Church leaders at Lambeth Palace (15 June 2005): www.archbishopofcanterbury.org/sermons_speeches/050615.htm.

[41] John Keane, *The Media and Democracy* (Polity Press, 1991), p. 154.

[42] Rowan Williams warns against the danger of the media exacerbating the tendency in society for people with different views to live in parallel universes: '...this movement into a parallel universe would be a disaster....'; 'The Media, Public Interest and the Common Good'.

[43] David Edgar, 'What are we telling the nation?', *London Review of Books* 27:13 (7 July 2005).

[44] Andrew Shanks, *Civil Society, Civil Religion* (Blackwell, 1995), p. 25.

[45] Beck, *Risk Society,* pp. 234–235.

[46] Reinhold Niebuhr, *Children of Light*, pp. 1, 3. Niebuhr, a close friend of William Temple's, had a profound influence both on two generations of American social theologians and on the makers of American foreign policy in the Roosevelt-Truman-Eisenhower eras.

[47] European Commission's White Paper on European Governance (25 July 2001): http://europa.eu.int/eur-lex/en/com/cnc/2001/com2001_0428en01.pdf.

[48] The Independent Commission on Good Governance in Public Services, whose members include the Chartered Institute of Public Finance and Accountancy and the Office for Public Management and the Joseph Rowntree Foundation, established in September 2003, a Governance and Public Services programme; *The Good Governance Standard for Public Services* (11 January 2005): www.opm.co.uk/ICGGPS/download_upload/Standard.pdf.

[49] *Public Service Governance: The Policy Context* (The Independent Commission on Good Governance in Public Services, 3 March 2004).

[50] COMECE, *Global Assessment 2003*, p. 79.

[51] Milbank, *Theology and Social Theory*; the passages in this section are from pp. 140, 335, 337, 403.

[52] John Milbank, *Being Reconciled*; the passages cited here are from the following chapters: 'Ecclesiology: The last of the last', pp. 129–132; 'Politics: Socialism by grace', pp. 182–183, and 'Culture: The gospel of affinity', pp. 192–193.

[53] Pope John Paul II, *Evangelium vitae* (25 March, 1995), para. 70.

[54] Rowan Williams, 'Christian Resources for the Renewal of Vision', in Alison J. Elliot and Ian Swanson (eds.) *The Renewal of Social Vision* (Centre for Theology and Public Issues: Occasional Paper No. 17, 1989), p. 4.

[55] The classical argument against democracy is a splendid example of ideology at work in so far as the case against was developed by those of the upper and middle classes. Nonetheless, it is interesting to note that, in contrast to Plato, Aristotle, always seeking to argue on the basis of actual human nature and always favouring the mean between extremes, sees the most stable and least corrupt form of government as containing a mix of democratic and oligarchic elements; Aristotle, *Politics,* Book IV, Chapter IX–XII, 1294a30–1297a13.

[56] Colonel Thomas Rainsborough in the Putney Debates, 1647, as cited in H. N. Brailsford, *The Levellers and the English Revolution* (Spokesman edition, 1976), p. 274.

[57] David Beetham, 'Democracy: Key Principles, Institutions and Problems', in Cherif Bassiouni, *Democracy: Its Principles and Achievement* (Inter-Parliamentary Union, 1998), p. 21.

[58] David Beetham and Kevin Boyle, *Introducing Democracy: 80 Questions and Answers*, UNESCO, 1995) pp. 1–2.

[59] David Beetham, 'Democracy: Key Principles', p. 22.

[60] John Dunn, *Setting the People Free: The Story of Democracy* (Atlantic Books, 2005), pp. 64, 135–137, 184–185.

[61] Walter Rauschenbusch, *A Theology for the Social Gospel* (first given as the 1917 Yale lectures; Abingdon Press, 1945), p. 174–5.

[62] H. R. Niebuhr, *Christ of Culture*, p. 100.

[63] Charles E. Curran observes: 'Until recently, Catholic scholars referred to the "indifference" of the church to forms of government. References to government were in terms of function rather than form. The transformation of the popes and Roman Catholicism into champions of democracy coheres with the methodological shift to the person as subject, with special emphasis on freedom, equality and participation.' *Catholic Social Teaching 1891–Present* (Georgetown University Press, 2002), p. 153.

[64] Leo XIII: *Libertas* (On the Nature of Human Liberty), 20 June 1888, para. 44.

[65] See Pontifical Council for Justice and Peace, *Compendium,* especially para. 406–417.

[66] Christian Democracy emerged briefly in the French Second Republic (1848–1852) and then remerged in the 1890s, first in Belgium, then in France, then in Italy. It clearly differentiated itself from capitalism, socialism, social democracy and liberalism but it was 'democratic' only in a very loose sense. It insisted on the privileged place of the Catholic Church, portraying the hierarchy as protectors and guides of the common people. Its vision of the unity and cohesion of all social groups gave it a strong corporatist bias, promoting structures which could bring together the main social actors, above all labour and capital. By the turn of the century, the popes were gradually backing away from Christian Democracy as a political project. In 1901 Leo XIII's encyclical *Graves de Communi* (On Christian Democracy) watered down the concept of Christian democracy as *'actio benefica in populum'* – 'beneficent action on behalf of the people' (para. 7) and his set of instructions issued the following year via his Secretary of State, Cardinal Rompolla, 'On Christian Popular or Christian Democratic Action in Italy' (27 January 1902) made it clear that: 'Catholic lay persons are not to go ahead of, but to follow behind their shepherds' has been described as giving Italian Christian Democracy its coup de grace. The history of Christian Democracy is treated by Paul Misner, *Social Catholicism in Europe: From the Onset of Industrialization to the First World War* (Darton, Longman and Todd, 1991) pp. 201, 220–261 241–246, and Michael Fogarty, *Christian Democracy in Western Europe 1820–1953* (Routledge and Kegan Paul, 1957).

[67] David Nichols, *God and Government in an 'Age of Reason'* (Routledge, 1995), p. 194.

[68] Macpherson, *Real World*; the passages cited in this section are from pp. 10, 35.

[69] The contrast in continental Europe between the failure of its inter-war democracies and the success of its post-World War II democracies is partially ascribed to the excessive reliance on 'the demos' in the earlier period and the soundness of constitutions in the latter by Yves Meny and Yves Samuel, eds., *Democracies and the Populist Challenge* (Palgrave, 2002).

[70] Elisha P. Douglass, *Rebels and Democrats* (University of North Carolina Press, 1953), pp. 24–27.

[71] Aristotle, *Politics*, Book IV, Chapter XIV–XVI, 1297b39–1301a15.

[72] Niccolo Machiavelli, *Discourses on the First Ten Books of Titus Livius* (1517, First Book, Chapters II–VI, Modern Library edition, 1950), pp. 110–130.

[73] Sir William Blackstone, *Commentaries on the Laws of England* (1787 ed), pp. 154–155 as cited in Asa Briggs, *The Age of Improvement 1783–1867* (Longman, 1979, originally 1959), pp. 88–96.

[74] Macpherson, *Possessive Individualism*, pp. 106–159.

[75] Niebuhr, *Children of Light*; the passages cited here are from pp. xiii, 118, 133, 174, 188.

[76] Figgis, *Churches in the Modern State* (Longmans, 1913), p. 101, as cited in Nicholls, p. 33.

[77] Figgis, 'A Puritan Utopia', *Church Quarterly Review* (1903): 126, as cited in Nicholls, p. 33.

[78] Nicholls, *Pluralist State*, p. 33.

[79] John Rawls, *Political Liberalism* (Columbia University Press, 1996; original edition 1993), pp. xl, xxvi.

[80] John Dewey, *The Richness of Democracy* (1885) as quoted by Jeffrey Stout, *Democracy and Tradition* (Princeton University Press, 2004).

[81] Brailsford, *The Levellers*, p. 274.

[82] Richard Rorty, 'The Priority of Democracy to Philosophy', in *Objectivity, Relativity and Truth: Philosophical Papers, Volume 1* (Cambridge University Press, 1991).

[83] Rorty stresses the moral obligation of loyalty to one's own community so that the most effective criticism comes from within; 'Postmodernist Bourgeois Liberalism', *Objectivity*, p. 210.

[84] Amartya Sen, 'The diverse ancestry of democracy', *Financial Times*, 13 June 2005.

[85] Hauerwas, 'The Church and Liberal Democracy', p. 75.

[86] Stanley Hauerwas, 'The Democratic Policing of Christianity', in *Dispatches from the Front: Theological Engagements with the Secular* (Duke University Press, 1994), pp. 93, 104. Hauerwas is not arguing that Christians should be forming Christian political parties, as was done in Europe, or forming Christian lobby groups as the Christian Right is currently doing in America. Hauerwas does not want Christians to win the game but to change the game.

[87] Hauerwas, *Community of Character*, pp. 84, 86.

[88] Condoleezza Rice as quoted in *The Guardian*, 22 October 2005.

[89] The World Bank's fears, of course, are only secondarily for democracy, and primarily for the sort of 'good governance' that will promote their understanding of social and economic development: 'Populist macroeconomic policy, sooner or later, is bad for equity and growth'; *World Development Report 2006: Equity and Development* (World Bank, September 2005) Overview, p. 16. Its own hopes are pinned on the emergence of a global middle class, which would encourage economic growth by increasing consumption, productive skill and more liberal attitudes to trade, all of which would, it is suggested help lay firmer foundations for democracy. *Global Economic Prospects 2007: Managing the Next Wave of Globalization* (World Bank, December 2006).

[90] As quoted by Gideon Rachman (*Financial Times*, 25 October 2006). Populism is less an ideology than a kind of behaviour – less like vegetarianism and more like alcoholism. It avoids deep-seated problems by offering solutions that address basic cravings (for security, comfort and the satisfaction of immediate needs). It ignores the very things that make for a sound constitution (defence of the rule of law, protection of minorities, respect for civil rights, acceptance of an independent judiciary, etc.). It creates dependency – which is why governments of all persuasions have been tempted to deploy such policies. And it lashes out at elites that attempt to warn that it is undermining the development of democracy and the health of the body politic.

[91] The democratic movements were most significant in North Carolina and Massachusetts, and above all in Pennsylvania, where a single-chamber, democratic Constitution – never put to 'the people' for ratification however – was in force from 1776–1790. See Douglass, *Rebels and Democrats*, especially pp. 263–286. Douglass argues that, in that period, economic and social conditions tended to create a harmony of interests between Whigs and potential democrats and that the limited rise of democratic movements was due to exceptional circumstances.

[92] William Hazlitt, 'What Is the People' (1818) as reproduced by Tom Paulin, *William Hazlitt: The Fight and Other Writings* (Penguin, 2000), p. 383. Hazlitt had in his sights 'Legitimacy – that detestable fiction' (p. 364).

[93] John Paul II, *Centesimus Annus*, para. 46. See also John Paul's earlier encyclical *Sollicitudo Rei Socialis*: (30 December 1987), para. 15 where the 'creative subjectivity of the citizen' is tied to the right of economic initiative; para. 15, and *Laborem Exercens* (14 September 1981), para. 13, with its emphasis on the 'subjectivity of human labour'.

[94] Machiavelli, *Discourses*, First Book, Chapter V, pp. 122–124. Elsewhere, Machiavelli

declares: '....it is the nature of the nobility to desire to dominate, yet those who have no share in such domination are the enemies of tyrants....' First Book, Chapter XL, p. 223.

[95] Hazlitt, 'On the Spirit of Monarchy' (1823), in Paulin, p. 340; 'On the Connection between Toad-Eaters and Tyrants' (1817), in Paulin, p. 356.

[96] Hazlitt, 'What Is the People?' in Paulin, p. 381.

[97] Hilary Wainwright, *The Guardian*, 20 February 2006.

[98] Hilary Wainwright, *Reclaim the State: Experiments in Popular Democracy* (Verso, 2003), p. 32.

[99] Charles Taylor, *Sources of the Self.* See especially his chapter 'God Loveth Adverbs', pp. 211–233.

[100] 'The antique "antinomy" of *polis [political arena]* and *oikos [domestic arena]*...is overcome because every household is now a little republic...or "unlimited society"...and the public itself is a household.' Milbank, *Theology and Social Theory*, p. 403.

[101] Hilary Wainwright, *Arguments for a New Left: Answering the Free Market* (Blackwell, 1994), pp. 50–56. It is not just at national level that technocrats fail to recognize the value of practical knowledge. The same tendency can be seen where local partnerships are shaped by professionals from the statutory sector, by self-appointed middle-class 'leaders' of local communities and by external consultants.

[102] Wainwright, *Reclaim the State*, p. 44.

[103] She chides them: 'They...take on the essential structure and features of the central leadership which they hope one day to be. Like the Elizabethan children who are dressed up as adults, the result at worst is absurd, puffed up and very constricting.' Hilary Wainwright, Sheila Rowbotham and Lynne Segal, *Beyond the Fragments: Feminism and the Making of Socialism* (Merlin Press, 1979), p. 241.

[104] Hirst, *Representative Democracy*, p. 82.

[105] Cohen and Arato refer to the 'explicitly self-limiting and evolutionary character [of new social movements]...repeatedly manifested in the search for compromise and transitional solutions and the deliberate acceptance of the slowing down of the rate of change....The term "self-limiting revolution"...extends the self-reflexive and self-critical discourse of modernity to its most important political concept, namely revolution.' Jean Cohen and Andrew Arato, *Civil Society and Political Theory* (MIT Press, 1992), pp. 73, 295, 562–564.

[106] Shanks, *God and Modernity*, p. 8.

[107] Shanks cites the definition of 'anti-politics' given by the Hungarian George Konrad and author of the book *Antipolitics*: 'Antipolitics is the political activity of those who don't want to be politicians and who refuse to share in power.' Shanks holds up East German churches as an example of church as agent of 'anti-political politics.' Such an attitude was justifiable in the context of life under state socialism when cooperation with the state did mean an unacceptable compromise of one's integrity and credibility. But the term 'anti-politics' may have outlived its usefulness. Shanks, *Civil Society*; the passages cited here are from, pp. 206–213.

[108] John Neville Figgis, 'The Great Leviathan', in Hirst, *Pluralist Theory*, p. 121.

[109] David Nicholls, *The Pluralist State* (Macmillan, 1975), p. 53.

[110] See the rather incomplete biography by Maurice G. Tucker, *John Neville Figgis: A Study* (SPCK, 1950). Figgis soon moved away from the church where his father was minister (the 'New Connexion' Church in Brighton) and, after a period of agnosticism, was confirmed in the Church of England. He served briefly as parish priest in Kettering, then as chaplain to Pembroke College in Cambridge. At the age of 35, he joined the Community at Mirfield in 1902, his father having declared that none of his money would go to his son as long as he remained a member of that community. Figgis wrote prolifically, primarily as an historian but also as a political and social theologian, lecturing both in the United States and in England.

[111] Nicholls identifies three dimensions of sovereignty: legal sovereignty (law as obliging everyone, even the lawmakers), political sovereignty (the state as being the final authority) and moral sovereignty (the autonomous subject). All three are flawed and dangerous, argues

Nicholls, for all three are founded ultimately on power and will. None have an adequate doctrine of freedom based on ethics as reflected in spontaneous associational life. Legal sovereignty (positive law) fails to acknowledge the limits set by the actual norms and customs and self-regulating systems of social groups. Political sovereignty (the state) fails to acknowledge the limits set by the claims of higher authorities than the state, such as the church. Moral sovereignty (individualism) fails to acknowledge the limits set by objective moral law. *The Pluralist State*, pp. 36–53.

[112] Nicholls, *Pluralist State*, p. 50.

[113] Figgis, *The Fellowship of the Mystery* (Longmans, 1915), p. 74, as cited in Nicholls, *Pluralist State*, p. 68.

[114] Maitland's 'Moral Personality and Legal Personality' was given as the Sidgwick Lecture in 1903 and is reproduced in Nicholls, *Pluralist State*, pp. 158–169.

[115] Nicholls attributes a similar expression 'society of societies' to the British Idealist philosopher T. H. Green; *Pluralist State*, p. 56.

[116] Figgis, *Churches in the Modern State* (Longmans, 1913), as reproduced in Hirst, *Pluralist Theory*, p. 122.

[117] Cole, *Social Theory*, in Hirst, *Pluralist Theory*, p. 72.

[118] Nicholls, *Pluralist State*, p. 60.

[119] Hirst, *Pluralist Theory*, p. 29.

[120] Erik Olin Wright, ed., *Associations and Democracy* (Verso, 1995). Others have also begun to develop the theory of associative democracy quite independently. John Matthews has used the term 'associative democracy' in *Age of Democracy: The Politics of Post-Fordism* (Oxford University Press, 1989), p. 92. Seyla Benhabib, who argues for a model of democratic deliberation which privileges 'a plurality of modes of association in which the affected can have the right to articulate their point of view'; 'Deliberative Rationality and Models of Democratic Legitimacy', *Constellations* 1.1 [April 1994]: 35.

[121] Cohen and Rogers, in Wright, *Associations and Democracy*; the passages cited here are from pp. 11, 32, 44–45, 71, 237, 248.

[122] For Cole: 'The essence of functional democracy is that a man should count as many times as there are functions in which he is interested.' *The Social Theory*, as cited in Hirst, *Pluralist Theory*, p. 89. But whereas Cole seems to have seen functional democracy as a complementary form of representative democracy, alongside that of territorial representation, Harold Laski saw functional democracy as taking the form of devolved self-management of the major industrial interests; Hirst. *Pluralist Theory*, pp. 35–36.

[123] Hirst, in Cohen and Rogers, *Associations and Democracy*, p. 111.

[124] Schmitter, in Cohen and Rogers, *Associations and Democracy*, p. 182.

[125] Wainwright, *Reclaim the State*; the passages cited here are from, p. xiii, 32, 44, 186–188, 198.

[126] Rowan Williams, 'Religion culture diversity and tolerance – shaping the new Europe' (Address at the European Policy Centre, Brussels, 7 November 2005): www.archbishopofcanterbury.org/sermons_speeches/2005/051107.htm.

[127] Wainwright, *Reclaim the State*, pp. 42–69. 'Reclaim the State' is a slogan which has been used in the World Social Forum and was also the title of the final chapter of Noreena Hertz's *The Silent Takeover: Global Capitalism and the Death of Democracy* (Heinemann, 2001).

[128] The historian Paul Ginsborg, who has been active in the 'Laboratory for Democracy' movement in Italy, describes the growth of new associational life in smaller towns as well as in major cities, involving especially the younger generation and the salaried middle class. Whilst they were formed around civic affairs – against nuclear arms, ecological destruction and crime – there was also a very marked development of cultural associations as well as in economic life; Ginsborg, *Italy and Its Discontents 1980–2001* (originally Allen Lane, 2001; Penguin, 2003), pp. 119–129. Ginsborg updates the picture in *New Left Review* 21: (May/June 2003): 58–64.

[129] Terry Eagleton, *The Ideology of the Aesthetic* (Blackwell, 1990), pp. 410, 413.

Conclusion: Church, Civil Society, Social Transformation

[1] People Paul VI, Address to a General Audience on the last day of the Holy Year of 1975.

[2] Jon Alterman, Director of the Middle East Program at the Center for Strategic and International Studies, has argued that significant political transformation in the Middle East will come only by a revitalizing of the centre, and when governments cease to try to maintain power by deligitimizing religious political opposition and by constantly portraying it in radical fundamentalist colours (*Financial Times*, 29 March 2005).

[3] A sign of the times was the publication by French Finance Minister Nicolas Sarkozy, *La republique, les religions, l'esperance* (Cerf, 2004). There Sarkozy, who is a Catholic with Jewish ancestors, calls for an amending of the 1905 law which establishes the separation of church and state, so that state assistance might be made available for Muslim places of worship. Since, however, Sarkozy is not of France's traditional elite and since he is setting his sights on a bid for the Presidency, his book has actually stiffened the resolve of many to retain the secularist Constitution.

[4] The survey drew responses from some 32,000 people from 103 countries. The result was interpreted as a sign of the Pope's crucial influence in regime change in Eastern Europe. *Financial Times Magazine*, Special Issue on Europe, 27 March 2004.

[5] The Faith Communities Unit – later absorbed into the Cohesion and Faiths Unit – included in its basic policy statement recommendations to: 'Ensure effective day-to-day consultation by supplementing formal consultation with an effective network of informal consultants…to engage with emerging regional inter-faith and single faith structures.…to support capacity building in Departments by servicing a new inter-departmental official committee, with the aim of mainstreaming faith issues.…Faith Communities Unit to include humanists and secularists among its contacts.' *Working Together: Cooperation between Government and Faith Communities* (Home Office, 29 March 2004): www.communities.gov.uk/index.asp?id=1503040.

[6] For information on US Faith Based action see the web site: www.faithbasedcommunityini-tiatives.org, as well as the official US government site: www.whitehouse.gov/government/fbci/mission.html.

[7] Richard Fletcher, *The Conversion of Europe: From Paganism to Christianity 371–1386 AD* (Fontana Press, 1998; originally published by Harper Collins, 1997).

[8] In Britain, one of the most remarkable was the convening by Joe Oldham, Secretary of the Council on Christian Faith and Common Life, of 'The Moot' which aimed at bringing together the 'best minds' in Britain to lay the foundations of a new Christian society. See the fascinating chapter on 'The Moot' in Clements, *Faith on the Frontier*, pp. 363–388. Different members exchanged different visions. Within the first year of The Moot, T. S. Eliot, for example, had spelt out his vision in 'The Idea of a Christian Society', lectures given in March 1939 and reproduced in in T. S. Eliot, *Christianity and Culture* (Harcourt, Brace and World, 1949).

[9] Ian Markham, 'Learning from Radical Orthodoxy: Challenging Sociological Assumptions', presentation delivered at the Association for Sociology of Religion in Atlanta, Georgia, August 2003.

[10] Paul's appeal for a 'civilization of love' was also developed by Cardinal Basil Hume in *Towards a Civilization of Love: Being Church in Today's World* (Hodder and Stoughton, 1988) and was endorsed Pope John Paul II, *Centesimus Annus*, para 10. The concluding paragraphs of the *Compendium of the Social Doctrine of the Church* bear the heading 'Building the "Civilization of Love"' (para. 575–583).

[10a] Niebuhr's insistence on the need to focus also on justice and power rather than love alone might best be seen not as a rejection of the social gospel as such but the way if retained elements of the perfectionist theology, of which traces could be found in Wesley but which is associated with Charles Finney and Oberlin Collegiate Institute in the 1830s. Even though that perfectionism was not based on a naive liberal assumption of the goodness of every human being but on the sanctifying power of the Holy Spirit which made possible perfect obedience to the will of God, it proved deeply divisive for both liberal and conservative Calvinists for decades

thereafter. See Timothy L. Smith, *Revivalism and Social Reform: American Fundamentalism on the Eve of the Civil War* (Harper Torchback, 1967; originally Abingdon Press, 1957), pp. 88, 157–161.

[11] John Milbank, 'The Poverty of Niebuhrianism', *The Word Made Strange: Theology, Language, Culture* (Blackwell, 1997), p. 240.

[12] For a study of the influences on King's thought see Kenneth M. Smith and Ira G. Zepp, Jr., *Search for the Beloved Community: The Thinking of Martin Luther King, Jr.* (Judson Press, 1974).

[13] Figgis, *Churches in the Modern State*, p. 112 (as quoted by Nicholls, *Pluralist State*, p. 104).

[14] In his fascinating sociological analysis of the interplay of political, economic and ideological power in the development of Europe, John A. Hall makes the pertinent observation: 'The Church…*was* civilization…if we ask what society was between 800 and 1050, the answer all mediaevalists agree, is that it was Latin Christendom.' John A. Hall, *Powers and Liberties: The Causes and Consequences of the Rise of the West* (Basil Blackwell, 1985), pp. 120–121. See especially Chapter 5: 'The Rise of Christian Europe'.

[15] Brown, *Augustine*, p. 240.

[16] Oliver O'Donovan, *The Desire of the Nations: Rediscovering the Roots of Political Theology* (Cambridge University Press, 1996); O'Donovan's language, however, could make some wonder just what kind of 'liberal' order the church has in mind: 'To display the liberal achievement correctly, we have to show it as the victory won by Christ over the nations' rulers'; or again: 'The church demands the obedience of society, and it demands the obedience of society's rulers. Communities are incorporated into Yhwh's Kingdom, rulers merely resign their pretensions. Yet these are two aspects of one conquest.' The passages cited here are from pp. 228–230, 233, 240, and 243.

[17] Milbank, *Theology and Social Theory*, p. 408.

[18] The Report of the Commission for Africa *Our Common Interest* (11 March 2005) contains a section on 'The growing importance of religious networks (3.4.4)'. Reference is there made to a paper by Ian Linden (leader of the 2004 Towards Social Transformation) 'New Thinking on Africa: Seminar Paper for Discussion on Culture and Development' for Bob Geldof's New Thinking Seminar (19 July 2004): www.commissionforafrica.org.

[19] Augustine contrasts Cicero's definition of a People – 'An assembly of people bound together by *legal consent* and by *common advantage*' ['coetus hominum iuris consensu et utilitatitis communione sociatus'] – with his own definition: 'An assembly of a multitude of rational beings bound together in *harmonious communion* about the objects of their *love*' ['coetus multitudinis rationalis rerum quas diligit concordi communione sociatus']. De *Civitate Dei,* Book XIX: 23–24.

[20] Hall, *Powers and Liberties*, p. 137.

[21] Samuel Brittan, as cited by Richard Tomkins, 'Goodbye, Cruel World', *Financial Times Magazine*, 4 February 2006, p. 25.

[22] Hall, *Powers and Liberties*, p. 117.

[23] David S. Landes, *The Wealth and Poverty of Nations: Why Some Are so Rich and Some Are so Poor* (Little, Brown and Co., Abacus edition, 1998), p. 37.

[24] Hall, *Power and Liberties*, p. 125.

[25] Milbank, 'On Complex Space', p. 274.

[26] Milbank, 'On Complex Space', pp. 283–284. Three even more critical paragraphs about John Paul II, contained in Milbank's original essay have not been reproduced. See his 'Against the Resignations of the Age', in Francis P. McHugh and Samuel M. Natale, eds., *Things New and Old: Catholic Social Teaching Revisited* (University Press of America, 1993), pp. 1–39.

[27] John Neville Figgis, *Hopes for English Religion* (Longmans and Co., 1919) p. 59 as quoted by Nicholls, *Pluralist State*, p. 96.

[28] Nicholls, *Pluralist State*, p. 7.

[29] Atherton, *Public Theology*, pp. 93–98.

[30] For details see Citizen Organizing Foundation: www.cof.org.uk.

[31] Keane, *Democracy and Civil Society*, pp. 21–22.

[32] Jessop, *Future of the Capitalist State*, pp. 189–90.

[33] Wainwright, *Reclaim the State*.

[34] Keane, *Global Civil Society?*, p. 92.

[35] See the biting essay of William Hazlitt, 'On the Connection between Toad-Eaters and Tyrants' (1817) in Paulin and Chandler, pp. 354–365.

[36] The approach associated with Stanley Hauerwas has performed an enormous service not only by boosting the self-confidence of the church in a post-Christian age but also by prodding church activists to ensure that their witness is distinctively Christian. But this is often at the price of failing to affirm the transformative power of God in other movements and institutions.

[37] Milbank, *Theology and Social Theory*, p. 397.

[38] Shanks, *Civil Society*; the passages cited here are from pp. 116, 151, 159, 186, 190, 205, 213.

[39] Hauerwas, *Community of Character*, p. 254. Hauerwas refers to Lindsay's *The Modern Democratic State* (Oxford University Press, 1962).

[40] Edward Farley, *Ecclesial Man: A Social Phenomenology of Faith and Reality* (Fortress Press, 1975), as cited by Gunton, *The Promise*, p. 78.

[41] Raymond Williams, *Culture and Society*; the passages in this section are from pp. 219, 274, 301, 304, 310, and 'The Idea of a Common Culture', p. 35.

[42] John Gray, *New Statesman*, 16 December 2002, as reprinted in *Heresies: Against Progress and Other Illusions* (Granta Books, 2004), p. 45.

[43] Studs Terkel, *Hope Dies Last: Making a Difference in an Indifferent World* (Granta Books, 2004; original edition The New Press, 2003).

[44] John Gray, *Al Qaeda: And What It Means to Be Modern* (Faber and Faber, 2003), pp. 114–115.

[45] Raymond Williams, 'Towards Many Socialisms', originally for the Tenth Round Table International Conference on Socialism at Cavtat, Yugoslavia, October 1985, as reprinted in *Resources of Hope: Culture, Democracy, Socialism* (Verso, 1989), p. 297.

[46] The theme has also been picked up in some Roman Catholic circles. See *Concilium* (5: 2004).

[47] An account of the Porto Alegre experiment is given by Hilary Wainwright, *Reclaim the State*, pp. 42–69, and more fully in Iain Bruce, ed., *The Porto Alegre Alternative: Direct Democracy in Action* (Pluto, 2004).

Select Bibliography

John Atherton, *Christianity and the Market: Christian Social Thought for Our Times,* London: SPCK, 1992.

Nicola Baker, ed., *Building a Relational Society: New Priorities for Public Policy,* Aldershot: Arena, 1996.

Pranab K. Bardhan and John E. Roemer, *Market Socialism: The Current Debate,* New York, Oxford: Oxford University Press, 1993.

Ulrich Beck, *Risk Society: Towards a New Modernity,* London: Sage, 1992.

Peter Berger and Michael Novak, *To Empower People: The Role of Mediating Structures in Public Policy,* Washington, D.C.: American Enterprise Institute, 1977.

David J. Bosch, *Transforming Mission: Paradigm Shifts in Theology of Mission,* Maryknoll, New York: Orbis Books, 1991.

Andrew Britton and Peter Sedgwick, *Economic Theory and Christian Belief,* Bern, Oxford: Peter Lang, 2003.

Keith Clements, *Faith on the Frontier: A Life of J. H. Oldham,* Edinburgh: T & T Clark, 1999.

Jean Cohen and Andrew Arato, *Civil Society and Political Theory,* London: MIT Press, 1992.

Charles E. Curran, *Catholic Social Teaching 1891–Present,* Washington, D.C.: Georgetown University Press, 2002.

Colin Crouch, *Coping with Post-democracy,* London: Fabian Ideas No. 598, December 2000.

Hernando de Soto, *The Mystery of Capital: Why Capitalism Triumphs in the West and Fails Everywhere Else,* London: Bantam Press, 2000.

Peter Dews, ed., *Autonomy and Solidarity: Interviews with Jurgen Habermas,* London: Verso, 1992.

Ulrich Duchrow, *Alternatives to Global Capitalism: Drawn from Biblical History and Designed for Political Action,* Heidelberg: International Books and Kairos Europa, 1995.

Ulrich Duchrow and Franz J. Hinkelammert, *Property for People, Not for Profit: Alternatives to the Global Tyranny of Capital,* London: Zed Books in association with the Catholic Institute for International Relations, 2004.

Terry Eagleton, *The Ideology of the Aesthetic,* Oxford: Blackwell, 1990.

Alison J. Elliot and Ian Swanson, eds., *The Renewal of Social Vision,* Edinburgh: Centre for Theology and Pubic Issues – Occasional Paper No. 17, 1989.

Ross B. Emmett, *Selected Essays by Frank H. Knight,* Chicago: University of Chicago, 1999.

William F. Fisher and Thomas Ponniah, *Another World Is Possible: Popular Alternatives to Globalization at the World Social Forum,* London: Zed Books, 2003.

Carl Joachim Friedrich, *Politica Methodice Digesta of Johannes Althusius (Althaus),* Cambridge, Mass.: Harvard University Press, 1932.

J. K Galbraith, *The Economics of Innocent Fraud: Truth for Our Time,* London: Allen Lane, 2004.

Ernest Gellner, *Conditions of Liberty: Civil Society and Its Rivals,* London: Hamish Hamilton, 1994.

Maurice Glasman, *Unnecessary Suffering: Managing Market Utopia,* London: Verso, 1996.

Jack Goody, *Capitalism and Modernity: The Great Debate,* Cambridge: Polity, 2004.

Timothy J. Gorringe, *Furthering Humanity: A Theology of Culture,* Aldershot: Ashgate, 2004.

Ian Gough, *The Political Economy of the Welfare State,* London: Macmillan, 1979.

Ian Gough, *Global Capital, Human Needs and Social Policies: Selected Essays 1994–99,* Basingstoke: Palgrave, 2000.

Ian Gough and Len Doyal, *A Theory of Human Need,* London: Macmillan, 1991.

John Gray, *Post-liberalism: Studies in Political Thought,* New York, London: Routledge, 1993.

John Gray, *Liberalism,* Maidenhead: Open University Press, rev. ed., 1995.

John Gray, *False Dawn: The Delusions of Global Capitalism,* London: Granta, 1998.

John Gray, *Al Qaeda: What It Means to Be Modern,* London: Faber and Faber, 2003.

Colin Gunton, *The Promise of Trinitarian Theology,* Edinburgh: T & T Clark, 1991.

Jurgen Habermas, *The Structural Transformation of the Public Sphere,* Cambridge: Polity Press, 1989.

John A. Hall, *Powers and Liberties: The Causes and Consequences of the Rise of the West,* Harmondsworth: Penguin, 1986; originally published by Basil Blackwell, 1985.

Stuart Hall, ed., *The Hard Road to Renewal: Thatcherism and the Crisis of the Left,* London: Verso, 1988.

David Held and Anthony McGrew, eds., *The Global Transformations Reader: An Introduction to the Globalization Debate,* Cambridge: Polity Press, second revised edition, 2003.

Peter S. Heslam, *Globalization: Unravelling the New Capitalism,* Cambridge: Grove Books, Ethics Series, 2002.

Paul Q. Hirst, *Asssociative Democracy: New Forms of Economic and Social Governance,* Cambridge: Polity, 1994.

Paul Q. Hirst, with Sunil Khilnani, *Reinventing Democracy,* Oxford: Blackwell, 1996.

Paul Q. Hirst, *The Pluralist Theory of the State: Selected Writings of G. D. H. Cole, J. N. Figgis and H.J. Laski,* London: Routledge, 1989.

Will Hutton and Anthony Giddens, eds., *On the Edge: Living with Global Capitalism,* London: Vintage, 2001.

Lewis Hyde, *The Gift: How the Creative Spirit Transforms the World,* Edinburgh: Canongate 2006 (originally New York: Random House, 1979).

David Jenkins, *Market Whys and Human Wherefores: Thinking Again about Markets, Politics and People,* London: Cassell, 2000.

Mary Kaldor, *Global Civil Society: An Answer to War,* Cambridge: Polity, 2003.

John Kay, *The Truth about Markets: Their Genius, Their Limits, Their Follies,* London: Allen Lane, 2003.

John Keane, *Civil Society and the State: New European Perspectives,* London: Verso, 1988.

John Keane, *Democracy and Civil Society,* London: Verso, 1988.

John Keane, *Civil Society: Old Images, New Visions,* Oxford: Polity, 1998.

John Keane, *Global Civil Society?,* Cambridge: Cambridge University Press, 2003.

Marjorie Kelly, *The Divine Right of Capital: Dethroning Corporate Aristocracy,* San Francisco: Berrett-Koehler, 2001.

Ian Linden, *A New Map of the World,* London: Darton, Longman & Todd, 2003.

C. B. Macpherson, *The Political Theory of Possessive Individualism: Hobbes to Locke,* Oxford: Clarendon Press, 1962.

C. B. Macpherson, *Democratic Theory: Essays in Retrieval,* Oxford: Clarendon Press, 1973.

Kenneth McRobbie ed., *Humanity, Society and Commitment: on Karl Polanyi,* Montreal: Black Rose Books: Critical Perspectives on Historic Issues, 1994.

John Milbank, *Theology and Social Theory: Beyond Secular Reason,* Oxford: Blackwell, 1990.

John Milbank, *The Word Made Strange: Theology, Language, Culture,* Oxford: Blackwell, 1997.

John Milbank, with Catherine Pickstock and Graham Ward, *Radical Orthodoxy: A New Theology,* London: Routledge, 1999.

John Milbank, *Being Reconciled: Ontology and Pardon,* London: Routledge, 2003.

Paul Misner, *Social Catholicism in Europe: From the Onset of Industrialization to the First World War,* London: Darton, Longman and Todd, 1991.

George Monbiot, *The Age of Consent: A Manifesto for a New World Order,* London: Flamingo, 2003.

David Morley and Kuan-Hsing Chen, eds., *Stuart Hall: Critical Dialogues in Cultural Studies,* London: Routledge, 1996.

Anthony J. Nicholls, *Freedom with Responsibility: The Social Market in Germany 1918–1963,* Oxford: Clarendon Press, 1994.

David Nicholls, *Three Varieties of Pluralism,* London: Macmillan, 1974.

David Nicholls, *The Pluralist State,* London: Macmillan, 1975.

David Nicholls, *Deity and Domination: Images of God and the State in the 19th and 20th Centuries,* London: Routledge, 1989.

David Nicholls, *God and Government in an 'Age of Reason',* London: Routledge, 1995.

Reinhold Niebuhr, *The Irony of American History,* New York: Charles Scribner's Sons, 1962.

Reinhold Niebuhr, *The Nature and Destiny of Man: A Christian Interpretation,* New York: Charles Scribner's Sons, vol. I, 1941; vol. II, 1943.

Oliver O'Donovan, *The Desire of the Nations: Rediscovering the Roots of Biblical Theology,* Cambridge: Cambridge University Press, 1996.

Thomas Paine, *The Thomas Paine Reader* (edited by Michael Foot and Isaac Kramnick), Harmondsworth: Penguin, 1987.

Raymond Plant, *Modern Political Thought,* Oxford: Basil Blackwell, 1991.

Raymond Plant, *Politics, Theology and History,* Cambridge: Cambridge University Press, 2001.

Raymond Plant, with Kenneth Hoover, *Conservative Capitalism in Britain and the United States: A Critical Approach,* London: Routledge, 1989.

Raymond Plant, ed., with Matt Beech and Kevin Hickson, *The Struggle for Labour's Soul: Labour's Political Thought since 1945,* London: Routledge, 2004.

John Plender, *Going Off the Rails: Global Capital and the Crisis of Legitimacy,* Chichester: Wiley, 2003.

Karl Polanyi, *Origins of Our Time: The Great Transformation,* London: Gollancz, 1945; later published as *The Great Transformation: The Political and Economic Origins of Our Time,* Boston: Beacon, 1957.

Pontifical Council for Justice and Peace, *Compendium of the Social Doctrine of the Church,* Vatican City: Libreria Editrice Vaticana, 2004.

Roy Porter, *Enlightenment: Britain and the Creation of the Modern World,* Harmondsworth: Penguin, 2000.

Patrick Riordan, *A Politics of the Common Good,* Dublin: Institute of Public Administration, 1996.

Philippe Sands, *Lawless World: America and the Making and Breaking of Global Rules,* London: Allen Lane, 2005.

Richard Sennett, *The Culture of the New Capitalism,* New Haven and London: Yale University Press, 2006.

Michael Schluter and the Cambridge Papers Group, *Christianity in a Changing World: Biblical Insight on Contemporary Issues,* London: Marshall Pickering, 2000.

Andrew Shanks, *Civil Society, Civil Religion,* Oxford: Blackwell, 1995.

George Soros, *The Crisis of Global Capitalism,* New York: Public Affairs, 1998; London: Little, Brown and Co., 1998.

George Soros, *Open Society: Reforming Global Capitalism,* New York: Public Affairs, 2000; London: Little, Brown and Co., 2000.

Glen H. Stassen, Dianne M. Yeager and John Howard Yoder, *Authentic Transformation: A New Vision of Christ and Culture,* Nashville, Tenn: Abingdon, 1996.

Jeffrey Stout, *Democracy and Tradition,* Princeton, N.J.: Princeton University Press, 2004.

Henry Tam, *Communitarianism: A New Agenda for Politics and Citizenship,* Basingstoke: Macmillan, 1998.

Charles Taylor, *Sources of the Self: The Making of Modern Identity,* Cambridge: Cambridge

University Press, 1989.

Studs Terkel, *Hope Dies Last: Making a Difference in an Indifferent World,* New York: The New Press, 2003; London: Granta Books, 2004.

Kevin J. Vanhoozer, ed., *The Cambridge Companion to Postmodern Theology,* Cambridge: Cambridge University Press, 2003.

Hilary Wainwright, *Arguments for a New Left: Answering the Free Market,* Oxford: Blackwell, 1994.

Hilary Wainwright, *Reclaim the State: Experiments in Popular Democracy,* London: Verso, 2003.

Hilary Wainwright with Sheila Rowbotham and Lynne Segal, *Beyond the Fragments: Feminism and the Making of Socialism,* London: Merlin Press, 1979.

Raymond Williams, *Culture and Society 1780–1950,* London: Chatto and Windus, 1958; Harmondsworth: Penguin Books, 1961.

Raymond Williams, *The Politics of Modernism: Against the New Conformity,* London: Verso, 1988.

Index

Abramoff case 202, 304n36
Abramovich, Roman 3
AccountAbility 169
accumulation of wealth 3; capital 32,
    50, 118; class 202–3; hyper-rich 154;
    inequality 156; personal 77, 79–80;
    profit 32; sharing 57
Active Community Unit 287n65
Acton, Lord 217, 232, 235
Adams, John 267n17
Adenauer, Konrad 180
Adorno, Theodor 43
adult education 284n10
aesthetics 98, 100
affluent society 119
Afghanistan 10, 196, 234
Africa 3, 4; *see also specific countries*
Africa Commission report 172
African Americans 91, 92
Agenda 2010 181, 182
Akbar, Emperor 221
Alaric, King 52
Alcatel 149
Alden, Edward 273n10
Ali, Ifzal 267n12
All China Federation of Trade Unions
    271n65, 294n96
Alterman, Jon 310n2
Althusius 85, 281n48
altruism 76, 288n81
Amaranth Advisors 151
Ambrose, Bishop 243
American Catholic label 109
American colonies 218, 224
American Constitution 224
American Enterprise Institute 88
American Social Gospel movement 215
Amnesty International 6
Anglican Association for Social
    Responsibility xiii, 1
Angola 192
Annan, Kofi 4, 297n143

anti-politics 250, 308n107
Anti-Social Behaviour Orders 83
anti-trust legislation 147
Aquinas, Thomas 123–4, 165, 241–2
Arato, Andrew 230, 308n105
Argentina 2
Arianism 93
Aristotle 123, 214, 217
Arrighi, Giovanni 17, 270n49
Asia 4, 19, 133–4, 239; *see also specific
    countries*
Asian Development Bank 267n12
asset redistribution 63
asset-stripping 142
Association of British Insurers 298n152
Association of Investment Trust Companies
    146
associational economic enterprises 185–6
associationalism 24; civic 75, 85–7,
    88–90; civil society 246; conservative
    88–90; dangers 90–2; economics 184–5;
    Milbank 210, 246; participation 245;
    popes 282n50; social ontology 127; social
    transformation 94–5; socialist 90, 186–7;
    state 86
associations 86–8, 232; political 86; civil
    87
Atherton, John 130; common good 123;
    economics 38, 123; historical review 160;
    local civil society 246–7, 276n58; markets
    161–2; social market 176–7
atonement 7, 11–13
Augur, Philip 135, 290n21
Augustine of Hippo 45, 66; biography 243;
    church/state 63, 64; Cicero 311n19; *City
    of God* 22–3, 28, 52–3, 110, 210, 222,
    242, 244, 276–7n64, 277n68; common
    good 123; community living 55;
    deconstruction of empire 53–4; giving
    182; goodness 163; Gunton on 93,
    283n72; hope, fallacious 9; intolerance
    57; *libido dominandi* 22–3, 53, 82; love

About the author

Pat Logan worked for the Diocese of Southwark from 1976 until 2002 as Adviser on Homelessness and on wider issues of Social Responsibility and was Co-ordinator of Church Action on Homelessness in London (UNLEASH). He also lectured for several years on the Southwark Ordination Course. Before coming to Britain, he taught moral theology for nine years in the United States. He holds degrees in theology and canon law from the Pontifical Gregorian University in Rome and a PhD in Religion and Human Nature from the Hartford Seminary Foundation in Connecticut. He has recently been serving as consultant to the London Churches Group for Social Action. Pat was the originator and one of the organisers of the Towards Social Transformation seminars on which this book is based.